CONSTITUTIONAL INTERPRETATION

Recent Titles in
Contributions in Legal Studies

Presidential Defiance of "Unconstitutional" Laws: Reviving the Royal Prerogative
Christopher N. May

Promises on Prior Obligations at Common Law
Kevin M. Teeven

Litigating Federalism: The States Before the U.S. Supreme Court
Eric N. Waltenburg and Bill Swinford

Law and the Arts
Susan Tiefenbrun, editor

Contract Law and Morality
Henry Mather

The Appearance of Equality: Racial Gerrymandering, Redistricting, and the Supreme Court
Christopher M. Burke

Religion, Law, and the Land
Brian Edward Brown

The Supreme Court's Retreat from Reconstruction: A Distortion of Constitutional Jurisprudence
Frank J. Scaturro

Respecting State Courts: The Inevitability of Judicial Federalism
Michael E. Solimine and James L. Walker

Basic Principles of Property Law: A Comparative Legal and Economic Introduction
Ugo Mattei

Inherent Rights, the Written Constitution, and Popular Sovereignty: The Founders' Understanding
Thomas B. McAffee

Constitutional Structure and Purposes: Critical Commentary
Michael Conant

CONSTITUTIONAL INTERPRETATION

Illusion and Reality

Jeffrey M. Shaman

Contributions in Legal Studies, Number 97

GREENWOOD PRESS
Westport, Connecticut • London

Library of Congress Cataloging-in-Publication Data

Shaman, Jeffrey M.
Constitutional interpretation : illusion and reality / Jeffrey M. Shaman.
p. cm.—(Contributions in legal studies, ISSN 0147–1074 ; no. 97)
Includes bibliographical references and index.
ISBN 0–313–31473–X (alk. paper)
1. Judicial review—United States. 2. Judicial process—United States. 3. Constitutional law—United States. I. Title. II. Series.
KF4575.S53 2001
347.73'12—dc21 00–032796

British Library Cataloguing in Publication Data is available.

Library of Congress Catalog Card Number: 00–032796
ISBN: 0–313–31473–X
ISSN: 0147–1074

First published in 2001

Greenwood Press, 88 Post Road West, Westport, CT 06881
An imprint of Greenwood Publishing Group, Inc.
www.greenwood.com

Printed in the United States of America

The paper used in this book complies with the Permanent Paper Standard issued by the National Information Standards Organization (Z39.48–1984).

10 9 8 7 6 5 4 3 2 1

This book is dedicated with love to my mother, Florence S. Shaman,
and to the memory of my father, Marvin A. Shaman

Contents

Preface

This book is an attempt to examine the process of constitutional interpretation through the lens of history, political science, and jurisprudence. This includes analysis of the major themes of constitutional interpretation developed by the Warren Court, the Burger Court, and the Rehnquist Court. In some respects the book is an assessment of the work of those courts, especially the latter two. While always observant of the historical development of constitutional interpretation, this study brings constitutional law up to date by describing the significant doctrinal developments of recent years. The aim of this examination is to trace the evolution of constitutional interpretation with a special focus on contemporary theory.

This book is the culmination of many years of reading, teaching, and thinking about the Supreme Court and constitutional law. Over those years, I have learned a great deal from discussions with colleagues in the field of constitutional law and related areas. I have benefited immeasurably from my colleagues' insights and ideas, as well as their comments and suggestions about my work. I am especially grateful to Susan Bandes, Erwin Chemerinsky, William Marshall, Marlene Nicholson, Jane Rutherford, Stephen Siegel, and Mark Weber. In addition, I have been very fortunate to have the support of two deans at the DePaul University College of Law, John Roberts and Teree Foster, both of whom appreciate research and scholarship. Further thanks are due to Emilie Bell for the two years of diligent research assistance that she provided for this work.

It will be difficult to finally bring the writing of this book to a close. I find that there is always another matter to be examined, another point to be made, another sentence or paragraph to be polished. But I once heard someone say that there comes a time when you have to take the page out of the typewriter, and that time has come for these pages.

Introduction

Originally adopted in 1787,[1] enhanced by the addition of a Bill of Rights two years later,[2] and amended from time to time over the ensuing years,[3] the Constitution stands today as the supreme law of the land. All governmental action—state and federal, legislative, executive, or judicial—must comply with the dictates of the Constitution.

In 1803, in the famous case of *Marbury v. Madison* the Supreme Court assumed for itself the responsibility of providing meaning for the Constitution.[4] The Court's ruling in *Marbury* is without parallel in its impact on the course of American history. *Marbury v. Madison* invested the Supreme Court with the power of judicial review and made the Court the final arbiter of the Constitution. Without *Marbury*, neither *Dred Scott v. Sandford*[5] nor *Brown v. Board of Education*[6] nor *Roe v. Wade*[7] nor, for that matter, any other constitutional decision would have been possible.

There are those who claim that the Court's assumption of judicial review in *Marbury* was an illegitimate usurpation of authority.[8] Nonetheless, it is an authority that the Court has continued to exercise again and again and again. The other branches of government as well as the people of the nation have accepted the Court's interpretative function in our constitutional scheme of government. Indeed, there has been such widespread acquiescence to judicial review that no one today would seriously challenge its legitimacy. Virtually everyone now agrees that the Supreme Court is the final arbiter of the meaning of the Constitution.

Of course, the opinion in *Marbury v. Madison*, written by the great Chief Justice John Marshall, makes it appear as if interpreting the Constitution is a relatively straightforward exercise. Marshall explains that if a law is "in opposition" or "repugnant" to the Constitution, the Court is obliged to declare the law void.[9] Unfortunately, Marshall's statement obscures the true nature of constitutional interpretation by suggesting that it is an uninvolved exercise consisting of nothing more than comparing two documents to see if they square with one another. But this sort of artless jurisprudence is a gross simplification of the nature of the judicial function in interpreting the Constitution. To say that judicial review is simply a matter of deciding if a law is "in opposition" or "repugnant" to the Constitution does not nearly begin to describe the complex process of constitutional interpretation.

Although for his time John Marshall was sophisticated about law and politics, the prevailing view in his day and age was that those two disciplines were separate from one another.[10] In following years that mistaken view would become even more pronounced. During the nineteenth century a shroud of myth and fiction descended over the legal process. Law came to be seen as a science that could be mechanically applied by judges. According to this view, law and the judicial function were thought to be essentially nonideological.[11] Law was thought to be neutral, objective, and devoid of values.[12] Hence, it was for the legislative and executive branches of our government, but not the judiciary, to make value judgments or policy choices.[13] Judicial decisions then did not require the exercise of will or discretion,[14] and certainly had nothing to do with making value choices. Judges were expected to be unconcerned about policy, or detached from it; it simply was none of their business.

This view of the judicial function persevered through the beginning of the twentieth century. So, for example, in 1905, while striking down a maximum hours law in *Lochner v. New York* on the ground that the law unduly interfered with liberty of contract and was not a valid health measure, the Supreme Court had either the myopia or the temerity to claim that it "was not substituting the judgment of the court for that of the legislature."[15] As late as 1936, Justice Owen Roberts, in an opinion written for the Court, declared that when a statute is challenged as unconstitutional, "the judicial branch of the Government has but one duty—to lay the article of the Constitution which is invoked beside the statute which is challenged and to decide whether the latter squares with the former. . . . This court neither approves nor condemns any legislative policy."[16]

By the time Justice Roberts penned those infamous words, however, serious doubt about the traditional view of the judicial function was well under way.[17] Indeed, the doubt first appeared in 1881, when Oliver Wendell Holmes, Jr., "a generation ahead of his time,"[18] and two decades before his appointment to the Supreme Court, published his groundbreaking opus, *The Common Law*. In chapter one, Holmes proclaimed:

> [T]he life of the law has not been logic: it has been experience. The felt necessities of the time, the prevalent moral and political theories, intuitions of public policy, avowed or unconscious, even the prejudices which judges share with their fellow-men, have had

a good deal more to do than the syllogism in determining the rules by which men should be governed. . . .

[I]n substance the growth of the law is legislative. . . . It is legislative in its grounds. . . . Every important principle which is developed by litigation is in fact and at bottom the result of more or less definitely understood views of public policy.[19]

After Holmes' book was published, the orthodox view of the law came under increasing criticism. In 1908 Roscoe Pound published his seminal article *Mechanical Jurisprudence*,[20] paving the way for a new school of thought, "Legal Realism," that was devoted to exploding the traditional myth that law was separate from policy and values.[21] Today, the orthodox view of mechanical jurisprudence has been thoroughly discredited as an extravagant distortion that bears little relationship to the reality of the judicial function.[22] Nonetheless, the traditional view has never been entirely abandoned, and still prevails in some corners more than others. Indeed, there seems to be a never ending quest to make the law objective and devoid of human value judgments. In the realm of constitutional law, which by character is one of the most political areas of the law, the Supreme Court and some constitutional scholars still seem bent upon constructing a network of abstract rules that give an appearance of objectivity and neutrality while masking the human value choices that the Court makes.[23]

A more realistic understanding of constitutional interpretation recognizes that it is a dynamic process, and one that involves a good deal of creativity on the part of the Supreme Court. Although the Court has always been reluctant to admit it, constitutional interpretation is a process that requires the exercise of imagination and discretion. Over the years since the original framing of the Constitution, the Supreme Court has created a substantial body of doctrine as it goes about interpreting the document. Through the continual interpretation and reinterpretation of the text, the Supreme Court perpetually creates new meaning for the Constitution. Although it is formally correct that we have a written Constitution, its words have been defined and redefined by the Supreme Court to the extent that in reality we have an unwritten Constitution—or, more precisely, we have a large body of constitutional doctrine, the great majority of which has been created by the Supreme Court.

Nonetheless, beginning with *Marbury* there has been a persistent inclination to deny the creative aspect of the Supreme Court in constitutional interpretation. For many years, the Court's creative function was hidden to a large extent by the use of a highly formalistic method of adjudication. In the past, formalism dominated legal thought and provided the appearance that law was an exercise in pure logic, devoid of value judgment or policy making. In the twentieth century, the rise of legal realism exposed the fallacies of formal legal thought and led to a more pragmatic approach to law, one that conceives of law as a social institution inherently intertwined with values and policy. This new realism removed much of the myth surrounding constitutional law, and thereby invigorated it. Unfortunately, the formal mode of thought has never been completely abandoned, and in recent years has enjoyed a resurgence despite the fact that it is a deeply flawed methodology. Indeed, one of the most disquieting aspects of constitutional interpretation during the Chief Justiceship of William Rehnquist has been a marked return to old, formalistic ways of thinking about the law.

The re-emergence of formalism, however, has been at most only a partially successful counter-revolution. The sweep of constitutional history and the power of a realistic constitutional jurisprudence are too compelling to be supplanted by outmoded formal ways of thought. Thus, the process of constitutional interpretation continues on its dynamic, restless course. In the last fifty years, the most striking development of constitutional jurisprudence has been the construction of an elaborate system of judicial review composed of multiple levels or tiers of scrutiny. During that period of time, the Supreme Court has devised three different levels of review, referred to as strict, intermediate, and minimal scrutiny. The levels of scrutiny are extremely important in constitutional adjudication. They involve both different standards and different methods of adjudication, and their impact upon the decision-making process cannot be overemphasized. But this hardly begins to tell the full story. With the Court adding one refinement and permutation after another to the levels of scrutiny, the system has become attenuated almost to the point of chaos.

Within this elaborate system, constitutional decision making depends, as it always has, on human perceptions of reality. Constitutional decisions, like all other legal decisions, are made by judges based upon their understanding of the world around them. The resolution of factual matters relevant to interpreting the Constitution is an inherent part of judicial review that cannot be eliminated, short of eliminating judicial review itself. Being mere mortals, however, judges often have very different perceptions of actuality. After all, no two human beings see things exactly the same. To the contrary, individuals often have differing or even contradictory perceptions of the world around them. As a result, it is not uncommon to find Supreme Court justices disagreeing, at times vehemently, about factual matters of constitutional import. Unfortunately, the Court has not developed a coherent methodology for dealing with constitutional facts. The Court is not above manipulating constitutional fact to suit its own purposes, and on occasion has been maddeningly close-minded about matters of constitutional fact.

In the process of constitutional interpretation, the Supreme Court also has struggled with a puzzle concerning the relationship between a law's constitutionality and its underlying motivation. In determining the constitutionality of legislation, the Court often professes that it will not inquire into the motive of the legislature. So long as a statute is within the authority of the legislature to enact, what may have motivated the legislature is irrelevant, even in situations where it seems obvious that the legislature has used a pretext to disguise an improper motive. On the other hand, it is not uncommon for the Court to simply ignore the tenet that motive is irrelevant and strike down laws because they were enacted for improper motives. In sum, the Court's treatment of legislative motive has been confusing and inconsistent.

The puzzle of legislative motive, the perception of reality, the levels of scrutiny, the dichotomy of formalism and realism, and constitutional creativity are important aspects of the process of constitutional interpretation that are operative in all areas of constitutional law. In other words, they transcend the provisions of the constitution and apply to all of them. These aspects of the interpretative process are all dramatically illustrated in cases involving the Freedom of Speech Clause of the First Amendment. Free speech cases are a microcosm of the constitutional process, and as such they function as a virtual observation tank to study the process of constitutional interpretation. They demonstrate the dynamic nature of constitutional law, its force, and its sweep as it progresses through history.

Dynamic movement has also characterized the three great clauses of the Fourteenth Amendment—the Privileges or Immunities Clause, the Due Process Clause, and the Equal Protection Clause. Enacted in 1868 after the Civil War, the Fourteenth Amendment stands as a powerful guardian against oppression and inequality. Each of its clauses, however, have gone through evolutionary swings from one extreme to another. Each clause has been debilitated by the Supreme Court, only to be restored later, then weakened again, and revived once again. Though perhaps more extreme when the Fourteenth Amendment is involved, this sort of evolutionary current runs throughout all of constitutional law. As we shall see, the interpretation of the constitution is a process of perpetual motion, first in one direction, then in another. Slow at some points and faster at others, constitutional law is an ongoing act of creation.

NOTES

1. The Constitution was approved and signed by the delegates to the Constitutional Convention on September 17, 1787. It was ratified by the necessary number of states in 1788. *See* Robert N. Clinton, *A Brief History of the Adoption of the United States Constitution*, 75 IOWA L. REV. 891 (1990).

2. The Bill of Rights consists of the first 10 amendments to the Constitution, which, along with two others that failed ratification, were proposed by Congress in 1789. Ratification of the Bill of Rights was completed in 1791.

3. In addition to the original Constitution, there are now 27 amendments. However, that includes the Eighteenth Amendment, which prohibited the manufacture, sale, or transportation of intoxicating liquors within the United States, as well as the Twenty-First Amendment, which repealed the Eighteenth.

4. Marbury v. Madison, 5 U.S. (1 Cranch.) 137 (1803).

5. Dred Scott v. Sandford, 60 U.S. (19 How.) 393 (1851).

6. Brown v. Board of Education, 394 U.S. 294 (1954).

7. Roe v. Wade, 410 U.S. 113 (1973).

8. *See. e.g.*, 2 William Crosskey, POLITICS AND THE CONSTITUTION 1008–1046

(1953). An admittedly "partial" but nonetheless very helpful bibliography of works criticizing and defending Marbury can be found at William W. Van Alstyne, *A Critical Guide to Marbury v. Madison*, DUKE L.J. 1, 45–47 (1969).

9. Marbury v. Madison, 5 U.S. (1 Cranch.) at 176–78.

10. *See* Laurence H. Tribe, AMERICAN CONSTITUTIONAL LAW 26 (2d ed. 1988).

11. *See* Morton J. Horwitz, THE TRANSFORMATION OF AMERICAN LAW 1870–1960: CRISIS OF LEGAL ORTHODOXY ch. 1 (1992).

12. *Id.* at 15.

13. *Id.* at 18.

14. *Id.*

15. Lochner v. New York, 198 U.S. 45, 56–57 (1905).

16. United States v. Butler, 297 U.S. 1, 62–63 (1936).

17. *See* Horwitz, *supra* note 11, *passim.*

18. Henry Steele Commager, THE AMERICAN MIND 376 (1950).

19. Oliver Wendell Holmes, Jr., THE COMMON LAW 1, 35 (1881).

20. Roscoe Pound, *Mechanical Jurisprudence*, 8 COLUM. L. REV. 605 (1908).

21. *See* Commager, *supra* note 18, at ch. XVIII.

22. *See* G. Edward White, INTERVENTION AND DETACHMENT—ESSAYS IN LEGAL HISTORY AND JURISPRUDENCE 275–78 (1994).

23. *See* Morton J. Horwitz, *The Constitution of Change: Legal Fundamentality Without Fundamentalism*, 107 HARV. L. REV. 30 (1993).

Chapter 1

Constitutional Creativity

[The Supreme Court is] a kind of Constitutional Convention in continuous session.

—Woodrow Wilson[1]

It is true that we live under a Constitution, but the Constitution is what the judges say it is.

—Charles Evans Hughes[2]

According to orthodox ideology, the Supreme Court's function in the constitutional process is essentially noncreative.[3] The proper role of the Supreme Court, it is said, is to "interpret" the Constitution, not rewrite it. Traditionally, it is believed that the Court's proper role is to ascertain the original understanding of the Constitution, as evidenced by its words and the intentions of those who adopted it.[4] "The whole aim of construction, as applied to a provision of the Constitution," Justice George Sutherland said, "is to discover the meaning, to ascertain and give effect to the intent of its framers and the people who adopted it."[5] As this view has it, constitutional interpretation consists of a search or quest for original intent, which leaves little room for creativity on the part of the Supreme Court.[6] The Court is supposed to find meaning for the Constitution, not create it. Hence, it is considered highly illegitimate for the Court to "revise" or "amend" the Constitution.[7] Similarly, it is thought to be extremely improper for the Court, when interpreting the Constitution, to engage in "judicial legislation" or "policy making."[8] Indeed, the oxymoronic character of the former phrase implies the illegitimacy of judicial lawmaking; legislating is for the legislature, not the judiciary.

For some period of time, the orthodox faith was referred to as "interpretivism," which implied that other methods of providing meaning for the Constitution, derided as "noninterpretivism," were illegitimate because they created new meaning for the document rather than interpreting it. These labels, however, proved to be misnomers, as all interpretation requires some degree of creativity. Even the author of those terms, Thomas Grey, eventually came to repudiate them, acknowledging that "the concept of interpretation is broad enough to encompass any plausible mode of constitutional adjudication."[9] It is clear, then, that the orthodox ideology is more accurately referred to as "originalism" rather than "interpretivism."

Like other matters concerning the Constitution, originalism at times finds expression in the political arena, where it is proclaimed that the justices of the Supreme Court should be "strict constructionists," adhering faithfully to the words of the Constitution and the intent of the framers who drafted the document.[10] Supreme Court justices who do otherwise are castigated as "judicial activists" who twist and bend the Constitution to their personal predilections.[11]

Over the years the orthodox articles of faith have been professed by a number of jurists.[12] Even some nominees to the high Court have joined the chorus, finding it convenient during their confirmation hearings to swear allegiance to the conventional wisdom.[13] These vows, however, should be taken with a healthy grain of salt because the confirmation process has devolved into a political rite of passage that may not reveal a nominee's true judicial philosophy, if, in fact, he or she has much of one at that point in time. Still, there are some nominees who, after being confirmed to the high Court, continue to champion the orthodox ideology.[14]

Others have disagreed; in fact, some have found the notion that the Constitution should be interpreted according to its original understanding barely worthy of a response. Chief Justice Charles Evans Hughes' opinion for the Court in the *Blaisdell* case[15] declares that the suggestion that "the great clauses of the Constitution must be confined to the interpretation which the framers, with the conditions and outlook of their time, would have placed upon them . . . carries its own refutation."[16] Yet the orthodox faith in originalism has persisted; in fact, it has enjoyed a resurgence of late, due primarily to the exhortation of its latest champion on the Supreme Court, Justice Antonin Scalia. Attention, after all, must be paid to Supreme Court justices, and Justice Scalia is a clever and forceful advocate, even if his analysis is sometimes deficient. After the publication of Justice Scalia's essay "A Matter of Interpretation" in 1997,[17] one commentator was moved to remark, "We are all originalists now."[18]

Even though that statement was not meant to be taken at face value,[19] it nonetheless is indicative of a renewed interest in the orthodox originalist faith. This is a sorry state of affairs because originalism is a severely flawed ideology. Indeed, over the years legal scholars have been extremely critical of the orthodox ideology.[20] They have, for example, described the notion of an original understanding of the Constitution as a "misconceived quest,"[21] an "impossibility,"[22] and even a "fraud."[23] Their criticism is well taken. Acute examination of the process of constitutional interpretation reveals a picture that differs fundamentally from the conventional school of thought. It is a picture that need not be approached apprehensively. Although perhaps startling to those who have believed in the old ideology, the picture is not necessarily an ugly one. More important, it portrays reality, and the time is long overdue for a realistic understanding of the constitutional process.

THE HISTORIC FOUNDATION OF CONSTITUTIONAL CREATIVITY

From its very inception, constitutional law has been a dynamic process of creativity. Through the continual interpretation and reinterpretation of the text, the Supreme Court perpetually creates new meaning for the Constitution. Although it is formally correct to state that we have a written Constitution, its words have been defined and redefined to the extent that, for the most part, we have an unwritten Constitution, the meaning of which originates in the Supreme Court. Notwithstanding the orthodox protestation that it is illegitimate for the Court to "revise" or "amend" the Constitution, that in fact is what the Court has always done by continually creating new constitutional meaning. Astute historical observer that he was, Woodrow Wilson captured the essence of the Supreme Court in describing it as "a kind of Constitutional Convention in continuous session."[24]

Much of the meaning that the Court creates for the Constitution can be traced to the language of the document only in the most tenuous sense and has little, if any, connection to the intention of the framers. In the words of Professor Thomas Grey, it is "a matter of unarguable historical fact" that over the years the Court has developed a large body of constitutional doctrine whose content derives neither from the text of the Constitution nor the intent of the framers.[25] This has been so since the earliest days of our history. Consider, for example, the case of *Hylton v. United States*,[26] which was decided in 1796 during the term of the Court's first chief justice, John Jay. The *Hylton* case involved a tax ranging from $1.00 to $10.00 that had been levied by Congress on carriages. Mr. Hylton, who was in the carriage trade and owned 125 carriages, understandably was unhappy about the tax, so he went to court to challenge it. He claimed that the tax violated section 9 of Article I of the Constitution, which states that "direct Taxes" shall be proportioned among the several states according to their populations. Hylton argued that this tax was a direct one, and therefore unconstitutional because it had not been apportioned among the states by population. This, of course, was years before the enactment of the Sixteenth Amendment in 1913, authorizing a federal income tax. Prior to 1913, Article I prohibited a federal income tax, but what about a tax on the use or ownership of carriages—

was that the sort of "direct" tax that was only permissible under Article I if apportioned among the states by population?

The Supreme Court, with several justices filing separate opinions (which was customary at that time) upheld the tax as constitutional on the ground that it was not direct and therefore not required to be apportioned. What is most significant about the *Hylton* case is how the Court went about making its decision. As described by Professor David Currie, the Court in *Hylton* "paid little heed to the Constitution's words," and "policy considerations dominated all three opinions" filed by the justices.[27] In fact, each of the opinions asserted that apportioning a carriage tax among the states would be unfair, because a person in a state with few carriages would have to pay a higher tax. While this may or may not be unfair, the justices pointed to nothing in the Constitution itself or the intent of the framers to support their personal views of fairness. Moreover, one of the justices, Justice William Paterson, went so far in his opinion as to assert that the constitutional requirement of apportioning direct taxes was "radically wrong," and therefore should not be extended to this case. In other words, Justice Paterson based his decision, at least in part, on personal antipathy to a duly enacted constitutional provision.

While Justice Paterson went too far in that respect, he and his colleagues on the high Court hardly could have made a decision in the case by looking to the text of the Constitution or the intent of the framers. That is because neither the language of the document nor the intentions of its framers provide an answer to the constitutional issue raised in *Hylton*. The text of the Constitution merely refers to "direct" taxes and offers no definition of what is meant by that phrase. Furthermore, as Professor Currie points out in his excellent historical study, the records of the debates at the Constitutional Convention reveal that "the framers had no clear idea of what they meant by direct taxes."[28] Thus, in order to fulfill their responsibility to decide the case and interpret the Constitution, the justices found it necessary to create meaning for the Constitution, and they sensibly chose to do so on the basis of policy, rather than making a decision for no reason at all. In either case, though, the Court was required to create meaning for the Constitution because it existed in neither the text nor the intent of the framers.

Hylton is but one example of the Supreme Court's creative role in constitutional adjudication. Over the years, the Court has created an immense amount of meaning for the Constitution. This is evident when considering that the document itself contains only 7,269 words,[29] yet the justices have written tens of thousands of pages in the official *United States Reports* explicating those words. Treatises explaining the meaning of the Constitution have been known to run to thousands of pages[30] and still are not able to capture everything there is to know about the document's meaning. The indisputable fact is that there is a vast amount of constitutional meaning that is not contained in the text of the document or its original understanding. To the contrary, most of the meaning of the Constitution consists of doctrine developed by the Supreme Court in the process of textual interpretation. Since the framing and adoption of the Constitution, a large body of doctrine has evolved through the course of constitutional adjudication. Legitimate or not, it is undeniable that constitutional doctrine has grown in great measure at the hands of the Supreme Court.

There is a constant ebb and flow to the Court's constitutional creativity. The Court expands and then contracts the meaning of constitutional provisions. The Court may energize one part of the Constitution while enervating another. Various areas of the law are "constitutionalized" by bringing them within the ambit of constitutional provisions and subjecting them to constitutional standards. For example, beginning in 1964 with the case of *New York Times v. Sullivan*, the Court brought the law of defamation within constitutional perimeters for the first time by applying First Amendment requirements to causes of action for libel. Similarly, in the 1970s the Court began to apply First Amendment principles to advertisements, thereby constitutionalizing the field of commercial speech and subjecting it to constitutional criteria for the first time. Over the years the Court also has expanded the scope of the Due Process Clause and Equal Protection Clause of the Fourteenth Amendment by recognizing various fundamental rights, such as the right to vote,[31] the right to interstate travel,[32] and the right to privacy.[33] In constitutionalizing these and other areas of the law, the Court gives new meaning to the Constitution by expanding its scope.

A dramatic example of the Court expanding the reach of the Equal Protection Clause can be seen in the Court's treatment of laws that discriminate on the basis of gender. Under the original understanding of the Equal Protection Clause there was nothing at all questionable about laws that discriminated on the basis of gender,[34] and for many years after the enactment of the Equal Protection Clause a similar attitude prevailed in the Court. In reviewing gender classifications, the Court almost always concluded that they were constitutional.[35] In fact, after a while the Court approached gender classifications with a strong presumption that they were reasonable and therefore needed only the most minimal scrutiny before being pronounced perfectly consistent with the Constitution.[36] In the 1970s, this all changed. No longer was there a presumption of constitutionality for laws that discriminated on the basis of gender. Henceforth, the Court would scrutinize such laws with heightened sensitivity, and as a result many of them were found to be constitutionally deficient.[37] This amounted to a sea change that significantly expanded the scope of the Equal Protection Clause. Before her appointment to the high Court, Ruth Bader Ginsberg pointed out that the reformulated approach to gender discrimination was only possible through "[b]oldly dynamic interpretation, departing radically from the original understanding."[38]

Of course, if the Court can giveth, it also can taketh away, and the Court has been known to contract constitutional meaning as well as to expand it. At times, the Court de-constitutionalizes areas of law by withdrawing them from constitutional oversight. For example, starting in the late 1930s the Court de-constitutionalized federal regulation of interstate commerce by granting

Congress virtually complete autonomy to regulate commercial transactions. In fact, the meaning of the Interstate Commerce Clause has undergone extreme fluctuation at the hands of the Supreme Court. At first, the Court interpreted the Interstate Commerce Clause to allow Congress to regulate any activity that "concerns more states than one."[39] Later, the Court retracted federal authority by ruling that Congress could regulate only those activities that had a "direct effect" on interstate commerce.[40] Still later, the Court changed its mind and reinstated federal authority by ruling that Congress could regulate any activity that had a "substantial effect" on interstate commerce.[41] Then the Court became more and more deferential in allowing Congress to decide for itself whether an activity had a substantial impact on interstate commerce.[42] This deference eventually became so extreme that there were no practical limits on the congressional authority to regulate commerce. The pendulum started to swing back in the other direction, with the result that the Court in 1995 struck down a federal regulation of commerce for the first time in nearly sixty years.[43] So, the Interstate Commerce Clause is a prime example of a constitutional provision that the Court has continuously reformulated—expanding its meaning, then contracting it, only to expand it again some time later.

In other instances it can be said that through the process of interpretation the Court revises the Constitution by nullifying certain constitutional provisions. For example, the Court has ruled that the so-called Guarantee Clause of Article IV, which provides that "[t]he United States shall guarantee to every State in this Union a Republican Form of Government," is unenforceable.[44] The effect of the Court's decisions regarding the Guarantee Clause is to read it out of the Constitution, almost as if it had never been included there. This sort of constitutional nullification is not an isolated occurrence. The Court also has ruled that the Article I requirement that "a regular Statement and Account of the Receipts and Expenditures of all public Money shall be published" was virtually unenforceable.[45] That provision remains in an incapacitated condition to this very day, as does the Guarantee Clause. Then, too, there are times when the Court vitiates a constitutional provision, only to revive it after a long period of quiescence. In the very first decision interpreting the Fourteenth Amendment after its enactment, the Court gave such a crabbed construction to the Privileges or Immunities Clause as to thoroughly nullify it.[46] Thus, one of the potentially great clauses of the Fourteenth Amendment was rendered nugatory in its very infancy and remained in that sorry state for 127 years until the Court, with a surprising change of mind, finally decided to breathe some life into it.[47] At times devitalizing constitutional provisions and at other times resuscitating them, the Court is able, as it were, to re-write the Constitution.

Constitutional law is dynamic, rather than static.[48] It is continuously evolving, sometimes slower, sometimes faster, but nonetheless perpetually in a state of flux. Although there are some people who like to deride the idea of a "living Constitution,"[49] the fact remains that it is an apt and accurate metaphor. Indeed, the Constitution may be conceived of as a process rather than a thing because its meaning is in a continuous state of evolution. "A poem should not mean, but be," Archibald MacLeish once said.[50] The same is true about the Constitution; it should not mean, but be.

The meaning that the Supreme Court creates for the Constitution finds its predominant source in the personal beliefs and values of the individual justices who comprise the Court at any given time. Deriving from neither the language of the document nor the intent of its framers, a great deal of constitutional doctrine perforce has its roots in the personal convictions of the Supreme Court justices whose "province and duty" it is to say what the Constitution means.[51] Throughout the Court's history, the justices have employed their own beliefs and values as the foundation of their constitutional rulings. From federal supremacy,[52] vested rights,[53] and commercial enterprise,[54] through autonomy of the individual,[55] gender equality,[56] and states' rights,[57] there is a long list of beliefs and values that the justices themselves have deemed worthy of constitutional shelter. The justices often turn inward to find values that will provide meaning for the Constitution. The policy considerations that dominated the three opinions filed in *Hylton*[58] flowed from the personal convictions of the justices who wrote those opinions. John Marshall's personal belief in a strong federal government led him to one decision after another expanding federal authority. Generations later, William Rehnquist's personal preference for states' rights would lead him to one decision after another to the extent, it has been said, that he would nullify the Civil War amendments.[59] Justice Oliver Wendell Holmes' faith in a marketplace of ideas, which came to be accepted as the guiding principle of the First Amendment, is a wonderful idea; despite his claim, however, it is not "the theory of our Constitution."[60] Rather, it is Holmes' theory of the Constitution, a theory that he devised, or, more likely, that he cribbed from John Milton or John Stuart Mill—and read into the Constitution. In the early part of the twentieth century, a strong personal belief in *laissez faire* economics animated a majority of the justices; A half-century or so later, a different group of justices was moved by a belief, no less strong or personal, in the value of individual autonomy.

Indeed, the justices often find it necessary to rely upon personal values in order to invest the Constitution with meaning. Certainly, the personal values of the justices are informed by the original understanding of the Constitution as well as by other historical sources and contemporary social mores. The personal values of the justices, however, are the heart of their decisions interpreting the Constitution. Even Justice Scalia, an ardent opponent of nonoriginalism, admits that, as an historical matter, the high majority of Supreme Court decisions have been rendered on the basis of what the justices currently believe is desirable, rather than on the basis of the original understanding of the Constitution.[61] Contemporary social ethos, along with history and tradition, shapes the beliefs of each justice. Once those beliefs have been formed they then become the source of meaning that the justices provide for the Constitution. The personal values of the justices are the ultimate source of the meaning that the Supreme Court creates for the Constitution.[62] Notwithstanding the orthodox protestation that it is improper for the Court to engage in "judicial legislation" or "policy making," that in fact is what the Court has always done by formulating constitutional meaning based upon the personal convictions of the justices.

In the pre-modern period prior to the twentieth century, the Court tended to effectuate the convictions of the justices beneath a cloak of natural law. Not surprisingly, the Court was hardly immune from the heavy influence that the natural law tradition exerted on early American thought. After all, there is a certain imprimatur, not to mention smug satisfaction, to be gained by professing that the law is not made by mere mortals, but rather preexists in a state of nature to be discovered by those with the extraordinary ability to find it. Being on the side of angels, history, or civilization is decidedly easier than standing up alone for your own beliefs. And so it was that in an earlier time the Court utilized an assortment of natural law concepts to proclaim constitutional doctrine. There were "the divine ordinance,"[63] "the natural order,"[64] "the fundamental laws of government,"[65] "the lessons of history,"[66] "the norms of civilization,"[67] "the concept of ordered liberty,"[68] and "the sense of justice."[69] (For the Anglophile, there was always Justice Felix Frankfurter's "canons of decency and fairness, which express the notions of justice of English-speaking peoples."[70]). When employing these natural law conceptions, the Court gave the impression that, rather than creating law, it was discovering or revealing law that preexisted in the nature of things. By resort to this artifice, the Court was able to constitutionalize the personal convictions held by the justices. Behind the facade of predetermination, the premodern Court read into the Constitution personal values and beliefs held by the justices. The guise, however, was transparent. The source of meaning for the Constitution was neither God, the natural order, history, nor civilization (English-speaking or otherwise); its true source was the personal value systems of the justices of the Supreme Court.

After the Civil War, the natural law tradition exerted little influence upon legal thought, except in the field of constitutional law,[71] and even in that field its influence soon waned.[72] Shortly after the breakdown of the natural law tradition, the Supreme Court became more willing to shed the disguise of predetermination for its constitutional preferences. Although the Court's practice of legal formalism (discussed in the next chapter) continued to partially obscure the Court's creative function, the reality of constitutional adjudication became increasingly apparent. Throughout the twentieth century, the Court typically has constitutionalized the convictions of the justices through the process of positive law,[73] which more openly manifests the Court's lawmaking function. Whether through the methodology of positive or natural law, however, the Supreme Court perennially has originated meaning for the Constitution, meaning that is rooted in the justices' own beliefs and values. Historically, then, the practice of judicial creativity in the constitutional process has deep and venerable roots.

The practice of attempting to find meaning in the original understanding of the Constitution parallels the natural law tradition in several respects. First, it denies creativity in the judicial function. Second, it posits a neutral judiciary devoid of values or beliefs that finds law rather than makes it. Finally, it insists that the Supreme Court functions as a disinterested medium revealing constitutional law that has a fixed meaning that preexists in history.[74] By viewing the text and history of the document as the only viable sources of constitutional meaning, originalism obscures the truth, which is that the Court creates meaning for the Constitution.

Under the guise of originalism, the Court frequently professes to discover constitutional doctrine strictly from the document's language or history, when in fact it is doing nothing of the sort.[75] Analysis of the written opinions of the Court often shows that its purported reliance upon the words of the Constitution or upon the framers' intent is more pretense than reality. First, the Court has faced few constitutional issues that can be definitively resolved by the Constitution's text. Second, the Court has not been above the use of forced readings of constitutional language as a means of concealing the fact that it is creating meaning for the Constitution from the justices' own beliefs and values. Two early instances of this technique can be observed in *Fletcher v. Peck*[76] and *Trustees of Dartmouth College v. Woodward.*[77] In the former, the Court stretched the meaning of the Contracts Clause of Article I to include a state legislative grant of land. In the latter, the Court extended the meaning of the same clause to encompass a college charter granted by King George III prior to the Revolution. In both instances, the Court may well be accused of manipulating constitutional language to revise its meaning. Indeed, no less than Thomas Jefferson accused Chief Justice Marshall, who wrote the Supreme Court's opinion in *Fletcher*, of "twistification" of the Constitution to conform to Marshall's personal biases.[78] A more modern example of "twistification" can be found in the Court's ruling in *United States v. Salerno*, upholding pretrial detention without bail on the ground that the Eighth Amendment's prohibition of excessive bail "says nothing about whether bail shall be available at all"[79]—a rationalization that so strains the text of the Constitution as to turn its meaning on its head.[80]

There are further instances where the Court has engaged in a more complex manipulation of constitutional language to obscure judicial creativity. An illustration of this phenomenon can be seen in *Marbury v. Madison*,[81] which is generally agreed to be the most important decision ever rendered by the Supreme Court because it established the power of judicial review. In *Marbury*, the Court declined to accept a grant of statutory jurisdiction on the ground that it was "repugnant to the Constitution."[82] Although the Court's decision purports to emanate directly from the document's text, in truth it does no such thing. Underlying the Court's professed reliance upon the constitutional text is a significant assumption—that the Court possesses the august authority to determine that a statute duly enacted by Congress and approved by the President (or enacted over his veto) is nevertheless "repugnant to the Constitution."[83] By making this unspoken assumption, the Court was able to establish judicial review as the law of the land and thereby to direct the course of the nation's history. That judicial review is nowhere mentioned in the Constitution and finds, at best, questionable support in the original understanding of the Constitution did not deter the Court from instituting it as a constitutional doctrine. Obtaining neither from the text of the Constitution nor its history, the power of judicial review was cut from whole cloth by the Supreme Court with the appearance that it was compelled by a plain reading of the document. The simplicity of the Court's reasoning in *Marbury* is deceptive, creating a facade behind which the Court worked its artfulness to institute judicial review.

It is tempting to suppose that the meaning of the Constitution is set in the text and its original understanding. However, as a matter of historical fact the Supreme Court "has never accepted that view."[84]

THE THEORETICAL FOUNDATION OF CONSTITUTIONAL CREATIVITY

As a theoretical matter, the Supreme Court's creative role is inevitable because it is the only practical way to interpret the Constitution. Attempts to find meaning for the Constitution in its text or history are, for the most part, doomed to failure.

The Text of the Document

It frequently is necessary for the Supreme Court to create meaning for the Constitution. This happens because the Constitution—a document designed, in the words of the great Chief Justice John Marshall, to "endure for ages"—is rife with generalities and abstract language.[85] As Marshall explained, for a constitution to contain accurate details of the various governmental powers it addresses and the means by which they may be executed would "partake of the prolixity of a legal code, and could scarcely be embraced by the human mind."[86] The very nature of a constitution requires "that only its great outlines should be marked,"[87] leaving it to the Supreme Court to supply meaning that will eventually fill in those outlines.

The original Constitution, for instance, uses extremely abstract language in granting "legislative Powers" to Congress, "executive Power" to the President, and "judicial Power" to the federal courts. Article IV speaks of "privileges and immunities," while Article V refers to "due process of law"—two obviously abstract concepts. Nor are the amendments to the Constitution free of generality. The Fourteenth Amendment, while reiterating the abstract concepts of privileges, immunities, and due process of law, adds the equally abstract (and equally, if not more, sublime) concept of equal protection of the laws. General language abounds in the Fourth Amendment's prohibition of "unreasonable" searches and seizures, not to mention the Eighth Amendment's ban of "cruel and unusual" punishment. The text of the Constitution, by necessity, teems with generality and abstraction.

Even many of the relatively specific provisions of the Constitution need to be supplied with meaning that cannot be found within the four corners of the document. The Commerce Clause grants Congress authority to regulate commerce among the several states. Does this mean that Congress may prohibit interstate transactions for moral reasons,[88] or intrastate transactions that affect commerce in other states?[89] The First Amendment states that Congress shall make no law prohibiting the free exercise of religion. Does this mean the government may not prohibit polygamy[90] or child labor if dictated by religious belief?[91] The First Amendment also states that Congress shall make no law abridging the freedom of speech. Does this mean that the government may not regulate obscene,[92] slanderous,[93] or deceptive speech?[94] These questions, which all arose in actual cases, cannot be answered by mere linguistic analysis of the Constitution. In that respect they are typical; most constitutional issues presented to the Court cannot be resolved simply by textual analysis. Much of the text of the Constitution is of little assistance in dealing with the various and sundry issues that arise. In many instances the Constitution itself is a prelude or remote starting place in the interpretative process. In reality there is no choice but to look beyond the document's text to provide meaning for it.

Certainly there are some provisions in the Constitution that are extremely specific in their wording. An example is Article II's directive that no person under the age of thirty-five shall be eligible for the office of President. But even with these very specific textual provisions, the Supreme Court has not always been content to strictly follow constitutional dictates. Thus, in *United States v. Richardson*[95] the Court ruled that the Article I requirement that "a regular Statement and Account of the Receipts and Expenditures of all public Money shall be published"[96]—a rather specific directive—was virtually unenforceable. So, while the meaning of this constitutional provision appears to be rather clear, in actual practice it has no meaning. One cannot help but wonder if the Court would take a similar approach, should the question ever arise, to Article II's age requirement for the Presidency. If someone under the age of thirty-five was elected President, it is very possible that the Court would hold that the age requirement of Article II was unenforceable. Specificity of constitutional wording, it seems, is not always enough to ensure the application of a constitutional provision by the Supreme Court.

Still, the larger point is that much of the text of the Constitution ranges from the moderately to the exceedingly general, and therefore needs a great deal of supplementation. Historically, that supplementation has been provided by the Supreme Court, which, incrementally, though persistently, has supplied meaning for a document riddled with generality and abstraction.

The Intent of the Framers

Relying upon the framers' intent to supply meaning for the Constitution has serious theoretical difficulties. Reconstructing what the framers intended when they drafted the Constitution in 1787 is a daunting task that may well be impossible to achieve. Justice Robert Jackson found it a staggering burden, as evidenced by his remark that "Just what our forefathers did envision or would have envisioned had they foreseen modern conditions, must be divined from materials almost as enigmatic as the dreams Joseph was called upon to interpret for Pharaoh."[97] There are several reasons why it is so difficult to ascertain the framers' intent. To begin, the evidentiary record of the Constitutional Convention is severely deficient. The *Journal of the Constitutional Convention*, which is the official record of the proceedings, is not a stenographic rendition and contains only the barest account of what transpired at the Convention.[98] To make matters worse, it is not entirely accurate. The notes for the *Journal* were carelessly kept and have been shown to contain a number of mistakes.[99] In many instances, the "very scanty history" contained in the records of the Convention "sheds little light" on the meaning of constitutional provisions.[100] Notes of the Convention also were taken by James Madison, but those were unofficial and frequently sketchy.[101] It has been estimated that at best Madison reported only one-fifth of what was said at the Convention,[102] and other estimates place the figure as low as ten percent.[103] *The Federalist Papers*, which is often mentioned as a source of the framers' intent, has no official status as such. Five or six of the eighty-five articles of the *Federalist* were written by John Jay, who was not a delegate to the Convention.[104] The remaining articles were written either by James Madison or Alexander Hamilton, both of whom were delegates, although after the first month of the Convention Hamilton's attendance was sporadic.[105] Most significantly, however, the *Federalist* was not written as an impartial account of the framers' intentions. Rather, it was more in the nature of an advocate's brief, written to convince others to ratify the Constitution.[106] For different reasons, then, neither the unofficial *Federalist*, Madison's unofficial and sketchy notes, nor even the official *Journal* of the Convention are fertile ground for unearthing the framers' intentions.

Furthermore, the historical record of the framers' intent concerning the Bill of Rights, which comprise the first ten amendments to the Constitution, is even more sparse. Enacted almost as an afterthought, the Bill of Rights was given relatively little consideration by the framers and there is practically no record of what the framers thought about the ten amendments contained in it.[107]

Even when the record cannot be faulted, ascertaining the framers' intent can be tricky. For one thing, there is the question of what level of abstraction to consider.[108] Human intention often can be interpreted at various levels of abstraction, ranging from the specific to the general. Did the framers of the Equal Protection Clause, for instance, intend only to prohibit unjust discrimination against African-Americans, or did they intend to prohibit other forms of racial discrimination, or even all forms of class-based discrimination? Was the Equal Protection Clause meant to protect minorities in general or only certain minorities? Whatever may be the answer to these questions and others like them depends on the level of abstraction one focuses upon, and hence gives the decision maker a good deal of discretion in interpreting what the framers meant.

In other words, the framers' intent is not set in stone. Rather, it is indeterminate and subject to varying plausible interpretations.

There are other difficulties in attempting to ascertain the intent of the framers. There are some matters about which the framers had little or no discernible intent. For instance, the Guarantee Clause of Article IV provides that "the United States shall guarantee to every State in this Union a Republican Form of Government," yet historical research shows that the framers had no clear idea of what they meant by a "Republican Form of Government."[109] In the days of the framing of the constitution, the phrase "republicanism" was little more than a hazy slogan.[110] As Robert Shalhope puts it, only one thing was certain about the Guarantee Clause: Americans believed that it meant an absence of an aristocracy and a monarchy.[111] Beyond that, there was no agreement about what constituted a republican form of government; in fact there was a great deal of disagreement that eventually led to harsh dissension.[112]

It would be a mistake to think that the Guarantee Clause is the only constitutional provision about which the framers had little discernible intention. Other examples certainly can be cited. As already noted, the records of the Constitutional Convention show that the framers did not have a clear idea of what they meant by the phrase "direct taxes" as used in Article I.[113] The records also are barren in providing any clue about the framers' intent regarding the Compact Clause of Article I.[114] There are a number of constitutional provisions, then, about which the framers had no cognizable intent.

At other times, the words of the framers and their actions contradict one another. Legal historian Stanley Kutler notes, for example, that while the Republican framers of the Fourteenth Amendment expressed a considerable amount of distrust of the federal judiciary, which could be taken as an indication that they did not want the courts to play an expansive role in construing that amendment, those same Republican framers, on the other hand, did nothing of substance to restrict the federal judicial power—to the contrary, they actively promoted new courts.[115] What is one to make of all this? Did the Republicans favor a restrained or an active judicial role in applying the Fourteenth Amendment? The answer, if indeed there is one, is a matter of debate; once again, we have an ambiguous historical record subject to differing plausible interpretations.

Furthermore, as might be expected, the framers did not express an intention about every constitutional issue that would arise after the document was drafted and adopted. No group of people, regardless of their talents, enjoys that sort of prescience. When the framers did address particular problems, often only a few of the framers spoke out. Frequently what is taken to be the intent of the framers as a group turns out to be the intent of merely a few or even only one of the framers, and it would be a mistake to suppose that those framers who expressed their views spoke for those who remained silent. As the Supreme Court noted in another context, "those who did not speak may not have agreed with those who did."[116]

There are also constitutional issues about which the framers expressed conflicting intentions.[117] A collective body of fifty-five individuals, the framers embraced a widely diverse and frequently inconsistent set of views. The two principal architects of the Constitution, James Madison and Alexander Hamilton, had extremely divergent political views. Madison also on occasion differed with George Washington over the meaning of the Constitution. When Washington, who had presided over the Constitutional Convention, became President, he claimed that the underlying intent of the Constitution gave him the sole authority as President to proclaim neutrality and to withhold treaty papers from Congress. Madison, who had been a leader at the Constitutional Convention, disagreed vehemently. And so, the man who would come to be known as the father of the nation and the man who would come to be known as the father of the Constitution[118] had opposing views of the original understanding of the document.[119]

This shows that it is anomalous to suppose that a multi-member group of human beings such as the framers can share a unitary intention about the sort of complex and controversial political issues addressed in the Constitution. As Ronald Dworkin explains, it is a mistake to think that the intention of the framers is some psychological fact locked in history waiting to be unearthed from old documents and proceedings.[120] "There is no such things as the intention of Framers waiting to be discovered, even in principle. There is only some such thing waiting to be invented."[121]

We can see, then, that the framers' intent is, at best, inadequately documented, ambiguous, and inconclusive; at worst, it is nonexistent, an illusion put together with smoke and mirrors.

The Intent of the Ratifiers

Some adherents of originalism shift the focus of inquiry by asserting that it is not the framers' original understanding of the Constitution that matters, but the ratifiers' original understanding. This may be taken to refer to the participants in the ratifying conventions or legislative sessions throughout the nation,[122] or even the people whom they represented. Ultimately, it is the people of the nation who adopted the Constitution, and hence it is their voices or the voices of their representatives who directly ratified the document that should count. According to this view, it is the original understanding of those who adopted or ratified the Constitution that should be plumbed to provide authoritative meaning for the document.[123] Statements made by the framers of the Constitution may be taken as evidence of the adopters' intent, but evidence only.[124] Thus revised, this version of originalism refers primarily to the original understanding of the ratifiers of the Constitution, as illuminated in the materials circa 1787 to 1788 that express their views.[125]

But if there are problems about finding a unified understanding of constitutional provisions among the fifty-five framers of the Constitution, imagine the problems in attempting to find a unified understanding among the hundreds of ratifiers of the Constitution or the people whom they represented! All the difficulties discussed concerning ascertaining the intent of the framers increase exponentially in attempting to determine the intent of the ratifiers. Even if we were to consider only the intentions of the delegates to the state ratifying conventions, and not consider the people whom they represented, the task obviously is overwhelming. The state ratifying conventions elicited, as might be expected, a wide range of opinions concerning the meaning of the Constitution.[126] Looking to the records of the state ratifying conventions only adds to the confusion. It has been shown that the records of the state ratifying conventions are extremely unreliable,[127] more so than the record of the Constitutional Convention in Philadelphia.[128] In a number of states the records contain gross inaccuracies and omissions; in some instances they are so fragmentary as to be useless.[129] In other states the records are obscure or even unintelligible.[130] In some states the records were blatantly doctored; in Pennsylvania, for example, the convention reporter was an ardent Federalist who "probably had no qualms about taking money from Pennsylvania Federalist leaders to delete all the Anti-Federalist speeches in the Convention."[131]

Ascertaining the original understanding of the ratifiers is, to put it mildly, next to impossible. Thus, some originalists, who believe that the intent of the ratifiers rather than the framers is decisive, nonetheless concede that "the difficulties of ascertaining the intent of the ratifiers leave little choice but to accept the intent of the Framers as a fair reflection of it,"[132] despite the fact that many states ratified the Constitution prior to receiving any report concerning the framers' intentions about the document.[133] This being so, it is nothing more than a fiction to suggest that the framers' understanding of the Constitution reflects that of the ratifiers.

Other originalists have acknowledged the difficulty in determining the original understanding of the ratifiers. Even Justice Scalia admits that:

> [I]t is often exceedingly difficult to plumb the original understanding of an ancient text. Properly done, the task requires the consideration of an enormous mass of material—in the case of the Constitution and its amendments, for example, to mention only one element, the records of the ratifying debates in all the states. Even beyond that, it requires an evaluation of the reliability of that material—many of the reports of the ratifying debates, for example, are thought to be quite unreliable. And further still, it requires immersing oneself in the political and intellectual atmosphere of the time.[134]

While admitting that this sort of undertaking is better suited to the historian than the lawyer,[135] Justice Scalia neglects to mention that the Supreme Court has had an abysmal record of playing historian. Experts agree that the Court's forays into historical exegesis have seen the Court ignoring, misunderstanding, and twisting historical information. Justice Scalia also seems unperturbed that, if pursued by the Supreme Court, a more accomplished effort of analyzing history would inundate the Court to the point of ineffectiveness. In fact, Scalia affectionately portrays an opinion written by Chief Justice William Howard Taft in the originalist mode, which took almost three years to write and was seventy pages long.[136] "Done perfectly," Scalia points out, "it might well take thirty years and 7,000 pages."[137] Even when done less than perfectly, this sort of undertaking would be such a burden that the Court would be able to decide precious few cases, a prospect that in all probability would be welcomed by Justice Scalia, who claims to be an adherent of judicial restraint.

For all his love of history, Justice Scalia seems to be unaware that "doing" history is a creative act. As any good historian knows, interpretation of the past entails considerably more than rummaging around in old archives to find hidden materials. Astute historian Edward Hallett Carr explains, "The belief in a hard core of historical facts existing objectively and independently of the interpretation of the historian is a preposterous fallacy."[138] Despite clichés to the contrary, historical events do not speak for themselves.[139] History easily can be misread if we are not careful to engage in thoughtful analysis of historical sources. Historical evidence often cannot be taken at face value; rather, it must be interpreted in light of its context, which is a complicated, though necessary, exercise.

The historian, therefore, is "necessarily selective" and the "element of interpretation enters into every fact of history."[140] Historical analysis, then, entails creativity as well as discovery. "In truth the actual past is gone; and the world of history is an intangible world, *re-created imaginatively*, and present in our minds."[141] Even when done properly, historical analysis leaves a good deal of room for the historian to make value judgments. The historian sees things from a particular point of view, according to a particular value system. The historical approach, therefore, would still leave the Supreme Court with the sort of discretion that Justice Scalia disdains.[142] Notwithstanding his disdain, however, judicial discretion is unavoidable. Whether the Court takes an historical or some other approach to constitutional interpretation, the exercise of judicial discretion is a necessary element of the process.

While the open-endedness of history should not be enough to scare the Court away from historical analysis of the Constitution, the Court should understand that the meaning of the Constitution is not fixed in history (or anywhere else, for that matter) and waiting to be found. Certainly there is no fixed meaning of the ratifiers' original understanding of the Constitution. If, as previously discussed, it is an illusion to suppose that the framers possessed a unified intent about Constitutional provisions, then it is nothing short of a grand illusion to suppose that the ratifiers possessed one. Given the number of delegates at even a single state's ratifying convention or legislative session, it is rare enough to find a unified understanding of constitutional provisions within one state. To expect to find a unified intent from state to state, obviously, is even more unlikely. This was especially so when the original Constitution was ratified, because varying interpretations of it were presented from one state ratifying convention to another.[143] To suppose that the delegates at all the state ratifying conventions or sessions—or even a majority of them—possessed a unified intent is absurd. And to suppose that a unified will can be found among the sovereign electorate—the people—is beyond absurd. The delegates to the state constitutional conventions held a wide variety of views about the Constitution they were ratifying, and the people whom they represented had an even wider variety of views.

In searching for the framers' or the ratifiers' original understanding, what one is more likely to discover is what one wants to discover.[144] A judge can always pretend that he or she is finding the ratifiers' will, but in truth it is the judge's own will that is being revealed. Justice Scalia's historical approach, then, suffers from the very flaw that he ascribes to non-originalist theories of constitutional interpretation: it gives judges a great deal of discretion to read their own values into the Constitution. Moreover, the historical approach is more insidious than non-originalist approaches, because it sneaks a judge's personal views into the Constitution by denying their true nature and pretending they are nothing more than the intention of the ratifiers.

Close examination of Supreme Court opinions reveals that the Court frequently uses the historical record to rationalize its own decisions and to create an illusion that it is doing nothing more than following the dictates of history.[145] In 1939, after an extensive analysis, Professor Jacobus tenBroek concluded that the Court most often relied upon the records of the Constitutional Convention "to affirm a conclusion which apparently, and sometimes assertedly, rests chiefly upon other grounds."[146] Unfortunately, it cannot be said that the Court's practice in that respect has improved much since the tenBroek study.

Originalism is a difficult faith to keep. What is one to do, after all, upon discovering an original meaning that is not very palatable to one's own values? The bane of originalism, it seems, is that originalists are forever slipping into a non-originalist mode. They tend to follow the original understanding of the Constitution when it suits their purposes to do so, but ignore the original understanding when it does not suit their purposes. Even Justice Scalia has stumbled from the orthodox way on a number of occasions. Perhaps this should come as no surprise. He did warn us back in 1989, over two years after his appointment to the Court, that "in a crunch I may prove a faint-hearted originalist."[147] Still, it came as somewhat of a shock when an astute observer of the Court exposed no less than three decisions in a single term when Justice Scalia let "his political passions overwhelm his originalist principles."[148] In each instance, it seems, Justice Scalia ignored an original understanding of a constitutional provision in favor of subjective policy preferences.[149] A cynic might see this as not so much a matter of faint-heartedness as hypocrisy.

Even if one could somehow overcome the insurmountable difficulties described above in reconstructing (or constructing) the original understanding of the framers or the ratifiers, it still might not be analytically valid to follow that path. Whatever understanding the framers or ratifiers may have had about the Constitution was formed in the context of a past reality and in accordance with past attitudes, both of which have changed considerably since the Constitution was drafted. History is inherently evolutionary, and a true historical approach to interpreting the Constitution would not come to an abrupt end with the adoption of the Constitution in 1787. Rather, it would recognize the evolving nature of history as an ongoing source of meaning for the Constitution. It is simplistic and ahistorical to believe that the Constitution can be interpreted simply by reference to the original intent of the framers or ratifiers. To transfer those intentions, fashioned under past conditions and attitudes, to contemporary situations may produce sorry consequences that even the framers would have abhorred had they been able to foresee them. Blindly following intentions formulated in reaction to past conditions and attitudes that have long since changed does not, in the end, effectuate the intent of the framers or ratifiers. Nor is it very likely to be an effective means of dealing with contemporary issues. Adherence to the original understanding thus reduces the capacity of the Constitution to be used to respond to the needs of modern society. As Woodrow Wilson stated, "The Constitution was not meant to hold the government back to the time of horses and wagons."[150]

Some scholars take this line of reasoning one step further by maintaining that the original understanding is inextricably locked into the past and has no meaning for the present. In other words, because the original understanding was formed in reference to a reality and ways of thinking that no longer exist, it has no meaning for the present day. The intent of framers and ratifiers is inextricably bound to the past and it is senseless to attempt to transplant it to the present or future. What the framers and ratifiers may have intended for their times is not what they may have intended for ours. Life constantly changes, and the reality and ideas that surrounded the framers are long since gone.

Consider, for instance, the authority granted to Congress by Article I to "regulate Commerce among the several States." Originally this was intended to allow Congress to regulate no more than interstate transactions, leaving it to each state to deal with internal transactions that have no impact beyond its borders. In those days, however, it was much simpler to draw a line between inter- and intrastate commerce. There was not much of a national economy, and many transactions were purely intrastate. By the end of the nineteenth century, the situation was radically different[151] and is even more so today. Now there is an immense national—even international—economy that affects every locality. There is a vast network of commerce, connecting its various elements to one another. Even transactions that occur entirely within one state's borders have repercussions in other states, not to mention other nations. These prodigious changes in our economy render the original understanding of the Commerce Clause irrelevant. The original understanding of "Commerce among the several States" was formulated when economic conditions were drastically different and simply has no application to the contemporary worldwide economic situation.

Another example of changed conditions has to do with the question of whether impeachment of the President or other government officials should follow the procedures the framers or ratifiers may have intended. In a book he wrote about impeachment well before presiding over the impeachment trial of President Clinton, Chief Justice Rehnquist observed that when the framers provided for impeachment in the Constitution, they "had not envisioned political parties as we now know them."[152] This led Chief Justice Rehnquist to ask whether "the dominant role played by political parties make[s] the Senate a partisan tribunal, which would be willing to undermine the fundamental principles of the Constitution in order to remove a political enemy from office?"[153] Seven years later, the House of Representatives impeached President Clinton in an extremely partisan manner. One wonders what the framers and ratifiers would have thought of this, but whatever intent the framers or ratifiers may have had about impeachment hardly seem applicable to the partisan affair it has become. If, as Chief Justice Rehnquist says, the framers did not envision the prominent role that political parties would play in our government, should the original understanding (assuming there was one) of how impeachment should operate be followed? Or should that original understanding be revised in light of the changed circumstances—the rise of political parties and partisan nature of impeachment—so that the "fundamental principles" of the Constitution are not undermined?

The futility of looking to the original understanding to resolve modern constitutional issues can be further illustrated by a number of cases that have arisen under the Fourth and Fifth Amendments of the Constitution. The Fourth Amendment prohibits unreasonable searches and seizures, and further requires that no search warrants be issued unless there is probable cause that a crime has been committed. Are bugging and other electronic surveillance devices "unreasonable searches"?[154] May they be used by the police without a warrant based on probable cause? What about the modern practice of some law enforcement agencies that use airplanes to fly over a suspect's property to take pictures with a telescopic camera? Is that an "unreasonable search"?[155] The Fifth Amendment states that no person shall be compelled in a criminal case to be a witness against himself. What about forcing a suspect to take a Breathalyzer test or a blood test,[156] or to have his or her stomach pumped?[157] Do these procedures amount to self-incrimination that violates the Fifth Amendment?

Whatever one thinks should be the answers to these questions, they cannot be found by looking to the original understanding of the Fourth or Fifth Amendments. Neither the framers nor the ratifiers had any intention or understanding concerning electronic surveillance, airplanes, telescopic cameras, Breathalyzer tests, blood tests, or stomach pumping for the simple reason that none of these things existed at that time. Not even Benjamin Franklin, for all his wisdom and inventiveness, was able to foresee that in the twentieth century constables would zip around in flying machines taking snapshots of criminal suspects through a telescopic lens.[158]

As Justice William Brennan, Jr. observed, an awareness of history does not always resolve the concrete problems of today, and, in fact, too literal a quest for past intentions may be counterproductive.[159] The framers of the Constitution may have been wise men, but not so wise that they could predict the future. That is not to say that the framers' or ratifiers' intentions should be ignored; certainly there are valuable lessons to be learned from history. It is to say, though, that the original understanding should not be used as an authoritative source to dictate the meaning of the Constitution. We should allow the framers and ratifiers to advise us, but not to rule us. As Chief Justice Earl Warren said on the occasion of his retirement from the high Court, "We, of course, venerate the past, but our focus is on the problems of the day and the future as far as we can see it."[160]

The framers themselves seemed to be aware that they could not predict the future, and they therefore took the sensible course of formulating the Constitution in a way that would allow it to be adapted to changing conditions as time passed.[161] Unfortunately, the sensibility of that course of action often is ignored by those who rigidly cling to the myopic myth of originalism.

Given the theoretical difficulties of the historical approach of relying on the original understanding to provide meaning for the Constitution, it should come as no surprise that this approach has been an abysmal failure when practiced by the Supreme Court. Scholars who have closely studied the Court agree that the Court's attempts at playing historian have been washouts. The Court often has been criticized for manipulating, revising, or even making up history when it purports to be following the original understanding. Perhaps it was inevitable that the Court would prove to be such a poor historian, because, as a theoretical matter, little meaning for the Constitution is fixed in history. Neither the document itself nor the original understanding of it is capable of providing much meaning for the Constitution. As a theoretical matter, meaning for the Constitution must be created by the Supreme Court.

THE POLITICAL FOUNDATION OF CONSTITUTIONAL CREATIVITY

Originalists frequently inveigh against the Supreme Court creating meaning for the Constitution on the ground that it is undemocratic.[162] It is argued that in a democratic system of government, Supreme Court justices—unelected officials who are unaccountable to the electorate—should not be able to create meaning for the highest law of the land. This theme echoes the criticism that was leveled during the Jacksonian era against the power of common law judges to make law.[163] Although the authority of common law judges to make law is now a widely accepted practice, aversion still exists to judicial creativity in the constitutional arena. That large bodies of tort law or contract law are made by judges is quite acceptable today; that constitutional law should be no different has been a more bitter pill to swallow. It does not seem to comport with democratic theory to find that the least representative branch of our government is creating no less than the supreme law of the land based for the most part on the personal convictions and beliefs of individual justices.

Therefore, originalists—or at least some of them—turn to the intentions of the framers as a source of interpreting the Constitution. According to this approach, there can be no better evidence of the meaning of constitutional text than the intent of those individuals who actually authored it. Words mean what their drafters intended them to mean, it is said, and therefore the goal should be to interpret the Constitutions by examining with the greatest possible care the intent of the framers.

Oddly enough, following the intent of the framers is not especially consistent with democratic theory. Of the fifty-five delegates to the Constitutional Convention, many of them had little to say and sixteen did not even sign the Constitution.[164] Adhering to the intention of such a small group of persons is hardly an exercise in democracy. Moreover, Ronald Dworkin pointed out that the fifty-five framers of the original Constitution "were remarkably unrepresentative of the people as a whole."[165] They were not chosen in any way approved by existing national law, and a majority of the population, including women, slaves, and the poor, were excluded from participating in selecting the framers as well as from the ratification process.[166] Furthermore, what the framers did not express in the Constitution itself has no binding force.[167] The Constitution was submitted to the representatives of (some of) the people and was ratified by them. Hence, legally speaking, the document represents the will of the people. The intent of the framers, however, was not voted upon by anyone and therefore does not express the will of the people. Lacking that imprimatur, it cannot be considered in any sense authoritative.[168] Once ratified, the words of the Constitution possess the force of law; the same cannot be said for what the framers did not express in the Constitution. Therefore, their unexpressed intention "has no binding force on us."[169]

In all probability, the framers did not intend their original understanding of the Constitution to be binding on future generations.[170] Therefore, the framers devised the document in a way that it could be molded to changing conditions by later generations. Constitutional scholars have noted that "[f]rom the text of the Constitution, it often seems plausible to suggest that the framers intended to delegate, to people in the future, the power to make decisions about what the provision means in the particular circumstances."[171] The Constitution contains a number of open-ended provisions that appear to be invitations to future constitutional creativity. The Ninth Amendment, in particular, which specifies that "[t]he enumeration in the Constitution, of certain rights, shall not be construed to deny or disparage others retained by the people," seems to encourage the notion of a living Constitution. If one insists upon strict adherence to the framers' intent, the ultimate irony is that the framers may well have intended that their intent not be honored. James Madison, the principal architect of the Constitution, stated that the debates and incidental decisions of the Constitutional Convention "have no authoritative character" and should not be consulted as a source of "legitimate meaning" for the Constitution.[172] He said that if meaning needed to be found for the Constitution, one should search elsewhere than "in the opinions or intentions of the Body which planned and proposed the Constitution.[173]

The "elsewhere" that Madison suggested as a more legitimate source of constitutional meaning was "in the sense attached to it by the people in their respective State Conventions where it recd. all the authority which it possesses."[174] This certainly enjoys the advantage of being a more democratic approach than looking to the intent of the framers. As Jack Rakove observes, Madison's stance has one great advantage: it is consistent with the idea that the Constitution derives its authority from the consent of the governed.[175] However, Professor Rakove continues, "if Madison's position has its logic, it creates as many problems as it solves."[176] First, there is considerable question as to why the intentions of the ratifiers should be considered authoritative, especially since no one voted on them, either. It was the words of the Constitution that were voted on at the state conventions, not the intentions of the ratifiers. Like the intent of the framers, the intent of the ratifiers was not put to any vote, and hence lacks the legitimacy that comes only through the ballot box. Moreover, as previously explained, ascertaining the intent of the ratifiers is an impossible task, if not a quest for something that simply does not exist.[177] Perhaps representative, but far from authoritative, and incomprehensible to the point of unreality, the understanding of the ratifiers is not a very viable source by which to provide meaning for the Constitution.

The premise of Madison's view is that the authority of the Constitution derives strictly from the people who enacted it. That view, however, does not preclude the notion of a living Constitution with an evolutionary meaning. While the original authority of the Constitution derives from the generation that ratified it, its continuing authority derives from following generations, who have retained the Constitution as the supreme law of the land. After all, the people possess the authority to amend the Constitution or even to repeal it. To the extent that they do not do so, the legitimacy of the Constitution is perpetually re-ratified. Constitutional legitimacy does not derive solely from the generation that originally enacted the document; it also derives from each succeeding generation. Ratification is a continual process, repeated by each generation that keeps the Constitution in force. Thus, while the original understanding of the people may be a legitimate source of constitutional meaning, the understanding of later generations is no less a legitimate source of constitutional meaning. It hardly is democratic to use the political convictions of a past generation to bind future generations. James Madison, I think, would agree that as far as legitimacy is concerned, each generation must define the Constitution for itself.

As the Supreme Court stated so eloquently in *Planned Parenthood v. Casey*:

> Our constitution is a covenant running from the first generation of Americans to us and then to future generations. It is a coherent succession. Each generation must learn anew that the Constitution's written terms embody ideas and aspirations that must survive more

ages than one. We accept our responsibility not to retreat from interpreting the full meaning of the covenant in light of all of our precedents.[178]

The originalist objection to the undemocratic aspects of the Supreme Court creating constitutional meaning disregards some rather explicit constitutional language. Article III of the Constitution states that there shall be a Supreme Court and, in combination with Article II, decrees the Court's independence from the electorate.[179] By its very terms, Article III establishes a countermajoritarian organ of government, the Supreme Court, in juxtaposition with the more democratic Congress and Presidency established by Articles I and II. This scheme reflects one of the guiding principles that underlies the Constitution: the principle of separate powers that check and balance one another. The Supreme Court's constitutionally mandated independence functions as a check and balance on the more majoritarian branches of the federal and state governments. It thereby provides a means of maintaining constitutional boundaries on majority rule.

It is the Supreme Court's role to enforce constitutional norms upon the majoritarian branches of government; otherwise they would be completely unbridled. As dictated by the Constitution, majority control should be the predominant feature of our governmental system subject to constitutional perimeters. The purpose of the Court's independence is to ensure that those perimeters will be honored by all branches of the state and federal governments. Constitutional constraint upon the majoritarian branches of government would be seriously reduced if the Supreme Court did not possess the authority to create meaning for the Constitution. In the absence of a creative power of judicial review, the majoritarian branches of government could move freely into new areas with little or no constitutional restraint. Elimination of the Court's creativity would destabilize the system of checks and balances that has characterized our government since its inception.

Although the Court is the least democratic branch of our government, it is not entirely undemocratic. While it is true that the justices who comprise the Court are appointed rather than elected and that they may be removed from office only for serious misbehavior, it should be remembered that they are appointed by a popularly elected President and must be confirmed by a popularly elected Senate. Turnover of the Court's personnel, which sometimes occurs frequently, enhances majority control of the Court through the recurrence of the appointment-confirmation procedure. In addition, the Court's constitutional rulings can be overridden by the people through constitutional amendment, which, although a difficult procedure, has been accomplished successfully on a number of occasions. Thus, while not directly answerable to the people, the Court is not entirely immune from popular control.

The people also have the ultimate authority to abolish the Supreme Court. They have not taken this step during our more than two centuries of constitutional experience, thus indicating popular acceptance of the Court's independent role in our system of government. Admittedly, some particular decisions rendered by the Court have aroused considerable public outcry, but given the many controversial issues that come before the Court, this is inevitable. More telling about the public attitude regarding the Court is that the people have taken no action to curtail its continual exercise of creativity. Indeed, the public has shown little, if any, inclination toward abolishing the Court or even restricting its powers. Despite widespread and intense dissatisfaction with the Court, one of the most popular presidents in our history, Franklin Delano Roosevelt, could not convince the Congress to enact his Court-packing plan.[180] In fact, the Senate Judiciary Committee was nothing short of vehement in rejecting the plan as "a needless, futile, and utterly dangerous abandonment of constitutional principle,"[181] and adding for good measure that the plan "should be so emphatically rejected that its parallel will never again be presented to the free representatives of the free people of America."[182] This political hyperbole is telling nonetheless in its message that even in the throes of the Great Depression the people's representatives would not tamper with the authority of judicial review.

Or consider the unsuccessful campaigns to impeach the eponymous Chief Justice Earl Warren and one of his most radical henchmen, Justice William O. Douglas. In not a few corners, the Warren Court was perceived as unduly activist, dangerously liberal, and atheistic to boot. This, after all, was the Court that outlawed prayer in the public schools and gave us decisions like *Escobedo v. Illinois*[183] and *Miranda v. Arizona*,[184] freeing vicious criminals on nothing more than "mere technicalities." Yet the campaigns to impeach these treacherous judicial villains never got off the ground. Those who campaigned to have Chief Justice Warren removed from office were unable to have impeachment proceedings instituted against him, and while impeachment proceedings were instituted against Justice Douglas, they never went beyond the subcommittee stage and were eventually forsaken.[185] Indeed, even legislative attempts to counteract Warren Court decisions by curtailing the jurisdiction of the federal courts were invariably rebuffed by Congress.[186] These experiences suggest that even in the face of intensely controversial constitutional decisions, there has been abiding public consent to the creative role of the Supreme Court in our scheme of government. By the time we reach the deep controversy engendered by *Roe v. Wade*,[187] there is little, if any, serious effort to impeach any of the justices who rendered that decision. Instead, the effort to counteract *Roe* is directed to amending the Constitution and to filling vacancies on the Court when they arise with anti-abortion justices in the hope that they will reverse *Roe* through the exercise of creative judicial authority! This shows that the creative role played by the Court has become an accepted part of our government system that the people have little desire to change.

Nevertheless, there are those who still question the force of popular consent to the Court. They argue that the Court enjoys public acceptance only by concealing its creativity and by duping the people into believing that the Court's decisions are compelled by the text of the Constitution or by the framers' intentions.[188] On one hand, this argument presumes that the public is aware of and persuaded by claims the Court makes in its written opinions that it is merely following the text of the document or the intent of the framers. On the other hand, it ignores that in the last sixty years or so the Court has become increasingly open about its creativity.[189] Even when the Court was less candid about its creative function, people must have sensed that it was engaging in the creation of constitutional meaning. What was the public to think, for instance, when Andrew Jackson, proclaiming that "Congress, the Executive, and the Court must each for itself be guided by its own opinion of the Constitution,"[190] felt free to veto a bill re-chartering the Bank of the United States on the ground that it was unconstitutional even though the Supreme Court had previously ruled that the bank charter was constitutional?[191] What was the public to think in the 1870s about the highly publicized controversy surrounding the *Legal-Tender Cases*,[192] in which a change in the Court's personnel was the obvious cause of an abrupt constitutional about-face that seemed clearly contrary to original intent?[193] What was the public to think during the New Deal Court crisis about President Roosevelt's Court-packing plan and Justice Roberts' switch in time that saved nine?[194] Could the people witness these and other momentous events, extremely visible to public scrutiny, and still be unaware that the Supreme Court was creating constitutional law?

Whether there is public comprehension of the Court's creative role, the fact remains that our constitutional system of checks and balances, which sets perimeters on majority rule, was adopted by the people and has been retained by them for over 200 years. That system, which is supported by popular consent, is dependent on the Court's capacity for creativity. Without creativity, the Court would be unable to fulfill the constitutional obligations prescribed for it by the people. In the final analysis, then, the creative authority of the Supreme Court derives from the people, that is, from the consent of the governed.

CONCLUSION

The Supreme Court's creativity is an integral part of our system of government, effectuating, as it does, the constitutional responsibility of the Court to enforce constitutional constraints upon the majoritarian branches of government. This creativity is necessary to furnish meaning for the Constitution, which cannot be adequately supplied by its text or its original understanding. Although from the very beginning the Court has continuously exercised creative authority, there are those who assert that its results have been mostly negative.[195] They argue that apart from the historical, theoretical, and political foundations of the Court's creativity, more often than not it has yielded unsound results. Justice Rehnquist, for instance, has written that the Court's creativity has resulted in several "disastrous experiences," most notably the decisions in *Dred Scott v. Sandford*[196] and *Lochner v. New York*,[197] and on balance "has done the Court little credit."[198]

This belief has not deterred Justice Rehnquist on numerous occasions from utilizing strong doses of creativity in his own constitutional decisions.[199] More important, his disparagement of the efficacy of creativity is based on an extremely slanted sampling of cases. To be fair, one cannot condemn the end product of the Court's creativity in *Dred Scott* while neglecting to praise it in *Brown v. Board of Education*.[200] Similarly, in condemning Lochnerism as wrongheaded creativity that misused the Fourteenth Amendment, one should not overlook the many Fourteenth Amendment cases in which creativity has been used to serve commendable purposes. The Court has used its creative authority to protect individuals from racial,[201] sexual,[202] and other forms[203] of unjust discrimination; to establish the "clear and present danger" test to protect freedom of speech[204]; and to protect the right of family members to live together,[205] to obtain a complete education for their children,[206] and to send their children to parochial school if they so choose.[207] Unless we are prepared to dismiss these and numerous other cases as wrongly decided, there simply is no basis to the claim that the Court's creativity has done it "little credit."

Yes, the Supreme Court has made its mistakes, including a few egregious ones. But so have the other branches of government. Possessed as they are of human fallibility, all three branches of government predictably will make their mistakes in the future. The time has come, however, to face the Supreme Court's mistakes directly on their merits rather than to ambush them on the pretense that they are illegitimate excursions into creativity. Attacks on the Court's creativity are spurious and should be entirely abandoned. It is time to admit, once and for all, that the Supreme Court has always been creative; otherwise, it would be unable to fulfill its constitutional responsibility of providing meaning for the Constitution.

NOTES

1. Quoted in J. W. Peltason, CORWIN & PELTASON'S UNDERSTANDING THE CONSTITUTION 125 (11th ed. 1988).

2. THE AUTOBIOGRAPHICAL NOTES OF CHARLES EVANS HUGHES 139 (David J. Danelski & Joseph S. Tulchin eds., 1973).

3. *See* Raoul Berger, GOVERNMENT BY JUDICIARY (1977); Bernard H. Siegan, ECONOMIC LIBERTIES AND THE CONSTITUTION (1980); Robert H. Bork, THE TEMPTING OF AMERICA (1990).

4. *Id.*

5. Home Bldg. & Loan Ass'n v. Blaisdell, 290 U.S. 398, 453 (1934) (Sutherland, J., dissenting).

6. *See* sources cited *supra* note 3.

7. *Id.*

8. *Id.*

9. Thomas Grey, *The Constitution as Scripture*, 37 STAN. L. REV. 1, 1 (1984).

10. "When Richard Nixon was running for President he promised that he would appoint to the Supreme Court men who represented his own legal philosophy, that is,

who were what he called 'strict constructionists.' . . . [T]hese men, he said, would enforce the law as it is, and not 'twist or bend' it to suit their own personal convictions, as Nixon accused the Warren Court of doing." Ronald Dworkin, TAKING RIGHTS SERIOUSLY 131 (1978).

11. *Id.*

12. *e.g.*, J. Clifford Wallace, *Interpreting the Constitution: The Case for Judicial Restraint*, 71 JUDICATURE 81 (1987).

13. *See* Hearing on Nomination of Warren E. Burger to be Chief Justice of the United States Before the Senate Comm. on the Judiciary, 91st Cong., 1st Sess. 5–7 (1969).

14. *See* William H. Rehnquist, *The Notion of A Living Constitution*, 54 TEX. L. REV. 693 (1976); Antonin Scalia, *Originalism: The Lesser Evil*, 57 U. CIN. L. REV. 849 (1989).

15. Home Bldg. & Loan Ass'n v. Blaisdell, 290 U.S. 398.

16. *Id.* at 443.

17. Antonin Scalia, A MATTER OF INTERPRETATION (1997).

18. Jeffrey Rosen, *Originalist Sin*, THE NEW REPUBLIC, May 5, 1997, at 26.

19. The author later explained: "That is to say, most judges and legal scholars who want to remain within the boundaries of respectable constitutional discourse agree that the original meaning of the Constitution and its amendments has some degree of pertinence to the question of what the Constitution means today." *Id.*

20. The negative response among scholars to the orthodox ideology, though, has not been universal. A small minority of scholars have advocated originalism. *See, e.g.*, Henry Monaghan, *Our Perfect Constitution*, 56 N.Y.U.L. REV. 353 (1981).

21. Paul Brest, *The Misconceived Quest for the Original Understanding*, 60 B.U.L. REV. 204, 204 (1980).

22. John H. Ely, *Constitutional Interpretivism: Its Allure and Impossibility*, 53 IND. L.J. 399, 399 (1978).

23. John E. Nowak, *Realism, Nihilism, and the Supreme Court: Do the Emperors Have Nothing But Robes?*, 22 WASHBURN L.J. 246, 257 (1983).

24. Peltason, *supra* note 1.

25. Thomas Grey, *Origins of the Unwritten Constitution: Fundamental Law in American Revolutionary Thought*, 30 STAN. L. REV. 843, 844 (1978). *See also* Michael Perry, THE CONSTITUTION, THE COURTS AND HUMAN RIGHTS 91 (1982), noting that virtually none of the constitutional doctrine regarding human rights fashioned by the Supreme Court in the twentieth century can be traced to the original understanding of the Constitution.

26. Hylton v. United States, 3 U.S. (3 Dall.) 171 (1796).

27. David Currie, THE CONSTITUTION IN THE SUPREME COURT 1789–1888 34 (1985).

28. *Id.* at 36.

29. This number refers to the Constitution as it stands today, including all of the amendments to the Constitution, except the Eighteenth Amendment, which was repealed by the Twenty-First Amendment.

30. *See* Lawrence H. Tribe, AMERICAN CONSTITUTIONAL LAW (3d ed. 2000).

31. Reynolds v. Sims, 377 U.S. 533 (1964); Harper v. Virginia Bd. of Elections, 383 U.S. 663 (1966).

32. Shapiro v. Thompson, 394 U.S. 618 (1969).

33. Griswold v. Connecticut, 381 U.S. 479 (1965); Roe v. Wade, 410 U.S. 113 (1973).

34. Geoffrey R. Stone *et al.*, CONSTITUTIONAL LAW (3d ed. 1996).

35. *See, e.g.*, Muller v. Oregon, 208 U.S. 412 (1908); Goesaert v. Cleary, 335 U.S. 464 (1948). A very rare exception during this period of time was Adkins v. Children's Hospital, 261 U.S. 525 (1923), in which the Court struck down a law providing a minimum wage for women but not for men.

36. *See, e.g.*, Muller v. Oregon, 208 U.S. 412 (1908); Goesaert v. Cleary, 335 U.S. 464 (1948); Hoyt v. Florida, 368 U.S. 57 (1961).

37. *See, e.g.*, Craig v. Boren, 429 U.S. 190 (1976); Taylor v. Louisiana, 419 U.S. 522 (1975); Kirchberg v. Feenstra, 450 U.S. 455 (1981).

38. Ruth Bader Ginsburg, *Sexual Equality Under the Fourteenth and Equal Rights Amendments*, WASH. U.L.Q. 161, 161 (1979).

39. Gibbons v. Ogden, 22 U.S. (9 Wheat.) 1, 194 (1824).

40. United States v. E. C. Knight Co., 156 U.S. 1 (1895).

41. NLRB v. Jones & Laughlin Steel Corp., 301 U.S. 1 (1937).

42. *See, e.g.*, United States v. Darby, 312 U.S. 100 (1941); Wickard v. Filburn, 317 U.S. 111 (1942).

43. *See* United States v. Lopez, 514 U.S. 549 (1995).

44. *See* Pacific States Tel. & Tel. Co. v. Oregon, 223 U.S. 118 (1912).

45. United States v. Richardson, 418 U.S. 166 (1974).

46. "[T]he privileges and immunities clause of the Fourteenth Amendment enjoys the distinction of having been rendered a 'practical nullity' by a single decision of the Supreme Court within five years after its ratification." Edward Corwin, THE CONSTITUTION OF THE UNITED STATES OF AMERICA 965 (1953).

47. *See* Saenz v. Roe, 526 U.S. 489, 119 S.Ct. 1518 (1999).

48. "In determining what lines are unconstitutionally discriminatory, we have never been confined to historic notions of equality, any more than we have restricted due process to a fixed catalogue of what was at a given time deemed to be the limits of fundamental rights. Notions of what constitutes equal treatment for purposes of the Equal Protection Clause *do* change." Harper v. Virginia State Bd. of Elections, 383 U.S. 663, 669 (1966) (emphasis in the original).

49. *See* Rehnquist, *supra* note 14; Scalia, *supra* note 14.

50. Archibald MacLeish, *Ars Poetica* (1926), collected in MODERN AMERICAN POETRY 453 (L. Untermeyer ed. 1962).

51. The quote is from Marbury v. Madison, 5 U.S. (1 Cranch.) 137 (1803).

52. *See, e.g.*, Gibbons v. Ogden, 22 U.S. (9 Wheat.) 1 (1824); McCulloch v. Maryland, 17 U.S. (4 Wheat.) 316 (1819); Martin v. Hunter's Lessee, 14 U.S. (1 Wheat.) 304 (1816).

53. *See, e.g.*, Trustees of Dartmouth College v. Woodward, 17 U.S. (4 Wheat.) 518 (1819); Terrett v. Taylor, 13 U.S. (9 Cranch.) 43 (1815); Fletcher v. Peck, 10 U.S. (6 Cranch.) 87 (1810).

54. *See, e.g.*, Allgeyer v. Louisiana, 165 U.S. 578 (1897); Swift v. Tyson, 41 U.S. (16 Pet.) 1 (1842); Charles River Bridge v. Warren Bridge, 36 U.S. (9 Pet.) 420 (1837).

55. *See, e.g.*, Roe v. Wade, 410 U.S. 113 (1973); Griswold v. Connecticut, 381 U.S. 479 (1965); Meyer v. Nebraska, 262 U.S. 390 (1923).

56. *See, e.g.*, Craig v. Boren, 429 U.S. 190 (1976).

57. *See, e.g.*, Younger v. Harris, 401 U.S. 37 (1971); National League of Cities v. Usery, 426 U.S. 833 (1976).

58. *See* Hylton v. United States, 3 U.S. (3 Dall.) 171 (1796).

59. *See* Owen Fiss & Charles Krauthammer, *The Rehnquist Court*, THE NEW REPUBLIC, Mar. 10, 1982, at 14, 20.

60. Abrams v. United States, 250 U.S. 616, 630 (1919) (Holmes, J., dissenting).

61. Scalia, *supra* note 14, at 852.

62. *See* Brest, *supra* note 21, at 226.

63. Bradwell v. State, 83 U.S. (16 Wall.) 130, 141 (1872) (Bradley, J., concurring).

64. Plessy v. Ferguson, 163 U.S. 537, 544 (1896).

65. Terret v. Taylor, 13 U.S. (9 Cranch.) 43, 52 (1815).

66. Ex Parte Milligan, 71 U.S. 2, 126 (1866).

67. Reynolds v. United States, 98 U.S. 145, 164 (1878).

68. Palko v. Connecticut, 301 U.S. 319, 325 (1937).

69. Rochin v. California, 342 U.S. 165, 173 (1952).

70. Adamson v. California, 332 U.S. 46, 47 (1947) (Frankfurter, J., concurring).

71. *See* Benjamin Fletcher Wright, Jr., AMERICAN INTERPRETATIONS OF NATURAL LAW: A STUDY IN THE HISTORY OF POLITICAL THOUGHT 330 (1931).

72. *See* John Hart Ely, DEMOCRACY AND DISTRUST 50–52 (1980).

73. *See* Thomas Grey, *Do We Have An Unwritten Constitution?*, 27 Stan. L. Rev. 703, 708 (1975).

74. "[T]he Constitution . . . has a fixed meaning ascertainable through the usual devices familiar to those learned in the law." Scalia, *supra* note 14, at 854.

75. *See* Jacobus tenBroek, *Use by the United States Supreme Court of Extrinsic Aids in Constitutional Construction*, 27 CAL. L. REV. 399, 404 (1939); Thomas Grey, *supra* note 73, at 706–709; Dean Alfange, Jr., *On Judicial Policymaking and Constitutional Change: Another Look at the 'Original Intent' Theory of Constitutional Interpretation*, 5 HASTINGS CONST. L.Q. 603, 617 (1978).

76. Fletcher v. Peck, 10 U.S. (6 Cranch.) 87 (1810).

77. Trustees of Dartmouth College v. Woodward 17 U.S. (4 Wheat.) 518 (1819).

78. 9 WRITINGS OF THOMAS JEFFERSON 275–76 (P. L. Ford ed. 1902).

79. United States v. Salerno, 481 U.S. 739, 752 (1987).

80. The opinion in Salerno brings to mind the famous dialogue in chapter six of Lewis Carroll's ALICE THROUGH THE LOOKING GLASS:

> "When *I* use a word," Humpty Dumpty said, in rather a scornful tone, "it means just what I choose it to mean—neither more nor less."
>
> "The question is," said Alice, "whether you *can* make words mean so many different things."
>
> "The question is," said Humpty Dumpty, "which is to be master—that's all."

81. Marbury v. Madison, 5 U.S. (1 Cranch.) 137 (1803).

82. *Id.* at 176.

83. " 'The question,' Marshall's opinion begins, 'whether an act repugnant to the Constitution, can become the law of the land, is a question deeply interesting to the United States; but, happily, not of an intricacy proportioned to its interest.' Marshall's confidence that he could traverse the path ahead with ease is understandable, since he had already begged the question-in-chief, which was not whether an act repugnant to the Constitution could stand, but who should be empowered to decide that the act is repugnant." Alexander Bickel, THE LEAST DANGEROUS BRANCH 3 (1962).

84. Planned Parenthood v. Casey, 505 U.S. 833, 847 (1992) (citation omitted):

> [I]t is tempting, as a means of curbing the discretion of federal judges, to suppose that liberty encompasses no more than those rights already guaranteed to the individual against federal inter-

ference by the express provisions of the first eight amendments . . . But of course this court has never accepted that view. It is also tempting, for the same reason, to suppose that the Due Process Clause protects only those practices, defined at the most specific level, that were protected against government interference by other rules of law when the Fourteenth Amendment was ratified. But such a view would be inconsistent with our law.

85. McCulloch v. Maryland, 17 U.S. (4 Wheat.) 316, 414 (1819).

86. *Id.* at 407.

87. *Id.*

88. *See* Champion v. Ames (The Lottery Case), 188 U.S. 321 (1903); Hoke v. United States, 227 U.S. 308 (1913); Hammer v. Dagenhart (The Child Labor Case), 247 U.S. 251 (1918).

89. *See* United States v. E. C. Knight Co. (The Sugar Trust Case), 156 U.S. 1 (1895); Schechter Poultry Corp. v. United States, 295 U.S. 495 (1935); Carter v. Carter Coal Co., 298 U.S. 238 (1936); NLRB v. Jones & Laughlin Steel Corp., 301 U.S. 1 (1937); Wickard v. Filburn, 317 U.S. 111 (1942).

90. *See* Reynolds v. United States, 98 U.S. 145 (1878).

91. *See* Prince v. Massachusetts, 321 U.S. 158 (1944).

92. *See* Roth v. United States, 354 U.S. 476 (1957).

93. *See* New York Times v. Sullivan, 376 U.S. 254 (1964).

94. *See* Central Hudson Gas & Elec. v. Public Serv. Comm'n of New York, 447 U.S. 557 (1980).

95. United States v. Richardson, 418 U.S. 166 (1974).

96. U.S. Const. art. I, § 9, cl. 7. The full clause states: "and a regular Statement and Account of the Receipts and Expenditures of all public Money shall be published from time to time." Admittedly, the last phrase, "from time to time," is somewhat general. However, that phrase was not at issue in the case. Rather, the issue presented was whether a statement and account would ever be published, and on that matter the wording of the clause is quite specific in stating that "a regular Statement and Account of the Receipts and Expenditures of *all* public Money shall be published." *Id.* (emphasis added).

97. Youngstown Sheet & Tube Co. v. Sawyer, 343 U.S. 579, 592 (1952) (Jackson, J., concurring).

98. John G. Wofford, *The Blinding Light: The Uses of History in Constitutional Interpretation*, 31 U. CHI. L. REV. 502, 504–505 (1964); Alpheus Thomas Mason & Donald Grier Stephenson, Jr., AMERICAN CONSTITUTIONAL LAW 51 (12th ed. 1999).

99. *See* 1 THE RECORDS OF THE FEDERAL CONVENTION OF 1787 xii–xiv (Max Farrand ed. 1937).

100. The quoted phrases are from the Supreme Court's opinion in Williams v. Florida, 399 U.S. 78, 93 (1970).

101. Leonard W. Levy, ORIGINAL INTENT AND THE FRAMERS' CONSTITUTION 286–88 (1988).

102. *Id.* at 288.

103. James H. Hutson, *The Creation of the Constitution: The Integrity of the Documentary Record*, 65 TEX. L. REV. 1, 12 (1986).

104. tenBroek, *supra* note 75, at 161 n.16.

105. *Id.* at 157–58.

106. *Id.* at 163.

107. *See* Levy, *supra* note 101 at 165–67, 291–94.

108. *See* Robert W. Bennett, *Objectivity in Constitutional Law*, 132 U. PA. L. REV. 445, 472 (1984).

109. Willi Paul Adams, THE FIRST AMERICAN CONSTITUTIONS: REPUBLICAN IDEOLOGY AND THE MAKING OF THE STATE CONSTITUTIONS IN THE REVOLUTIONARY ERA 99 (Rita & Robert Kimber trans. 1980).

110. *Id.* at 99–100.

111. Robert Shalhope, *Toward a Republican Synthesis: The Emergence of an Understanding of Republicanism in American Historiography*, 29 WM. & MARY Q. 49, 72 (1972).

112. *Id.*

113. *See* text *supra*, at notes 26–28.

114. The Compact Clause states, "No State shall, without the Consent of Congress . . . enter into any Agreement or Compact with another State." U.S. Const. art I, §10. The Supreme Court has noted that the records of the Constitutional Convention are "barren of any clue as to the precise contours of the agreements and compacts governed by the Compact Clause." United States Steel Corp. v. Multistate Tax Comm'n, 434 U.S. 452, 460–61 (1978). This case is discussed in more detail in Chapter 2, *infra* at notes 177–92.

115. Stanley I. Kutler, *Raoul Berger's Fourteenth Amendment: A History or Ahistorical?*, 6 HASTINGS CONST. L.Q. 511, 520 (1979).

116. United States v. Trans-Missouri Freight Ass'n, 166 U.S. 290, 318 (1897).

117. "[On] our precise problem the historical record is at best ambiguous, and statements can readily be found to support either side of the proposition." School Dist. of Abington Township v. Schempp, 374 U.S. 203, 237 (1963) (Brennan, J., concurring).

118. *See* Irving Brant, JAMES MADISON: FATHER OF THE CONSTITUTION, 1787–1800 (1950).

119. James MacGregor Burns, THE VINEYARD OF LIBERTY 101–104 (1982).

120. Ronald Dworkin, *The Forum of Principle*, 56 N.Y.U.L. REV. 469, 477 (1981).

121. *Id.*

122. The original Constitution was ratified through conventions held for that purpose in the states. All of the amendments to the Constitution except the Twenty-First Amendment, which was ratified in state conventions, were ratified by the state legislatures. *See* Brest, *supra* note 21, at 214–15.

123. *See* Charles A. Lofgren, *The Original Understanding of Original Intent?*, in INTERPRETING THE CONSTITUTION—THE DEBATE OVER ORIGINAL INTENT 117, 142–43 (J. Rakove ed. 1990).

124. Brest, *supra* note 21, at 214.

125. Lofgren, *supra* note 123, at 143.

126. *See* Jack N. Rakove, *Mr. Meese, Meet Mr. Madison*, in INTERPRETING THE CONSTITUTION—THE DEBATE OVER ORIGINAL INTENT, *supra* note 123, at 179, 183.

127. *See* James H. Hutson, *The Creation of the Constitution: The Integrity of the Documentary Record*, in INTERPRETING THE CONSTITUTION—THE DEBATE OVER ORIGINAL INTENT, *supra* note 123, at 151.

128. "The reliability of the records degenerates with a shift of focus from Philadelphia to the state ratifying conventions." Levy, *supra* note 101, at 288.

129. *Id.* at 289–91.

130. *Id.* at 290.

131. Hutson, *supra* note 127 at 161.

132. Henry P. Monaghan, *Our Perfect Constitution*, 56 N.Y.U.L. REV. 353, 375 n.130 (1981).

133. *See* tenBroek, *supra* note 75 at 171.

134. Scalia, *supra* note 14, at 856.

135. *Id.* at 857.

136. *Id.* at 851–52. The case to which Justice Scalia refers is Myers v. United States, 272 U.S. 52 (1926).

137. Scalia, *supra* note 14, at 852.

138. Edward Hallett Carr, WHAT IS HISTORY? 10 (1962).

139. *Id.* at 9.

140. *Id.* at 10–11.

141. Carl L. Becker, *What Are Historical Facts?*, 8 W. POL. Q. 327, 333 (1955) (emphasis added).

142. *See* Antonin Scalia, A MATTER OF INTERPRETATION 18, 22–23 (1997).

143. Wofford, *supra* note 98, at 508–09.

144. *See* Ely, *supra* note 72, at 60.

145. Michael Perry, *Interpretivism, Freedom of Expression, and Equal Protection*, 42 Ohio St. L.J. 261, 265 (1981).

146. tenBroek, *supra* note 75, at 443.

147. Scalia, *supra* note 14, at 864.

148. Jeffrey Rosen, *The Leader of the Opposition*, THE NEW REPUBLIC, Jan. 18, 1993, at 21. The three decisions were Lucas v. South Carolina Coastal Council, 505 U.S. 1003 (1992); Lujan v. Defenders of Wildlife, 504 U.S. 555 (1992); and Lee v. Weisman, 505 U.S. 577 (1992).

149. *Id.* at 21, 24.

150. Woodrow Wilson, CONSTITUTIONAL GOVERNMENT IN THE UNITED STATES 169 (1908); quoted in Arthur M. Schlesinger, Jr., THE POLITICS OF UPHEAVAL 285 (1960).

151. *See* Robert Stern, *That Commerce Which Concerns More States Than One*, 47 HARV. L. REV. 1335 (1934); *The Commerce Clause and the National Economy, 1933–1946*, 59 HARV. L. REV. 645 (1946).

152. William H. Rehnquist, GRAND INQUESTS: THE HISTORIC IMPEACHMENTS OF JUSTICE SAMUEL JOHNSON AND PRESIDENT ANDREW JOHNSON 277 (1992).

153. *Id.*

154. Katz v. United States, 389 U.S. 347, 359 (1967).

155. California v. Ciraolo, 476 U.S. 207, 215 (1986).

156. Schmerber v. State, 384 U.S. 757, 772 (1996).

157. Rochin v. California, 342 U.S. 165, 172 (1952).

158. Yet another example of changed conditions can be seen in the religious make-up of the nation. As Justice Brennan pointed out:

> [O]ur religious composition makes us a vastly more diverse people than were our forefathers. They knew differences chiefly among Protestant sects. Today the Nation is far more heterogeneous religiously, including as it does substantial minorities not only of Catholics and Jews but as well of those who worship according to no version of the Bible and those who worship no God at all. . . . In the face of such profound changes, practices which may have been objectionable to no one in the time of Jefferson and Madison may today be highly offensive to many persons, the deeply devout and the nonbelievers alike.

School Dist. of Abington Township v. Schempp, 374 U.S. 203, 240–41 (1963) (Brennan, J., concurring).

159. *Id.* at 237.

160. Retirement Address by Chief Justice Warren, Supreme Court of the United States (June 23, 1969), *reprinted in* 395 U.S. X–XII.

161. *See* H. Jefferson Powell, *The Original Understanding of Original Intent*, 98 HARV. L. REV. 885 (1985); Suzanna Sherry, *The Founders' Unwritten Constitution*, 54 U. CHI. L. REV. 1127 (1987).

162. *See* Scalia, *supra* note 14; Robert Bork, *Neutral Principles and Some First Amendment Problems*, 47 IND. L.J. 1, 2–12 (1971); Rehnquist, *supra* note 14, at 704–06; Raoul Berger, GOVERNMENT BY JUDICIARY *passim* (1977).

163. *See* Morton Horowitz, *The Jurisprudence of Brown and the Dilemmas of Liberalism*, 14 HARV. C.R.-C.L. L. REV. 599, 601 (1979).

164. Levy, *supra* note 101 at 296–97.

165. Ronald Dworkin, LAW'S EMPIRE 364 (1986).

166. *Id.*

167. *See* Ely, *supra* note 72, at 411–12.

168. Charles P. Curtis, LIONS UNDER THE THRONE 2 (1947).

169. *Id.*

170. Powell, *supra* note 161, at 903.

171. Stone, *supra* note 34, at 42.

172. James Madison, letter to Thomas Ritchie (Sept. 15, 1821), reprinted in 9 THE WRITINGS OF JAMES MADISON at 71–2 (G. Hunt ed. 1910).

173. *Id.*

174. *Id.* (The abbreviation "recd." is in the original.)

175. Rakove, *supra* note 126.

176. *Id.*

177. *See* text *supra*, at notes 122–60.

178. Planned Parenthood v. Casey, 505 U.S. 833, 901 (1992).

179. U.S. Const. art. III, § 1; art. II, § 2.

180. "Not all the influence of a master politician in the prime of his popularity was quite enough to carry a program that would impair judicial review." Robert McCloskey, THE AMERICAN SUPREME COURT 177 (1960).

181. Senate Comm. on the Judiciary, Reorganization of the Fed. Judiciary, Adverse Report, S. Rep. No. 711, 75th Cong., 1st Sess. 23 (1937).

182. *Id.*

183. Escobedo v. Illinois, 378 U.S. 478 (1964).

184. Miranda v. Arizona, 384 U.S. 436 (1966).

185. *See* Special Subcomm. on H. Res. 920 of the House Comm. on the Judiciary, 91st Cong., 2d Sess., Final Report, Associate Justice William O. Douglas (Comm. Print 1970).

186. *See* Max Baucus & Kenneth R. Kay, *The Court Stripping Bills: Their Impact on the Constitution, the Courts, and Congress*, 27 VILL. L. REV. 988 (1982).

187. Roe v. Wade, 410 U.S. 113 (1973).

188. *See* Bork, *supra* note 162, at 3–4; Berger, *supra* note 162, at 319–20.

189. *See* text *supra*, at notes 72–73.

190. Andrew Jackson, *Veto Message of July 10, 1832*, in 2 MESSAGES AND PAPERS OF THE PRESIDENTS 576, 581–82 (J. Richardson ed. 1896).

191. The Supreme Court upheld the constitutionality of the bank charter in McCulloch v. Maryland, 17 U.S. (4 Wheat.) 316 (1819).

192. Hepburn v. Griswold, 75 U.S. (8 Wall.) 603 (1870); Knox v. Lee, 79 U.S. (12 Wall.) 457 (1871).

193. *See* Kenneth W. Dam, *The Legal Tender Cases*, SUP. CT. REV. 367 (1981).

194. In the 1930s, a narrow majority of the Supreme Court persisted in striking down as unconstitutional one New Deal program after another designed to ameliorate the dire conditions of the Great Depression. The Court's rulings evoked tremendous political and popular criticism, as well as President Roosevelt's Court-packing plan, attacking the Court's authority. Finally, one justice, Owen Roberts, began to change his votes, thus shifting the majority in favor of New Deal legislation. This led Thomas Reed Powell, a Harvard law professor who at the time was a faculty colleague of Felix Frankfurter, to quip about Justice Roberts: "A switch in time saves nine." Quoted in Kenneth S. Davis, FDR, INTO THE STORM 1937–1940 81 (1993).

195. *See* Rehnquist, *supra* note 14; Philip B. Kurland, *Government by Judiciary*, 2 U. ARK. LITTLE ROCK L.J. 307 (1979).

196. Dred Scott v. Sandford, 60 U.S. (19 How.) 393 (1856).

197. Lochner v. New York, 198 U.S. 45 (1905).

198. Rehnquist, *supra* note 14, at 699–704.

199. *E.g.*, in Edelman v. Jordan, 415 U.S. 651 (1974), he created the rule that the Eleventh Amendment shelters the states from being ordered by federal courts to make retroactive payments from their treasuries; in Sosna v. Iowa, 419 U.S. 393 (1975), he created an exception to the previously established constitutional right to travel interstate; in National League of Cities v. Usery, 426 U.S. 833 (1976), he created an exception to the federal commerce power in order to protect state sovereignty; in Fitzpatrick v. Bitzer, 427 U.S. 445 (1976), and Quern v. Jordan, 440 U.S. 332 (1979), he created constitutional exceptions to his previously created rule that the Eleventh Amendment shelters the states from being ordered by federal courts to make retroactive payments from their treasuries; in Nevada v. Hall, 440 U.S. 410, 432 (1979) (Rehnquist, J., dissenting), he sought to create an implied sovereign immunity among the states.

200. Brown v. Board of Educ., 349 U.S. 294 (1954).

201. *See, e.g., id.*; Loving v. Virginia, 388 U.S. 1 (1967); Hunter v. Erickson, 393 U.S. 385 (1969).

202. *See, e.g.*, Reed v. Reed, 404 U.S. 71 (1971); Mississippi Univ. for Women v. Hogan, 458 U.S. 718 (1982); United States v. Virginia, 518 U.S. 515 (1996).

203. *See, e.g.*, Levy v. Louisiana, 391 U.S. 68 (1968); United States Dep't of Agric. v. Moreno, 413 U.S. 528 (1973); Sugarman v. Dougall, 413 U.S. 634 (1973); City of Cleburne v. Cleburne Living Ctr., Inc., 473 U. S. 432 (1985); Romer v. Evans, 517 U.S. 620 (1996).

204. *See, e.g.*, Abrams v. United States, 250 U.S. 616, 624 (1919) (Holmes, J., dissenting); Brandenburg v. Ohio, 395 U.S. 444 (1969).

205. *See* Moore v. City of East Cleveland, 431 U.S. 494 (1977).

206. *See* Meyer v. Nebraska, 262 U.S. 390 (1923).

207. *See* Pierce v. Society of Sisters, 268 U.S. 510 (1925).

Chapter 2

Formalism v. Realism

> [T]he provisions of the Constitution are not mathematical formulas having their essence in their form; they are organic living institutions. . . . Their significance is vital not formal.
>
> —Oliver Wendell Holmes, Jr.[1]

Throughout its history, constitutional interpretation, particularly as practiced by the United States Supreme Court, has been characterized by two distinct modes of thought. One of them, which was the predominant mode of constitutional adjudication during the Supreme Court's first 150 years or so, can be referred to as "categorizing" or "defining."[2] The other mode of thought, which was developed in more modern times, is called "balancing."[3] Where categorization is a formal mode of thought, balancing is functional or realistic. In the first half of this century, legal formalism was subject to withering criticism that sought to reveal that it was fundamentally flawed.[4] Since the 1940s, balancing has been used with such increasing frequency that it is considered the dominant judicial style that distinguishes constitutional interpretation in the modern era.[5] Nonetheless, categorization has never been completely abandoned, and in recent years there has been a resurgence of categorization.[6] The Supreme Court has increasingly reverted to formalism in making constitutional decisions, to the extent that there is "a significant movement afoot at the Supreme Court" to discard balancing and revive categorization.[7] Over his years on the high Court, Chief Justice William Rehnquist has frequently employed the formal mode of thought in his written opinions.[8] Justice Antonin Scalia, on several occasions since his appointment to the high Court, has taken the opportunity to criticize balancing while advocating a return to formalism, at least in some areas.[9] Other justices, whether unintentionally or not, have slipped back into the categorizing mode more often than might have been expected.[10]

At the same time, a small group of constitutional scholars have questioned the validity of balancing, and urged a return to more formal means of adjudication.[11] This movement is, perhaps, part of a larger trend toward a revival of legal formalism in general.[12]

These recent occurrences call for a re-examination of the methods by which the Constitution is interpreted, especially because the meaning of the Constitution is determined in no small measure by the way we think about it. Old ways of thinking, though not to be scorned by virtue of their age, are to be scorned if they previously have been discarded due to their flaws. The return to formalism, therefore, ought to be cause for concern, if not alarm.

THE NATURE OF CATEGORIZATION

As its name suggests, the categorizational, or definitional, mode of constitutional adjudication consists of setting forth definitions—that is, meaning or content—for the words in the Constitution. Under the definitional mode, constitutional phrases are treated as categories that refer to relatively discrete phenomena. Categories posit differences of kind, rather than differences of degree, and they purport to make bright-line delineations. Categorization has been described as similar to taxonomy—concerned with classification and labeling.[13] The function of a judge working in this mode also is similar to the function performed by a lexicographer, who determines the meaning of words and provides definitions for them.[14] In fact, in the famous case of *Gibbons v. Ogden*, Chief Justice John Marshall's opinion for the Court likens constitutional interpretation to lexicography by remarking that in deciding the case, "it becomes necessary to settle the meaning of the word 'commerce' " as used in the Constitution.[15] *Gibbons*, decided in 1824, marks the beginning of a series of decisions in which the Supreme Court, operating in the definitional mode, sought to provide meaning for section 8 of Article I, which grants Congress authority to "regulate Commerce among the several States." In *Gibbons* itself, Justice Marshall's opinion for the Court defined that constitutional phrase as meaning any "commercial intercourse that concerns more states than one."[16] Seventy-one years later, in *United States v. E. C. Knight Co.*, the Court redefined "Commerce among the several States" to mean any activity that has a "direct effect" upon interstate business.[17] Under the *Gibbons* definition, interstate commerce included navigation; under the *Knight* definition, it did not include manufacturing or production. But in still later cases in the 1930s, the Supreme Court would once again redefine the meaning of "Commerce among the several States" to refer to any activity that had a substantial interstate impact, which would include a good deal of manufacturing and production, as well as navigation.[18]

All of this, of course, is classic categorization. In each of these cases the Court is setting forth formal categories—commerce that "concerns" several states, or that has a "direct effect" upon several states, or that has a "substantial impact" upon several states—to define the meaning of the Constitution. In setting forth each category, the Court necessarily implies—and at times expressly states—that there is an counter-category that is subject to an opposite rule of law. According to the approach in *Knight*, for example, there are two kinds of commerce—one that has a "direct effect" upon several states, and another that has only an "indirect effect" upon several states. The former is within the congressional authority granted by section 8 of Article I, while the latter is not. Or, to look at the definitional mode as it operates under a different constitutional provision, the Court has set forth the opposing categories of "rights" and "privileges" to determine the meaning of the word "property" as used in the Due Process Clause.[19] If a particular benefit claimed by an individual is viewed by the Court as a right, it will be considered a property interest entitled to the protection of due process of law.[20] Therefore, it may not be revoked by the state without prior notice and a hearing.[21] But if a benefit is viewed by the Court as a mere "privilege," it will not be considered a property interest, and hence goes unprotected by the Due Process Clause.[22] A mere "privilege," unlike a "right," does not rise to the level of a property interest and may be revoked by the state without prior notice or a hearing.[23]

Constitutional categorization is a formal mode of interpretation. Legal formalism was the prevalent mode of thought throughout the pre-modern stage of American law, and its predominant characteristic was categorization.[24] Legal historian Morton Horwitz points out, "Nothing captures the essential difference between the typical legal minds of nineteenth- and twentieth-century America quite as well as their attitude toward categories."[25] Nineteenth-century legal thought, he continues, was overwhelmingly under the sway of categorical thinking, whereas twentieth-century thought emphasizes balancing of values and policies.[26] Twentieth-century thought recognizes that the differences of kind presumed to be at the foundation of categories are actually differences in degree.[27] Thus, we have come to see reality "not as a series of mutually exclusive black-white bright-line boundaries . . . but rather as a series of continua involving shades of gray requiring line-drawing."[28]

A pertinent question arises concerning the definitional mode of constitutional interpretation: Where do the justices of the Supreme Court (or the judges of whatever court is interpreting the Constitution) obtain the definitions that they provide for constitutional provisions? What is the source of the definitions or categories announced by the justices? An examination of Supreme Court opinions in which the definitional mode is operative makes it obvious that in the vast majority of instances the source of the definitions or categories is the justices themselves. That that is, the justices devise the categories on their own. On occasion, the justices might turn to the intent of the framers as a source of defining the constitution,[29] or to the lessons of history,[30] social mores,[31] or even the wisdom of learned persons.[32] When the justices purport to rely upon these sources to define the constitution, what they often really find is what they themselves set out to find, consciously or not.[33] In other words, the justices may profess that they are relying upon these sources, and even honestly believe that they are doing so, when in fact the true source of their decisions is themselves; the framers' intent, history, or whatever is in reality a pretext that masks the fact that the justices themselves are creating meaning for the Constitution. As John Hart Ely observed, when judges attempt to ascertain meaning for the Constitution from an external "objective" source, what they usually end up "discovering" are their own values.[34]

In most definitional instances, the justices make little or no attempt to cloak constitutional categories with the intent of the framers, the imprimatur of history, or some other external source. The justices simply announce the definitions, as if they were a given. For example, in the *Knight* case[35] the Court made no pretense that there was an extrajudicial source for its ruling that Congress only possessed authority to regulate commercial activities that have a "direct effect" upon several states. The Court made no suggestion that the "direct-indirect" distinction came from anywhere but the justices themselves. Similarly, in later cases when the Court redefined congressional authority to encompass any commercial activity that had a "substantial impact" upon several states, it made no attempt to link its new rule to the framers' intent or any other extrajudicial source.[36] These rules were simply announced by the Court with no explication of their source. In fact, the Court seems to feel little or no obligation to identify the source of these constitutional definitions, because the definitions are treated by the Court as *a priori* categories. The Court seems to believe that the definitions are fixed entities that have a prior existence or supernatural essence, and hence call for no explanation. To the Court, the categories simply "are," and therefore their content needs no justification.

Insofar as the justices themselves create definitions for constitutional phrases, their function differs in degree from that of the true lexicographer. Whereas the true lexicographer finds meaning for words primarily from how others use those words,[37] the justices for the most part devise their own meaning for words. Lexicography, like any act of interpretation, does involve some measure of creativity, but the lexicographer functions more as an editor than as an author. On the other hand, constitutional interpretation involves a greater quantum of creativity or authorship. The lexicographer looks outward to find meaning, while the Supreme Court justice looks inward to create meaning.

Whether creative or not, the formal aspects of lexicography seem to have a recurring appeal to some members of the legal profession. In recent years, we have witnessed a return to some extent of constitutional formalism. A small but influential group of what might be called "neo-formalists" have taken their places on the bench or in the academy.[38] They accept some of the old categories[39] and reject others as mistaken, but would replace them not with balancing but rather with revised categories. Neo-formalism in the field of constitutional law parallels the rise of neo-territorialism in the field of conflict of laws,[40] which also signals a return to formal categories that are revised in light of more modern ideas, but still are highly formalistic rather than realistic.

This resuscitation of old ways of thought that previously had been abandoned is perhaps surprising, but not entirely so. Categorization can never be entirely eliminated from the process of constitutional interpretation. Indeed, it can never be entirely eliminated from any form of human thought. Words themselves are categories. Human beings inescapably think in categories, and write and speak in categories. Nonetheless, categorization can be emphasized or de-emphasized in a human thought process, and it can maximized or minimized in constitutional interpretation. There is an essential difference between the categorization or definitional mode of thought and the balancing mode that in more modern times has become the predominant method of constitutional interpretation.

THE CATEGORICAL ILLUSION

In the twentieth century, legal formalism came under serious and sustained criticism, and by the 1940s its influence was collapsing.[41] The collapse of legal formalism was part of a larger movement that recognized the general invalidity of all formal modes of thought.[42] Philosophers explained that formal categories of any kind were Platonic ideals that were a mere illusion with no real existence.[43] "The truth of an idea," William James proclaimed, "is not a stagnant property inherent in it."[44] He explained that "truth happens to an idea" when it is verified by events in the real world.[45] James and other pragmatic philosophers, such as Charles Peirce and John Dewey, saw that formal categories were abstractions that had no inherent truth; rather, any truth they possessed came from the effects they had in reality.[46] Above all, pragmatism was purposive. It stressed function over form, and held that the validity of any concept depends upon its purpose.[47]

Similar to James, Dewey stressed that there were no transcendental truths.[48] Reality, he explained, is tentative, indeterminate, and has meaning only in relation to the situation in which it occurs.[49] The meaning of reality has no innate form, but rather depends upon context and consequences.[50] Dewey also assailed false dualisms, such as mind and body, means and ends, and subject and body; he noted that they were precarious and contingent.[51] Dualisms and forms are valid, he said, only insofar as they are pragmatic.[52]

The lessons of pragmatism were not lost on the natural or social sciences.[53] In physics,[54] chemistry,[55] medicine,[56] anthropology,[57] history,[58] economics,[59] and sociology,[60] the light of functionalism permeated the American mind. Of the social sciences, it was probably law that took the longest to assimilate the new learning.[61] Led by Holmes, and then Roscoe Pound, followed by Morris Cohen, Felix Cohen, Llewellyn, Frank, and others, the law finally was dragged into the twentieth century, if not kicking and screaming, then growling and muttering.

The new dawning revealed that as an epistemological matter, categorization is not a valid method of constitutional interpretation. Constitutional concepts such as "interstate commerce," "freedom of speech," or "due process of law," like all other concepts, are human constructs that have no inherent meaning. Constitutional dualisms, such as the direct or indirect effect upon interstate commerce, are artificial, tenuous, and precarious. As alluring as it may be, there is no juristic heaven where Platonic ideals defining legal concepts magically exist.[62] Holmes put it well when he said that law is not a "brooding omnipresence in the sky."[63] Law is a human creation of judges, and the meaning of the Constitution is created by the Supreme Court justices as they go about interpreting the document. The definitions of the Constitution that the justices set forth come from the justices' minds and have no existence apart from that.

Certainly, it is possible to make up a definition for a constitutional provision or for any other concept. But to create a definition for a constitutional provision does not by that act alone make the definition a sensible one. In and of itself, one definition makes as much sense or as much nonsense as any other definition. In and of itself, one definition is no better than any other definition and is no more effective or valid than any other definition. If definitions are to be created, they ought to be created teleologically, that is, they ought to be created with some purpose in mind. After all, the creation of a definition (or, to put it another way, the interpretation of a constitutional provision) will have an impact in the real world; it will effect the way cases are decided. Therefore, the definition ought to be constructed in a thoughtful way that looks to the achievement of public policy or purposes. Constitutional interpretation ought to proceed in a purposeful rather than a desultory way. And that is where balancing enters the picture. Balancing is purposeful; it looks to reasons, policies, or purposes. Categorization, on the other hand, is haphazard; it sets forth definitions for no apparent reason. It is non-teleological.

Operating as they do as *a priori* entities, constitutional categories have a beguiling appeal because they seem to be natural or even supernatural, handed down by some transcendental authority.[64] They satisfy what seems to be a perpetual quest to find meaning for the Constitution from an external authoritative source other than the Supreme Court itself. At base, however, *a priori* categories provide nothing more than a false security. They are based on the sort of artificial dualisms that John Dewey revealed as having only spurious meaning.[65] They can be neither proven nor disproven because they are founded neither upon empirical observation nor policy considerations.[66] Having no basis in reality or policy, *a priori* categories tend to be non-teleological—lacking in purpose—and therefore the results they lead to when used to decide cases are random and desultory. As Felix Cohen observed:

> In every field of law we should find peculiar concepts which are not defined either in terms of empirical fact or in terms of ethics but which are used to answer empirical and ethical questions alike, and thus bar the way to intelligent investigation of social fact and social policy. . . . Legal arguments couched in these terms are necessarily circular, since

these terms are themselves creations of law, and such arguments add precisely as much to our knowledge as Moliere's physician's discovery that opium puts men to sleep because it contains a dormitive principle. . . . *Legal concepts* . . . are supernatural entities which do not have a verifiable existence.[67]

The supernatural and irrational nature of constitutional categories can be readily seen in the Supreme Court's vicissitudes in dealing with the authority of Congress to regulate interstate commerce. As noted above,[68] after originally defining interstate commerce as including any commercial activity that "concerns more states than one," the Court later recategorized interstate commerce to encompass only those activities that had a "direct" effect upon interstate business. The "direct-indirect" distinction had a restrictive effect upon the scope of federal authority to regulate business practices throughout the nation, and was a major factor which led to the New Deal Court struggle.[69] That struggle was defused after President Roosevelt appointed several new justices to the Supreme Court whose constitutional philosophy was decidedly more sympathetic to the New Deal than a majority of their predecessors' philosophy had been.[70] With a new majority on the Court, the justices once again redefined interstate commerce, returning to a definition similar to the original one.[71] The refurbished definition of interstate commerce, which included any activity that had a substantial effect on interstate commerce, allowed expansive—some would say, unlimited—federal regulation of business.[72]

As a theoretical matter, distinct from a political one, each of the various categories that the Supreme Court has used over time to define interstate commerce is arbitrary. Each category is "equally logical and equally unrealistic," because "the line to be drawn between interstate and intrastate commerce is necessarily artificial."[73]

There are also contemporary examples that illustrate the irrational nature of constitutional categories. One of the formal constitutional categories that has been resuscitated in recent times is the dichotomy between rights and privileges. This dichotomy or doctrine was previously used to determine what interests were protected by the Due Process Clause and other constitutional provisions. Interests, such as the right to do business[74] or practice law[75] within a state, that were designated as "rights" were thereby considered within the protection of the Constitution and could only be regulated if the government could show a strong need to do so and if the dictates of procedural fairness were followed. Interests, such as employment[76] or Social Security benefits,[77] that were designated "privileges" could be regulated by the government virtually at will, with no showing of a justification for regulation and no requirement of procedural fairness.

Beginning in the 1960s, constitutional scholars subjected the right-privilege dichotomy to severe criticism, pointing out that it amounted to little more than a tautology that operated by arbitrarily assigning labels—now "right," then "privilege"—with little rhyme or reason.[78] This revealed that to denominate an interest as a privilege rather than a right was merely to declare a conclusion, with no explanation or justification, that the interest was unprotected by the Constitution.[79] Some years earlier, Carl Sandburg had said much the same thing, though more poetically:

> Stocks are property, yes.
> Bonds are property, yes.
> Machines, land, buildings are property, yes.
> A job is property,
> No, nix, nah nah.[80]

Heedful of the scholarly criticism, the Supreme Court moved to dismantle the right-privilege dichotomy and replace it with a balancing test. In a 1970 decision, *Goldberg v. Kelly*,[81] the Court ruled that the application of due process of law is to be determined by balancing the weight or importance of the individual interest at stake in relation to the weight or importance of the governmental interest in the regulation in question. Accordingly, the Court concluded that whether welfare benefits are considered a right or privilege, they are a significant property interest that must be afforded the protection of due process of law, and therefore may not be terminated without a prior hearing.[82] Similarly, in a subsequent case, *Bell v. Burson*,[83] the Supreme Court used the same balancing test in ruling that the Due Process Clause required a prior hearing before revocation of a driver's license.

By 1972 the Supreme Court could state that it had "fully and finally rejected the wooden distinction between 'rights' and 'privileges' " and cite no less than seven cases for that proposition.[84] A few years earlier an esteemed Court watcher observed that the right-privilege doctrine had been "utterly repudiated by the Supreme Court."[85] Not so utterly repudiated, though, that it could not be revived in a slightly disguised form by a Supreme Court of different composition with more formalist leanings. Thus, in *Board of Regents v. Roth*[86] and subsequent cases,[87] the Court relinquished the balancing test in favor of a formal approach that limited the protection of the Due Process Clause to a category referred to as "entitlements." At first in adopting the criterion of entitlement, the Court "avoided the forbidden terminology of 'right' and 'privilege,' " but later "almost completely dropped all pretense of having abandoned the [right-privilege] distinction."[88] In *Roth* and following decisions, the Court ruled that there is no entitlement and hence no due process protection for public employment, Social Security benefits,[89] individual reputation,[90] or nursing care.[91] As a result, as far as the Supreme Court was concerned, due process of law was not offended by the denial or termination of such interests without a prior hearing.

Of course, the entitlement standard is nothing more than a synonym for the right-privilege dichotomy, and is prone to all of the flaws that previously led the Court to abandon that dichotomy. The designation of entitlement is a tautological label that can be manipulated with little rhyme or reason. And while it provides constitutional protection to entitlements, it allows the state to decide at its discretion what is or is not an entitlement. So, what the state gives with one hand, it is free to take away with the other.

The entitlement standard, the right-privilege dichotomy, and the direct-indirect test of interstate commerce are legal constructs of a highly formal character. Similar to other formal categories, they make no sense and have no reason. They are transcendental nonsense. Being abstractions, they are empty shells that exalt form over function.

Despite the deficiencies of formalism, the Supreme Court occasionally, though repeatedly, returns to it. While balancing clearly is the predominant mode of constitutional adjudication, it is not unusual for the Court to slip into the categorization mode. Chief Justice Rehnquist, in particular, is a practitioner of categorization. Indeed, his opinion in *United States v. Lopez* comes close to resuscitating the old "direct-indirect" dualism under the Interstate Commerce Clause.[92] For whatever reasons, Chief Justice Rehnquist seems to have a formalistic turn of mind; a number of his opinions rely heavily upon formal categories. In one case, he decreed that there is no violation of the First Amendment if a law is aimed at the "secondary effects" of speech rather than its "content."[93] In another case, he proclaimed that pretrial detention does not violate the Due Process Clause if it is "regulatory, not penal."[94] And in yet another case, he declared that a forfeiture order did not amount to an unconstitutional prior restraint because it was a deprivation of assets, rather than a prohibition of expressive activity.[95] It would not be unfair to describe these conceptions as highly formalistic hairsplitting. Moreover, they are plagued by one of the common pitfalls of categorization; each of them is a false dichotomy. After all, a law regulating speech may well be aimed at both its content and its secondary effects. Pretrial detention may well have a regulatory function as well as a penal one. Forfeiture may well operate as both a prior restraint and a deprivation of assets. False dichotomies, therefore, should come as no surprise when the formalistic mode of thought is being used. Indeed, given the artificiality of formal constructs, false dichotomies are an occupational hazard of categorization. In Chief Justice Rehnquist's opinion for a 5–4 majority of the Court in *Rust v. Sullivan*,[96] they even came in a double-barreled variety. In *Rust*, the Court upheld a federal regulation that prohibited programs that received funds under the Public Health Services Act from counseling women about abortion while requiring counseling about continuing a pregnancy to term. The parties challenging the regulation asserted that it violated the First Amendment by impermissibly discriminating on the basis of viewpoint. Chief Justice Rehnquist's opinion dismissed this assertion by proclaiming that "the government has not discriminated on the basis of viewpoint; it has merely chosen to fund one activity to the exclusion of the other."[97] Obviously, the two categories here constitute a false dichotomy. That the government has chosen to fund one activity to the exclusion of another does not preclude the possibility that the government has engaged in viewpoint discrimination. To the contrary, the government may well have chosen to fund one activity and not the other precisely because the government approves of one viewpoint and not the other. In *Rust*, it is undeniable that the government, as often occurs, has done two things at the same time: it has chosen to fund one activity over another while also engaging in viewpoint discrimination.

The parties challenging the federal regulation in *Rust* additionally asserted that it impermissibly conditioned the receipt of a benefit on the relinquishment of a constitutional right (freedom of expression). Chief Justice Rehnquist rejected this assertion by declaring that "the government is not denying a benefit to anyone, but is instead simply insisting that public funds be spent for the purposes for which they were authorized."[98] This, too, is a false dichotomy. While insisting that the funds be spent in a particular way, at the same time the government denied benefits to any program that would not forgo the right to counsel about abortion. The two actions of the government were simply two sides of the same coin.

Rust is a vivid illustration of the pitfalls of formal categories. Prone to false dichotomies, not to mention abstraction and arbitrariness, categorization appears to be a most precarious way to interpret the Constitution.

THE NATURE OF BALANCING

The constitutional methodology of balancing arose in response to the basic deficiency of categorization. In law as well as other fields, the realization was dawning that formal modes of thought were invalid.[99] As a result, more functional modes were developed to replace formalism.

Balancing is a realistic or functional mode of constitutional adjudication that operates by weighing or balancing the interests involved in a case. The term "balancing" is a metaphor that suggests that the Court is "weighing" competing interests. Interests, however, cannot be literally weighed. For example, in a libel case, which involves the competing interests of freedom of speech and integrity of reputation, the values of speech and reputation cannot be measured like ounces or pounds. Their value can be compared on a qualitative, rather than a quantitative, basis. Constitutional values can be compared, weighed, or balanced qualitatively. Balancing, then, entails the making of value judgments; that is, choosing among values. Justice Scalia has argued that the "scale analogy is not really appropriate, since the interests on both sides are incommensurate."[100] This argument, however, misconceives the nature of balancing by casting it as a quantitative measure rather than a qualitative one. The balance or scale certainly is an appropriate analogy—or more precisely, an appropriate metaphor—which refers to the assessment of governmental and individual interests.

Balancing is a realistic mode of constitutional interpretation that, unlike categorization, conceives of law as a social institution rather than an asocial entity isolated in pure logic. Balancing recognizes that constitutional interpretation, like all other legal decision making, depends upon the ideology of judges. Balancing is realistic because it acknowledges that all legal decisions necessarily entail value judgments. It therefore brings those value judgments out into the open, and directs that they be made in a considered, thoughtful way.

The balancing approach recognizes that the essential issue in any constitutional case is whether there is sufficient justification for the governmental action that is being challenged. Do the ends and means of the government action justify the deprivation or harm they have caused? This is a question of both constitutional policy and constitutional fact. When the Supreme Court examines the ends of governmental action, it is making a policy determination; when it examines the means of governmental action, it is making a factual determination.

There are number of cases involving the free speech provision of the First Amendment that provide a clear, if uncharacteristically simple, illustration of the balancing test. For example, in *Schneider v. State*,[101] the Supreme Court found that the First Amendment was violated by several ordinances that prohibited the distribution of leaflets. In reaching that decision, the Court explained that while a state may enact regulations "in the interest of the public safety, health, welfare or convenience," it may not do so in a way that infringes freedom of speech.[102] As a consequence, "the delicate and difficult task falls upon the courts to weigh the circumstances and to appraise the substantiality of the reasons advanced in support of the regulation."[103] In making that "delicate and difficult" balance in *Schneider*, the Court rejected the state's argument that the ordinances were justified by the governmental interest in keeping streets clean by the prevention of littering.[104] In the Court's view, keeping the streets clean was "insufficient to justify" this restriction on speech.[105] Thus, as the Court struck the metaphorical balance in *Schneider*, free speech was more important than clean streets.

In another speech case, *Cox v. New Hampshire*,[106] the Court struck a different balance in ruling that the state interest in protecting pedestrian safety was strong enough to justify a restriction on free speech that required a prior license for a parade or procession. In the view of the Supreme Court, protection of life and limb is a value that justifies restricting freedom of speech, but prevention of litter is not.

These cases vividly illustrate how the balancing approach operates by a comparative, qualitative choice of values. Moreover, the different results reached in the cases illustrate that balancing is neither inherently liberal nor inherently conservative. The decision reached in any case under a balancing approach depends upon the values, whatever they may be, of the justices who are doing the balancing.

Since the 1950s, balancing has become the predominant mode of constitutional adjudication. It is so predominant, in fact, that it can hardly be doubted that we live in, to borrow a phrase coined by T. Alexander Aleinikoff, "the age of balancing."[107] In fact, balancing has become the predominant mode of adjudication not only in the sphere of constitutional law, but also in the spheres of common law and statutory interpretation.[108] Patrick McFadden points out that state courts have used balancing to decide issues of tort law, conflict of laws, domestic relations, civil procedure, estates, taxation, zoning, and others.[109] The ubiquitous use of balancing should come as no surprise because it reflects what philosophers and legal scholars have been telling us for years, namely, that formal modes of thought are spurious and need to be replaced by purposive thinking.[110]

The purposive nature of balancing, which involves choosing among values, is seen by its critics as a fundamental flaw. In their view, choosing among values or making policy is an illegitimate function for the judiciary, and should be left to the more representative branches of government, the executive and especially the legislature.[111] This criticism, however, seriously misperceives the true nature of the judicial process, not to mention misperceiving categorization.

The truth is that judicial decision making, whether done by balancing or categorization, necessarily involves policy or value choices. Balancing brings he policy-making out into the open, and renders it an informed process, whereas categorizing does it covertly or unconsciously, and therefore in a desultory manner.[112]

The Supreme Court has always been more or less reluctant to display its policy-making role.[113] As the only unelected and least democratic branch of the federal government, the judiciary has long operated under the burden that policy making is not a legitimate judicial function. But the fact remains that judicial decision making is impossible without some choosing among values or policies. Judging, after all, is precisely that: determining policy, choosing among values.[114]

Categorization does not avoid value choices, it merely cloaks them. For instance, when the Court formulated the direct-indirect effect test to determine the extent of federal authority, the Court most decidedly was making a policy choice about the allocation of federal and state power. It may be that in devising such categories, the justices were not consciously aware of the social or political consequences the categories would have, but one suspects that more often than not, the justices were consciously aware of the policies that would be effectuated by the rules they were devising. Certainly, in cases like *Lochner v. New York*,[115] it appears that in excluding the authority to regulate working conditions from the police power of the state, the Court was making the policy judgment that freedom of contract was more important than safe working conditions. While the mode of thought in *Lochner* is formalistic, the Court can barely hide the fact that the results in *Lochner* are value laden. By formally defining the police power to preclude the regulation of working conditions, the Court in effect elevated the value of freedom of contract over and above the value of a safe working environment.

SOME COMPARATIVE OBSERVATIONS ABOUT CATEGORIZATION AND BALANCING

Some constitutional provisions may seem to be more prone to being interpreted by categorization, while others may appear more susceptible to balancing.

For example, because the Commerce Clause operates as a limit on state authority, the Court often is called upon to define the scope of permissible state regulation. The delineation of federal and state power seems to call for categories that define and separate the two spheres of authority. Cases that question the constitutionality of state regulations look like they can be neatly resolved by categories that distinguish federal and state realms. It is hardly surprising, therefore, that categorization is the method the Supreme Court originally used to define the extent of state regulatory activities. Indeed, at an early date the Court devised formal categories that supposedly were mutually exclusive to differentiate federal and state power. In the Court's view, the states possessed "police power" to regulate health, welfare, and morals, but no authority to regulate "interstate commerce," which was exclusively within the federal domain. An activity was considered to be within either the (state) police power or the (federal) commerce power, and never the twain shall meet. It was these cut-and-dried categories that the Court used to give meaning to the Constitution in regard to state regulatory authority.

Appearances, we know, can be deceptive. Regardless of what may appear to be appropriate, the truth is that any constitutional provision may be interpreted either through a categorizing mode or a balancing mode. The formal categories of "police power" and "interstate commerce" that the Court created did not prove to be entirely appropriate or effective, and eventually gave way to a balancing methodology as the Court realized that federal and state authority often overlap and cannot be neatly cabined in mutually exclusive categories. As early as 1851 in *Cooley v. Board of Wardens*,[116] the Supreme Court began to determine the scope of state authority by balancing the state interest in regulating a particular activity as compared to the interest in national uniformity regarding the activity in question. By the 1940s it was recognized that interpreting the Constitution to ascertain state regulatory authority entailed "deliberately balancing national and local interests and making a choice as to which of the two *should* prevail."[117]

Other constitutional provisions, such as the Due Process Clause, may appear to be more appropriately interpreted by a balancing approach. Due process seems to be a relatively open-ended concept that does not fit neatly into categories; it should be determined by balancing and weighing a variety of interests. Nonetheless, at one time the Supreme Court used formal categories to define due process.[118] Due process of law, the Court ruled, protected "fundamental rights," such as freedom of contract,[119] ownership of property,[120] and freedom to control the upbringing of one's children,[121] but did not protect non-fundamental rights, such as the right to safe working conditions,[122] freedom from double jeopardy,[123] or freedom from self-incrimination.[124] In time, these categories proved to be internally inconsistent[125] as well as externally specious,[126] so the Court moved to a balancing approach to determine the scope of due process of law. Whether dealing with procedural matters, such as the right to a hearing,[127] or substantive matters, such as the right to marriage, procreation, or family living arrangements,[128] the Court found that the Due Process Clause was just as amenable to balancing as it was to categorization.

The Supreme Court's experience with the Due Process Clause, the Commerce Clause, and other constitutional provisions illustrates that either categorization or balancing can be used in conjunction with any constitutional concept. Whether a question involves the scope of state regulatory authority, interstate commerce, due process of law, freedom of speech, or any other constitutional issue, it can be determined either by categorizing or by balancing. As discussed later, one method may be more valid than the other. Setting aside for now the question of validity, however, the Supreme Court has the choice of utilizing either method to interpret any provision of the Constitution.

Whichever method the Court chooses to use, some degree of creativity is unavoidable. In fact, categorization and balancing are equally creative techniques. That is, both are interpretative acts that require the Supreme Court to create meaning for the Constitution rather than find it from an external source. On occasion, categorization may seem less creative than balancing because its creative aspect is hidden under a cloak of superficial logic and pretense. When the cloak is lifted, however, it is clear that categorization is no less a creative act than is balancing. Justice Scalia has said that balancing is "vague and open-ended."[129] He prefers a more formal approach that is "anchored in rules, not set adrift in some multifactored 'balancing test.' "[130] This position overlooks the value of balancing, while ascribing much too steadfastness to rules. After all, rules are a species of categorization, and, like other formal categories, tend to be artificial, arbitrary, and irrational. Hence, rules are highly susceptible to manipulation. The "anchor" or certainty they provide can be illusory, liable to shatter at the slightest tremor. Although balancing may be open-ended, nonetheless it is decidedly more circumspect than the formalism of a rule-oriented approach. In contrast to rules, balancing is realistic and purposive; these two qualities make for more genuine certainty than the shell game of categorization.

It should also be noted that categorization and balancing possess an equal propensity to be used for either conservative or liberal purposes. Historically, the categorizers have tended to be conservative and the balancers have tended to be liberal, but that phenomena has nothing to do with the nature of categorization or balancing. Neither mode is necessarily tied to a particular ideology.

In fact, in the hands of the same justice or justices, categorization and balancing can lead to the same result in some cases. A 1981 decision, *Jones v. Helms*,[131] illustrates this. In *Jones*, the Court upheld the constitutionality of a state statute that made it a crime for a parent to willfully abandon a dependent child. The statute had been challenged as violative of the Equal Protection Clause because, according to the statute, the crime was a misdemeanor unless the parent left the state after abandoning the child, in which case the crime was elevated to a felony. By making that distinction, the statute affected the right to interstate travel, which the Court previously had held was a fundamental right protectable by strict judicial scrutiny. However, in *Jones*, the Court refused to apply strict scrutiny by ruling that although the right to travel is fundamental, it is not "unqualified," and may be lost, as it was here, by the commission of a crime. In other words, the Court carved out a categorical exception to the fundamental right of interstate travel. And the exception, like other formal categories, was tautological: The right to travel is fundamental, but not always. It is only fundamental when it has not been qualified, or it is only fundamental when it is fundamental.

The same result could have been reached in *Jones* without the sophistry by following precedent and admitting that the right to interstate travel is fundamental, applying strict scrutiny, and then ruling that the fundamental right to travel is outweighed by a compelling state interest in protecting dependent children. That is the exact value judgment that the Court's decision effectuates in the case without actually saying so. Instead of admitting this balance that was occurring, the Court disguised its policy determination by using a circular formalism.

The categorization approach used in *Jones* was unnecessary to the result in the case; the same result could have been reached by a balancing approach. Not only was it unnecessary, but, like other formal approaches, it made little sense. Categories, then, unnecessarily involve the Court in tautology.

CATEGORICAL BALANCING

As the words indicate, categorical balancing is a combination of categorization and balancing. It operates by devising general constitutional categories by balancing the interests relevant to the constitutional provision in question. For instance, the Supreme Court has held that to impose liability in libel actions involving public officials, the free speech provision of the First Amendment requires a showing that the libelous speech was made with "actual malice," that is, either knowledge that the speech was false or reckless disregard that it was false. The rule of actual malice functions as a First Amendment category. Libelous speech that is accompanied by actual malice is not protected by the First Amendment, whereas libelous speech that is not accompanied by actual malice is protected by the First Amendment. Unlike traditional categories, which are *a priori* or transcendental, the category of actual malice was devised by balancing the interests pertinent to libel cases. On one side of the balance is the value in robust public discourse and "breathing space" for freedom of speech. On the other side is the recognition that false statements of fact do not enhance public discourse and the value in protecting the integrity of an individual's reputation from being falsely maligned. In an attempt to accommodate or balance these interests, the Court formulated the actual malice standard, which delineates constitutionally protected speech from that which is unprotected.

It has been pointed out that whether *ad hoc* or categorical balancing provides more protection for constitutional rights depends upon the specific content that the Court chooses to provide for each of those balancing approaches.[132] Certainly the Court could devise a categorical balancing test that is highly protective of constitutional rights and could devise a pure balancing test that is less so. In practice, however, it appears that *ad hoc* balancing, as used by the Court, provides decidedly more protection for constitutional rights than definitional balancing does. Categorical balancing seems to be a method used by the Court to decrease the degree of protection afforded to constitutional rights, although there is nothing about the nature of either of those forms of balancing that would dictate that result.

Unlike categorical balancing, pure balancing is particularized; that is, it focuses upon the particular facts of the case at hand. For example, in free speech cases involving advocacy of illegal action, the Court will inquire whether the particular speech in question actually amounted to a clear and present danger of provoking the illegal action.

In a categorical balancing situation, the balancing focuses on the general category rather than on the particular instance involved in the case. Thus, in a libel case the Court does not inquire whether the specific speech involved in the case added greatly to the marketplace of ideas or whether it caused great harm to the reputation of the plaintiff. Having already made the balance between speech and individual reputation in general, the Court now will merely apply the actual malice standard. That standard or category operates as a kind of clumsy accommodation of the conflicting interests of free speech and individual reputation.

Categorical balancing rules, however, are haphazard. That is, they do not always accomplish the goals for which they are meant. While they are motivated by a balancing of interests, they are not composed in terms of those interests. In other words, their substance does not speak to the interests that motivated them. The actual malice rule in libel cases, for instance, was motivated by weighing the interests of free speech and individual reputation, but the rule itself says nothing about either of those interests. Categorical balancing, then, begins on a teleological basis, but accomplishes its ends in an erratic way, and is not nearly as purposive as *ad hoc* balancing. Because of this deficiency, categorical balancing has a tendency to collapse. As Kathleen Sullivan notes, just when it seems that a category has been devised to avoid *ad hoc* balancing, the formula inevitably breaks down.[133]

THE NECESSITY OF BALANCING

Alternatives to Balancing

A number of constitutional scholars have noted that balancing is a necessary process in constitutional interpretation.[134] "One way or another . . . the Court is always deciding whether in its judgment the harm done to the disadvantaged class by the legislative classification is disproportionate to the public purposes the measure is likely to achieve."[135] What this really seems to mean is that "all *thoughtful* decision-making involves a balance."[136] Decisions can be made through categories that do not balance, but those decisions are hardly thoughtful or purposive. Admittedly, categorization can and has been used to decide cases and in the process of deciding cases also will determine how the competing interests involved in those cases will be resolved. Categorization resolves the competing interests, but does so without consciously considering them. Categorization is random decision making without purpose. On the other hand, balancing is considered decision making with purpose. In that sense, balancing is unavoidable in constitutional adjudication; that is, it is the only thoughtful mode of constitutional interpretation.

T. Alexander Aleinikoff disputes the necessity of balancing. He argues that balancing seems to be inevitable when in reality it is not.[137] As Professor Aleinikoff sees it, the case for balancing has been overestimated because it has been used in opposition to absolutism or literalism.[138] He claims that "there is plenty of room between literalism and balancing."[139] What that "room" is, however, seems to be nothing more than a thinly disguised return to formalism or categorization. An absolute principle, says Professor Aleinikoff, can be limited in scope, and thereby can be absolute when applied but cannot be applied in every situation.[140] In other words, formal categories can be devised to circumscribe the range of absolute principles. Unfortunately, these formal categories have all the deficiencies of formal categories discussed above. While there may be an alternative to balancing without going so far as to embrace absolutism, that alternative is formalism, which is a sterile, invalid mode of adjudication. Certainly Professor Aleinikoff is correct to suggest that balancing is not the sole method of constitutional adjudication, but the fact remains that it is the only valid method of constitutional adjudication.

Professor Aleinikoff also asserts that balancing is not a necessary component of constitutional adjudication.[141] Other methods, he claims, may be used to interpret the Constitution.[142] Exactly what those methods are, however, is something about which Professor Aleinikoff says little. He does note that "constitutional history belies the claim that balancing is inescapable,"[143] but fails to acknowledge that while that history may reveal alternatives to balancing, it does not reveal any sound alternatives to it.

Professor Aleinikoff briefly mentions four possible sources that may be used as alternatives to balancing in interpreting the Constitution: precedent, original intent of the framers, history, and constitutional purpose.[144] A closer examination of these sources, however, reveals that either they are not alternatives to balancing or that they are not viable alternatives to it.

Precedent

Almost in passing, Professor Aleinikoff suggests that precedent may be used instead of balancing.[145] What this overlooks is that the balancing may have occurred in the precedent opinion. Following precedent is not an alternative to balancing, but rather merely shifts the occurrence of balancing to an earlier case.

Or, if the case is one that relied upon categorization, it may be an alternative to balancing, but hardly a sound one. In other words, the use of precedent does not avoid balancing; it merely shifts the balancing to another time or replaces it with categorization and all of its deficiencies.

Original Intent

Professor Aleinikoff also briefly asserts that original intent may be used in lieu of balancing.[146] This ignores that it has been demonstrated again and again that there are serious limits and drawbacks in trying to find meaning for the Constitution by turning to the original intent of the framers or the ratifiers. As discussed in Chapter 1, original intent simply is not a fruitful source of meaning for the Constitution.

There are a number of reasons why the framers' intent is not a determinate source of constitutional meaning. First, the framers of the Constitution were a collective body of fifty-five individuals who did not possess a unitary view of the Constitution.[147] In fact, they embraced a widely diverse, often inconsistent view of most of the provisions in the Constitution.[148] Second, a great number of constitutional issues have risen about which the framers expressed little or no intention whatsoever.[149] Despite the awe in which they are held, the framers were, after all, human beings with human limitations. Like other human beings, they did not think of everything and did not have the ability to foresee the future. They could express no intent about matters such as electronic surveillance,[150] radio and television broadcasting,[151] life-support systems,[152] or the Internet.[153] Nor is it only technological advances that the framers could not foresee. For example, in the days of the framers public schooling was rare, and universal mandatory education would not be conceived for many years. Thus, whatever intentions the framers may have expressed about separation of church and state tell us very little about the framers' views concerning school prayer in the context of elementary and secondary education today.[154] Similarly, the intent of the framers of the Fourteenth Amendment is difficult, if not impossible, to translate to the question of desegregation of public schools in the 1950s, when state-run mandatory education was the rule rather than the exception.[155]

Whether the framers foresaw a particular matter or not, there are a number of constitutional provisions about which they had very little or even nothing to say.[156] There are other provisions about which the framers expressed conflicting ideas, and there are times when the words of the framers are contradicted by their actions.[157] As noted in Chapter 1, it makes little sense to ascribe a unitary intention about complex political issues to a multi-member group such as the framers of the Constitution. Their intentions are poorly documented, extremely ambiguous, and, in some instances, illusory.

Ascertaining the original intent of the ratifiers—that is, the people or their representatives at state ratifying conventions—of the Constitution is even more problematic. The records of the ratifying conventions are notoriously unreliable, and in some instances are so fragmentary or unintelligible that there is little, if anything, to be gained from consulting them.[158] There were hundreds of delegates to the state ratifying conventions, and, as might be expected, the delegates had an extremely broad range of opinions regarding the meaning of the Constitution.[159] To think that anyone could find a unified intent among the hundreds of ratifiers borders on the preposterous.

Moreover, whatever intentions the framers or ratifiers may have had about the Constitution were formulated in the context of a past reality and in accordance with past beliefs, both of which have changed significantly in ensuing years.[160] To transplant those intentions, formulated under past conditions and beliefs, to contemporary situations may result in sad consequences contrary to what the framers themselves would have wanted. Old intentions, fashioned under the conditions of the past, are not readily transportable to later times. What the framers or ratifiers may have intended for their times is not what they may have intended for ours. Life constantly changes, and the reality and ideas that surrounded the framers are long since gone.

Considering the innate restrictions of original intent, it should come as no surprise that the originalist approach has been a failure when attempted by the Supreme Court. Scholars who have studied the Court's use of this approach commonly agree that it has not been a satisfactory method of constitutional decision making because the Court ends up manipulating, revising, or creating intent for the framers under the guise of following historical dictates.[161] When judges claim or even believe that they are engaged in an objective, impersonal search for the framers' intent, what they actually unearth are their own values.[162] Hence, it should come as no surprise that various scholars have concluded that the attempt to interpret the Constitution by following the framers' intent is a "misconceived quest,"[163] an "impossibility,"[164] a "fraud,"[165] and "only slightly stronger than the case for the proposition that we inhabit a flat earth."[166] Justice William Brennan, Jr. has pointed out that the originalist approach "feigns self-effacing deference . . . [b]ut in truth is little more than arrogance cloaked in humility."[167] Given the judicial and scholarly exposure of the masquerade of originalism, it is time to stop pretending that it is a viable means of finding meaning for the Constitution.

History

Professor Aleinikoff suggests that instead of balancing, the Court should look not only to the framers' intentions, which are part of history, but also should look to a more broad view of history. By this he apparently means that the Court should look to any portion of history relevant to the Constitution in addition to looking to the framers' original intentions. It is worth noting that turning to history or original intent does not necessarily avoid balancing; it merely may shift the balancing process from the present to the past and allow persons other than the current Supreme Court justices to be the ones who do the balancing.

More significantly, though, if we turn to a broader view of history to interpret the Constitution, we face many of the same problems attendant upon turning to the intent of the framers. History is infinitely more indeterminate than original intent. John Hart Ely has described how amorphous history, or what he refers to as "tradition," can be:

> "[T]radition" can be invoked in support of almost any cause. There is obvious room to maneuver, along continua of both space and time, on the subject of which tradition to invoke. . . . Top all this off with the tremendous uncertainties in ascertaining anything very concrete about the intellectual or moral climates of ages passed, and you're in a position to prove almost anything to those who are predisposed to have it proved or, more candidly, to admit that tradition doesn't really generate an answer, at least not an answer sufficiently unequivocal.[168]

Given the amorphous nature of history, not to mention its complexity and vastness, it is hardly surprising that on the occasions when they do turn to the past as a source of constitutional meaning, the Supreme Court justices have proven to be rather inept historians.[169] If history was a more predominant fount of meaning for the Constitution, then we should appoint historians rather than lawyers to the high Court, so that something more than a shabby job of historical interpretation could be achieved.

Like the framer's intent, history is inherently locked to the past. It is backward looking,[170] and does not take into account changed conditions. Following history to interpret the Constitution runs the risk of freezing past practices into the law of the land. This is precisely what happened in *Plessy v. Ferguson*[171] when the Supreme Court turned to historical custom and tradition to interpret the Fourteenth Amendment and thereby gave constitutional shelter to racial segregation.[172] By equating the reasonableness of legislation—and hence its constitutionality—with custom and tradition,[173] the Court approved discriminatory practices, no matter how pernicious, so long as they were customary or traditional in society. This approach has the effect of freezing the *status quo* and eroding the capacity of the Constitution to be responsive to changing conditions. It is a truly conservative approach in the sense that it conserves the past by retarding, if not completely blocking, progress. Justice Brennan has noted that this is a "political choice" that is antipathetic to minority rights and ignores the changing nature of the world around us.[174]

Criticism of the historical approach, though, should not be taken to suggest that in interpreting the Constitution the Court should ignore history or the framers' intentions; certainly there are important lessons to be learned from history. But history should not be expected to provide definitive solutions to contemporary constitutional issues. As much as there may be a desire to find an external or determinate source of meaning for the Constitution, unfortunately history cannot fulfill that desire. History can and should be used to inform the balancing process; it should not, however, replace it. Although the justices should look to history as an aid and should learn well its lessons, the fact remains that they themselves cannot avoid creating meaning for the Constitution.

Constitutional Purpose

Finally, Professor Aleinikoff mentions, again almost in passing, that in lieu of balancing, the Supreme Court should look to constitutional purpose to determine the meaning of the document.[175] Undoubtedly, the Court can and should look to the purpose of constitutional provisions in interpreting and applying them. To do so, however, is not a substitute for balancing. To the contrary, it is an integral part of the balancing process. Balancing looks to and weighs interests, and evaluating constitutional purposes helps the Court to decide what those interests are. Deciding constitutional purpose informs the balancing process, which is, if nothing else, teleological. That is, the balancing process is purposeful, it operates by evaluation of purpose. The determination of constitutional purpose, then, is part and parcel of the balancing process.

United States Steel Corp. v. Multistate Tax Commission

Professor Aleinikoff argues that "to recognize a role for balancing in the extreme and rare case is not to demonstrate its validity as a mode of interpretation for the vast majority of constitutional cases."[176] This, however, greatly understates the role of balancing and inverts the focus of proper inquiry concerning the constitutional process. Balancing has proven to be an effective, valid mode of constitutional interpretation not only in the "extreme and rare case," but in virtually all cases. That the Court at times may look to history or the intent of the framers as an aid in interpreting the Constitution in no way replaces the pure balancing mode. Similarly, although the Court on occasion may engage in categorical balancing, this is not a replacement for the pure balancing mode. These techniques may supplement the pure balancing mode, but they hardly can supplant it. Supplemented on occasion by those implements, balancing remains the predominant mode of constitutional interpretation and as such has no valid alternative. Actually, the correct observation is the one that is virtually the opposite of Professor Aleinikoff's: To recognize a role for history, the framers' intent, or other instruments hardly demonstrates that balancing does not remain the predominant and only valid framework of constitutional adjudication.

In an attempt to prove his point that balancing is not ineluctable, Professor Aleinikoff points to *United States Steel Corp. v. Multistate Tax Commission*,[177] a relatively modern case that he views as presenting an alternative to balancing. This case arose when United States Steel challenged a Multistate Tax Compact that a group of states had entered to promote uniformity and compatibility among state tax systems and to facilitate the ascertainment of tax liability of multistate taxpayers. United States Steel claimed that the Multistate Tax Compact violated the Compact Clause, a seldom-used constitutional provision that reads: "No State shall, without the Consent of Congress . . . enter into any Agreement or Compact with another State."[178] In *United States Steel*, the Court admitted that a literal reading of the Compact Clause would require the states to obtain approval from Congress before entering into any agreement whatsoever.[179] But, as Professor Aleinikoff notes, the Court rejected an absolute view of the clause and instead reaffirmed a previous decision that limited the application of the Compact Clause to agreements that are "directed to the formation of any combination tending to the increase of political power in the States, which may encroach upon or interfere with the just supremacy of the United States."[180] Applying this rule, the Court found no violation of the Compact Clause because the Multistate Tax Compact did not grant to the states any authority that impinged upon federal supremacy.

In Professor Aleinikoff's view, the Court's opinion in *United States Steel* does not frame the issue as one of competing interests, and it does not attempt to weigh or compare the strength of federal versus state interests.[181] As he sees it, *United States Steel* is "decidedly not a balancing opinion."[182] This may overstate the point a bit.[183] After all, the Court did describe the rule of the case as "stat[ing] the proper *balance* between federal and state power with respect to compacts and agreements among States."[184] Professor Aleinikoff attempts to minimize this description by suggesting that the Court made it merely "[b]ecause we live in balancing times."[185] Still, A good deal of the Court's opinion, not to mention the rule of the case, certainly looks to the federal interest that underlies the Compact Clause. The Court's opinion also acknowledges that the Compact Clause further functions to prevent any compact between states that might injure the "interests" of other states.[186] In addition, the Court points out that there is no "advantage" or "benefit" to giving an absolute interpretation to the Compact Clause.[187] Thus, the Court seems to recognize that there is an interest in allowing some interstate compacts, and the interest needs to be weighed against the interest of the federal government and the other states in protecting their sovereignty. Accordingly, the rule that the Court follows can be taken as one that amounts to categorical balancing rather than pure categorization.

On the other hand, insofar as Professor Aleinikoff is correct that *United States Steel* is "decidedly not a balancing opinion,"[188] the Court's method of decision making is not particularly satisfactory. If the Court is not taking federal and state interests into account, the rule of the case and the decision itself are non-teleological. That is, if they are not based upon a consideration of interests, they have no purpose and make no sense. If not to balance federal and state interests, what reason is there to have a rule that limits application of the Compact Clause to "agreements directed to the formation of any combination tending to the increase of political power in the States, which may encroach upon or interfere with the just supremacy of the United States"?

United States Steel is one of those cases where any intention on the part of the framers is notably lacking to shed light on the meaning of a constitutional provision. As the Court says, the records of the Constitutional Convention "are barren of any clue as to the precise contours of the agreements and compacts governed by the Compact Clause."[189] Professor Aleinikoff, however, points to the Court's use of precedent, history, and the purpose of the Compact Clause to decide the case without balancing.[190]

Certainly the Court did rely on precedent in deciding *United States Steel*. However, insofar as the Court relied on precedent, that reliance is not an alternative to balancing. As noted above,[191] the use of precedent either shifts the balancing to another time or utilizes categorization, which is not a sensible alternative to balancing.

Nor is there any denying that part of the Court's opinion in *United States Steel* is devoted to a discussion of the history of the Compact Clause. However, a good part of that discussion, although interesting, is surplusage that adds little to actually deciding the case. In reading the historical passages in the opinion, one gets the sense that the Court is filling up pages with historical material that makes the same point over and over again. To the extent that the Court's use of history actually aided the decision, it included consideration of the interests noted above, and thus informed the categorical balance that the Court struck in the case. *United States Steel* is not simply a case where the Supreme Court turned to history to find a preexisting answer. Rather, it is a case where the Court used history partially as an interesting makeweight and partially to help mold an answer that did not previously exist.

Finally, insofar as the Court relied upon the purpose of the Compact Clause, it was engaging in balancing. When the Court determines the purposes of a constitutional provision and applies them to the case at hand, it is balancing; that is, it is weighing relevant interests and deciding their respective weight. The opinion in *United States Steel*, then, is one in which the Court relies upon a bit of balancing that occurred previously, combined with a categorical rule that may be an alternative to balancing, but hardly is a viable one. It is a case that is far from a shining example of a sensible alternative to balancing.

A Last Grasp at an Alternative to Balancing

At a later point in his article, Professor Aleinikoff asserts that constitutional decisions can be made without balancing by "constructing a theory" for the constitutional provision in question.[192] But Professor Aleinikoff offers little explanation as to how a theory is actually constructed without balancing. He does say that many important moral and legal issues are decided without balancing by using principles, and he cites a number of cases to illustrate that claim.[193] Nowhere, however, does he explain how principles are to be determined and applied without balancing. In lieu of balancing, Professor Aleinikoff proposes "theories" and "principles," but he says nothing about how they are to be derived. He appears to ignore that the determination of theory and principle requires either balancing or categorization with all of its attendant flaws. In fact, Professor Aleinikoff admits that proponents of balancing would observe that principles "are simply the products of earlier balances,"[194] and he proffers no rebuttal of that observation.

Judgments of principle, Professor Aleinikoff continues, "may be leaps of faith . . . [b]ut they form the bedrock of our moral systems."[195] This sounds suspiciously like the old categories, such as "freedom of contract" or "direct effect on interstate commerce," that were once taken as leaps of faith and created a terrible morass. Whether referred to as "categories," "principles," or "theories," if they are formulated without considering purposes and without weighing interests, they are not bedrock, but rather are a rickety structure built on illusion that can support nothing of substance.

CONCLUSION

We live in an age of balancing because balancing is the only sound way to interpret the Constitution. Balancing is the only sound way to make any legal decision as well as any well-considered human decision. Balancing is realistic decision making; it is thoughtful and purposive. Balancing may not be inevitable, but it is necessary if we want a viable system of constitutional interpretation.

Balancing replaced categorization as the predominant mode of constitutional interpretation when legal formalism collapsed under the weight of its own fallibility. The revival of categorization, although not very widespread, is a disturbing trend in the law. In the past, the use of formal categories proved to be an unworkable way of interpreting the Constitution, but evidently that lesson of history is being ignored in some corners. Although disturbing, the resuscitation of formalism is not entirely surprising. Formal categories provide an illusion of certainty that is reassuring to those who fail to look beyond legal facades. It is, however, a false security. Behind its facade, categorization is no more certain than balancing, and perhaps even less so. More significantly, categorization is an aimless method of decision making, whereas balancing is utilitarian.

NOTES

1. Oliver Wendell Holmes, Jr., in Gompers v. United States, 233 U.S. 604, 610 (1914).

2. *See* Henry S. Commager, THE AMERICAN MIND: AN INTERPRETATION OF AMERICAN THOUGHT AND CHARACTER SINCE THE 1880's ch. XVII (1950); Craig R. Ducat, MODES OF CONSTITUTIONAL INTERPRETATION 42–115 (1978); Duncan Kennedy, *Toward an Historical Understanding of Legal Consciousness: The Case of Classical Legal Thought in America, 1850–1940*, 3 RES. L. & SOC. 3, 7–9 (1980).

3. *See* Commager, *supra* note 2, at ch. XVIII; Ducat, *supra* note 2, at 116–192; T. Alexander Aleinikoff, *Constitutional Law in the Age of Balancing*, 96 YALE L.J. 943, 943–72 (1987).

4. The breakthrough occurred before the turn of the century when Oliver Wendell Holmes, Jr. published The Common Law in 1881. Oliver W. Holmes, Jr., THE COMMON

LAW (1881). Subsequent influential works include: Roscoe Pound, *Mechanical Jurisprudence*, 8 COLUM. L. REV. 605 (1908); Walter W. Cook, *The Logical and Legal Bases of the Conflict of Laws*, 33 YALE L.J. 457 (1924); Karl N. Llewellyn, *A Realistic Jurisprudence—The Next Step*, 30 COLUM. L. REV. 431 (1930); Max Radin, *Legal Realism*, 31 COLUM. L. REV. 824 (1931); Jerome Frank, *Mr. Justice Holmes and Non-Euclidean Thinking*, CORN. L.Q. 568 (1932); Felix S. Cohen, *Transcendental Nonsense and the Functional Approach*, 35 COLUM. L. REV. 809 (1935).

5. Morton J. Horwitz, THE TRANSFORMATION OF AMERICAN LAW, 1870–1960: THE CRISIS OF LEGAL ORTHODOXY 17 (1992); Aleinikoff, *supra* note 3, at 963–72; Patrick M. McFadden, *The Balancing Test*, 29 B.C.L. Rev. 585, 588, 603–22 (1988).

6. Kathleen M. Sullivan, *Post-Liberal Judging: The Roles of Categorization and Balancing*, 63 U. COLO. L. REV. 293, 294 (1992).

7. *Id.* Although Professor Sullivan's article notes the revival of categorization, the article does not address the theoretical flaws of categorization as a method of constitutional interpretation. The article is directed to other concerns.

8. *See, e.g.*, Renton v. Playtime Theatres, Inc. 475 U.S. 41 (1986) ("the ordinance is not aimed at the *content* of the films . . . but rather at [their] *secondary effects*"); DeShaney v. Winnebago County Dep't of Soc. Servs., 489 U.S. 189 (1989) (the Due Process Clause is phrased as "a limitation on the State's power to act" and does not impose an "affirmative obligation" upon the State to protect its citizens from private actors; therefore, no cause of action arose from the failure of county-employed social workers to protect a child from an abusive father); Rust v. Sullivan, 500 U.S. 174, 196 (1991) ("the government has not discriminated on the basis of viewpoint; it has merely chosen to fund one activity to the exclusion of another"), ("the government is not denying a benefit to anyone, but is instead simply insisting that public funds be spent for the purposes for which they are authorized"). At times, Justice Rehnquist seems either disingenuous about the use of formal methodology or uninformed about it. Thus, in United States v. Salerno, 481 U.S. 739 (1987), his opinion for the Court purported to use a balancing approach and eschewed any "categorical imperative," *id.* at 748–51, but could not escape being accused of "sterile formalism" by the dissent. *Id.* at 758 (Marshall, J., dissenting).

9. *See* Bendix Autolite Corp. v. Midwesco Enters., Inc., 486 U.S. 888, 897 (1988) (Scalia, J., concurring) ("I would therefore abandon the 'balancing' approach to these negative Commerce Clause cases"); Morrison v. Olson, 487 U.S. 654, 711–12 (1988) (Scalia, J., dissenting); Employment Div. v. Smith, 494 U.S. 872, 888–89 (1990); Itel Containers Int'l Corp. v. Huddleston, 507 U.S. 60, 79 (1993) (Scalia, J., concurring).

10. *See, e.g.*, Jones v. Helms, 452 U.S. 412 (1981) (upholding a state law that elevates willful child abandonment from a misdemeanor into a felony when accompanied by departure from the state); Hazelwood Sch. Dist. v. Kuhlmeier, 484 U.S. 260 (1988) (holding that a high school newspaper published as part of a journalism class is not a public forum, therefore, it was not a violation of the First Amendment for school administrators to impose reasonable restrictions on content); Boos v. Barry, 485 U.S. 312 (1988) (striking down, as violative of the First Amendment, a municipal ordinance prohibiting the display of disparaging signs within 500 feet of a foreign embassy, while upholding a similar ordinance prohibiting congregations of people within 500 feet of a foreign embassy).

11. Aleinikoff, *supra* note 3; Frederick Schauer, *Categories and the First Amendment: A Play in Three Acts*, 34 VAND. L. REV. 265 (1981).

12. *See, e.g.*, Frederick Schauer, *Formalism*, 97 YALE L.J. 509 (1988); Ernest J. Weinrib, *Legal Formalism: On the Immanent Rationality of Law*, 97 YALE L.J. 949 (1988).

13. Sullivan, *supra* note 6, at 293.

14. Samuel I. Hayakawa, LANGUAGE IN THOUGHT AND ACTION 49–50 (4th ed. 1978).

15. Gibbons v. Ogden, 22 U.S. (9 Wheat.) 1 (1824) (holding that a New York grant of a steamboat monopoly affecting navigation between New York and New Jersey conflicted with a federal statute licensing such interstate commerce and was therefore void under the Supremacy Clause).

16. *Id.* at 194.

17. United States v. E.C. Knight Co., 156 U.S. 1 (1895) (holding that "manufacture" was different from "commerce," therefore, the Sherman Antitrust Act did not apply to stock purchases by which the American Sugar Refining Company had acquired almost total control over the manufacture of domestic sugar).

18. *See, e.g.*, NLRB v. Jones & Laughlin Steel Corp., 301 U.S. 1 (1937) (holding that Congress could regulate labor relations at any manufacturing plant operated by an integrated manufacturing and sales concern because of the serious effect that a work stoppage at such a plant would have on interstate commerce); Wickard v. Filburn, 317 U.S. 111 (1942) (holding that Congress's regulatory power is not restricted to acts which taken alone would have substantial economic effect upon interstate commerce, but also encompasses acts which, in the aggregate, have such a significant economic effect); United States v. Darby, 312 U.S. 100 (1941) (holding that Congress may follow its own public policy conceptions in determining appropriate restrictions on interstate commerce, and may exclude from such commerce those articles which it concludes are injurious to public health, morals or welfare, even though the individual states have not sought to regulate such articles).

19. *See* text *infra* notes 20–23.

20. *See* Goldberg v. Kelly, 397 U.S. 254 (1970) (holding that there is a property right in the continued receipt of welfare benefits, which entitles the recipient to a hearing before said benefits may be terminated).

21. Fuentes v. Shevin, 407 U.S. 67 (1972) (holding unconstitutional a state law permitting replevin, without a hearing, of household goods bought on contract).

22. Board of Regents of State Colleges v. Roth, 408 U.S. 564 (1972) (holding *inter alia* that a university's decision to deny contract renewal to a nontenured assistant professor without a hearing did not create a constitutional claim as the plaintiff's expectation of contract renewal did not amount to a protectable property interest).

23. *Id.*

24. Horwitz, *supra* note 5, at 16–17.

25. *Id.* at 17.

26. *Id.*

27. *Id.*

28. *Id.* at 199.

29. McCulloch v. Maryland, 17 U.S. (4 Wheat.) 316 (1819) (holding *inter alia* that the framers intended the Constitution to set forth only its "great outlines" and "important objects," leaving the "minor ingredients" to be "deduced from the objects themselves").

30. Muller v. Oregon, 208 U.S. 412, 421 (1908) ("[H]istory discloses the fact that woman has always been dependent upon man . . . she has been looked on in the courts

as needing especial care that her rights may be preserved"); Reynolds v. United States, 98 U.S. 145, 164 (1878) ("[F]rom the earliest history of England polygamy has been treated as an offence against society"); Bradwell v. State, 83 U.S. (16 Wall.) 130, 141 (1872) ("[I]t certainly cannot be affirmed, as an historical fact, that [the right of women to engage in any profession or occupation] has ever been established as one of the fundamental privileges and immunities of the sex. On the contrary, civil law has always recognized a wide difference in the respective spheres and destinies of man and woman").

31. Adamson v. California, 332 U.S. 46, 60–68 (1947) (Frankfurter, J., concurring) (arguing that the concepts of a "progressive democracy" and a "truly free society" were inconsistent with the notion that the Fourteenth Amendment automatically imposed the first eight constitutional amendments upon the states); Reynolds v. United States, 98 U.S. 145, 164 (1878) ("Polygamy has always been odious among the northern and western nations of Europe").

32. *See, e.g.*, Slaughter-House Cases 83 U.S. (16 Wall.) 36, 110 (1872) (Field, J., dissenting) (quoting Adam Smith).

33. *See* Jacobus tenBroek, *Use by the United States Supreme Court of Extrinsic Aids in Constitutional Construction*, 27 CAL. L. REV. 399 (1939); Alfred H. Kelly, *Clio and the Court: An Illicit Love Affair*, SUP. CT. REV. 119 (1965), John Hart Ely, DEMOCRACY AND DISTRUST 48–70 (1980); Jeffrey M. Shaman, *The Constitution, the Supreme Court, and Creativity*, 9 HASTINGS CONST. L.Q. 257 (1982).

34. Ely, *supra* note 33, at 44.

35. United States v. E. C. Knight Co., 156 U.S. 1 (1895).

36. *Supra* note 18.

37. *See* Hayakawa, *supra* note 14, at 49–50:

> The task of writing a dictionary begins with the reading of vast amounts of the literature of the period or subject that it is intended to cover. As the editors read, they copy on cards every interesting or rare word, every unusual or peculiar occurrence of a common word, a large number of common words. . . . For a really big job of dictionary writing, . . . millions of such cards are collected and the task of editing occupies decades . . . [T]here will be for each word anywhere from two or three to several hundred illustrative quotations . . . [The dictionary editor] writes his definitions, following the hard-and-fast rule that each definition *must* be based on what the quotations in front of him reveal about the meaning of the word. The editor cannot be influenced by what *he* thinks a given word *ought* to mean. He must work according to the cards, or not at all.

It should be noted, however, that Professor Hayakawa overstates the point that an editor cannot be influenced by what he or she thinks a given word ought to mean, and that the editor must work according to the cards or not at all. In fact, the editor will be influenced by what he or she thinks a word ought to mean, and the editor's work will not be strictly limited by the cards. Editing the cards, like interpreting the Constitution, necessarily will entail some degree of creativity.

38. *See* text *supra*, at notes 8–12.

39. *Id.*

40. *See* Jeffrey M. Shaman, *The Choice of Law Process: Territorialism and Functionalism*, 22 WM. & MARY L. REV. 227, 231–40 (1980).

41. *See* sources cited notes 4–5.

42. *See* Commager, *supra* note 2, at ch. XVII.

43. *Id.* at 3–107.

44. William James, PRAGMATISM, A NEW NAME FOR SOME OLD WAYS OF THINKING: POPULAR LECTURES ON PHILOSOPHY 201 (1907).

45. *Id.*

46. *See* Commager, *supra* note 2, at 91–107.

47. *Id.*

48. John Dewey, EXPERIENCE AND NATURE ch. 8 (1929).

49. *Id.*

50. John Dewey, LOGIC, THE THEORY OF INQUIRY ch. 3 (1938).

51. Dewey, *supra* note 48, at 241–44.

52. *Id.*

53. *See* Commager, *supra* note 2, at chs. X, XI, XIV; William Quine, FROM A LOGICAL POINT OF VIEW 30–46 (1961); Alfred N. Whitehead, ADVENTURES OF IDEAS chs. XI–XV (1937).

54. *See, e.g.*, Bertrand Russell, HUMAN KNOWLEDGE part I, ch. III; part III, ch. IV (1948); Bertrand Russell, OUR KNOWLEDGE OF THE EXTERNAL WORLD lecture IV (1914).

55. Russell, *supra* note 54, at 214–15.

56. *See, e.g.*, Francis G. Crookshank, *The Importance of a Theory of Signs and a Critique of Language in the Study of Medicine*, in THE MEANING OF MEANING: A STUDY OF THE INFLUENCE OF LANGUAGE UPON THOUGHT AND OF THE SCIENCE OF SYMBOLISM 337 (Supp. II 1938).

57. *See, e.g.*, Bronislaw Malinowski, *The Problem of Meaning in Primitive Languages*, in THE MEANING OF MEANING: A STUDY OF THE INFLUENCE OF LANGUAGE UPON THOUGHT AND OF THE SCIENCE OF SYMBOLISM 296 (Supp. I 1938); Benjamin L. Whorf, LANGUAGE, THOUGHT, AND REALITY: SELECTED WRITINGS (1956).

58. *See, e.g.*, Commager, *supra* note 2, at chs. XIII, XIV (1950).

59. *See, e.g., id.* at ch. XI.

60. *See, e.g., id.* at ch. X.

61. *See id.* at 360 ("Of all the social sciences, law retained longest its Newtonian character, resisted most successfully the impact of evolution and economic realism").

62. *See* Von Jhering, IM JURISTISCHEN BERGRIFFSHIMMEL, IN SCHERZ UND ERNST IN DER JURISPRUDENZ 245 (11th ed. 1912).

> A great German jurist had a curious dream. He dreamed that he died and was taken to a special heaven reserved for the theoreticians of the law. In this heaven one met, face to face, the many concepts of jurisprudence in their absolute purity, freed from all entangling alliances with human life. Here were the disembodied spirits of good faith and bad faith, property, possession, *laches* and rights *in rem*. Here were all the logical instruments needed to manipulate and transform these legal concepts and thus to create and to solve the most beautiful of legal problems. Here one found a dialectic-hydraulic-interpretation press, which could press an infinite number of meanings out of any text or statute, an apparatus for constructing fictions, and a hair-splitting machine that could divide a single human hair into 999,999 equal parts and, when operated by the most expert jurists, could split each of these parts into 999,999 equal parts. The boundless opportunities of this heaven of legal concepts were open to all properly qualified jurists, provided only they drank the Lethean draught which induced forgetfulness of terrestrial human affairs. But for the most accomplished jurists the Lethean draught was entirely superfluous. They had nothing to forget.

Cohen, *supra* note 4, at 809.

63. Southern Pac. Co. v. Jensen, 244 U.S. 205, 222 (1912) (Holmes, J., dissenting).

64. Cohen, *supra* note 4, at 814–21.

65. *See* Dewey, *supra* note 48, at 241–44.

66. *Id.*

67. Cohen, *supra* note 4, at 820.

68. *See* text *supra*, at notes 17–18.

69. Leo Pfeffer, THIS HONORABLE COURT: A HISTORY OF THE UNITED STATES SUPREME COURT 299–321 (1965).

70. Bernard Schwartz, A HISTORY OF THE SUPREME COURT 238–41 (1993).

71. United States v. Darby, 312 U.S. 100, 118 (1940) ("The power of Congress over interstate commerce . . . extends to those activities intrastate which so affect interstate commerce . . . as to make regulation of them appropriate means to a legitimate end"); Wickard v. Filburn, 317 U.S. 111, 125 (1942) ("But even if . . . activity be local and though it may not be regarded as commerce, it may still, whatever its nature, be reached by Congress if it exerts a substantial economic effect on interstate commerce").

72. Darby, 312 U.S. at 118; Wickard, 317 U.S. at 125.

73. Martin M. Shapiro, *The Constitution and Economic Rights*, in ESSAYS ON THE CONSTITUTION OF THE UNITED STATES 74, 79 (Mont J. Harmon ed. 1978).

74. *See* Frost & Frost Trucking Co. v. Railroad Comm'n, 271 U.S. 583 (1926) (holding that the government may not condition the receipt of its benefits upon the nonassertion of constitutional rights, even if the receipt of the benefit is otherwise merely a privilege).

75. *See* Willner v. Commission on Character & Fitness, 373 U.S. 96 (1963) (holding that New York denied procedural due process to an individual by refusing him admittance to the practice of law on the basis of an adverse report from the bar association character committee that he was given no opportunity to contest).

76. *See* Cafeteria & Restaurant Workers Union v. McElroy, 367 U.S. 886 (1961) (holding that the unexplained revocation of the security clearance of a privately employed cook at a naval base caused no constitutionally actionable damage to the individual's reputation, even though she was terminated as a result, since her employment opportunities elsewhere were not shown to have been hindered); Board of Regents of State Colleges v. Roth, 408 U.S. 564 (1972) (holding that a university's decision to deny contract renewal to a nontenured assistant professor without a hearing did not create a constitutional claim as a protectable property interest must stem from an independent source, such as state law which, in this case, left the decision to the unfettered discretion of the university); *but cf.* Greene v. McElroy, 365 U.S. 474 (1959) (construing a federal statute in such a way as to avoid the question whether revocation of a defense industry engineer's security clearance without a full hearing and confrontation violated the right to due process); Perry v. Sindermann, 408 U.S. 593 (1972) (holding that, even if a person has no right to a valuable government benefit, and it may be denied for any number of reasons, the government may not deny in a way that infringes upon a persons's freedom of speech).

77. *See* Flemming v. Nestor, 363 U.S. 603 (1960) (holding that the expectation of Social Security benefits is not a property right, therefore, termination of Social Security benefits to certain deported aliens did not violate due process); Weinberger v. Salfi, 422 U.S. 749 (1975) (holding that a requirement of nine months of marriage to the wage earner prior to receipt of Social Security benefits did not violate due process for lack of an individualized determination).

78. *See* Charles Reich, *The New Property*, 73 YALE L.J. 733 (1964); Robert O'Neill, *Unconstitutional Conditions: Welfare Benefits with Strings Attached*, 54 CAL. L. REV. 443 (1996); William W. Van Alstyne, *The Demise of the Right-Privilege Distinction in Constitutional Law* 81 HARV. L. REV. 1439 (1968).

79. Van Alstyne, *supra* note 78, at 1458–60.

80. Carl Sandburg, THE PEOPLE, YES 77 (1936).

81. Goldberg v. Kelly, 397 U.S. 254 (1970) (holding that a welfare recipient's interest in continued receipt of benefits is a statutory entitlement amounting to property under the Due Process Clause, which necessitates a hearing prior to termination of benefits).

82. *Id.*

83. Bell v. Burson, 402 U.S. 535 (1971) (holding that aperson involved in an accident has an entitlement to a driver's license under state law and, thus, has a federal constitutional right to a due process hearing on the issue of fault prior to any suspension of his license).

84. Board of Regents of State Colleges v. Roth, 408 U.S. 564, 571 n.9 (1972).

85. Van Alstyne, *supra* note 78, at 1445.

86. Board of Regents of State Colleges v. Roth, 408 U.S. 564 (1972) (holding that a university's decision to deny contract renewal to a nontenured assistant professor without a hearing did not create a constitutional claim as a protectable property interest must stem from an independent source, such as state law which, in this case, left the decision to the unfettered discretion of the university).

87. *E.g.*, Perry v. Sindermann, 408 U.S., 593 (1972) (holding that, even if a person has no right to a valuable government benefit, and it may be denied for any number of reasons, the government may not deny in a way that infringes upon that person's freedom of speech); Bishop v. Wood, 426 U.S. 341 (1976) (holding that public employees are entitled to procedural due process protection only if the law or contract defining their job expressly provides that discharge can occur only for cause); Meachum v. Fano, 427 U.S. 215 (1976) (holding that the Due Process Clause does not entitle a state prisoner to a hearing when transferred to a prison with less favorable conditions unless a state law or practice conditions such transfers upon proof of serious misconduct or other events).

88. Rodney A. Smolla, *The Reemergence of the Right-Privilege Distinction in Constitutional Law: The Price of Protesting Too Much*, 35 STAN. L. REV. 69, 73 (1982).

89. Weinberger v. Salfi, 422 U.S. 749 (1975) (holding that a requirement of nine months of marriage to the wage earner prior to receipt of Social Security benefits did not violate due process for lack of an individualized determination).

90. Paul v. Davis, 424 U.S. 693 (1976) (holding that reputation, alone, is neither property nor liberty, therefore, inclusion of a person's name on a flyer listing "known" active shoplifters did not violate due process).

91. O'Bannon v. Town Court Nursing Ctr., 447 U.S. 773 (1980) (holding that the unwilling transfer of elderly patients, without a hearing, from a nursing home decertified by Medicare/Medicaid did not violate due process as the patients had no interest in receiving benefits for care in a particular facility).

92. *See* United States v. Lopez, 514 U.S. 549, 559 (1995).

93. *See* Renton v. Playtime Theatres, Inc., 475 U.S. 41, 47 (1986).

94. *See* United States v. Salerno, 481 U.S. 739, 746 (1987).

95. *See* Alexander v. United States, 509 U.S. 544, 550–51 (1993).

96. Rust v. Sullivan, 500 U.S. 173 (1991).

97. *Id.* at 193.

98. *Id.* at 195.

99. *See supra* text accompanying notes 41–61.

100. Bendix Autolite Corp. v. Midwesco Enters., Inc., 486 U.S. 888, 897 (1988) (Scalia, J., concurring).

101. Schneider v. State, 308 U.S. 147 (1939) (holding city antihandbill ordinances unconstitutional as restrictions on free speech despite the state's legitimate interests in litter control and traffic safety).

102. *Id.* at 160.

103. *Id.* at 161.

104. *Id.* at 162–63.

105. *Id.* at 162.

106. *See* Cox v. New Hampshire, 312 U.S. 569 (1941) (upholding convictions under a state licensing statute for parades and processions where the state supreme court had subsequently narrowly construed the statute as limited to restrictions on time, place and manner); *see also* Heffron v. International Soc'y for Krishna Consciousness, 452 U.S. 460 (1981) (holding that a rule requiring state fair vendors and exhibitors to rent booths was content-neutral and was not an unconstitutional restriction on free speech).

107. Aleinikoff, *supra* note 3, at 943–44. One person, however, has doubted the predominance of balancing; *see* Sullivan, *supra* note 6, at 295–96, although her attempt to prove her case is not convincing.

108. McFadden, *supra* note 5, at 603–11.

109. *Id.* at 609–10.

110. *See supra* note 4.

111. *See, e.g.*, Robert Bork, *Styles in Constitutional Theory*, 26 S. TEX. L.J. 383 (1985); Raoul Berger, *New Theories of "Interpretation": The Activist Flight from the Constitution*, 47 OHIO ST. L.J. 1 (1986); Bendix Autolite Corp. v. Midwesco Enters., Inc., 486 U.S. 888, 897 (1988) (Scalia, J., concurring).

112. *See* Jerome D. Frank, COURTS ON TRIAL: MYTH AND REALITY IN AMERICAN JUSTICE 353 (1963):

> It is high time that we put an end to the device of referring to Nature as the justification for any particular social or economic program or method of government. That device has always led to the worst kind of casuistry. It is oblique, indirect, lacking in forthrightness. The candid approach is to say: Here is my program. Whether or not it is "right" depends upon whether it is in accord with, and will effectively promote, values and ideals which you think both desirable and possible of accomplishment. Here are values and ideals which I favor. And here are my reasons for believing that they will be furthered by my program, and that that program is feasible.

See also David L. Shapiro, *In Defense of Judicial Candor*, 100 HARV. L. REV. 731 (1978).

113. *See* Morton J. Horwitz, *The Rise of Legal Formalism*, 19 AM. J. LEGAL HIST. 251, 254–55 (1975) ("The desire to separate law and politics has always been a central aspiration of the American legal profession. . . . [T]he attempt to place law under the banner of 'science' was designed to separate politics from law, subjectivity from objectivity and layman's reasoning from professional reasoning").

114. *See* William J. Brennan, Jr., *Reason, Passion, and "The Progress of the Law,"* The Forty-Second Annual Benjamin Cardozo Lecture Delivered at the Association of the Bar of the City of New York (Sept. 17, 1987), *reprinted in* 10 CARDOZO L. REV. 3, 4–5 (1988):

> Having admitted and demonstrated that judges inevitably confront value choices, Cardozo did not shrink from the implications of that admission. He rejected the prevailing myth that a judge's

personal values were irrelevant to their decision process . . . He attacked the myth that judges were oracles of pure reason, and insisted that we consider the role that human experience, emotion, and passion play in the judicial process.

115. Lochner v. New York, 198 U.S. 45 (1905). This case is discussed more fully in Chapter 3 at notes 22–36.

116. Cooley v. Board of Wardens, 53 U.S. (12 How.) 299 (1851) (holding that states are free to regulate those aspects of interstate commerce that are so local in character as to demand diverse treatment, while Congress can regulate the aspects of interstate and foreign commerce that are so national as to require uniform treatment).

117. Dowling, *Interstate Commerce and State Power*, 27 VA. L. REV. 1, 21 (1940) (emphasis in original).

118. *See, e.g.*, Allgeyer v. Louisiana, 165 U.S. 578 (1897) (striking down Louisiana law that prohibited buying insurance for property in Louisiana from any company which has not complied with Louisiana law); Coppage v. Kansas, 236 U.S. 1 (1915) (striking down state law prohibiting "yellow dog" contracts); Lochner v. New York, 198 U.S. 45 (1905) (holding unconstitutional a state-imposed 60-hour limit on bakery employees' work week).

119. *Id.*

120. *Id.*

121. *See* Meyer v. Nebraska, 262 U.S. 390 (1923) (striking down state law prohibiting the teaching of foreign languages to children); Pierce v. Society of Sisters, 268 U.S. 510 (1925) (striking down state law prohibiting children from attending parochial schools).

122. Lochner v. New York, 198 U.S. at 45.

123. Palko v. Connecticut, 302 U.S. 318 (1937) (holding that the Fifth Amendment protection against double jeopardy was not made applicable to the states by the Fourteenth Amendment).

124. Twining v. New Jersey, 211 U.S. 78 (1908) (holding that the Fifth Amendment protection against self-incrimination was not made applicable to the states by the Fourteenth Amendment).

125. Laurence H. Tribe, AMERICAN CONSTITUTIONAL LAW 442–46 (1978).

For example, the Court's decisions in Holden v. Hardy and Muller v. Oregon indicated that, insofar, as such groups as coal miners and women were concerned, states could attempt to assist the protected group even at the expense of others, because of its supposedly vulnerable and dependent position. These recognized exceptions were cast in terms that rendered the entire theory potentially vulnerable to an argument that, as social and economic patterns change or as existing patterns are reassessed, other groups—ultimately, industrial laborers in general—may become unable, or may come to be *regarded* as unable, to protect their own interest effectively, so that governmental intervention on their behalf becomes justifiable in terms of an already available theory.

Id. at 442.

126. *Id.* at 446–49.

In large measure, however, it was the economic realities of the Depression that graphically undermined Lochner's premises. No longer could it be argued with great conviction that the invisible hand of economics was functioning simultaneously to protect individual rights and produce a social optimum. The legal "freedom" of contract and property came increasingly to be seen as an illusion, subject as it was to impersonal economic forces. Positive government intervention came to be more widely accepted as essential to economic survival, and legal doctrines would henceforth have to operate from that premise.

Id. at 446–47.

127. *See, e.g.*, Greene v. McElroy, 365 U.S. 474 (1959) (construing a federal statute in such a way as to avoid the question whether revocation of a defense industry engineer's security clearance without a full hearing and confrontation violated the right to due process); Goldberg v. Kelly, 397 U.S. 254 (1970) (holding that a welfare recipient's interest in continued receipt of benefits is a statutory entitlement amounting to property under the Due Process Clause, which necessitates a hearing prior to termination of benefits); Boddie v. Connecticut, 401 U.S. 371 (1971) (holding a state law conditioning a judicial decree of divorce upon the claimant's ability to pay court fees and costs unconstitutional under the Due Process Clause).

128. *See, e.g.*, Roe v. Wade, 410 U.S. 113 (1973) (holding that the fundamental right to privacy encompasses a woman's decision whether or not to terminate her pregnancy); Moore v. City of East Cleveland, 431 U.S. 494 (1977) (holding unconstitutional, under substantive due process, a city ordinance limiting occupancy of any single dwelling to members of the same family where "family" was limited to only a few categories of related individuals); Zablocki v. Redhail, 434 U.S. 374 (1978) (holding unconstitutional, under substantive due process, a state law forbidding parents with court-ordered child support obligations to remarry without a judicial determination of compliance with such obligations).

129. Itel Containers Int'l Corp. v. Huddleston, 507 U.S. 60, 79 (1993) (Scalia, J., concurring).

130. Granfinanciera v. Nordberg, 492 U.S. 33, 70 (1989) (Scalia, J., concurring).

131. Jones v. Helms, 452 U.S. 412 (1981).

132. Steven H. Shiffrin, THE FIRST AMENDMENT, DEMOCRACY, AND ROMANCE 15–17 (1990).

133. Sullivan, *supra* note 6, at 299.

134. Steven Shiffrin, *The First Amendment and Economic Regulation: Away from a General Theory of the First Amendment*, 78 NW. U.L. REV. 1212, 1249 (1984). "[B]alancing is nothing more than a metaphor for the accommodation of values. Everyone balances." *Id.*

135. Archibald Cox, Book Review, 94 HARV. L. REV. 700, 706 (1981).

136. Aleinikoff, *supra* note 3, at 997 (emphasis added). Professor Aleinikoff goes on to dispute the notion that all thoughtful decision making involves a balance. *Id.* Others, however, would readily agree that all thoughtful decision making does involve a balance and would probably find that way of putting it quite to the point.

137. *Id.* at 995–96.

138. *Id.*

139. *Id.* at 996.

140. *Id.* "Absolute in force is not the same as unlimited in range. A principle or right can be absolute when applied without being applicable to every situation" (quoting Frederick Schauer, *Speech and "Speech"—Obscenity and "Obscenity": An Exercise in the Interpretation of Constitutional Language*, 67 GEO. L.J. 899, 903 [1979]).

141. *Id.* at 995.

142. *Id.* at 995–96.

143. *Id.* at 995.

144. *Id.* at 995–96.

145. *Id.* at 996.

146. *Id.* at 996, 1002.

147. *See* Chapter 1, *supra* at notes 114–20.

148. *Id.*

149. *Id.*

150. *See, e.g.*, Olmstead v. United States, 277 U.S. 438 (1928) (holding that conversations transmitted to the government by an undercover agent wearing a hidden microphone did not violate the Fourteenth Amendment); Silverman v. United States, 365 U.S. 505 (1961) (holding that conversations recorded via insertion of a microphone into a heating duct intruded into a constitutionally protected area, thereby violating the Fourteenth Amendment).

151. *See, e.g.*, Red Lion Broad. Co. v. FCC, 395 U.S. 367 (1969) (holding that the FCC's fairness doctrine, requiring radio and television broadcasters to present all sides of public issues, was not an unconstitutional abridgement of freedom of speech and press); CBS, Inc. v. Democratic Nat'l Comm., 412 U.S. 94 (1973) (holding that broadcasters were not constitutionally required to accept editorial advertisements from groups or individuals wishing to express their views on public issues).

152. *See, e.g.*, Cruzan v. Director, Missouri Dep't of Health, 497 U.S. 261 (1990) (upholding a state law requiring clear and convincing evidence of an incompetent patient's wish that life support be terminated).

153. *See* Reno v. American Civil Liberties Union, 521 U.S. 844 (1997) (holding unconstitutional a federal provision prohibiting indecent or patently offensive material on the Internet if the communication might reach someone under the age of 18).

154. *See* Abington Sch. Dist. v. Schempp, 374 U.S. 203 (1963) (holding unconstitutional the practice of devotional Bible reading in public schools); Wallace v. Jaffree, 472 U.S. 38 (1985) (holding unconstitutional a state law authorizing public schools to set aside one minute each day for voluntary prayer or meditation).

155. *See* Brown v. Board of Educ., 347 U.S. 483 (1954) (holding unconstitutional legally compelled racial segregation in public schools).

156. *See* Chapter 1 *supra* at notes 108–113.

157. *Id.* at notes 114–18.

158. *Id.* at notes 126–30.

159. *Id.* at notes 124–25.

160. *Id.* at notes 148–60.

161. *See* Paul Brest, *The Misconceived Quest for the Original Understanding*, 60 B.U.L. REV. 204 (1980); John H. Ely, *Constitutional Interpretivism: Its Allure and Impossibility*, 53 IND. L.J. 399 (1978); John E. Nowak, *Realism, Nihilism, and the Supreme Court: Do the Emperors Have Nothing But Robes?*, 22 WASHBURN L.J. 246, 257 (1983); Lief H. Carter, CONTEMPORARY CONSTITUTIONAL LAWMAKING: THE SUPREME COURT AND THE ART OF POLITICS 41 (1985).

162. Ely, *supra* note 33, at 44. "[A]lthough the judge or commentator in question may be talking in terms of some 'objective,' nonpersonal method of identification, what he is really likely to be 'discovering,' whether or not he is fully aware of it, are his own values." *Id. See also* Patricia M. Wald, *Some Observations on the Use of Legislative History in the 1981 Supreme Court Term*, 68 IOWA L. REV. 195, 214 (1983) ("It sometimes seems that citing legislative history is still, as my late colleague Harold Leventhal once observed, akin to "looking over a crowd and picking out your friends").

163. Brest, *supra* note 161, at 204.

164. Ely, *supra* note 161, at 399.

165. Nowak, *supra* note 161, at 257.

166. Carter, *supra* note 161, at 41.

167. William J. Brennan, Jr., Speech at Georgetown University, reprinted in *The Great Debate* 14–15 (Washington, D.C., THE FEDERALIST SOCIETY, 1986). Justice Brennan continues:

> It is arrogant to pretend that from our vantage we can gauge accurately the intent of the Framers on application of principle to specific, contemporary problems. All too often, sources of potential enlightenment such as the records of the ratification debates provide sparse or ambiguous evidence of the original intention. Typically, all that can be gleaned is that the Framers themselves did not agree about the application or meaning of particular constitutional provisions, and hid their differences in cloaks of generality. Indeed, it is far from clear whose intention is relevant—that of the drafters, the congressional disputants, or the ratifiers in the state?—or even whether the idea of an original intention is a coherent way of thinking about a jointly drafted document drawing its authority from a general assent of the states. And apart from the problematic nature of our sources, our distance of two centuries cannot but work as a prism refracting all we perceive. One cannot help but speculate that the chorus of lamentations calling for interpretation faithful to "original intention"—and proposing nullification of interpretations that fail this quick litmus test—must inevitably come from persons who have no familiarity with the historical record.

Id.

168. Ely, *supra* note 33, at 60.

169. *See* Kelly, *supra* note 33, at 119–37; Ely, *supra* note 33, at 27–30, 60–63.

170. Ely, *supra* note 33, at 62.

171. Plessy v. Ferguson, 163 U.S. 537 (1896) (holding that racial segregation of black and white railroad passengers in equal accommodations did not unconstitutionally discriminate against blacks).

172. *Id.* at 550–51.

173. *Id.*

174. Brennan, *supra* note 167, at 15.

175. Aleinikoff, *supra* note 3, at 996, 1001.

176. *Id.* at 1000.

177. United States Steel Corp. v. Multistate Tax Comm'n, 434 U.S. 452, 460–61 (1978) (holding that the formation and operation of a 21-state cooperative tax commission did not violate the Compact Clause of the Constitution).

178. U.S. Const. art. 1, § 10.

179. United States Steel Corp. v. Multistate Tax Comm'n 434 U.S. at 459.

180. Aleinikoff, *supra* note 3, at 996.

181. *Id.* at 997.

182. *Id.* at 997.

183. United States Steel Corp, v. Multistate Tax Comm'n, 434 U.S. at 471: "[The] application of the Compact Clause is limited to agreements that are 'directed to the formation of any combination tending to the increase of political power in the States, which may encroach upon or interfere with the just supremacy of the United States' " (quoting New Hampshire v. Maine, 426 U.S. 363, 369 [1976]).

184. *Id.* (emphasis added).

185. Aleinikoff, *supra* note 3, at 996–97.

186. United States Steel Corp. v. Multistate Tax Comm'n 434 U.S. at 467.

187. *Id.*

188. Aleinikoff, *supra* note 3, at 997.

189. United States Steel Corp. v. Multistate Tax Comm'n, 434 U.S. at 460–61.

190. Aleinikoff, *supra* note 3, at 996–97.

191. *Id.* at 997.

192. *Id.* at 999. "But this conflict can and ought to be resolved by constructing a theory of the Fourteenth Amendment." *Id.* "[W]e need a theory of the Amendment." *Id.* at 1002.

193. *Id.* at 997–99.

194. *Id.* at 997.

195. *Id.* at 998.

Chapter 3

The Levels of Scrutiny

Contemporary constitutional adjudication is characterized by an elaborate system of judicial review composed of multiple levels or tiers of scrutiny. This elaborate structure, built by the Supreme Court, step by step over several decades, is the most significant feature of modern constitutional analysis. By the Court's own admission, there are at least three distinct levels of judicial review, referred to as strict, intermediate, and minimal scrutiny. But this hardly begins to tell the full story. With the Court adding one refinement and permutation after another, the system has become attenuated almost to the point of chaos. In actual practice, there are at least four levels of scrutiny each with its own twists and turns, if not a sliding scale of scrutiny calibrated to an infinite number of degrees.[1]

The levels of scrutiny consist of different methods and standards that the Supreme Court uses to evaluate the constitutionality of government action. The differences between strict, intermediate, and minimal scrutiny are not merely rhetorical; they are real differences that have decisive consequences. In fact, the practice of judicial reviews varies considerably under each level of scrutiny, and the results of cases often are determined by the operative level of scrutiny.

Under minimal scrutiny, which sometimes is called "rationality review," there is a presumption in favor of legislation, and the Court will not strike it down unless the party challenging it can prove that it is completely irrational, that is, that it bears no rational relationship to any legitimate state interest at all. Under minimal scrutiny, the ends of legislation need be nothing more than valid, and there need be no more than a rational relationship between the ends of legislation and the means chosen to accomplish them. Thus, when this low level of scrutiny is employed, both the ends and means will be subject to a minimal criterion of reasonableness or rationality.

At the other extreme—strict scrutiny—legislation will be struck down unless the government can prove that the legislation is precisely tailored to achieve a compelling state interest. In other words, there is a presumption against the legislation that can only be overcome by showing an extremely strong justification—a compelling state interest—to support it, as well as the closest possible fit between legislative means and ends.

Minimal scrutiny operates by granting deference to the legislature; under strict scrutiny such deference is inappropriate either because legislative action is tainted by a suspicious property or because it impinges upon the exercise of a basic right of constitutional magnitude. Thus, if legislation contains an invidious suspect classification, such as race, or affects a fundamental right, such as the right to vote, strict scrutiny will be used.

Strict scrutiny is not the only tier of heightened judicial review; an intermediate tier also exists. As the term indicates, intermediate scrutiny is somewhere between strict and minimal scrutiny. While strict scrutiny starts off with a finger on one side of the scale and minimal scrutiny starts off with a finger on the other side of the scale, supposedly intermediate scrutiny starts off with an equal balance. While strict scrutiny asks if there is a compelling state interest and minimal scrutiny asks only if there is a valid state interest, intermediate scrutiny asks for something in between—an important or substantial state interest. While strict scrutiny asks if the legislative means are absolutely necessary to accomplish their ends and minimal scrutiny asks only if the means are reasonably related to the ends, intermediate scrutiny requires a close, though not perfect, fit between means and ends. Intermediate scrutiny seems to offer more flexibility than strict or minimal scrutiny; it suggests a meaningful form of judicial review, less predisposed to one side or the other of a constitutional issue.

This multi-level structure of judicial review evolved over the years into a complex system of constitutional adjudication. Further additions, qualifications, and exceptions to the multi-tier system have been made by the Supreme Court, reflecting the perpetual vicissitudes of constitutional jurisprudence.

The multi-level system cuts across a wide spectrum of constitutional provisions. Its basic outline was originally articulated under the Due Process Clause,[2] then more fully elaborated in equal protection cases,[3] and did not take long to spread to other areas of constitutional law. The system of tiers has completely permeated free speech jurisprudence,[4] and also is prominent in cases involving the dormant Commerce Clause,[5] the Free Exercise Clause,[6] the Takings Clause,[7] the Privileges and Immunities Clause,[8] and the Contracts Clause.[9] Its details may vary a bit under different constitutional provisions. For example, the standards of intermediate scrutiny have yet to make an appearance in a due process case. But in its essential characteristics, the same system is used extensively, regardless of what constitutional provision is in question. In fact, in constitutional adjudication, the level of scrutiny to be used is more meaningful than the respective constitutional provision to be applied. Determining the level of scrutiny to be utilized in a particular case has a greater impact on its outcome than deciding what constitutional provision will be applied to it. At times, it becomes almost irrelevant whether a case is treated under, say, the Equal Protection Clause or the Free Speech Clause; what really matters is what level of scrutiny will be chosen.[10] In fact, if one steps back from individual constitutional provisions and takes a broad view of constitutional law, the individual provisions of the document seem to coalesce to form a single overarching principle: Government action must be properly related to a sufficiently strong governmental purpose. In other words, both the ends and the means of governmental action must be justifiable. This comprehensive constitutional dictate is given more specific content from case to case as it is put into practice through the levels of scrutiny.

There are those who think that the existence of multiple tiers of scrutiny is anomalous in light of the language of the Constitution.[11] They see a discrepancy, for instance, between the presence of levels of review and the fact that there is only one Equal Protection Clause, which does not direct the Court to apply one standard of review in some cases and a different standard in other cases. The same could be said, of course, about other constitutional provisions; there is a single Commerce Clause and only one Free Speech Clause, neither of which directs the Court to use varying standards of review.

This point of view, however, is much too literalist. As related in Chapter 1, there are volumes upon volumes of constitutional doctrine that do not derive literally from the text of the Constitution.[12] There is a multitude of constitutional rules, principles, and tests that cannot be connected to the text of the document any more than the levels of scrutiny. These rules, principles, and tests, like the levels of scrutiny, are the result of doctrinal accretion that evolves over the years through constitutional adjudication one case at a time. To mention but one example, the Court has noted that in the course of time it has erected a "structure" within which there are three broad spheres of activity that Congress may regulate under its interstate commerce authority.[13] "First, Congress may regulate the channels of interstate commerce. Second, Congress is empowered to regulate and protect the instrumentalities of interstate commerce, or persons or things in interstate commerce, even though the threat may come only from intrastate activities. Finally, Congress's commerce authority includes the power to regulate those activities having a substantial relation to interstate commerce . . . those activities that substantially affect interstate commerce."[14] None of these rules, nor the "structure" they embody, can be "found" in the text of the Interstate Commerce Clause or anywhere else in the Constitution. Rather, like vast amounts of other constitutional rulings, they were devised by the Court through the process of constitutional interpretation. The vast majority of constitutional law has been created to augment the constitutional text, and in that respect the tiered system of judicial review is no different than any other constitutional doctrine.

Superficially, it may well seem anomalous that there is only one Equal Protection Clause and only one Free Speech Clause, yet three different modes of enforcing them. When we look deeper that anomaly disappears. There are reasons for the existence of the various levels of scrutiny, and if those reasons are sufficient, there should be no objection because the levels of scrutiny do not match the literal wording of the Constitution.

In the last five decades, the Supreme Court has engaged in a continuous reworking of the multi-tier system, attempting to refine it in case after case. Through this ongoing exercise, the system has become highly rarefied to the point where it threatens to collapse of its own complexity.

MINIMAL SCRUTINY

The system's lower tier of judicial review, minimal scrutiny or rationality review, has a deceptive lineage to the past. It can be traced linguistically to a number of early cases in which the Supreme Court purported to bestow a presumption of constitutionality upon legislation.[15] However, in the past the presumption of constitutionality was ignored more often than not, and on those occasions when evoked it was used more as a rhetorical makeweight than as a working principle.[16] It was not until after the New Deal Court crisis in the 1930s that the presumption of constitutionality was utilized with any regularity as something more than a rhetorical flourish.

The minimalism of rationality review also can be traced to an article written in 1893 by James Bradley Thayer, a Harvard law professor.[17] Thayer posited that a court should not strike down an act as unconstitutional unless "those who have the right to make laws have not merely made a mistake, but have made a very clear one,—so clear that it is not open to rational question."[18] In Thayer's view, the Constitution was susceptible to different interpretations and allowed the legislature a range of choices.[19] Hence, as long as a legislative choice was rational, it could not be said to be unconstitutional.[20] At the time it was articulated and for some years thereafter, Thayer's formula had little influence upon the Supreme Court, which embarked on one of its most activist periods just a few years after Thayer's article appeared.[21] Justice Oliver Wendell Holmes, then Justice Louis Brandeis, and still later Justice Felix Frankfurter would take Thayer's stance,[22] but for many years few justices paid any attention to Professor Thayer's exhortation.

Thayer's standard of rationality, like the presumption of constitutionality, had little practical impact until historical forces combined to bring them to the forefront. The call for judicial restraint would finally find fertile soil and blossom—if not explode—into genuine minimal scrutiny as a reaction to the culmination of "Lochnerism" in the New Deal Court crisis. The term "Lochnerism" refers to the Court's practice, in the early part of the twentieth century, of incorporating extreme *laissez faire* economic policy into constitutional provisions, thereby invalidating many remedial statutes designed to regulate wages, prices, and working conditions. In *Lochner v. New York* itself, the Court ruled that a labor law setting maximum hours of work for bakers unduly interfered with liberty of contract and therefore was a violation of the Due Process Clause of the Fourteenth Amendment.[23] A slim five-person majority of the Court equated due process of law with an extremely conservative economic policy and in the bargain bestowed an undeserved constitutional status upon the concept of liberty of contract. *Lochner* has come to symbolize the excesses of judicial intervention; which saw the Court equating constitutional provisions with an outmoded, discredited economic policy to the point of inhumanity.[24]

The majority's opinion in *Lochner* provided Justice Holmes, who had a genius for aphorisms, with the opportunity for one of his better ripostes. "The 14th Amendment," he retorted in dissent, "does not enact Mr. Herbert Spencer's *Social Statics*."[25] In addition to being cleverly put, Holmes' point was well taken; the majority did seem to be excessively active in reading external values into the Fourteenth Amendment. Still, a separate dissenting opinion written by Justice John Harlan (and later joined by Justices Edward White and William Day), though less clever, offered an alternative basis for sustaining the law in question.[26] Justice Harlan pointed out that liberty of contract was not absolute and could be limited by state regulations reasonably designed to protect health.[27] To demonstrate that the law in question was a reasonable health measure, Justice Harlan's dissenting opinion included a good deal of empirical evidence describing the health hazards faced by bakers and showing that in fact their health was substandard.[28]

For Holmes, however, neither Harlan's empirical evidence nor the majority's value judgments were relevant to deciding the case or interpreting the Constitution. As Holmes put it in his dissenting opinion, his "agreement or disagreement has nothing to do with the right of a majority to embody their opinions in law."[29] The state may regulate life in many ways "as injudicious or if you like as tyrannical as this."[30] That the Court finds a statute to be "novel or even shocking" was no reason to strike it down, as far as Justice Holmes was concerned.[31]

It was the same philosophy of restraint that also led Holmes to dissent from the Court's decision in *Meyer v. Nebraska*, striking down a statute that prohibited the teaching of foreign languages to young children.[32] In the majority's view, the statute violated the right of teachers to engage in a common occupation of life, the right of children to acquire knowledge, and the right of parents to bring up their children, all of which the majority thought were protected by the Due Process Clause of the Fourteenth Amendment. To Holmes, this was the same sort of illegitimate activism that plagued the majority in *Lochner*. In his dissent in *Meyer*,[33] Holmes professed to appreciate the objection to the statute, but since it presented a question about which reasonable persons might differ, he was unable to find a constitutional violation.

While the majority in *Lochner* certainly was guilty of wrongheaded activism, Holmes' extreme acquiescence may not be the best antidote for it. Holmesian forbearance, after all, is not without its own problems. By abnegating judicial authority to enforce the Fourteenth Amendment, it runs the risk of allowing too much latitude for the legislature to enact unjust laws. Although there is much to criticize about the majority opinion in *Lochner*, including its result, the majority did strike at least one telling note with its observation that there must be some limit to legislative authority: "Otherwise the 14th Amendment would have no efficacy."[34]

In *Lochner*, Holmes denounced the majority for providing meaning for the Fourteenth Amendment by incorporating values external to it. This, however, was exactly what Holmes himself did in cases involving the First Amendment. In fact, to this day Holmes enjoys a good deal of well-deserved acclaim for advocating the theory that the First Amendment was meant to create a free marketplace of ideas so that freedom of speech would flourish.[35] Echoing the philosophic thought of John Milton and John Stuart Mill, Holmes proclaimed that a free marketplace of ideas was "the theory of our Constitution." In truth, it was no such thing. While there is much to commend about the free marketplace of ideas theory, it was not "the theory of our Constitution." To the contrary, it was Holmes' theory of the Constitution, and cynics might well have objected that "the First Amendment does not enact Mr. John Stuart Mill's *On Liberty*."[36]

Although willing to engage in activism under the First Amendment, Holmes remained steadfast in his view that in Fourteenth Amendment cases the rule should be judicial restraint and deference to the legislature. However, Holmes' counsel of restraint—some have called it detachment[37]—did not prevail in *Meyer* and emphatically not in the *Lochner* line of cases involving economic matters. A majority of the Court went on its merry way, striking down statute after statute that interfered with the precious right of liberty of contract or similar economic prerogatives. Eventually the Holmesian philosophy would have its day, although not until a span of years after its author, the Yankee from Olympus, had left the Court and Lochnerism reached its apogee in the New Deal Court crisis.

Holmes retired from the high Court in 1932, the same year that Franklin Delano Roosevelt was elected President. With the nation mired in the Great Depression, the Court would soon find itself on a collision course with Roosevelt's New Deal that would culminate in a constitutional crisis before it was over. While the exceedingly popular Roosevelt and a compliant Congress were enacting one program after another in an attempt to ameliorate the desperate conditions of the Depression, their efforts were being frustrated by a slim majority of the Court that viewed much of the New Deal legislation as unconstitutional. Frequently by votes of either 5–4 or 6–3, the Court struck down one New Deal program after another on the ground that they were beyond federal authority.[38]

At the same time, the Court was becoming schizophrenic toward state efforts to enact progressive economic legislation. While some state laws designed to counteract the Depression fell to the Court's ideological axe, others were spared that fate. In one case the Court invalidated an Oklahoma statute regulating the ice industry,[39] in another a Vermont income tax law,[40] and in a third a New York minimum wage law.[41] Yet the Court upheld a Minnesota moratorium on mortgage foreclosures[42] and a New York statute fixing the price of milk.[43] In both of the latter cases, decided by 5–4 votes, the majority opinions endorsed the Holmesian notion that judicial deference to legislative policy was the better part of discretion.[44] To Justice James McReynolds, one of the Court's hardline fundamentalists, the majority approach spelled "the end of the Constitution."[45]

After being reelected to a second term, Roosevelt proposed his Court-packing plan.[46] Precluded by the Constitution from removing Supreme Court justices, Roosevelt sought instead to control the composition of the Court by adding new seats to it. Thinly disguised as a means to relieve an over-burdened federal judiciary that supposedly could not keep up with its caseload, the plan dictated that if an incumbent federal judge did not resign six months after reaching the age of seventy, the president could nominate another judge to sit on the same court. At the time of the plan's proposal, six of the justices on the Supreme Court were over age seventy. Had the plan passed, Roosevelt would have been able to nominate six additional justices to assemble a majority more sympathetic to economic reform.

The Court-packing plan provoked considerable opposition, even among those who favored the New Deal.[47] Many viewed it as an improper attempt to tamper with the constitutional system of government. As controversy mounted concerning the plan, the Court announced a decision that would prove to be the beginning of the end of the New Deal Court crisis. *NLRB v. Jones & Laughlin Steel Corporation* was a major case in which the Court, by vote of 5–4, upheld the constitutionality of the National Labor Relations Act of 1935.[48] Most significantly, the case signaled that Justice Owen Roberts had undergone a constitutional change of heart,[49] which shifted the majority so that it now favored New Deal legislation by a single vote. That would not take long to increase. Less than two weeks later, one of the Court's economic fundamentalists, Justice Willis Van Devanter, retired, providing President Roosevelt with his first opportunity to appoint a justice to the high Court. In succeeding years, the remaining three fundamentalists—George Sutherland, Pierce Butler, and finally McReynolds—left the Court.[50] In the meantime, Roosevelt's Court-packing plan, no longer needed to change the make-up of the Court, was reported adversely out of the Senate Judiciary Committee and never enacted into law. Roosevelt ultimately would have the opportunity to appoint eight new justices to the high Court, all of whom proved to be hospitable to economic reform.

The constitutional crisis occasioned by the Supreme Court's clash with Franklin Delano Roosevelt and his New Deal proved to be one of the most traumatic encounters ever suffered by the Supreme Court. Not since the hostile reaction to its decision in the *Dred Scott* case[51] had the Court's prestige been at such a low ebb. Maligned and ridiculed—even hung in effigy—for striking down New

Deal and state legislation needed to ameliorate the severe conditions of the Depression,[52] the Court was deeply shaken. President Roosevelt's Court-packing plan challenged the very legitimacy of the Court and especially its right to be the final arbiter of the meaning of the Constitution. With the "switch in time that saved nine," the Court barely escaped with its authority intact.

The lesson was not lost on the Court. Indeed, the Court can be accused, not unjustly, of over-reacting to its traumatic collision with the New Deal; the Court's response to it was to renounce its power. It did this by adopting Holmes' posture of judicial restraint, granting great deference to the legislature. By 1942 the Court had abandoned all of the doctrines it had previously used to limit congressional authority over interstate commerce.[53] Until 1995 not one federal law was struck down as beyond the authority of Congress to regulate interstate commerce. Judicial review of federal regulations of commerce became a mere formality, allowing Congress carte blanche over interstate commerce.

As far as state legislation was concerned, again following the lead of Holmes, the Court adopted a posture of extreme deference. "We do not sit as a super legislature," the Court declared in an opinion written by Roosevelt-appointed Justice William O. Douglas.[54] And in another opinion also written by Justice Douglas, the Court stood firm that "[t]he day is gone when this Court uses the Due Process Clause of the Fourteenth Amendment to strike down state laws, regulatory of business and industrial conditions, because they may be unwise, improvident, or out of harmony with a particular school of [thought]."[55] Under this approach, state laws were granted a presumption of constitutionality that could be overcome only by showing them to be clearly irrational or unreasonable.[56] This meant that legislation was presumed to rest on a rational basis and the party calling it into question had the difficult burden of proving the presumption to be wrong.[57] In other words, minimal judicial scrutiny became the Court's modus operandi.

As first conceived, minimal scrutiny seemed to allow some room for a party challenging legislation to demonstrate that it was irrational. Originally, the Court at least professed that it was possible to overcome the presumption of constitutionality that rationality review affords to legislation.[58] It did not take the Court long, however, to completely defang minimal scrutiny. It did this by devising three mechanisms to divest minimal scrutiny of any bite whatsoever.[59]

One of these mechanisms is the doctrine that a statute will not be found unconstitutional as long as "any state of facts reasonably may be conceived to justify it."[60] That in itself makes for a rather minimal version of judicial review, acceding to legislation, no matter how irrational it may be, as long as any purpose can be imagined that is arguably furthered by it.[61] Moreover, that small measure of scrutiny was decreased even further by the Court's added requirement that a party who challenges legislation must "negate every conceivable basis which might support it."[62] As a logical matter, this is an impossible task, requiring as it does the proof of a negative.[63] Indeed, it requires a good deal more than the proof of a negative; it requires a party challenging legislation to imagine every conceivable basis of the legislation and then negate each and every one of them. Certainly this amounts to an insurmountable burden imposed upon the party challenging a law, which reduces minimal scrutiny to no scrutiny whatsoever.

Another mechanism created by the Court to enervate minimal scrutiny is the doctrine allowing the state to regulate a problem "one step at a time." This doctrine enables the Court to wink at legislation that is grossly under-inclusive. For instance, in *Williamson v. Lee Optical*, the Court upheld a statute prohibiting opticians from fitting or duplicating eyeglass lenses without a prescription from an ophthalmologist or optometrist, while exempting all sellers of ready-to-wear glasses from the prohibition.[64] The Court's submissive explanation for its decision was that "reform may take one step at a time."[65]

The third mechanism by which minimal scrutiny can be devitalized is the Court's willingness to accept speculative or hypothetical purposes for legislation by presuming or pretending that the legislature had a valid reason for a statutory classification. For example, in *Railway Express Agency v. New York* the Court upheld a New York City ordinance prohibiting owners of trucks from placing advertisements on their vehicles, supposedly because they caused traffic accidents by distracting motorists and pedestrians.[66] The ordinance, however, contained an exception allowing trucks to display advertisements for the owner's business, even though such advertisements may be just as distracting, if not more so, than others that were prohibited. Because the extent to which an advertisement on a truck is distracting depends on the appearance of the advertisement and not at all on who owns the business in question, the ordinance drew a line that had nothing to do with traffic safety. The Court, deferential to a fault, closed its eyes to the irrational nature of the ordinance by offering the lame excuse that "local authorities may well have concluded that those who advertise their own wares on their trucks do not present the same traffic problem in view of the nature or extent of the advertising which they use."

The best that the Court could do in *Railway Express* was to postulate a phantom explanation for the ordinance by claiming that there "may" have been some reason for it.[67] This, of course, is a pretense and as such amounts to the height of judicial deference. Minimal scrutiny is thus depleted to the point of nullity.

The *Railway Express* case typifies the Supreme Court's practice of minimal scrutiny from the late 1930s until the early 1970s. Throughout this period of time, minimal scrutiny functioned as virtually no scrutiny at all. While professing to require a modicum of rationality in legislation, the Court blindly accepted the legislative judgment supposedly under review with no real critical examination. During these years, the Court struck down only one statute while using minimal scrutiny, and later overruled that decision.[68] In actuality, then, rationality review operated as nothing more than a rubber stamp for legislation, and a "sharp difference" developed between the two extant tiers of scrutiny. Scrutiny that was supposed to be strict in theory turned out to be fatal in practice, while scrutiny that was supposed to be minimal in theory turned out to be illusory in practice. The nullification of even minimal scrutiny was complete.

The Court now deferred to the legislature with a vengeance. It went to extremes to dream up rationalizations for the most ill-conceived statutes,[69] and sustained legislation even though its under- or over-inclusiveness clearly demonstrated that its actual basis was something other than that asserted by the state.[70] With all of the bite taken out of minimal scrutiny, the Court routinely upheld laws that, by any realistic measure, were lacking adequate explanation.

Statutes that seemed to grant unjustifiable favors to special interest groups likewise were blindly approved. For example, in *Williamson v. Lee Optical Co.*, the Court upheld an Oklahoma law that forbid opticians from fitting or duplicating lenses without a prescription and also barred opticians from fitting lenses into new frames or from duplicating a broken lens by reading its prescription (no matter how recent) through a lens reader.[71] As the Court admitted, the "Oklahoma law may exact a needless, wasteful requirement in many cases."[72] Moreover, although the Court did not mention it, perhaps it was no coincidence that the law had the effect of diverting customers away from opticians and toward optometrists (who also fit and duplicate lenses). Still, the Court sustained the law because "it is for the legislature, not the courts, to balance the advantages and disadvantages" of legislation.[73]

The Court also went so far as to uphold a state practice of nepotism in the granting of licenses. This occurred in *Kotch v. Board of River Pilot Commissioners*, in which the Court used rationality review to sustain the administration of Louisiana pilotage laws that granted river pilot licenses to no one other than relatives or friends of incumbent pilots.[74] And in the *Carolene Products* case,[75] a deferential Court upheld a statute that one knowledgeable observer described as "an utterly unprincipled example of special interest legislation" that ruined an industry and deprived people of a healthful, nutritious low-cost food.[76]

In other cases where this sort of minimal scrutiny prevailed, the Court condoned legislation based on assumptions that were factually dubious or even demonstrably incorrect. Unfortunately, there are times when legislation is founded on mistaken information, not to mention prejudice, stereotypical thinking, myth, or even outright lies and deception, none of which will be exposed by toothless minimal scrutiny. For instance, in *Vance v. Bradley*,[77] under the sway of rationality review, the Court sustained a federal mandatory retirement law based on outdated and stereotypical assumptions about elderly persons that were contradicted by more recent empirical studies produced by Congress itself.[78] In *Carolene Products*, the Court used minimal scrutiny to uphold a federal law enacted in response to an ongoing campaign by the dairy industry making false claims that a competing product was unhealthy.[79] And in one of the Court's most tragic decisions, *Korematsu v. United States*[80] the Court approved the internment of 120,000 persons of Japanese descent by meekly accepting assertions based on evidence that had been falsified by government officials.[81] In *Kore-*

matsu, misinformation and lies went hand in hand with prejudice and invidious stereotyping. Unfortunately, none of these fallacies can be revealed when rationality review is nothing more than an empty pretense.

UPGRADING MINIMAL SCRUTINY

After forty-odd years of toothless minimal scrutiny, the Supreme Court finally, albeit on rare occasions, began to re-invest minimal scrutiny with a bit more bite. The first case to do this was *U.S. Department of Agriculture v. Moreno*, decided in 1973.[82] In *Moreno*, the Court struck down an amendment to the Food Stamp Act that disqualified unrelated persons who lived together from eligibility for food stamps. The legislative history of the amendment indicated that it was motivated by a desire to penalize "hippies," which the Court found to be an illegitimate governmental goal. In so ruling, the Court enunciated the principle that "a bare congressional desire to harm a politically unpopular group cannot constitute a *legitimate* governmental interest."[83] This contradicted the Court's usual practice under minimal scrutiny, which was to deem legislative motive irrelevant and to posit hypothetical or speculative ends for legislation that has no discernible legitimate purpose. By taking a more critical view of the governmental objective in *Moreno*, the Court invested minimal scrutiny with an acuity it ordinarily did not possess.

The same technique was employed in a subsequent decision, *Zobel v. Williams*, which concerned an Alaska statute distributing annual dividends from windfall oil revenues to state residents.[84] According to the statute, the value of the dividend paid to each recipient depended upon his or her length of residence within the state—the longer the residency, the larger the dividend. In evaluating this statutory scheme, the Court was presented with a dilemma concerning the proper tier of scrutiny to use. Arguably, either strict or minimal scrutiny could appropriately be applied to the Alaska legislation, since it possessed some, but not all, of the attributes of a durational residency requirement, which ordinarily evokes the stricter form of review. The Court, however, sidestepped this dilemma by stating that "if the statutory scheme cannot pass even the minimal test . . . we need not decide whether any enhanced scrutiny is called for."[85] Then, purportedly using minimal scrutiny, the Court went on to hold that the Alaska statute could not be justified by any of the purposes advanced in defense of it. One of those purposes was to reward citizens for contributions, both tangible and intangible, made in the past to the state, on the theory that the longer a person had resided in Alaska, the more he or she had contributed to the state. The Court ruled, though, that this was not a legitimate governmental objective. To support this ruling, the Court reached beyond the bounds of minimal scrutiny by relying on two cases, *Shapiro v. Thompson*[86] and *Vlandis v. Kline*,[87] both of which utilized the strict form of review. By relying on those cases, the Court increased the degree of scrutiny beyond traditional minimalism. Further, in rejecting the governmental goal in *Zobel*, the Court contravened its usual practice under minimal scrutiny of either accepting or postulating objectives to bolster the validity of legislation.

It is also possible to upgrade minimal scrutiny by reducing the deference it customarily allows for governmental means. When utilizing minimal scrutiny, the Court regularly sustains legislation that bears little, if any, relationship to a legitimate end by exercising extreme tolerance for over- and under-inclusive legislative means. This sort of tolerance was notably lacking in both *Moreno* and *Zobel*, as well as in another decision, *Logan v. Zimmerman Brush Co.*,[88] which also supposedly employed the minimal tier of review. In *Moreno*, the Court ruled that the amendment in question could not be sustained as a means of preventing fraud, because it was not rationally related to that purpose. Similarly in *Zobel*, the Court held that the Alaska statute could not be justified as a means of encouraging residence in the state or of ensuring prudent management of the dividend fund, because it was not rationally related to either of those objectives. In *Logan*, a majority of the Court found that a statutory condition requiring the dismissal of a complaint unless a fact-finding conference was convened within 120 days was not rationally related to the goal of discouraging unfounded claims or of expediting resolution of disputes. Thus, in these three cases the Court contracted the indulgence that normally prevails under minimal scrutiny for over- and under-inclusive legislation, and thereby sharpened the level of review.

The cases discussed above illustrate that minimal scrutiny may be upgraded by granting less obeisance than usual to either the ends or means of government action. A leading constitutional scholar, Gerald Gunther, has proposed a model that would consistently upgrade minimal scrutiny of legislative means but not ends.[89] Professor Gunther believes that the Court should regularly put some bite into rationality review of legislative means, while remaining absolutely deferential toward legislative ends.[90] This certainly would enhance minimal scrutiny, but only to a limited extent. Focused solely on legislative means, the Gunther model does nothing to address laws that are based on illegitimate ends. For example, neither the statute in *Moreno* nor the one in *Zobel* would be struck down under the Gunther model. The Supreme Court was able to invalidate those statutes only by putting some bite into the review of legislative ends, which led to a finding that they were illegitimate. Still, Professor Gunther's model has much to recommend it. Some bite should at least be put into the review of legislative means. Unfortunately, a majority of the Court apparently thought otherwise, as indicated in recently released documents showing that at one time the justices considered adopting something like the Gunther model, but a majority of them were not willing to do so.[91]

Ironically, had the Court been willing on a regular basis to put some bite into its review of both legislative ends and means, the effect would have been to restore minimal scrutiny to its original nature, which may have obviated the need to create an intermediate tier of review. As first conceived by the Supreme Court, minimal scrutiny afforded substantial, but not absolute, deference to the other branches of government. This was quickly modulated to total deference, which led the Court to uphold government action that was not in actuality reasonably related to a legitimate state interest, and thus widened the gap between the strict and minimal tiers of review. Had the original version of minimal scrutiny been maintained, an intermediate level might not have been necessary to alleviate this situation.

After intermediate scrutiny became well-established as a mode of constitutional analysis, the Court occasionally returned to a minimal scrutiny with bite and, in so doing, reaffirmed the principle enunciated in the *Moreno* case that "a bare congressional desire to harm a politically unpopular group cannot constitute a *legitimate* governmental interest."[92] This principle would prove to be important in *Cleburne v. Cleburne Living Center, Inc.*[93] and especially in *Romer v. Evans.*[94] In *Cleburne* the Court found that the Equal Protection Clause was violated by a city zoning ordinance that barred a home for persons who were mentally retarded. Explicitly declining to recognize mental retardation as even a quasi-suspect classification, the Court insisted that minimal scrutiny was the appropriate tier of review to use in the case. Nonetheless, the Court found that the city's action could not pass even mere rationality review, because it was founded on nothing more than "an irrational prejudice against the mentally retarded." Quoting *Moreno*, the Court noted that "some objectives—such as 'a . . . bare desire to harm a politically unpopular group'—are not legitimate state interests."[95]

The *Moreno* principle was given even more emphasis in *Romer v. Evans*, in which the Court struck down a Colorado state constitutional amendment that prohibited the state or any subdivision of the state from enacting, adopting, or enforcing any law or policy whereby homosexual, lesbian, or bisexual orientation is the basis of a claim of entitlement or protection.[96] Once again professing to use nothing more than rationality review, the Court concluded that the amendment violated the Equal Protection Clause by singling out a group of persons for disfavored treatment. Relying heavily on *Moreno*, the Court stressed that "a bare desire to harm a politically unpopular group cannot constitute a legitimate governmental interest."[97]

Professors Daniel Farber and Suzanna Sherry describe this as the "Pariah Principle," a principle that bars the government from designating any group, whether entitled to special constitutional protection or not, as untouchable.[98] As Farber and Sherry see it, the government may not target someone for who they are rather than what they do; the government may not treat people as pariahs. Professor Akhil Amar makes a similar point, which he links to the Bill of Attainder Clause found in Article I of the Constitution.[99] In his review, the Attainder Clause is related to the Equal Protection Clause in logic and spirit, by establishing a mandate that prohibits the government from penalizing persons simply because it does not like them.

In *Romer*, as well as *Cleburne* and *Moreno*, the Court professed to be using minimal scrutiny although it could be accused of using a more heightened form of scrutiny under the guise of rationality. In fact, in *Cleburne* Justice Thurgood

Marshall's separate opinion accused the majority of doing exactly that.[100] Justice Marshall asserted that the majority was able to strike down the ordinance only by departing from traditional rationality review and using "precisely the sort of probing inquiry associated with heightened scrutiny."[101] The majority in *Cleburne*, however, devoted a good deal of attention to explaining why only minimal scrutiny would be used in the case, and the majority explicitly professed to be using nothing more than minimal scrutiny. Similarly in *Moreno* and *Romer* the Court professed to be using nothing more than rationality review.

If so, it certainly is minimal scrutiny with bite. As one astute observer of the Court, Cass Sunstein, sees it, this trilogy of cases does not establish a new tier of scrutiny, but does allow "the possible use of rationality review as a kind of magical trump card, or perhaps joker, hidden in the pack and used on special occasions."[102] On these occasions, Professor Sunstein continues, minimal scrutiny is given an added edge, "used to invalidate badly motivated laws without refining a new kind of scrutiny."[103]

On the other hand, the decision in *Romer* can be viewed as, if not establishing a new level of scrutiny, creating a new doctrine that circumvents or transcends the levels of scrutiny. An amicus curiae brief submitted in the case by a group of law professors asserted that the Colorado amendment, by setting a class of persons apart from others on the basis of a personal characteristic, was a rare instance of a per se violation of the Equal Protection Clause and hence did not implicate the traditional analysis relying upon the levels of scrutiny.[104] According to this novel though compelling theory, apart from the levels of scrutiny, the Colorado amendment was unconstitutional on its face by virtue of the plain meaning of the Equal Protection Clause.

In parts of the majority opinion in *Romer* the Court comes close to adopting this theory. The Court, after all, does say that a state "cannot so deem a class of persons a stranger to its laws."[105] And even more to the point, the Court states, "A law declaring that in general it shall be more difficult for one group of citizens than for all others to seek aid from the government is in itself a denial of equal protection of the laws in the most literal sense."[106] This is a strong statement and a significant one. The Colorado amendment did, in fact, operate to deny a group of persons protection that was readily available to other groups of persons. As such, the amendment appeared to be, literally, a denial of equal protection of the laws, not unlike the denial of equal protection of the laws to freed slaves after the Civil War, which was the paradigm that inspired the Equal Protection Clause.

Since *Moreno* was announced in 1973, a small group of cases has been decided in which minimal scrutiny has been upgraded to possess some degree of efficacy. It should be emphasized, however, that this is a small group of cases, and absolute deference to the legislature remains the rule in the minimal tier of scrutiny. Especially in cases involving economic legislation or social welfare legislation, the Court has been extremely deferential in allowing the legislature to draw lines and make whatever allocations it sees fit. In the high majority of cases, minimal scrutiny still functions as no scrutiny at all.

A typical example of this can be seen in a 1980 decision, *U.S. Railroad Retirement Board v. Fritz*, in which the Court upheld a statute that allocated retirement benefits to various groups of railroad employees and former employees according to a complicated scheme that depended on, among other factors, how long an individual had worked for a railroad and the individual's last date of employment.[107] Some of the lines drawn by this statutory scheme seemed to make no sense, particularly the one that granted benefits to former employees whose last date of employment was 1974 and who worked for a railroad for eleven years, while denying benefits to employees whose last date of employment was 1973 and who had worked for a railroad for twenty-four years. The scheme appeared to be nothing more than a reflection of the private interests of railroad labor and management who had drafted the legislation at the request of Congress. Tellingly, the class of persons denied benefits were no longer employed by a railroad and no longer active union members, and hence their interests were not represented among the individuals who drafted the statutory scheme.[108] Moreover, the legislative record indicated that Congress had little understanding of this complex statutory scheme when it was enacted. In other words, it appeared that Congress did not know what it was voting for. Nevertheless, Justice William Rehnquist's opinion for the majority of the Court upheld the constitutionality of the statute on the ground that Congress could have concluded that the line drawn by the statutory scheme was "equitable."

Justice Rehnquist's opinion in *Fritz* harkened back to the old *Railway Express* approach with the Court speculating that the legislature may have had some reason for drawing a line where it did. About the best Justice Rehnquist could do here was to offer the vague supposition that the legislature may have thought the statute was equitable. This conforms to one of the early precepts of minimal scrutiny, namely, that legislation will be upheld so long as there is "any conceivable basis to justify it." This meant, among other things, that it was not the legislature that had to conceive of the justification for a statute; the justification could be conceived by the Court itself or by a government attorney arguing as an advocate in response to litigation challenging the statute.

It was that aspect of minimalism that finally proved to be too much for Justice William Brennan. In *Fritz*, he entered a dissenting opinion, maintaining that minimal scrutiny had become excessively deferential to the point of providing virtual immunity for legislation from judicial review.[109] In Justice's Brennan's view, the Court had gone too far by blindly accepting after-the-fact rationalizations proffered by attorneys to justify legislation. Justice Brennan thought that more skepticism was in order, even under minimal scrutiny. He stressed that "the actual purposes of Congress, rather than the post hoc justifications offered by Government attorneys, must be the primary basis for analysis under the rational basis test."[110] Even under minimal scrutiny Justice Brennan believed that it should not be enough that attorneys can suggest some "conceivable" rational basis for legislation. Legislation should pass minimal scrutiny "only if it is rationally related to achievement of an *actual* legitimate governmental purpose."[111]

Justice Brennan seems to be suggesting that it is one thing for the Court to be deferential to the legislature, and quite another for it to be deferential to government attorneys. If there was some indication in the legislative record that the legislature actually believed that the lines drawn in *Fritz* were equitable, perhaps the Court should be deferential to that legislative determination. There is no reason, however, why the Court should defer to the assertion of a government attorney arguing a case in response to litigation that legislation is equitable. In reviewing the constitutionality of legislation, deference may be due to the judgment of the legislature, it is hardly due to the judgment of an attorney-advocate for the legislation in question.

Surely Justice Brennan is correct in situations similar to the one in *Fritz*, where the only justification offered for the lines drawn in the legislation is the vague assertion that they may be "equitable." If it could be demonstrated that Congress actually thought that the lines drawn were equitable, perhaps the Court should defer to that legislative judgment. It could be argued that even under minimal scrutiny Congress should be required to do more than that; Congress should have a reason that is a bit more specific to support its enactment. But even if a vague claim like "equitableness" is thought to be enough when it comes from Congress, certainly it should not be enough when it comes from an attorney-advocate in the course of litigation. If any deference is due in regard to legislation, it is due to the legislature that enacted it and not to the attorneys who might think up post hoc rationalizations for statutes.

When some degree of heightened scrutiny is operative, it is inappropriate for the Court to submissively accept hypothetical purposes proffered after-the-fact to rationalize legislation, and the Court will not do so. As the Court stated in *United States v. Virginia*, the justification for a statute must be genuine, not hypothesized or invented post hoc in response to litigation."[112] For instance, in *Plyler v. Doe* the Court rejected the suggestion that congressional policy favored the denial of a free public education to school-age children who were living in the United States as illegal aliens.[113] The Court expressly stated that it was reluctant to impute such a policy to Congress in the absence of any support for it in the legislative record.[114] Because the case involved "an area of special constitutional sensitivity" (that is calling for heightened scrutiny), deference to Congress was not appropriate.[115] Accordingly, where there was no genuine indication in the record that Congress did in fact have such a policy, the Court was not willing to impute it to Congress.[116]

However, to say that hypothetical justifications for legislation are not acceptable under heightened scrutiny should not be taken to mean that the legislature must actually articulate the justification for a statute. Justification for a statute invented post hoc in response to litigation does not necessarily preclude the fact that the justification is genuine. The justification for a statute may be real despite the fact that the legislature never articulated or even imagined it. As Justice David Souter explained, the "appropriate focus is not an empirical enquiry into the actual intent of the enacting legislature, but rather the existence or not of a current governmental interest in the service of which the challenged application of the statute may be constitutional."[117]

Justice Souter's point is well taken. The purpose of *legislation* may exist independently of the legislature. If a law actually serves a beneficial function, it cannot be said that the law itself is irrational. There may be times when legislation should be upheld because it serves a real purpose in fact, although not one conceived by the legislature. That is, legislation may have a function or effect in the real world that was not imagined by the legislative body that enacted it. "Actual" legislative purpose should be understood as referring to legislation rather than to the legislature. If a law does in fact function to accomplish a legitimate purpose in the real world, the law itself is rational, regardless of what was or was not in the mind of the legislature.

In considering an actual purpose in the sense of realness and specificity—not some vague, ephemeral purpose like "equitableness"—it should not make any difference that the legislature was unaware of the actual function served by a statute. If the statute works, if it does something beneficial, it should be considered rational—that is, having a reason—and upheld as constitutional, even if its actual purpose is articulated for the first time as a post hoc rationalization by an attorney-advocate or even by the Supreme Court itself. That most emphatically does not mean the Court should make up half-baked purposes for legislation; the Court though, should recognize real purposes that legislation serves in actuality, regardless of whether they were conceived by the legislature. Legislation is enacted to accomplish real things in a real world. If it does so, it should be upheld, regardless of whether the legislature that enacted it conceived of its actual function or not.

The functions of legislation in the real world may change over time. A law enacted by the legislature for one purpose later may be recognized as serving a different function in actuality. For example, in *McGowan v. Maryland* the Court admitted that the state's Sunday closing laws were originally enacted for religious motives.[118] Nevertheless the Court upheld the laws because, as circumstances evolved over the years, the laws acquired the secular function of mandating a uniform day of rest for state citizens. While one might quibble with the Court's assessment of these particular laws, they illustrate that a statute enacted for one purpose by the legislature may in fact serve a different purpose in the real world, and that with the evolution of time, the actual function served by a statute may change.

To return to *Fritz*, however, despite Justice Brennan's best efforts in that case to provide some degree of bite to minimal scrutiny, complete deference remains the rule in a high majority of cases where minimal scrutiny is operative. There is, however, a small group of minimal scrutiny cases where the deference is not total and the scrutiny has a small degree of effectiveness. At this point in time, it is probably accurate to say that minimal scrutiny comes in two varieties: minimal scrutiny with a bit of bite and minimal scrutiny with none. To state it another way, there are two versions of minimal scrutiny, which vary enough from each other to be designated as two different tiers of scrutiny.

STRICT SCRUTINY

After the New Deal Court crisis, the Court uniformly used the most minimal form of scrutiny in all cases involving economic legislation. However, it did not take the Supreme Court long to realize that this method of judicial review, which grants complete deference to the legislature, could not appropriately be used to evaluate all kinds of legislation. After all, if the Court applied the same sort of minimal scrutiny across the board in all situations it would amount to a repudiation of *Marbury v. Madison*[119] and a total abdication of the Court's authority of judicial review. It would render judicial review meaningless and make judicial enforcement of constitutional norms impossible. Obviously, the Supreme Court was not about to embark on such a momentous upheaval in our constitutional system of government. The question then became when to use minimal scrutiny and when to use a more genuine form of judicial review.

The Supreme Court recognized soon after the New Deal Court crisis that minimal scrutiny was not appropriate in all circumstances. In fact, in the *Carolene Products* case, which was one of the first decisions to articulate the minimalist "rational basis" test, the Court acknowledged the need for a more searching form of scrutiny in matters other than commercial transactions.[120] Justice Harlan Fiske Stone's footnote 4 in his opinion for the Court was astonishingly prescient in charting a future course for the evocation of strict scrutiny. It explained, "There may be narrower scope for the operation of the presumption of constitutionality" when legislation appears on its face to be within a specific Constitutional prohibition, restricts the political process, is directed at particular religions, or is directed at discrete and insular minorities.[121] This lowly footnote would prove to be a prescription for the future by paving the way for the development of strict judicial scrutiny.

The rise of modern strict scrutiny can be traced to *Korematsu v. United States*, in which the Court upheld Executive Order 9066, issued during World War II, incarcerating persons of Japanese ancestry in relocation camps.[122] The Court's decision was a horrible travesty of justice and has since been widely recognized as such. Nevertheless, there is one noteworthy ingredient in the Court's opinion in *Korematsu*. For the first time the Court expressly enunciated the principle that racial classifications were "suspect" and therefore subject to "the most rigid scrutiny."[123] Sadly, after announcing that principle, the Court proceeded to water it down by applying much less than searching scrutiny to the government's action in the case. The government had attempted to justify Order 9066 on the ground that it was necessary to prevent espionage and sabotage during wartime.

While the prevention of espionage and sabotage during times of war undoubtedly is enough of a compelling state interest to satisfy even strict scrutiny, the government's use of a racial classification to achieve that interest was hardly rational. While the government's ends in *Korematsu* were compelling, the means chosen to accomplish those ends were grossly over- and under-inclusive. While allowing that nothing short of "the gravest imminent danger to the public safety" could constitutionally justify Order 9066,[124] Justice Hugo Black's opinion for the majority offered no explanation as to why this egregiously over- and under-inclusive racial classification should be allowed to stand. Turning a blind eye to the executive order's flaws, the majority opinion hardly amounts to genuine strict scrutiny.

Justice Frank Murphy's dissenting opinion recognized the government's shameful action for what it was: "obvious racial discrimination."[125] He further asserted that the government's attempt to justify Order 9066 was based on "questionable racial and sociological grounds not ordinarily within the realm of expert military judgment . . . [and] an accumulation of much of the misinformation, half-truths and insinuations that for years have been directed against Japanese Americans by people with racial and economic prejudices."[126] It was those very unproven assertions, misinformation, and half-truths that the majority, while smugly proclaiming to use "the most rigid scrutiny," readily swallowed.

Time, of course, has proven Justice Murphy right. In 1982, the Commission on Wartime Relocation and Internment of Civilians, established by an act of Congress, concluded that the internment was "not justified by military necessity" and was "a grave injustice" caused by "race prejudice, war hysteria, and a failure of political leadership."[127] Other historical research has shown that to bolster support for Executive Order 9066 in the Supreme Court, government officials not only permitted mistaken facts to go uncorrected, but also altered, suppressed, and discarded crucial evidence, including reports from the FBI and the Office of Naval Intelligence, that exonerated Japanese Americans of wrongdoing.[128]

The watered-down version of strict scrutiny that was used in *Korematsu* did not prevail. The Supreme Court soon came to apply a brand of judicial scrutiny that was in fact strict in its operation. The Court actually meant what it said when it proclaimed that under strict scrutiny laws would be struck down unless proven to be necessary to achieve a compelling state interest. In case after case when using strict scrutiny, the Court rigorously assessed both the ends and means of legislation. Later, the Supreme Court, composed of a combination of Roosevelt appointees and newer justices, finally made good on some of the Court's previous promises. Under the Chief Justiceship of Earl Warren, the Court faithfully adhered to the principle that racial classifications were suspect and therefore subject to the most exacting scrutiny. This accorded with footnote 4 of *Carolene Products*, which indicated that a more searching form of review was called for in reviewing legislation directed at discrete and insular minorities. Hence, the Warren Court further used strict scrutiny to review classifications based on ethnic origin or alienage. Taking another cue from footnote 4, the

Warren Court also made it clear that rigorous judicial scrutiny would be employed in cases involving express constitutional rights, such as freedom of speech. In addition, the Warren Court ruled that there were certain implicit fundamental rights, such as the right to vote, the right to interstate travel, and the right to access to the justice system, that deserved the protection of demanding scrutiny. Laws that impinged on fundamental rights, like those which contained invidious suspect classifications, were subject to genuine strict scrutiny.

In fact, as put into operation by the Warren Court, there was a sharp difference[129] between strict and minimal scrutiny. Scrutiny that was supposed to be strict in theory turned out to be fatal in practice, while scrutiny that was supposed to be minimal in theory turned out to be nonexistent in practice.[130] The levels of scrutiny became the entire ball game, so to speak. That is, in the hands of the Warren Court, the selection of the level of scrutiny effectively dictated the outcome of a case, and the Court was accused, not unjustly, of using the tiers of scrutiny to mask the value judgments needed to be made in deciding a case. Any balancing of interests that was necessary for making a decision occurred covertly at the stage of selecting a level of scrutiny rather than occurring overtly at the next stage when the ends and means of legislation were to be assessed.

As time passed and justices left the Court to be replaced by newcomers, the deadly force of strict scrutiny as practiced by the Warren Court proved to be too rigid for its successor, the Burger Court. During the Chief Justiceship of Warren Burger, the Court sought ways to escape the rigidity of the Warren Court's variety of strict scrutiny. Unfortunately, the means of escape devised by the Burger Court were not always analytically sound. One of the most erratic defections from the system occurred in *Fullilove v. Klutznick*,[131] even though it was decided after the creation of an intermediate level of scrutiny that to some degree eased the rigidity of the tiered system. Evidently that was not enough for Chief Justice Burger, who authored a plurality opinion in *Fullilove* that, while approving a federal affirmative action program, tersely declined to adopt any tier of review. Burger's opinion, jumping from one mode of scrutiny to another, concluded with a frank refusal to follow any of the "tests" or "formulas" adopted in previous cases. Apparently, Chief Justice Burger had become exasperated with the levels of scrutiny, so he decided to freelance without them. His defection from the system, on the heels of fluctuating from one level to another, in an opinion that did not garner a majority vote, can be dismissed as a brief aberration.

Unfortunately, the same cannot be said for other endeavors of the Burger Court to escape the application of strict scrutiny. One technique the Court used to accomplish this was to carve out exceptions to the situations where strict scrutiny was supposed to be used. The Court did this in several areas, one of which was the right of interstate travel. In a line of cases that began with *Shapiro v. Thompson*[132] in 1969, the Court has ruled that interstate travel is a fundamental right implicitly guaranteed by the Constitution. Accordingly, state residency requirements that impinge on this right are subject to strict scrutiny, and will be struck down unless shown to be necessary to achieve a compelling state interest. Under this standard, the Court has invalidated residency requirements that condition eligibility for welfare benefits, voting, and free medical care. On the other hand, the Court has summarily affirmed a lower court decision upholding a state university's practice of charging higher tuition rates to nonresidents.[133] Additionally, in *Memorial Hospital v. Maricopa County* the Court said that strict scrutiny is not applicable to residency requirements that do not penalize the right to interstate travel by conditioning another fundamental right or a necessity of life.[134] Although the Court made little use of this distinction in later cases, at the time it did open the door for the development of a substantial exception from the application of strict scrutiny to residency requirements.

In several cases after *Maricopa*, however, the Court found other ways to exempt state laws that affect the right to travel from being strictly scrutinized. The first of these decisions, *Sosna v. Iowa*[135] sustained a requirement that a person reside in the state for at least one year before being allowed to file a divorce action against a nonresident. Although the state residency requirement in *Sosna* affected no less than two fundamental rights—the right of marital association as well as the right of interstate travel—a majority of the Court saw fit to use only minimal scrutiny, on the ground that the area of domestic relations "has long been regarded as a virtually exclusive province of the States." In a feeble attempt to support this proposition, Justice Rehnquist's opinion for the Court cited three cases, the latest of which had been decided in 1899, while overlooking at least ten more recent and more apposite decisions that take an opposite position. Through this belaboring of precedent, the Court was able to contrive an exception to the scope of strict scrutiny.

The approach taken in *Sosna* was eschewed in a later decision, *Jones v. Helms*,[136] which involved a state statute that made it a crime for a parent to willfully abandon a dependent child. According to the statute, the crime was a misdemeanor unless the parent left the state after abandoning the child, in which case it was raised to a felony with a harsher penalty. Although the statute obviously concerned domestic relations, the Court made only passing reference to the *Sosna* rationale, choosing instead to fashion a different exception to strict scrutiny. Although the right to interstate travel is fundamental, the Court explained in an opinion written by Justice John Paul Stevens that it is not "unqualified," and may be lost, as it was here, through the commission of a crime. Therefore it was concluded that strict scrutiny would not be applied to the state statue because it "did not penalize the exercise of the constitutional right to travel." In other words, the right to travel is fundamental, but not always; it is only fundamental when it has not been qualified. Although the Court's decision in *Jones* may be correct, its reasoning is open to considerable question. The premise of the Court's opinion amounts to the tautology that the right to travel is fundamental when it is fundamental. This sophistry could have been avoided without changing the result in *Jones* by holding that under strict scrutiny the fundamental right to travel was outweighed by a compelling state interest in protecting dependent children. Instead, the Court elected to devise yet another exception to the scope of strict scrutiny.

In *Jones* and *Sosna* the Court was able to avoid the application of heightened scrutiny by devising an exception to what otherwise would have been recognized as a fundamental interest calling for the strict level of review. Not only fundamental interests, however, are subject to this technique; the Court has also avoided the application of strict scrutiny by formulating an exception to the suspect classification of alienage. State classifications based on alienage,[137] like those based on race or national origin, have been found suspect by the Court and therefore held to evoke strict scrutiny. Under this analysis, the Court has struck down state laws that preclude aliens from eligibility for welfare benefits, civil service employment, admission to the bar, scholarships, and the practice of civil engineering. In subsequent cases, however, the Court has had second thoughts about alienage classifications, stating that it is "inappropriate" to subject all state restrictions upon aliens to strict scrutiny because "to do so would 'obliterate all the distinctions between citizens and aliens.' "[138] Therefore, the Court has decided to exempt state alienage classifications from strict scrutiny when they concern "matters firmly within a State's constitutional prerogative."[139] Using only minimal scrutiny for such matters, the Court has upheld state laws that bar aliens from employment as state troopers, public school teachers, and deputy probation officers. By the Court's own admission, its decisions concerning alienage classifications have not been entirely consistent. Dissenters from the majority approach maintain that the Court's decisions concerning alienage are impossible to reconcile because a state has no greater interest in excluding aliens from employment as state troopers, teachers, or probation officers than it does in excluding them from employment as civil servants, attorneys, or engineers. Nonetheless, a slim majority of the Court seemed to be more intent upon evading the use of strict scrutiny in this area than in achieving consistency in the cases. Whether consistent with precedent or not, what the Court has done in decisions dealing with alienage classifications is to contrive yet another exception to the use of strict scrutiny.

These exceptions to the use of strict scrutiny and an occasional upgrading of minimal scrutiny were the means by which the Burger Court attempted to alleviate the rigidity of the two-tiered system that had been put into place by its predecessor, the Warren Court. The Burger Court, however, found that these efforts were not up to the task of providing sufficient flexibility to the system. As a result, the Burger Court was moved to take a more radical step by formulating a third tier of judicial review that operates as an intermediate form of scrutiny.

INTERMEDIATE SCRUTINY

Actually, intermediate scrutiny made its first appearance in a case decided by the Warren Court; the opinion in fact was written by Chief Justice Warren himself. It would be the Burger Court, however, that would take the ball and run with it, just a few years after the Warren Court had not only fumbled the ball but apparently forgotten about it as well. Although the inception of intermediate scrutiny is usually associated with equal protection cases involving gender classifications, the debut of an intermediate level of scrutiny occurred in a First Amendment case involving symbolic speech, *United States v. O'Brien.*[140] Some confusion about the genesis of intermediate scrutiny is understandable because the Supreme Court itself may not have fully appreciated exactly what it was creating in *O'Brien.* Confusion may also have been engendered because, after enunciating what appeared to be a new version of meaningful judicial scrutiny, the Court was quick to water down its actual application, much as the Court had watered down the actual application of strict scrutiny after first enunciating it in *Korematsu v. United States.* Perhaps it is more than coincidental that the two cases first articulating heightened levels of judicial scrutiny only to water them down in application both involved military regulations during times of war.

Be that as it may, the creation of an intermediate level of scrutiny was quite logical in a case like *O'Brien.* Mr. O'Brien was being prosecuted for burning his draft card in violation of a federal law prohibiting the mutilation or destruction of a draft card. O'Brien argued that he had destroyed his draft card as an act of symbolic expression to protest the war in Viet Nam. Therefore, he claimed that his conduct was an exercise of freedom of speech protected by the First Amendment. O'Brien's conduct has elements of both speech and action. On one hand, it expresses an idea—in fact, a political idea—that, if expressed in a more pure form of speech such as the printed page or the spoken word, would be entitled to the protection of strict scrutiny under the First Amendment. On the other hand, O'Brien is taking action—burning a draft card—of the sort that ordinarily would evoke only minimal constitutional protection. Why not compromise, then, and follow a middle course, a level of scrutiny intermediate to strict and minimal? And that is exactly what the Court did in *O'Brien*, or, to describe it more accurately, what the Court said it was doing. It said that "when 'speech' and 'non-speech' elements are combined in the same course of conduct," the government may regulate the conduct if the regulation "furthers an important or substantial governmental interest."[141] This statement articulated a new constitutional standard—namely, an "important or substantial" government interest—that sets a higher standard than a mere rationality test of minimal scrutiny, but a lower standard than the compelling state interest required under strict scrutiny. Thus, the Court chartered an intermediate course of constitutional review.

What the Court says, however, is not always what the Court does, and in

O'Brien the Court seemed to stray from its articulated program by accepting a justification for the law in question that did not appear particularly important or substantial. The Court found that the federal law prohibiting mutilation or destruction of a draft card was a "substantial administrative aid" to the functioning of the selective service system. Although the Court described this as a substantial governmental interest, it sounded suspiciously like nothing more than administrative convenience, which ordinarily does not rise to anything more than a legitimate state interest. Moreover, the law was flawed in other respects. It added little to a preexisting regulation that required draft registrants to be in possession of their draft cards, and there was strong indication that it had been enacted for the impermissible purpose of suppressing dissent. All in all, the Court went through considerable machinations in *O'Brien* to demonstrate that the law served an important government interest, and the Court's efforts were far from convincing.

Still an articulated version of a new level of judicial scrutiny was on the books, and in a few years the Court would return to it, as the Court had previously done with strict scrutiny, to apply it with more realistic vigor. Intermediate scrutiny would first be given a vigorous enforcement in cases involving gender discrimination. Prior to the 1970s, the Court had consistently used minimal scrutiny to review gender classifications and always upheld laws that treated women differently than men. The Court took the position that gender was a valid basis of classification and upheld laws that provided special protection for women or denied women rights commonly enjoyed by men. For example, the Court upheld laws that prohibited women from serving on juries, from being admitted to the practice of law, from working as bartenders, and so on. As late as 1961, a complacent Supreme Court could be found employing minimal scrutiny to sustain a law automatically exempting women, but not men, from jury service.[142]

In the early 1970s the Court began to question its previous acceptance of gender discrimination. The watershed case was *Reed v. Reed*, in which the Court was faced with an Idaho law that gave a preference to men over women in the appointment of administrators of estates.[143] The Court, apparently applying minimal scrutiny, nonetheless struck the law down on the ground that it was irrational, and therefore violated the Equal Protection Clause. This was baffling to Court watchers, because under minimal scrutiny as it was then practiced, the Court was not supposed to strike laws down; it was supposed to defer to the legislature. Then, a few years later in *Frontiero v. Richardson*, the Court invalidated a federal law granting certain dependency allowances to male members of the armed services but not to female members.[144] In this case, Justice Brennan wrote an opinion suggesting that sexual classifications should be considered suspect, similar to racial classifications, and therefore should evoke strict scrutiny. But Justice Brennan could only convince three other justices to join what turned out to be a plurality opinion, so a majority of the Court was not willing to declare gender to be a suspect classification calling for strict scrutiny.

So the confusion about the Court's treatment of gender classifications continued for a while, but in subsequent cases, the Court settled on a less confusing pathway. What the Court decided to do was to adopt the new level of intermediate judicial scrutiny recently formulated in *O'Brien*. The compromise of an intermediate tier of scrutiny, which had seemed logical enough for situations involving symbolic speech, also possessed a certain logic as a compromise for those justices who were forced to admit the invidious nature of gender classifications but could not bring themselves to allow the recognition of another suspect classification. Thus, avoiding both the acuity of strict scrutiny and the short-sightedness of minimal, the Court embarked on an intermediate path to review classifications based on gender.

After a few decisions using intermediate scrutiny, without calling it that, the Court finally came out in 1976 in *Craig v. Boren* and openly acknowledged that there now was a third—intermediate—level of scrutiny, that would be used in equal protection cases to evaluate the constitutionality of gender classifications.[145] Following *Craig*, the Court explicitly applied intermediate scrutiny in a number of cases involving gender classifications. In fact, the Court ruled that intermediate scrutiny should be used for gender classifications that discriminate against women as well as those that discriminate against men. For example, in *Kirchberg v. Feenstra*, the Court used intermediate scrutiny to strike down a Louisiana law that gave a husband, as "head and master" of property owned jointly with his wife, the unilateral right to dispose of their community property.[146] In *Mississippi University for Women v. Hogan*, the Court applied intermediate scrutiny to declare unconstitutional a state nursing school open only to women.[147]

Evidently, a majority of the Burger Court was pleased with its elaboration of an intermediate level of scrutiny because it did not take the Court long to extend its use to areas other than gender discrimination. The Court next decided to use intermediate scrutiny to review classifications of nonmarital children, and shortly thereafter employed intermediate scrutiny to deal with a variety of free speech situations, including content-neutral regulations of speech, regulations of commercial speech, and regulations of symbolic speech. In dealing with the latter, moreover, the Burger Court saw it fit to apply genuine intermediate scrutiny, rather than a watered-down application of it, as the Warren Court initially had done in *O'Brien*. Eventually, however, in cases involving the Equal Protection Clause, the Burger Court reached a point of unwillingness to further expand the ambit of intermediate scrutiny. While the Court eagerly extended the reach of intermediate scrutiny into various areas of the First Amendment, in equal protection cases the Court appeared to reach a stopping place for further use of heightened scrutiny.

This can be observed in the Court's opinion in the *Cleburne* case,[148] which manifests considerable reluctance to extend heightened scrutiny to new areas within the ambit of the Equal Protection Clause. In *Cleburne*, the Court declined to recognize mental retardation as a quasi-suspect classification, when it easily could have done so. The class of mental retardation, after all, unfortunately possesses a number of the indicia of an invidious classification, and seems to fall within the Court's own definition of a suspect class.[149] Persons who are mentally retarded embody a "discrete and insular minority" that has been "saddled with such disabilities, or subjected to such a history of purposeful unequal treatment, or regelated to such a position of political powerlessness as to command extraordinary protection from the majoritarian political process." Brushing all of that aside, however, the Court explicitly declined to recognize mental retardation as a quasi-suspect classification because it was loathe to open the door to the recognition of other classes that might be entitled to the protection of heightened judicial scrutiny.[150] No more suspect or quasi-suspect classifications, the Court seemed to be protesting. No more expansion of heightened scrutiny under the Equal Protection Clause.

Still, intermediate scrutiny continues to be an integral part of constitutional analysis, especially in equal protection and First Amendment cases. The presence of this intermediate tier of judicial review remains extremely significant in constitutional adjudication, and its impact should not be minimized. Indeed, the development of intermediate scrutiny, if not the most important legacy of the Burger Court, is certainly one of them. By establishing this intermediate tier of scrutiny, the Court opened entire new areas to heightened judicial review and provided a flexibility to judicial review that improved it substantially. As we shall see though, this was not enough to rectify the basic flaws of the tiered system.

REHNQUIST AND SCALIA: FORAYS INTO WEAKENING INTERMEDIATE SCRUTINY

While most of the justices on the Supreme Court were directing their attention to developing a definitive intermediate tier of judicial review, Justice Rehnquist stood in solitary opposition to this movement. He was not pleased by the emergence of this new genus of heightened judicial review and frequently found himself a sole dissenter, inveighing against the Court's invocation of intermediate scrutiny.[151] As a professed adherent of judicial restraint,[152] Justice Rehnquist believed that all legislative classifications, with the exception of those based on race or national origin, should be treated with the most minimal judicial scrutiny. As far as Justice Rehnquist was concerned, aside from one or two areas, rationality review should be the Supreme Court's watchword. Accordingly, the emergence of any form of heightened scrutiny was anathema to Justice Rehnquist, and he made it crystal clear that he was opposed to the very creation of intermediate scrutiny.[153] In a series of cases, Justice Rehnquist parted company with all eight of his colleagues on the Court by objecting to the use of anything stronger than minimal scrutiny to evaluate the constitutionality of gender-based classifications.[154] When the Court extended the reach of intermediate scrutiny to evaluate classifications against nonmarital children, Justice Rehnquist reiterated his objection.[155]

Despite his best efforts, Justice Rehnquist could not dissuade his colleagues from firmly establishing intermediate scrutiny as an integral part of judicial review. When it became apparent to Justice Rehnquist that he could not convince the other members of the Court to dismantle what they had recently constructed, he changed his strategy. Justice Rehnquist appeared to grudgingly accept this new tier of intermediate review, while attempting sub rosa to undermine it by converting it into something more akin to minimal scrutiny.

This dissimulation first occurred in *Michael M. v. Superior Court of Sonoma County*,[156] a 1981 decision in which a splintered Supreme Court sustained the constitutionality of a California statutory rape law that made it a crime for a male to have sexual relations with a female under the age of eighteen, but did not make it a crime for a female to have sex with a male under the same age. Justice Rehnquist's plurality opinion in this case is a tour de force of disingenuousness that three other Justices were somehow persuaded to join. Dissimulation appears early in the Rehnquist opinion, with the statement that prior cases show that "the Court has had some difficulty in agreeing upon the proper approach and analysis" in cases involving gender-based classifications.[157] This statement neglects to mention that the Court had previously reached agreement on this matter and by the time of *Michael M.* had established in a number of cases that intermediate scrutiny was the "proper approach and analysis" for reviewing gender-based classifications. While the Rehnquist opinion goes on to reluctantly acknowledge the existence of an intermediate level of scrutiny, the opinion depreciates the character of intermediate scrutiny by portraying it as merely "somewhat" sharper than minimal scrutiny.[158] This is faint praise, which, if not damning of intermediate scrutiny, certainly is degrading of it. As put into practice in the *Michael M.* plurality opinion, intermediate scrutiny loses even that slight edge, being blunted upon contact with the essential issue, which had to do with the California law's under-inclusiveness. It had been argued to the Court that by excluding females from its coverage, the law was impermissibly under-inclusive, because the law's purpose of deterring teenage pregnancy could be achieved just as well by a gender-neutral statute under which males as well as females would be subject to prosecution. This argument was dismissed by Justice Rehnquist with a rebuke, "The relevant inquiry, however, is not whether the statute is drawn as precisely as it might have been, but whether the line chosen by the California legislature is within constitutional limitations."[159] This, of course, is a regression to minimalism—an observation so abstract as to be virtually meaningless and thereby allow great deference to the legislature. It is a far cry from the previous requirement of intermediate scrutiny that calls for a close, though not perfect, fit between legislative means and ends.

Furthermore, as support for this approach Justice Rehnquist cited only a single case, *Kahn v. Shevin*, a decision from the embryonic stage of intermediate scrutiny, which saw the Court momentarily regress to the use of minimal scrutiny to deal with a gender-based classification. By using a solitary precedent that was an aberration when decided and thereafter was disregarded to support a misplaced rationale, Justice Rehnquist was able to transmute intermediate scrutiny, which he always disdained, into minimal scrutiny, which is his favorite mode of review.

Not content with this handiwork, Justice Rehnquist found yet another way to indulge under-inclusiveness—by refusing to recognize its presence. His opinion avows an unwillingness to admit that a gender-neutral statutory rape provision would be as effective as a gender-based one, because the former "may well be incapable of enforcement."[160] As pointed out in a dissenting opinion, this overlooks the fact that at the time of the case thirty-seven states had enacted gender-neutral statutory rape laws, and had shown no difficulty in enforcing them. This pertinent data is ignored in Justice Rehnquist's opinion, which heedlessly assumes that the legislative classification is sufficiently related to its purpose. In persisting in this assumption despite factual data that belies it, the opinion displays an uncritical deference to government that is typical of minimal, not intermediate, scrutiny.

In a second case also decided in 1981, *Rostker v. Goldberg*,[161] Justice Rehnquist once again wrote an opinion, although this time for a majority of the Court, that in part seemed to devolve into minimalism in order to sustain a gender-based classification. In *Rostker*, the Court upheld a federal law mandating a male-only draft registration for the armed services.[162] With his categorical turn of mind, Justice Rehnquist viewed the case as presenting one of those false dichotomies of which he is so fond of fabricating. On one hand, the Rehnquist opinion dwells on the point that the case involved national defense and military affairs, an area where the Court grants the greatest deference to Congress.[163] This would call for the weakest variety of rationality review. On the other hand, there was no avoiding the fact that the federal law in question set forth a gender-based classification, which would call for a more heightened form of review.[164] Having constructed this gratuitous dilemma, Justice Rehnquist then declined to resolve it by simply stating that there was no reason to further refine the multi-tier system.[165] The levels of scrutiny, the opinion explained, "may all too readily become facile abstractions used to justify a result."[166] This seemed to signal a defection from the established system of judicial review, which allowed Justice Rehnquist to skip back and forth from intermediate to minimal scrutiny. While purporting, at least in places, to apply intermediate scrutiny, a close examination of the opinion reveals that, similar to the one in *Michael M.*, it employs a watered-down version of intermediate scrutiny.

In cases following *Michael M.* and *Rostker*, a majority of the Court returned to a more genuine use of intermediate scrutiny.[167] Nonetheless, those two decisions indicated that the Court's commitment to intermediate scrutiny might be faltering. This raised concerns that the Court's actual exercise of intermediate scrutiny was weaker than originally promised.[168]

That original promise, however, was reinvigorated in 1996, in the case of *United States v. Virginia*,[169] when the Supreme Court ruled that it violated the Equal Protection Clause for the Commonwealth of Virginia to exclude women from the Virginia Military Institute. VMI had argued that it had a good reason to exclude women—namely, that they are unable to withstand the rigorous military training, called the "adversative method," that VMI requires of all of its students. Therefore, to admit women would spell the end of military education as it has been known at VMI since its inception in 1839. The Supreme Court rejected this argument because it was based entirely on stereotypical thinking about men and women. In fact, the Court pointed out, the successful integration of women at West Point and Annapolis belied VMI's assertion that excluding women from a military institution is necessary to maintain the character of the institution. In short, the Court concluded that VMI offered no justification for the exclusion, except archaic stereotypes about women that no longer were valid, if, indeed, they ever were.

Obviously, the VMI decision is important for what it says about gender discrimination and education, but it also is important for what it says about equal protection doctrine. The Court's opinion in VMI, written by Justice Ruth Bader Ginsburg, resolves an important question about the level of scrutiny to be used in cases involving gender classifications.

The VMI case shores up or rebuilds the prior weakening of intermediate scrutiny. It does that by picking up some language that actually was used in an earlier decision, but the VMI case stresses it more. What the VMI opinion says is that to sustain a gender classification there must be an "exceedingly persuasive justification."[170] Previously, the Court required an "important" or "substantial" state interest, but the VMI case describes it as "exceedingly persuasive." It sounds almost like the "compelling" state interest standard used with strict scrutiny and indeed in his dissenting opinion in the VMI case, Justice Antonin Scalia accuses the majority of transforming the intermediate scrutiny of gender classifications into strict scrutiny.[171] When the case is viewed from another perspective, however, Justice Scalia's accusation turns out to be incorrect. More accurately, what the majority is doing in the VMI case is returning intermediate scrutiny to the status it enjoyed before being watered down in *Michael M.* and *Rostker*. In the VMI case the majority, concerned that intermediate scrutiny was being transformed into minimal scrutiny, took action to reverse that trend. In effect the majority was saying, "Look, we're serious about intermediate scrutiny and we are not going to allow it to be watered down. Intermediate scrutiny calls for an important state interest, and by important we mean 'exceedingly persuasive.' "

In the meantime, Chief Justice Rehnquist, later followed by Justice Scalia, led another attempt to downgrade intermediate scrutiny, this time in the area of commercial speech. In a 1980 decision, *Central Hudson Gas v. Public Service Commission*, the Court set forth a four-part test to be used to evaluate the constitutionality of laws regulating commercial speech.[172] By requiring such laws to be justified by a substantial state interest and be no more extensive than necessary to achieve that interest, the *Central Hudson* test clearly is an expression of intermediate scrutiny. The decision in *Central Hudson* was the culmination of a series of cases, beginning with the 1976 decision in *Virginia Pharmacy Board*, in which the Supreme Court concluded that commercial speech was entitled to a significant degree of constitutional protection.[173] The Court's decision in *Central Hudson* confirmed that intermediate scrutiny was the appropriate level of protection for commercial speech. The Court adhered to that position in commercial speech cases following *Central Hudson*,[174] until its decision in *Posadas de Puerto Rico Associates v. Tourism Company of Puerto Rico*, authored by Chief Justice Rehnquist.[175] In *Posadas*, by a vote of 5–4 the Court upheld a Puerto Rican statute that prohibited local casinos from advertising their gambling facilities to residents of Puerto Rico, while leaving them free to advertise to persons residing anywhere else.[176] In addition, the statute applied only to advertising for casino gambling, while freely allowing advertising for other kinds of gambling that were conducted in Puerto Rico. The statute, then, discriminated in several ways; it discriminated on the basis of the intended audience of advertising as well as on the basis of the activity being advertised. In his dissenting opinion, Justice Stevens described the statute as a "bizarre [restraint] . . . [that] blatantly discriminates in its punishment of speech depending on the publication, audience, and words employed."[177]

Nonetheless, a slim majority of the Court voted to uphold the statute. After noting that the activity of casino gambling itself could be banned, Justice Rehnquist's opinion for the majority concluded that "the greater power to completely ban casino gambling necessarily includes the lesser power to ban advertising of casino gambling."[178] While this may or may not be so, it does not address the core issue, which is whether a selective or discriminatory ban on casino advertising is permissible.[179] It has been pointed out that the rationale offered by Justice Rehnquist does not address the discriminatory aspects of the Puerto Rican law.[180] In this way, Justice Rehnquist once again was able to debase the effectiveness of intermediate scrutiny. While professing to follow the *Central Hudson* test of intermediate scrutiny, in actuality the Rehnquist opinion applied a diminished degree of scrutiny in evaluating the legislative means employed in the statute.

Whereas Justice Rehnquist's approach in *Posadas* is to depreciate intermediate scrutiny sub silencio, in another case involving commercial speech, *Board of Trustees of the State University of New York v. Fox*,[181] Justice Scalia is more open in his effort to weaken intermediate scrutiny. In this case, the Court upheld a state regulation that prohibited commercial solicitation in campus dormitory rooms. The plaintiff's assertion that the regulation was unduly discriminatory was dismissed by the Court on the ground that because of its subordinate value under the First Amendment, commercial speech was entitled only to a limited measure of constitutional protection, which does not include the requirement that the state employ the least restrictive means to accomplish its purposes. In fact, Justice Scalia's opinion for the Court expressly rejected the "least restrictive means" test for reviewing regulations of commercial speech. *Posadas* raised the suspicion that intermediate scrutiny was being diminished for commercial speech cases, and *Fox* confirmed that suspicion.

In subsequent decisions, however, a majority of the Court reversed the *Posadas-Fox* approach and completely restored the forcefulness of the *Central Hudson* test. In a 1993 decision, *City of Cincinnati v. Discovery Network, Inc.*, the Court struck down a regulation of commercial speech because its means were not sufficiently related to its ends.[182] And in the same year in *Edenfield v. Fane*, the Court concluded that a regulation of commercial speech was fatally flawed because the state could not show that it materially advanced a substantial state interest.[183]

More recent cases further illustrate the renewed vigor of the *Central Hudson* test. Thus, in *Rubin v. Coors Brewing Company*,[184] the Supreme Court struck down a provision of the Federal Alcohol Administration Act that prohibited beer labels from displaying alcohol content. The Court found that since the regulation prohibited the disclosure of truthful, verifiable, and nonmisleading factual information, analysis must focus on "the substantiality of the interest" behind the FAAA rule and whether the rule advanced that interest "in a direct and material way."[185] In order to meet this burden, the government could not rely on "mere speculation and conjecture," but rather must give proof that its means will alleviate the real harms to a material degree.[186] The Court described this requirement as "critical."[187] In addition, the Court found that the regulation was wanting because several alternatives were available to advance the government's interest in a manner less intrusive to speech. All of these standards clearly are characteristic of heightened scrutiny rather than mere rationality review.

In *44 Liquormart v. Rhode Island*,[188] the Court invalidated a Rhode Island restriction that prohibited the advertisement of liquor prices. There was no majority in this case. Justice Stevens, who wrote the principal opinion concerning the First Amendment issue, concluded that the ban failed the *Central Hudson* standard because the state did not present sufficient evidence that the ban directly advanced its asserted interest and because there were less restrictive alternatives available to meet the government's goal.[189] Justice Stevens, joined in this part of his opinion by Justices Anthony Kennedy, Clarence Thomas, and Ruth Bader Ginsburg, also addressed the viability of *Posadas*, stating that "*Posadas* erroneously performed the First Amendment analysis."[190] The opinion went on to say that because the 5–4 decision in *Posadas* "marked such a sharp break from our prior precedent . . . we decline to give force to its highly deferential approach."[191]

Justice Sandra Day O'Connor, joined by Chief Justice Rehnquist and Justices Souter and Stephen Breyer, also concluded that the restriction failed the *Central Hudson* test because the restriction was more extensive than necessary and Rhode Island had other, less intrusive means to advance its interest.[192] Justice O'Connor's opinion further addressed the *Posadas* question and found that in decisions since *Posadas*, the Court has "examined more searchingly" the state's professed goal and its means to further it.[193] Her opinion stated, "The closer look that we have required since *Posadas* comports better with the purpose of the analysis set out in *Central Hudson*, by requiring the State to show that the speech restriction directly advances its interest and is narrowly tailored."[194] Between the Stevens and O'Connor opinions, fully eight justices (including of all people, Chief Justice Rehnquist) found that the *Posadas-Fox* approach was no longer good law. Those two cases have been repudiated and now can be considered aberrational. Both before and after them, the Supreme Court has consistently applied the *Central Hudson* test with full force.

JUSTICE MARSHALL'S SLIDING SCALE OF SCRUTINY

The most thoughtful criticism of the multi-level system from a Supreme Court justice was articulated by Thurgood Marshall in a series of dissenting and concurring opinions that began in 1970 prior to the emergence of intermediate scrutiny and continued after the intermediate tier was in place.[195] Justice Marshall believed that the multi-tier system is an over-simplification that does not accurately reflect the adjudicative process in constitutional cases.[196] He claimed that a more discerning reading of the Court's opinions reveals a spectrum or sliding scale of scrutiny that is calibrated by degrees rather than two or three tiers.[197] According to this conception, the operative degree of scrutiny depends upon a mix of factors: the constitutional and societal importance of the interest adversely affected; the recognized invidiousness of the basis upon which a particular classification is drawn; and the state interests asserted in support of the classification in question.[198] Assessment of these factors determines the operative degree of scrutiny along a spectrum decidedly more finely attuned than the tiered structure.

Moreover, Justice Marshall maintained that the multi-level system is a "rigidified approach" that hinders proper constitutional analysis in two respects. First, it misdirects constitutional analysis by deflecting the focus of inquiry toward abstractions (the tiers of scrutiny) that have little to do with the specific merits of a case.[199] Second, it inhibits constitutional analysis by relying upon *a priori* categories (such as "fundamental right" and "suspect classification") to trigger the operative tier of scrutiny.

Originally, Justice Marshall's criticism was directed at the multi-level system when it consisted of two tiers, strict and minimal scrutiny. In Justice Marshall's view, the addition of a third level of review, intermediate scrutiny, did little to address his concerns about the system, and he remained critical of it in its revised form. In fact, around the time that intermediate scrutiny was in an incipient stage, Justice Marshall authored a majority opinion for the Court in the case of *Police Department of Chicago v. Mosley*,[200] which adapted his sliding scale of review to a single overall standard of review offered as an alternative to the multi-tier approach. Marshall's opinion in *Mosley* stated that the crucial question in all equal protection cases is whether there is "an appropriate governmental interest suitably furthered" by the government regulation in question.[201] This comprehensive inquiry consolidates the levels (or, as may be the case, the degrees) of scrutiny into a unified criterion for all cases. However, use of the *Mosley* standard was short-lived; a majority of the Court evidently preferred to concentrate its attention upon further refining the levels of scrutiny, especially the newest intermediate level.

Another case, however, that marks an apparent conversion to Justice Marshall's way of thinking is *Plyler v. Doe*,[202] where the Court employed a flexible comprehensive standard in lieu of the *a priori* categories that normally obtain under the multi-level approach. Justice Brennan wrote the 5–4 majority opinion in *Plyler*, striking down a Texas law that denied free public education to the children of illegal aliens.[203] Although the state law fell into none of the categories previously held to invoke either of the forms of heightened scrutiny, the Court nevertheless concluded that the intermediate tier was the appropriate standard of review.[204] This conclusion was reached through an analysis that bore a striking resemblance to the analysis suggested by Justice Marshall—that is, by evaluating the extent of invidiousness of the classification at hand and the relative importance of the individual and state interests at stake. The Court devoted six pages to this analysis,[205] in the course of which it stated that more was involved in the case than the "abstract question" of whether the law discriminates against a suspect class or whether education is a fundamental right.[206]

Given the various refinements and permutations that the Court has developed in utilizing the tiered structure, Justice Marshall seems to be close to the truth in his observation that in actuality there is a spectrum of scrutiny calibrated by degrees rather than tiers. To say that there are three or even four tiers of scrutiny hardly begins to describe the Court's exercise of judicial review.

FLAWS IN THE MULTI-TIER SYSTEM

Rigidity

Justice Marshall outlined a number of flaws in the multi-tier system that can be taken as a starting point for a deeper comprehension of the system's defects. When Justice Marshall began to criticize the system, it was composed of two tiers, strict and minimal scrutiny. He continued to be critical of the system even after an intermediate tier was established. When the system was composed of only two tiers, its most obvious flaw was its rigidity, especially as administered by the Warren Court. In those days, decision making was initiated with a heavy hand pressing upon one or the other side of the constitutional scale. As a result, the ultimate acceptance or rejection of government action was determined by the level of scrutiny chosen in a given case. In situations calling for minimal scrutiny, government action was almost automatically sustained; in situations calling for strict scrutiny, it was almost automatically struck down. This extreme rigidity was not inherent to the system and could have been alleviated to some degree if the Court was willing to be a bit less deferential with minimal scrutiny and a bit less disapproving with strict. Still, even if the Court had eased up a bit, the two-tiered structure itself caused a fair amount of rigidity, which, at times, forced the Court to manipulate the system by questionable means.

Eventually, this situation led to the formulation of an intermediate tier, which provided a degree of flexibility to the overall structure of judicial review. However, the presence of intermediate scrutiny did little to reduce the rigidity that remained within the other two tiers. This was most pronounced in the lowest tier of review. With minimal scrutiny functioning in reality as virtually no scrutiny, the Court had no other option but to uphold legislation that in truth was irrational. Under this mode of review, the Court sustained a number of laws despite the fact that they were grossly over- or under-inclusive or were supported by nothing more than flimsy or implausible justifications proffered after-the-fact by government attorneys. While the creation of intermediate scrutiny was able to elevate some cases from the rigidity of the lowest tier, it did nothing to enhance the options available in those cases that remained subject to the minimalism of rationality review. Thus, the inflexibility within the minimal tier of scrutiny persisted.

Finally, this moved the Court in a few cases to restore minimal scrutiny to its original status, which granted substantial but not total deference to the legislature. By doing so, the Court has created what in fact is a fourth level of scrutiny—minimal scrutiny with bite. As might be expected, this causes some confusion in the law, especially because it is difficult to determine exactly what factors will induce the Court to invest rationality review with a bit of bite. Nonetheless, this is a welcome development, because, while still granting deference to the legislature, it eases the rigidity of minimal scrutiny and makes rationality review something more than an empty pretense. After all, if nomenclature is any indication, minimal scrutiny should be minimal but not nonexistent, and rationality review should require at least a modicum of reason. Unfortunately, this welcome development is utilized only on rare occasions; in a high majority of cases minimal scrutiny still is nothing more than a rubber stamp for legislation. Albeit with a few exceptions now, rationality review continues to be nothing more than a pretext.

Even if minimal scrutiny were to be more thoroughly rehabilitated, it is not certain that the multi-tier system would provide sufficient flexibility for the Court. It already has been observed that manipulation of the standards of the system occurs not only in the lowest tier, but in all three of them. This is a strong indication that the Court finds the overall system to be too rigid. In equal protection cases, the Court has found it necessary to resort to dubious logic to escape from both strict and intermediate scrutiny.[207] Some justices feel pressured by the dictates of heightened scrutiny; others feel constrained by the limits of minimal scrutiny. Whether there are two tiers or three, the Court always seems to be manipulating them by questionable means. It may be that this shows a lack of intellectual integrity or ability on the part of some of the justices, rather than undue inflexibility in the system itself. But the fact remains that in the hands of the Supreme Court the tiered system has not manifested enough flexibility. It may be, then, that even with further refurbishing of the system here and there, the Court will not have adequate room to develop a principled and cohesive body of law.

Inhibition of Analysis

Justice Marshall was correct when he stated that another deficiency of the multi-tier approach is that it hampers legal analysis by deflecting the focus of inquiry toward abstractions that are divorced from the specific merits of a case. Under the system, attention is concentrated on conceptions about classifications, interests, levels of scrutiny, and the like, to the extent that the actual merits of a case are neglected, if not altogether lost in the shuffle. The system channels attention away from the particular issues and factual details of cases toward general questions about which tier of scrutiny should be utilized and why and how. After reading the Court's opinions in constitutional cases, or the briefs submitted therein, one often feels a sense of having seen the forest but not the trees. Under the multi-level system, cases become primarily concerned with issues about judicial review, to the exclusion of the specific concerns that gave rise to them.

The multi-level system additionally impedes legal analysis, in a most serious way, by imposing categorical thinking upon the constitutional balancing process. All constitutional adjudication, regardless of the structure through which it is accomplished, necessarily entails a balancing or comparative evaluation of governmental and individual interests. The essential issue in all constitutional cases is whether the governmental interests promoted by state regulations are sufficiently important to outweigh the individual interests that they restrict. Short of abolishing judicial review, there is no way to eliminate the balancing process from constitutional decision making, and the multi-tier system certainly does not do so. However, it does filter the appraisal of interests through *a priori* categories. The level of scrutiny to be selected is determined through categories such as "suspect classification" or "fundamental right." In turn, each level functions through its own categories such as "valid state interest," "important state interest," and "compelling state interest." Rather than focus purely upon the evaluation of governmental and individual interests, the multi-level system refracts it through pre-set compartments. This results in a species of constitutional adjudication that might well be described as categorical balancing.

The *a priori* categories by which the multi-level approach operates are abstract generalizations. As such, they dilute constitutional analysis. Individual rights are conceptualized as either fundamental or not, with nothing in between. Classifications of individuals are thought of as suspect, quasi-suspect, or non-suspect, but nothing else. Governmental ends may be compelling, important, or valid, but no other possibilities are conceivable. Governmental means may be necessary, substantial, or reasonable, but there the list ends. This sort of categorical thinking squeezes the appraisal of interests into prefabricated boxes that allow for no variation beyond their own dimensions. Stringently confined as it is, categorical balancing does not provide adequate calibration for evaluating the diverse interests that arise in constitutional litigation.

Categorical balancing exacerbates the rigidity of the multi-tier approach by increasing its propensity to predetermine the result of cases. The *a priori* labels ascribed to governmental and individual interests tend to preordain their constitutional fate. Through the categorization of governmental and individual interests, their evaluation is fettered and their relative merit is prejudged.

Internal Inconsistency

The *a priori* categories used in the multi-level system have not always been capable of providing internal stability for the system. In fact, internal inconsistency has plagued several of the categories that have been stalwarts of the system, beginning with the category of suspect classifications. Early in the history of the multi-tier approach, the Court defined a suspect classification as one directed at a "discrete and insular minority."[208] Later cases describe a suspect class as consisting of persons "subjected to such a history of purposeful unequal treatment, or relegated to such a position of political powerlessness as to command extraordinary protection from the majoritarian political process."[209] A suspect classification often flows from invidious stereotypes about people and operates as a badge or stigma of inferiority. Suspect classifications usually are based on an immutable trait, accident of birth, or condition that has nothing to do with a person's ability, and hence is irrelevant as far as any proper government purpose is concerned. Race is the paradigm suspect classification and has been recognized as such by the Supreme Court.[210] Although the historical impetus for the enactment of the Fourteenth Amendment was the abolition of racial discrimination, that amendment, unlike the Fifteenth, makes no mention of race, and the Court has not limited the application of the Fourteenth Amendment to racial discrimination. The Court has not restricted the category of suspect classifications to race; it also has ruled that classifications based on national origin or alienage are suspect, and, similar to those based on race, are therefore subject to strict scrutiny.[211]

However, there are other legislative classifications that appear to fit the Court's own definition of being suspect that the Court has declined to acknowledge as such. In *Frontiero v. Richardson*,[212] a majority of the Court was unwilling to declare gender a suspect classification, despite the strong case made by Justice Brennan to show that classifications based upon gender possess the characteristics of a suspect classification and despite the fact that women have been subjected to "a history of purposeful unequal treatment" as well as being relegated to "a position of political powerlessness."[213] While it is true that in cases after *Frontiero* the Court agreed to treat gender as what is referred to as a "quasi-suspect" classification subject to intermediate scrutiny, there still are lingering doubts about the Court's logic in refusing to recognize gender as a suspect classification.

It has been even more disconcerting to see the Court decline to recognize other suspect or quasi-suspect classifications, despite the fact that they bear many suspicious attributes. The Court refused to recognize classifications based on wealth as suspect or based on age as quasi-suspect, leaving them both to linger in the lowest confines of minimal scrutiny.[214] The Court bypassed several opportunities to rule that sexual orientation is suspect or quasi-suspect (although in the last instance the Court did strike down a law that discriminated against gay and lesbian persons).[215] The Court sidestepped one opportunity to hold that mental illness was a suspect or quasi-suspect classification,[216] and later adamantly refused to recognize mental retardation as a suspect or quasi-suspect classification (although striking down a zoning law that discriminated against persons who were mentally retarded).[217] Brushing aside the dubious properties of these classifications, the Court has been unwilling to find that any one of them is suspect or quasi-suspect. These rulings manifest an internal inconsistency within the multi-level system. Unwilling to abide by its own definition of a suspect classification, the Court takes classifications that, according to the Court's own logic, should be grouped together, and randomly scatters them among four different tiers of review.

Internal inconsistency also afflicts another multi-level category, that of fundamental rights or interests. Originally, an interest was deemed fundamental because the Court thought it to be of extreme social significance.[218] This approach opened the Court to the criticism that it was reverting to natural law formulations in deciding constitutional matters.[219] This criticism, however, was not entirely accurate because the modern Court, unlike some of its predecessors, did not pretend to discover fundamental rights in the nature of things, but rather designated certain rights to be fundamental because of their social importance. Although the difference may seem to be obscure, it nevertheless is real; presuming to discover fundamental rights that supposedly preexist somewhere is a very different process than evaluating which rights are important enough to be approved as fundamental. Still, the modern Court's approach to the recognition of fundamental rights left it open to the charge that it was reading its own values into the Constitution, *a la* Lochnerism. The only difference was that the Court's values had changed; where once the Court favored conservative values, now it esteemed liberal ones. Admittedly, the Court's approach to fundamental rights has been subjective, and hence prone to inconsistency. The right of privacy, for example, was fundamental to the Court's way of thinking, but property rights were not. The right to vote was fundamental,[220] but not by absentee ballot.[221] At any rate, in *San Antonio Independent School District v. Rodriguez*, decided in 1973, the Court moved to curtail the conception of fundamental rights by ruling that henceforth only those rights explicitly or implicitly guaranteed by the Constitution itself are to be considered fundamental.[222] The focus now would be on the text of the Constitution, in lieu of the social importance of interests.

This definition of fundamental rights, while more objective than the former one, does not eliminate all subjectivity. What the Constitution explicitly guarantees is not always a matter of indeterminate judgment. Unfortunately, the constitutional text is not in all instances that exact. And what the Constitution implicitly guarantees is even more debatable.

After *Rodriguez*, the Court was moved in due process cases to acknowledge a possible source of fundamental rights other than those indicated in the text of the Constitution. In *Moore v. City of East Cleveland*, Justice Powell's plurality opinion announced that fundamental rights include those liberties "deeply rooted in this Nation's history and tradition."[223] It should not be thought, however, that this is a particularly objective standard. To the contrary, as seen in Chapter 1, the interpretation of history is notoriously subjective[224] Moreover, in looking to tradition to ascertain fundamental rights, differing results will be reached depending on the level of abstraction by which a right is conceived.[225] At a general level of abstraction, numerous liberties will be found; at a narrow one, very few.[226] Despite, or perhaps because of, this inexactitude, Justice Powell's standard was utilized in subsequent cases by a majority of the Court,[227] although the Court seemed to confuse the standard by combining it with an older one that defined fundamental rights as those "implicit in the concept of ordered liberty" such that "neither liberty nor justice would exist if they were sacrificed."[228] This formulation was among the most subjective of the old natural law notions, and sets the Court on a false track. As Holmes stated so well, many years ago, "law is not a brooding omnipresence in the sky."[229]

The Court's delineation of fundamental rights has remained inconsistent. For example, the right to vote in a state election,[230] to interstate travel,[231] to access to the justice system,[232] to decide to have an abortion,[233] or to live in an extended family,[234] are all fundamental; the right to an education,[235] housing,[236] employment,[237] subsistence,[238] or physician-assisted suicide[239] are not.

These, then, are the basic flaws that beset the multi-level system of judicial review: inconsistency, faulty analysis, and rigidity. They are the source of the Court's recurrent frustration with the system as well as the continual tinkering with it, by which the Court is often led astray. Given the vicissitudinous career of the tiers of scrutiny, one cannot help but wonder if there is not a better way of structuring constitutional adjudication.

RESTRUCTURING THE SYSTEM

A viable alternative to the multi-level system of judicial review is the unified structure championed by Justice Marshall. The multiple tiers readily could be transformed or replaced by a comprehensive system based on the unitary standard announced in the *Mosley* case, which in all instances would inquire whether there is "an appropriate governmental interest suitably furthered" by the government action in question.[240] Like the multiple tier approach, a unified system would provide a framework for the evaluation of governmental and individual interests. The unified system, though, would differ in several important respects from the current tiered one. First, a unified structure would eliminate the rigidity that pervades the present multi-level approach. With the abolition of tiers, the constitutionality of government action would not be predetermined by the level of scrutiny that applied in a particular instance. This would obviate the need now felt by the Court in a considerable number of cases to manipulate principle and precedent in order to reach a proper result. In the absence of tiers, there obviously would be no reason for the Court to abruptly refuse to deal with them, as happened in *Fullilove v. Klutznick* and *Rostker v. Goldberg*.[241] Nor would the Court have reason to manufacture devices to contort the tiers, as happens in a variety of cases. Thus, adoption of the proposed uniform structure would remedy the inconsistency and confusion that now prevails due to the court's unpredictable but not uncommon deviations from the multi-level approach.

Second, a unified system would promote more accuracy in the appraisal of both individual and governmental interests. Under the proposed system, attention would not be diverted away from the specific merits of a case toward abstract questions concerning judicial review. The eradication of tiers would make such questions largely irrelevant, so that the Court could concentrate its inquiry upon the actual merits of cases. At the same time, the unitary approach would purify judicial review of categorical thinking. By lifting the shroud of *a priori* categories, the new structure would sharpen the Court's focus upon governmental and individual interests, thereby fostering a more precise evaluation. Judicial review would be more direct, more realistic, and more finely attuned.

The essential differences between a unified system of judicial review and a tiered one can be illustrated by comparing the majority and dissenting opinions in *Plyler v. Doe*.[242] As previously mentioned, in *Plyler* the Court was faced with a Texas law that deprived free public education to the children of illegal aliens. The dissenting opinion in the case, written by Chief Justice Burger, exemplified the multi-level approach in its most pristine form. Relying upon the prefabricated categories of the multi-tier approach, Chief Justice Burger pointed out that the case involved neither a suspect class nor a fundamental right. As he saw it, however unfair it might be to hold these children responsible for their illegal status, the fact was that illegal alienage was not a suspect classification.[243] Although he conceded that the "importance of education is beyond dispute," the fact was that the Court had previously ruled that education was not a fundamental right.[244] As far as the Chief Justice was concerned, that dictated the outcome in *Plyler*. With no suspect classification or fundamental right present, rationality review was the only choice. As a result, Chief Justice Burger and the other dissenters voted to sustain the law on the ground that it was not irrational for a state to take the position that it does not have the same obligation to provide education to children who are illegally present in the country as it does to children who are lawfully present.[245]

In reaching this point in the dissenting opinion of Chief Justice Burger, the reader might be struck by a certain anomaly, namely, that Chief Justice Burger insisted that the Texas law was not irrational only after describing the policy of the law in the very beginning of his opinion as "senseless," "folly," and "wrong."[246] How a law can make no sense yet be rational is, indeed, puzzling. This sort of oxymoron, however, is one of the occupational hazards of minimal scrutiny with no bite. By pretending that even senseless laws are not irrational, a minimalist opinion written with too much candor or perhaps too little care incurs the risk of self-contradiction.

The senselessness of the state laws in *Plyler* was more fully explained in the Court's majority opinion, which was written by Justice Brennan. He was able to deal more thoroughly with the state law by adopting a flexible approach along the lines suggested by Justice Marshall.[247] While noting that the state law fell into none of the categories that invoke heightened scrutiny, Justice Brennan's opinion stated that more was involved in the case than the "abstract question" of whether the law discriminated against a suspect class or infringed a fundamental right.[248] This extricated the majority from the categorical thinking of the multi-level approach, making it possible to analyze the state law in more depth. Justice Brennan's opinion then pointed out that the state law imposed a lifetime hardship—the stigma of illiteracy—upon a discrete class of children who were not responsible for their status as illegal aliens. While admitting that illegal alienage is not entirely irrelevant to a proper legislative goal, Justice Brennan observed that the Texas law was directed against children and imposed a discriminatory burden on the basis of a status over which the children had little control. His opinion also admitted that the Court had previously ruled that education was not a fundamental right. Nonetheless, Brennan continued, education is not an ordinary government benefit. Education is extremely important both to the individual and to society. It has a lasting impact upon individuals and provides them with the basic tools to lead productive lives. At the same time, it sustains our basic societal institutions. "In sum, education has a fundamental role in maintaining the fabric of our society."[249]

The majority opinion recognized that the classification of children who are illegal aliens was not suspect and perhaps not even quasi-suspect, but it did bear some of the attributes of a suspect classification and therefore should not go unexamined. The opinion further recognized that while education was not a fundamental right, it was extremely important to both individuals and society; therefore, it should have some degree of constitutional protection. Putting these two considerations together, the majority was able to employ a meaningful degree of scrutiny, under which all of the interests asserted by the state in support of its law were revealed to be wanting. Examining the asserted state interests, the majority demonstrated that the state law was indeed senseless; it accomplished not one of the objectives that state claimed for it.[250]

On the other hand, Chief Justice Burger, mired in the rigidity and categorical thinking of the tiered approach, could only stand by helplessly, blinking an eye at the senselessness of the Texas law before the Court. Burger accused the majority of "patching together bits and pieces" of constitutional doctrine to spin out a theory "unabashedly result-oriented."[251] A more perceptive appraisal, however, should appreciate that the majority's way of thinking was analytically sound.

CONCLUSION

Justice Brennan's majority opinion in *Plyler v. Doe* demonstrates that the Court need not be bound by the artificial constraints that plague the multi-tier system and that have forced the Court on numerous occasions to manipulate constitutional principles. Sadly, since *Plyler* was decided in 1982, the Court has not gained enough insight to return to the circumspect mode of analysis adopted in *Plyler*. Instead, the Court has continued using the multi-level system: refining it here, qualifying it there, and continually revamping it.

At this point in our constitutional history, it seems fair to say that the multi-level system has become exceedingly convoluted. With two levels of heightened scrutiny and two varieties of minimal, each with its own twists and turns, the tiered system approximates, in operation if not in name, Justice Marshall's sliding scale of scrutiny, which is calibrated by degrees rather than levels. Unlike the sliding scale, however, the tiered system is unable to provide a theoretically sound framework for constitutional adjudication. As a system of judicial review, the multi-level approach has proven to be a rigid structure that retards constitutional analysis by diverting thought away from the merits of cases and by constricting thought through *a priori* categories. Recurrent tinkering with the multi-level system over the years since its inception has not been able to remedy its fundamental defects, and, in fact, may actually have made matters worse. Even the more major revision of adding an intermediate tier of scrutiny has not been enough to remedy the system's flaws.

Due to its basic defects, the multi-tier system severely restricts the ability of the Supreme Court to establish a healthy constitutional jurisprudence. The system frequently leaves the Court with no other choice but to distort precedent and logic, thereby infesting constitutional law with a considerable amount of confusion. It is no exaggeration to say that the multi-level system has reached a point of substantial disarray. Deviation from the system has become so common as to render constitutional adjudication a desultory affair. Given the basic flaws of the multi-tier system, it is most improbable that this deviation will abate in the future. The inevitable changes in the Court's personnel are unlikely to improve the situation without a corresponding change in the Court's methodology of decision making. If constitutional law is ever to enjoy a fair measure of coherence and stability, it will be necessary for the Supreme Court to abandon the multi-level edifice of judicial review.

NOTES

1. One observer of the Court believes it is possible to identify six levels of scrutiny. *See* R. Randall Kelso, *Filling Gaps in the Supreme Court's Approach to Constitutional*

Review of Legislation Standards, Ends, and Burdens Reconsidered, 33 S. TEX. L. REV. 493, 497–508 (1992); *Three Years Hence: An Update on Filling Gaps in the Supreme Court's Approach to Constitutional Review of Legislation*, 36 S. TEX. L. REV. 1, 1–7 (1995). My colleague Jane Rutherford suggested during a conversation that in actual practice there is a sliding scale of scrutiny. The sliding scale is discussed in the text *infra*, at notes 195–206, 239–51.

2. *See* United States v. Carolene Prods. Co. 304 U.S. 144 (1938). *See also* Kelso, *Filling Gaps in the Supreme Court's Approach, supra* note 1, at 525–29 and cases cited therein.

3. *See* Erwin Chemerinsky, CONSTITUTIONAL LAW—PRINCIPLES AND POLICIES. 526–533 (1997) and cases cited therein.

4. *See* Ashutosh Bhagwat, *Purpose Scrutiny in Constitutional Analysis*, 85 CAL. L. REV. 297, 304–305 (1997) and cases cited therein.

5. *See* Kelso, *Three Years Hence, supra* note 1, at 16–18 and cases cited therein.

6. *See* Chemerinsky, *supra* note 3, at 1021–34 and cases cited therein.

7. *See* Kelso, *Three Years Hence, supra* note 1, at 12–15 and cases cited therein.

8. *See* Laurence H. Tribe, AMERICAN CONSTITUTIONAL LAW 532–45 (2d ed. 1988) and cases cited therein.

9. *See id.* and cases cited therein.

10. Perhaps the most dramatic example of this is Police Dep't v. Mosley, 408 U.S. 92 (1972), in which the Court used strict scrutiny to strike down an ordinance regulating picketing—a form of speech—under the Equal Protection Clause rather than the First Amendment. The Court's opinion in Mosley merges a number of free speech and equal protection principles.

11. *See* Justice Rehnquist's dissenting opinion in Craig v. Boren, 429 U.S. 190, 220 (1976); compare Justice Stevens concurring opinion in the same case, *id.* at 211–12.

12. *See* Chapter 1 *supra*, at notes 27–30.

13. United States v. Lopez, 514 U.S. 549, 558 (1995).

14. *Id.*

15. *See, e.g.*, Fletcher v. Peck, 10 U.S. (6 Cranch.) 87, 128 (1810); Ogden v. Saunders, 25 U.S. (12 Wheat.) 213, 270 (1827); Legal-Tender Cases, 79 U.S. (12 Wall.) 457, 531 (1870); Sinking-Fund Cases, 99 U.S. 700, 718 (1878); Trade-Mark Cases, 100 U.S. 82, 96, (1879).

16. Willard Hurst, *Review and the Distribution of National Powers*, in SUPREME COURT AND SUPREME LAW 140, 156 (Edmond N. Cahn ed. 1954).

17. James Bradley Thayer, *The Origin and Scope of the American Doctrine of Constitutional Law*, 7 HARV. L. REV. 129 (1893).

18. *Id.* at 144.

19. *Id.*

20. *Id.*

21. In Allgeyer v. Louisiana, 165 U.S. 578 (1897), the Court struck down a law on substantive due process grounds for the first time. This initiated the rise of "Lochnerism," discussed in the text *infra*, at notes 22–37.

22. *See* Harlan B. Phillips, FELIX FRANKFURTER REMINISCES 299–300 (1960); Richard Posner, *Against Constitutional Theory*, 73 N.Y.U.L. REV. 1, 4 (1998).

23. Lochner v. New York, 198 U.S. 45 (1905).

24. "Justice Peckham's opinion striking down the law has been a continuing source of outrage, both because of the inhumanity of the result and because it contains language

that can be reasonably interpreted as violently hostile to all attempts to use the legal system as a conscious mechanism to redress the bargaining position of workers in their dealings with employers." Duncan Kennedy, *Toward An Historical Understanding of Legal Consciousness: The Case of Classical Legal Thought In America, 1850–1940*, in RESEARCH IN LAW AND SOCIOLOGY Vol. 3 at pp. 9–10 (Steven Spitzer ed. 1980).

25. Lochner v. New York, 198 U.S. at 75 (Holmes, J., dissenting).

26. *Id.* at 65–74 (Harlan, J., dissenting).

27. *Id.* at 66–67 (Harlan, J., dissenting).

28. *Id.* at 70 (Harlan, J., dissenting).

29. *Id.* at 75 (Holmes, J., dissenting).

30. *Id.*

31. *Id.* at 76 (Holmes, J., dissenting).

32. Meyer v. Nebraska, 262 U.S. 390 (1923).

33. Holmes' dissent in Meyer was published as part of its companion case, Bartels v. State, 262 U.S. 404, 412 (1923).

34. Lochner v. New York, 198 U.S. at 56.

35. *See* Abrams v. United States, 250 U.S. 616, 630 (1919) (Holmes, J., dissenting).

36. *See* Paul Brest, PROCESSES OF CONSTITUTIONAL DECISIONMAKING 798 (1975).

37. "Detachment seems the most accurate term to characterize Holmes' stance on the Supreme Court. He was not merely skeptical; his emotions were for the most part not engaged. To put it more precisely, his emotions were stimulated by the professional features of his work but not by its substance. Few judges could pack more emotion into an opinion, but the emotion was not often generated from compassion for the litigants or concern for the seriousness of the issue at stake. It was the emotion of a literary talent, a person who liked the sound of memorable phrases. Holmes' aphorisms were original and incisive; they were also repeated often." G. Edward White, *The Integrity of Holmes' Jurisprudence*, 10 HOFSTRA L. REV. 633, 654 (1982).

38. *See* Railroad Retirement Bd. v. Alton R. R. Co., 295 U.S. 330 (1935); Carter v. Carter Coal Co., 298 U.S. 238 (1936); United States v. Butler, 297 U.S. 1 (1936).

39. New State Ice Co. v. Liebmann, 285 U.S. 307 (1932).

40. Colgate v. Harvey, 296 U.S. 404 (1935).

41. Morehead v. New York *ex rel.* Tipaldo, 298 U.S. 587 (1936).

42. Home Bldg. & Loan Ass'n v. Blaisdell, 290 U.S. 398 (1934).

43. Nebbia v. New York, 291 U.S. 502 (1934).

44. *See id.* at 537–38; Home Bldg. & Loan Ass'n v. Blaisdell, 290 U.S. at 422–23, 447–48.

45. *See* Arthur M. Schlesinger, Jr., THE POLITICS OF UPHEAVAL 254 (1960). On the occasion of another decision McReynolds declared, this time from the bench, that "[t]he Constitution as we know it is gone!" *See* Michael E. Parrish, ANXIOUS DECADES 355 (1992).

46. *See* Leo Pfeffer, THIS HONORABLE COURT 311–320 (1965).

47. *See id.* at 314–20.

48. NLRB v. Jones & Laughlin Steel Corp., 301 U.S. 1 (1937).

49. *See* Fred Rodell, NINE MEN 223 (1955); Schlesinger, *supra* note 45, at 464–67, 474–79 (1960).

50. Justice Sutherland retired in 1938, Justice Butler died in 1939, and Justice McReynolds retired in 1941.

51. Dred Scott v. Sandford 60 U.S. (19 How.) 393 (1856).

52. Harsh criticism of the Court was widespread. *See* Schlesinger, *supra* note 45, at 484–90. In Iowa, the six justices who voted to strike down the Agricultural Adjustment Administration were hung in effigy. *See id.* at 488. When the Court invalidated a New York minimum wage law in Morehead v. New York *ex rel.* Tipaldo, 298 U.S. 587 (1936), even former President Herbert Hoover was moved to assail the Court for going too far in denying state authority to regulate working conditions, and the Republican party platform of 1936 called for reversing the decision by a constitutional amendment. *See* Parrish, *supra* note 45, at 367.

53. *See* Wickard v. Filburn, 317 U.S. 111 (1942); United States v. Darby, 312 U.S. 100 (1941); Chemerinsky, *supra* note 3, at 187–91.

54. Day-Brite Lighting, Inc. v. Missouri, 342 U.S. 421, 423 (1952).

55. Williamson v. Lee Optical Co., 348 U.S. 483, 488 (1955). *See also* Olsen v. Nebraska, 313 U.S. 236, 246 (1941): "We are not concerned . . . with the wisdom, need, or appropriateness of legislation."

56. United States v. Carolene Prods. Co., 304 U.S. 144, 152–53 (1938).

57. *Id.*

58. "Where the existence of a rational basis for legislation whose constitutionality is attacked depends upon facts beyond the sphere of judicial notice, such facts may properly be made the subject of judicial inquiry, and the constitutionality of a statute predicated upon the existence of a particular state of facts may be challenged by showing to the court that those facts have ceased to exist. Similarly we recognize that the constitutionality of a statute, valid on its face, may be assailed by proof of facts tending to show that the statute as applied to a particular article is without support in reason because the article, although within the prohibited class, is so different from others of the class as to be without the reason for the prohibition." *Id.* at 153–54.

59. Professor Gerald Gunther deserves credit for coining this extremely apt metaphor. *See* Gerald Gunther, *Forward: In Search of Evolving Doctrine on a Changing Court: A Model for a New Equal Protection*, 86 HARV. L. REV. 1, 12, 20 (1972).

60. McGowan v. Maryland, 366 U.S. 420, 426 (1961).

61. *See* Dandridge v. Williams, 397 U.S. 471, 508 (1970) (Marshall, J., dissenting).

62. *E.g.*, Madden v. Kentucky, 309 U.S. 83, 88 (1940); Lehnhausen v. Lake Shore Auto Parts Co., 410 U.S. 356, 364 (1973); FCC v. Beach Communications, Inc., 508 U.S. 307, 308 (1993).

63. In a different context where the Court was intent upon upholding legislation, it has recognized the difficulty of proving a negative. *See* Miller v. California 413 U.S. 15, 22 (1973).

64. Williamson v. Lee Optical Co., *supra* note 55.

65. *Id.* at 489.

66. Railway Express Agency v. New York, 336 U.S. 106 (1949).

67. *Id*, at 110.

68. Morey v. Doud, 354 U.S. 457 (1957), which was overruled in New Orleans v. Dukes, 427 U.S. 297 (1976).

69. *See* Dandridge v. Williams, 397 U.S. at 520 (Marshall, J., dissenting).

70. *Id.* at 508.

71. Williamson v. Lee Optical Co., *supra* note 55.

72. *Id.* at 487.

73. *Id.*

74. Kotch v. Board of River Pilot Commissioners, 330 U.S. 522 (1947).

75. United States v. Carolene Prods. Co., 304 U.S. 144, 152–53 (1938).

76. Geoffrey P. Miller, *The True Story of Carolene Products*, SUP. CT. REV. 397, 398–99 (1987).

77. Vance v. Bradley, 440 U.S. 93 (1979).

78. *See id.* at 119–20 (Marshall, J., dissenting).

79. *See* Miller, *supra* note 76, at 408–20.

80. Korematsu v. United States, 323 U.S. 214 (1944).

81. In Korematsu, while the Supreme Court professed to be using "the most rigid scrutiny," in fact it accepted the government's factual assertion with no examination at all. *See* discussion in text *infra*, at notes 122–28.

82. United States Dep't of Agric. v. Moreno, 413 U.S. 528 (1973).

83. *Id.* at 534 (emphasis in original).

84. Zobel v. Williams, 457 U.S. 55 (1982).

85. *Id.* at 60–61.

86. Shapiro v. Thompson, 394 U.S. 618 (1969).

87. Vlandis v. Kline, 412 U.S. 441 (1973).

88. Logan v. Zimmerman Brush Co., 455 U.S. 422 (1982).

89. *See* Gunther, *supra* note 59, at 20–24.

90. *See id.* at 21–24.

91. *See* Mark Tushnet, *Justice Lewis F. Powell and the Jurisprudence of Centrism*, 93 MICH. L. REV. 1854, 1856–62 (1995).

92. United States Dep't of Agric. v. Moreno, 413 U.S. at 528, 534 (emphasis in original).

93. City of Cleburne v. Cleburne Living Ctr., Inc., 473 U.S. 432 (1985).

94. Romer v. Evans, 517 U.S. 620 (1996).

95. City of Cleburne v. Cleburne Living Ctr., Inc., 413 U.S. at 446–47.

96. Romer v. Evans, 517 U.S. at 620.

97. *Id.* at 634.

98. Daniel Farber & Suzanna Sherry, *The Pariah Principle*, 13 CONST. COMMENTARY 257 (1996).

99. Akhil Reed Amar, *Attainder and Amendment 2: Romer's Rightness*, 95 MICH. L. REV. 203, 208–10 (1996).

100. City of Cleburne v. Cleburne Living Ctr., Inc., 473 U.S. at 458 (Marshall, J., concurring in part and dissenting in part).

101. *Id.*

102. Cass Sunstein, *Foreword: Leaving Things Undecided*, 110 HARV. L. REV. 4, 61 (1996).

103. *Id.*

104. Brief of Laurence H. Tribe, John Hart Ely, Gerald Gunther, Philip B. Kurland, and Kathleen M. Sullivan as Amici Curiae in Support of Respondents, Romer v. Evans, 517 U.S. 620 (1996) (No. 94–1039).

105. Romer v. Evans, 517 U.S. at 635.

106. *Id.* at 633.

107. United States R.R. Retirement Bd. v. Fritz, 449 U.S. 166 (1980).

108. *Id.* at 190 (Brennan, J., dissenting).

109. *Id.* at 183 (Brennan, J., dissenting).

110. *Id.* at 187 (Brennan, J., dissenting). Similarly, in a later case, Justice Lewis Powell argued in dissent that the Court should not acquiesce to "post hoc hypotheses

about legislative purpose, unsupported by the legislative history." Schweiker v. Wilson, 450 U.S. 221, 244 (1981) (Powell, J., dissenting).

111. United States R.R. Retirement Bd. v. Fritz, 449 U.S. at 183 (Brennan, J., dissenting) (emphasis in original).

112. United States v. Virginia, 518 U.S. 515, 516 (1996).

113. Plyler v. Doe, 457 U.S. 202 (1982).

114. *Id.* at 226.

115. *Id.*

116. *Id.* at 224–26.

117. Barnes v. Glen Theatre, Inc., 501 U.S. 560, 582–83 (1991) (Souter, J., concurring).

118. McGowan v. Maryland, 366 U.S. 420 (1961).

119. Marbury v. Madison, 5 U.S. (1 Cranch) 137 (1803).

120. United States v. Carolene Prods. Co., 304 U.S. 144, 153 n.4 (1938).

121. *Id.*

122. Korematsu v. United States, 323 U.S. 214 (1944).

123. *Id.* at 216.

124. *Id.* at 218.

125. *Id.* at 234 (Murphy, J., dissenting).

126. *Id.* at 236–39 (Murphy, J., dissenting).

127. Personal Justice Denied, The Report of the Commission on Wartime Relocation and Internment of Civilians 18 (December 1982).

128. *See* Peter Irons, Justice at War 202–218, 280–307, 354–67 (1983).

129. The phrase "sharp difference" is from Gunther, *supra* note 59, at 17.

130. *See id.* at 8.

131. Fullilove v. Klutznick, 448 U.S. 448 (1980).

132. Shapiro v. Thompson, 394 U.S. 618 (1969).

133. Starns v. Malkerson, 326 F. Supp. 234, off'd, 401 U.S. 985 (1971).

134. Memorial Hospital v. Maricopa County, 415 U.S. 250 (1974).

135. Sosna v. Iowa, 419 U.S. 393 (1975).

136. Jones v. Helms, 452 U.S. 412 (1982). This case also is discussed in Chapter 2 *supra*, at note 131.

137. While state classification based on alienage are subject to strict scrutiny, federal ones are not because the Constitution expressly grants Congress authority to regulate immigration and naturalization. Given this express constitutional grant of authority, the Court has ruled that it should ordinarily defer to Congress in this area. *See* Mathews v. Diaz, 426 U.S. 67 (1976); *compare* Hampton v. Mow Sun Wong, 426 U.S. 88 (1976).

138. Folie v. Connelie, 435 U.S. 291, 295 (1978).

139. *Id.* at 296.

140. United States v. O'Brien, 391 U.S. 367 (1968).

141. *Id.* at 376–77.

142. Hoyt v. Florida, 368 U.S. 57 (1961).

143. Reed v. Reed, 404 U.S. 71 (1971).

144. Frontiero v. Richardson, 411 U.S. 677 (1973).

145. Craig v. Boren, 429 U.S. 190 (1976).

146. Kirchberg v. Feenstra, 450 U.S. 455 (1981).

147. Mississippi Univ. for Women v. Hogan, 458 U.S. 718 (1982).

148. City of Cleburne v. Cleburne Living Ctr., Inc., 473 U.S. 432 (1985).

149. *See* Jeffrey M. Shaman, *Persons Who Are Mentally Retarded: Their Right to Marry and Have Children*, 12 FAM. L.Q. 61, 67–70 (1978); City of Cleburne v. Cleburne Living Ctr., Inc., 473 U.S. at 467 (Marshall, J., concurring in the judgment in part and dissenting in part).

150. "[I]f the large and amorphous class of the mentally retarded were deemed quasi-suspect, for the reasons given by the Court of Appeals, it would be difficult to find a principled way to distinguish a variety of other groups who have perhaps immutable disabilities setting them off from others, who cannot themselves mandate the desired legislative responses, and who can claim some degree of prejudice from at least part of the public at large. One need mention in this respect only the aging, the disabled, the mentally ill, and the infirm. We are reluctant to set out on that course, and we decline to do so." City of Cleburne v. Cleburne Living Ctr., Inc., 473 U.S. at 445–46.

151. Justice Rehnquist was the sole dissenter in the following cases: Weber v. Aetna Cas. and Sur. Co., 406 U.S. 164 (1972); New Jersey Rights Org. v. Cahill, 411 U.S. 619 (1973); Frontiero v. Richardson, 411 U.S. 677 (1973); Jimenez v. Weinberger, 417 U.S. 628 (1974); Stanton v. Stanton, 421 U.S. 7 (1975); Zablocki v. Redhail, 434 U.S. 374 (1978); Duren v. Missouri, 439 U.S. 357 (1979); Wengler v. Druggists Mut. Ins. Co., 446 U.S. 142 (1980).

152. *See* William Rehnquist, *The Notion of a Living Constitution*, 54 TEX. L. REV. 693 (1976).

153. *See* especially Justice Rehnquist's dissenting opinion in Craig v. Boren, 429 U.S. 190, 220–22 (1976).

154. *See* Justice Rehnquist's dissenting opinions in Frontiero v. Richardson, 411 U.S. 677 (1973); Stanton v. Stanton, 421 U.S. 7 (1975); Wengler v. Druggists Mut. Ins. Co., 446 U.S. 142 (1980).

155. *See* Justice Rehnquist's dissenting opinions in Weber v. Aetna Cas. and Sur. Co., 406 U.S. 164 (1972); New Jersey Rights Org. v. Cahill, 411 U.S. 619 (1973); Jimenez v. Weinberger, 417 U.S. 628 (1974); Zablocki v. Redhail, 434 U.S. 374 (1978).

156. Michael M. v. Superior Court of Sonoma County, 450 U.S. 464 (1981).

157. *Id.* at 468.

158. *Id.*

159. *Id.* at 473.

160. *Id.* at 474.

161. Rostker v. Goldberg, 453 U.S. 57 (1981).

162. *Id.*

163. *Id.* at 64–73.

164. *Id.* at 69.

165. *Id.*

166. *Id.* at 69–70.

167. *See* Mississippi Univ. for Women, 458 U.S. 718 (1982); Heckler v. Mathews, 465 U.S. 728 (1984).

168. "Cases such as Michael M. and Rostker . . . raised concerns that the Court's actual exercise of Craig-level scrutiny was weaker than the Craig standard's words had promised." Gerald Gunther & Kathleen Sullivan, CONSTITUTIONAL LAW 698 (13th ed. 1997).

169. United States v. Virginia, 518 U.S. 515 (1996).

170. *Id.* at 531 (citing Mississippi Univ. for Women v. Hogan, 458 U.S. at 724).

171. *Id.* at 571 (Scalia, J., dissenting).

172. Central Hudson Gas v. Public Serv. Comm'n, 447 U.S. 557 (1980).
173. Virginia Pharmacy Bd. v. Virginia Consumer Council, 425 U.S. 784 (1976).
174. *See, e.g.*, Metromedia, Inc. v. San Diego, 453 U.S. 490 (1981); *In re* R.M.J., 455 U.S. 191 (1982); Bolger v. Youngs Drug Prods. Corp., 463 U.S. 60 (1983).
175. Posadas de Puerto Rico Assoc. v. Tourism Co., 478 U.S. 328 (1986).
176. *Id.*
177. *Id.* at 359 (Stevens, J., dissenting).
178. *Id.* at 345–46.
179. *See* Tribe, *supra* note 8, at 903.
180. *Id.* at 903–904.
181. Board of Trustees of the State Univ. of New York v. Fox, 492 U.S. 469 (1989).
182. City of Cincinnati v. Discovery Network, Inc., 507 U.S. 410 (1993).
183. Edenfield v. Fane, 507 U.S. 761 (1993).
184. Rubin v. Coors Brewing Co., 514 U.S. 476 (1995).
185. *Id.* at 486.
186. *Id.* at 487.
187. *Id.*
188. 44 Liquormart v. Rhode Island, 517 U.S. 484 (1996).
189. *Id.* at 1509–10.
190. *Id.* at 1511.
191. *Id.*
192. *Id.* at 1521 (O'Connor, J., concurring).
193. *Id.* at 1522 (O'Connor, J., concurring).
194. *Id.* at 1522.
195. *See* Dandridge v. Williams, 397 U.S. 471, 519 (1970) (Marshall, J. dissenting); Richardson v. Belcher, 404 U.S. 78, 88 (1971) (Marshall, J., dissenting); San Antonio Indep. Sch. Dist. v. Rodriguez, 411 U.S. 1, 70 (1973) (Marshall, J., dissenting); Massachusetts Bd. of Retirement v. Murgia, 427 U.S. 307, 317 (1976) (Marshall, J., dissenting); Plyler v. Doe, 457 U.S. 202, 230 (1982) (Marshall, J., concurring); City of Cleburne v. Cleburne Living Ctr., Inc., 473 U.S. 432, 455 (1985) (Marshall, J., concurring); Kadrmas v. Dickinson Pub. Sch., 487 U.S. 450, 469 (1988) (Marshall, J., dissenting).
196. *See* Massachusetts Bd. of Retirement v. Murgia, 427 U.S. at 318 (Marshall, J., dissenting).
197. *See* San Antonio Indep. Sch. Dist. v. Rodriguez, 411 U.S. at 98–99 (Marshall, J. dissenting).
198. Massachusetts Bd. of Retirement v. Murgia, 427 U.S. at 318 (Marshall, J., dissenting); Plyler v. Doe, 457 U.S. at 230 (Marshall, J., concurring).
199. Dandridge v. Williams, 397 U.S. at 519 (Marshall, J., dissenting).
200. Police Dep't of Chicago v. Mosley, 408 U.S. 92 (1972).
201. *Id.* at 95.
202. Plyler v. Doe, 457 U.S. 202 (1982).
203. *Id.*
204. *Id.* at 224.
205. *Id.* at 218–24.
206. *Id.* at 223.
207. *See* text *supra*, at notes 131–39, 156–66.
208. United States v. Carolene Prods. Co., 304 U.S. 144, 153 n.4 (1938).

209. San Antonio Indep. Sch. Dist. v. Rodriguez, 411 U.S. 1, 28 (1973).

210. *See* Korematsu v. United States, 323 U.S. 214 (1944); Brown v. Board of Educ., 347 U.S. 483 (1954); Loving v. Virginia, 388 U.S. 1 (1967).

211. *See* Hirabayashi v. United States, 320 U.S. 81 (1943); Korematsu v. United States, 323 U.S. 214 (1944); Oyoma v. California, 332 U.S. 633 (1948); Graham v. Richardson, 403 U.S. 365 (1971); Sugarman v. Dougall, 413 U.S. 634 (1973); Nyquist v. Mauclet, 432 U.S. 1 (1977).

212. Frontiero v. Richardson, 411 U.S. 677 (1973).

213. *See id.* at 684–88.

214. *See* James v. Valtierra, 402 U.S. 137 (1971); San Antonio Indep. Sch. Dist. v. Rodriguez, 411 U.S. 1 (1973); Massachusetts Bd. of Retirement v. Murgia, 427 U.S. 307 (1976); Vance v. Bradley, 440 U.S. 93 (1979).

215. *See* Doe v. Commonwealth's Attorney, 425 U.S. 901 (1976); Bowers v. Hardwick, 478 U.S. 186 (1986); Romer v. Evans, 517 U.S. 620 (1996).

216. *See* Schweiker v. Wilson, 450 U.S. 221 (1981).

217. *See* City of Cleburne v. Cleburne Living Ctr., Inc., 473 U.S. 432 (1985).

218. *See, e.g.*, Skinner v. Oklahoma, 316 U.S. 535 (1942); Griffin v. Illinois, 351 U.S. 12 (1956); Douglas v. California, 372 U.S. 353 (1963); Griswold v. Connecticut, 381 U.S. 479 (1965); Harper v. Virginia Bd. of Elections, 383 U.S. 663 (1966); Kramer v. Union Free Sch. Dist. No. 15, 395 U.S. 621 (1969).

219. *See* Kenneth L. Karst, *Invidious Discrimination: Justice Douglas and the Return of the "Natural-Law-Due-Process Formula,"* 16 UCLA L. REV. 716 (1969).

220. Harper v. Virginia Bd. of Elections, 383 U.S. 663 (1966); Kramer v. Union Free Sch. Dist. No. 15, 395 U.S. 621 (1969).

221. McDonald v. Board of Election, 394 U.S. 802 (1969).

222. San Antonio Indep. Sch. Dist. v. Rodriguez, 411 U.S. 1, 33–34 (1973).

223. Moore v. City of East Cleveland, 431 U.S. 494, 503 (1977).

224. *See* Chapter 1 *supra*, at notes 136–42.

225. *See* Michael H. v. Gerald D., 491 U.S. 110 (1989), for a pointed debate between Justices Brennan and Scalia about the appropriate level of abstraction to use to determine fundamental rights. *See also* Laurence H. Tribe & Michael C. Dorf, ON READING THE CONSTITUTION, ch. 5 (1991).

226. Chemerinsky, *supra* note 3, at 641.

227. *See* Bowers v. Hardwick, 478 U.S. 186 (1986); Washington v. Glucksberg, 521 U.S. 702 (1997).

228. Bowers v. Hardwick, *id.* at 191–92 (citing Palko v. Connecticut, 302 U.S. 319, 325, 326 [1937]); Washington v. Glucksberg, *id.* at 721 (citing Palko v. Connecticut, 302 U.S. at 319, 325, 326).

229. Southern Pac. Co. v. Jensen, 244 U.S. 205, 222 (1917).

230. *See* Harper v. Virginia Bd. of Elections, 383 U.S. 663 (1966); Kramer v. Union Free Sch. Dist. No. 15, 395 U.S. 621 (1969); Kusper v. Pontikes, 414 U.S. 51 (1973).

231. *See* Shapiro v. Thompson, 394 U.S. 618 (1969); Dunn v. Blumstein, 405 U.S. 330 (1972); Memorial Hosp. v. Maricopa County, 415 U.S. 250 (1974).

232. *See* Griffin v. Illinois, 351 U.S. 12 (1956); Douglas v. California, 372 U.S. 353 (1963); Williams v. Illinois, 399 U.S. 235 (1970); Boddie v. Connecticut, 401 U.S. 371 (1971); M.L.B. v. S.L.J., 519 U.S. 102 (1996).

233. *See* Roe v. Wade, 410 U.S. 113 (1973); Planned Parenthood v. Casey, 505 U.S. 833 (1992).

234. *See* Moore v. City of East Cleveland, 431 U.S. 494 (1977).

235. *See* Antonio Indep. Sch. Dist. v. Rodriguez, 411 U.S. 1 (1973).

236. *See* Lindsey v. Normet, 405 U.S. 56 (1972).

237. *See* Massachusetts Bd. of Retirement v. Murgia, 427 U.S. 307 (1976).

238. *See* Dandridge v. Williams, 397 U.S. 471 (1970); Jefferson v. Hackney, 406 U.S. 535 (1972).

239. *See* Washington v. Glucksberg, 521 U.S. 702 (1997); Vacco v. Quill, 521 U.S. 793 (1997).

240. *See* text *supra*, at notes 200–201.

241. *See* text *supra*, at notes 131–32, 161–67.

242. Plyler v. Doe, 457 U.S. 202 (1982).

243. *Id.* at 244–45 (Burger, J., dissenting).

244. *Id.* at 247 (Burger, J., dissenting).

245. *Id.* at 250 (Burger, J., dissenting).

246. *Id.* at 242 (Burger, J., dissenting).

247. *See* text *supra*, at notes 240–41.

248. Plyler v. Doe, 457 U.S. at 223.

249. *Id.* at 221.

250. *Id.* at 244.

251. *Id.* (Burger, J., dissenting).

Chapter 4

Constitutional Fact: The Perception of Reality by the Supreme Court

Being a species of human decision making, the constitutional law process is dependent on human perceptions of reality.[1] Constitutional decisions, like all other legal decisions, are made by judges based on their understanding of the world around them.[2] Thus, constitutional law is determined by the judicial perception of factual reality. This includes not only the "adjudicative" facts that concern the immediate case before a court, but also the "legislative" facts that concern the general situation confronted by a court.[3] Indeed, more often than not courts must focus on general situations rather than particular instances.[4] Legislative facts are no less essential to the judicial function than they are to the legislative one, and therefore are more appropriately referred to, at least in the constitutional arena, as "constitutional" facts.

Questions of constitutional fact lie at the core of every case involving the Constitution. In pre-modern decisions, they may be obscured by the mantel of legal formalism,[5] but they are nonetheless present. Examples of questions of constitutional fact are not difficult to find: Does racial segregation generate feelings of inferiority?[6] Is it harmful to children's well-being for them to distribute religious literature on the streets?[7] Does the distribution of obscene materials cause criminal behavior?[8] Does limiting the length of trucks prevent traffic accidents?[9] The list, of course, could go on and on; the point is that questions of constitutional fact permeate the process of constitutional decision making.

Issues of constitutional fact often cannot be resolved merely from the record of a case. Nevertheless, courts cannot avoid resolving them, except by avoiding deciding cases altogether. If a case is to be heard and decided, the factual questions posed therein must be resolved along with it, if not explicitly then implicitly.[10] Obviously, explicit treatment of constitutional facts is the preferable method for engendering informed decision making. Whether explicit or implicit, resolution of constitutional facts is an inherent part of the judicial process that cannot be eliminated. To properly fulfill their responsibilities, judges necessarily must pass upon questions of constitutional fact.

It is not uncommon to find judges disagreeing, at times vehemently, about constitutional facts. Even (or perhaps especially) at so lofty a level as the Supreme Court, judges can be found accusing their colleagues of drawing conclusions of constitutional fact that are "unfounded,"[11] "speculative,"[12] "questionable,"[13] "facile,"[14] "improbable,"[15] and even "fantastic."[16] This is hardly surprising when the phenomenon that no two persons ever have the same perception of any object or event is taken into account.[17] In observing an aspect of reality, individuals consider it from different points of view, focus upon various elements of it, and filter it through diverse conceptual schemata.[18] As a result, each person's perception of reality is unique.

Given this state of affairs, Supreme Court justices merely manifest human fallibility when they hold differing perceptions of constitutional fact. Human though this may be, it remains a fallibility, and an extremely consequential one at that, considering the determinative role that human perceptions play in the constitutional process. It therefore becomes particularly perplexing to find that over the years the Supreme Court's treatment of constitutional facts has been most undisciplined. Throughout its history, the Court has devoted little attention to developing proper methodology to deal with constitutional facts.

In the absence of adequate methodology, the Supreme Court has rendered many constitutional decisions based on factual assumptions that are extremely questionable. Indeed, in applying contemporary knowledge to older cases, it now appears that numerous factual pronouncements made by the Supreme Court in the past were mistaken and in some instances egregiously so. From a more current perspective it can be said that the Court erred when it proclaimed that "[t]he natural and proper timidity and delicacy" of women make them unfit to be attorneys,[19] or that a law limiting the hours a person may work in a bakery "bears but the most remote relation" to safeguarding health,[20] or that "[i]t is better for all the world, if instead of waiting to execute degenerate offspring for crime, or to let them starve for their imbecility, society can prevent those who are manifestly unfit from continuing their kind."[21]

On occasion, the Court admits its past mistakes. In a 1992 opinion, the Court acknowledged that an earlier line of cases identified with *Lochner v. New York*,[22] which severely restricted the government's ability to regulate business, "rested on fundamentally false factual assumptions about the capacity of a relatively unregulated market to satisfy minimal levels of human welfare."[23] Those facts, the Court continued, "proven to be untrue, and history's demonstration of their untruth" required their repudiation.[24] In the same opinion, the Court further noted that *Plessy v. Ferguson*,[25] the 1896 decision establishing the separate but equal doctrine, needed to be overruled because it was based on a notion "so clearly at odds with the facts apparent to the Court in 1954."[26] These sort of admissions of error by the Court, though laudable, are unfortunately rare. It would be somewhat reassuring if the factual mistakes of the past could be explained as the result of a relatively immature jurisprudence that has since been improved. However, the passage of time is not always attended by increasing enlightenment, and examination of more recent cases reveals little, if any, progress in the Supreme Court's treatment of constitutional fact. The Court's approach to constitutional facts has remained rudimentary, and it still produces extremely questionable decisions.

THE MANIPULATION OF CONSTITUTIONAL FACT

In reading modern Supreme Court opinions, one is struck by a curious repetition of words and phrases; There is a certain terminology that appears again and again in the Court's written decisions. The Court recurringly uses phrases such as "there is no reason to believe,"[27] "we are not convinced,"[28] "the record does not show,"[29] and "we are unwilling to assume."[30] In the same vein, the Court frequently uses words such as "unclear,"[31] "uncertain,"[32] and "unproven."[33] The repetition of this language is telling; it is a manifestation of a strong strain of negativism in the Court's thought processes.

Negativism serves the Court as a means of rejecting assertions of constitutional fact. A prime example of this can be seen in *Branzburg v. Hayes*,[34] in which the Court ruled that the First Amendment right to freedom of speech and press was not abridged by a court order compelling reporters to identify their confidential sources of information to a grand jury. In reaching this conclusion, the Court rejected the contention made by journalists that a refusal to recognize a reporter's privilege to keep sources confidential would have a substantial chilling effect upon the free flow of information to the press. This contention is an empirical matter, which can be neither proved nor disproved absolutely. While it is a contention that seems to make sense as a matter of logic, the journalists did not rest their position on logic alone. Rather, they took the additional step of submitting a considerable amount of evidence to support their contention that a ruling against them would undermine the free flow of information to the press. The record in the case was replete with surveys, studies, and testimony from reporters and editors, all of which indicated that compelled disclosure of sources caused formerly cooperative press informants to become silent.[35] In fact, in one case (*Branzburg* was a consolidation of several cases) the trial judge made a special finding of fact that to compel journalists to reveal their sources of information had the effect of deterring potential informants from speaking to members of the press.[36]

Despite his strong factual record, not to mention logic, the Supreme Court saw little threat to news gathering from the compelled disclosure of confidential press sources. The claim of the journalists that compelled disclosure of their sources would have a chilling effect upon communication of news was dismissed by the Court as "unclear," "uncertain," "speculative," and "doubtful."[37] By thus erecting a wall of negativism around the journalists' assertions, the Court was able to rebuff constitutional fact that appeared to be both logically sound and supported by a good deal of evidence in the record.

When it is not possible to dismiss constitutional facts through negativism, the Court may simply ignore them. This was done in *Wisconsin v. Yoder*,[38] in which the Court held that for a state to compel Amish children to attend school beyond the eighth grade violated their parents' constitutional right to the free exercise of religion. In *Yoder* the state sought to justify its compulsory laws on the ground that more complete schooling was necessary for those Amish children who one day would leave their community to join society at large.[39] In response, the Court stated that this argument was "highly speculative"[40] because there was "no specific evidence of the loss of Amish adherents by attrition."[41] This statement completely disregarded several statistical studies cited in the dissenting opinion of Justice William Douglas showing that a significant number of persons do leave the Amish community.[42]

The same sort of judicial myopia was present in *Michael M. v. Sonoma County Superior Court*,[43] in which the Court ruled that it was not unconstitutional for a state to make statutory rape a crime for men but not for women. The Court's plurality opinion, written by Justice William Rehnquist, was able to sustain this form of sexual discrimination by presuming that gender-neutral statutory rape laws "may well be incapable of enforcement."[44] What this presumption overlooked was that thirty-seven states previously had enacted gender-neutral statutory rape laws, and had shown no difficulty in enforcing them.[45]

The use of negativism can be accompanied, as it was in *Branzburg*, by a perverse twist of logic: A fact that is unclear or unproven is treated as establishing the existence of its opposite. Thus, the Court leapfrogs from the uncertainty that compelled disclosure of confidential sources chills speech to the exact opposite conclusion, namely, that it is certain that compelled disclosure does not chill speech.[46] In doing this, the Court ignores that a speculative or undocumented assertion of fact may nevertheless be correct, or that its antithesis may not be correct. For example, if it is uncertain or unproven that Jane Doe was at home on the evening of April 16, it does not establish that she was not at home at that time. For all that is known about Ms. Doe, it is entirely possible that she was in fact at home on the sixteenth, and it would be unwarranted to say that she was not. It is a logical fallacy to treat the uncertainty of an assertion as amounting to proof of its antithesis.

In *Branzburg*, this leap of logic was openly manifest; after impugning the assertion that compelled disclosure deters speech, the Court went on to proclaim expressly that compelled disclosure does not deter speech.[47] In other cases, such as *Zurcher v. Stanford Daily*,[48] this sort of sophistry is more tacit. In *Zurcher*, seeing "no reason" to believe that unannounced, forcible searches of newspaper offices threatened the ability of the press to gather or publish information, the Court implicitly assumed that the opposite was true; that is, that the press was not threatened by such searches.[49] This implicit leap of logic has the same result as its explicit cousin: the fallacious assumption of constitutional fact.

The Court's employment of negativism can be highly selective.[50] In *Branzburg*, the negativism displayed by the Court toward the possible constitutional evils of compelled disclosure was held in abeyance for assertions of fact that tended to bolster the constitutionality of such disclosure. In its opinion, the Court stated unqualifiedly that the press has always flourished without constitutional protection of confidential sources, and that the relationship between the press and its informants was unlikely to be inhibited by the threat of compelled disclosure.[51] These statements were made with absolutely no evidence in the record to support them.[52] Obviously, the Court's use of negativism in *Branzburg* is extremely discriminatory. The Court readily accepts one crucial factual assertion (favorable to compelled disclosure) that had no support whatsoever in the record, while rejecting another crucial factual assertion (adverse to compelled disclosure) that had substantial support in the record. The skepticism shown by the Court toward one set of constitutional facts suddenly becomes inoperative for another set of constitutional facts.

This kind of selective negativism also abounds in *Yoder*, in which virtually every factual argument made by the state to justify its compulsory education law was met with critical disdain by the Court. To the Court, the state's position was "highly speculative," and unsupported by the record.[53] In addition to ignoring statistical evidence showing that numerous persons do leave the Amish community,[54] the Court refused to accept the proposition that more education might be helpful to the Amish in the larger world.[55] Indeed, the Court stated repeatedly that there was no reason to believe that if Amish persons leave their community, they will be hindered in the larger society by their educational shortcomings.[56] While playing the skeptic toward the state's argument, the Court was being extremely receptive to arguments beneficial to the Amish position. Further education was unnecessary for the Amish people, the Court professed, because even without it they are "productive,"[57] "effective,"[58] "highly self-sufficient,"[59] and "highly successful."[60] While the Court's view of the Amish is not unfounded, it is somewhat exaggerated and does ignore several less desirable characteristics of Amish communities.[61] The point here is not to disparage the Amish, who certainly seem to be no more deserving of censure than any other group of persons. Rather, the point is that in *Yoder*, as far as the Court was concerned, the Amish could do no wrong and the state could do no right.

The opinions in *Yoder* and *Branzburg* demonstrate that the Court is quite capable of suspending its disbelief when it is inclined to do so. In both cases the Court readily accepted assertions of constitutional fact that were highly questionable: the press will flourish despite compelled disclosure of sources, and the Amish will flourish (even in the world at large) despite their limited education. In adopting these disputable assertions of constitutional fact, the Court displayed a pronounced facility for acquiescence to dubious factual matters.

In numerous other cases, the Court has been quick to accede to factual assertions of dubious validity. For example, in *Heffron v. International Society for Krishna Consciousness, Inc.*,[62] the Court upheld a state regulation that prohibited the distribution of literature on the grounds of a state fair except at assigned booths at fixed locations. The Court sustained the regulation on the ground that it prevented "widespread disorder."[63] As Justice William Brennan pointed out in dissent, however, there was no showing whatsoever that the distribution of literature caused any more disorder than already existed at the state fair, where face-to-face speechifying was freely permissible.[64] The majority's failure to deal with this point evinces an eager willingness to accept a crucial constitutional fact that stands on rather shaky footing.

Supreme Court justices are human, and human beings have a proclivity to view facts in conformity with the values to which they subscribe.[65] Whatever wisdom they may enjoy, Supreme Court justices are hardly immune from this tendency. Frequently, constitutional facts that displease the Court are treated with great skepticism, while facts that the Court finds agreeable are readily accepted. By selectively applying its critical faculties to some constitutional facts, but not to others, the Court is able to maneuver an opinion toward its goal. Along the way, the Court picks and chooses constitutional facts by their congeniality to the desired result rather than by their apparent validity. Critical in one instant, then indiscriminate or even neglectful in the next, the Court manipulates constitutional fact to suit its own purposes.

The Court's method of ascertaining constitutional fact parallels its method of ascertaining the original understanding of the Constitution.[66] Inasmuch as the original understanding of the Constitution is a matter of historical constitutional fact, the Court's treatment of the original understanding is predictably similar to its treatment of other kinds of constitutional fact. There is little reason to suppose that the Court would treat contemporary constitutional fact differently than it treats historical constitutional fact. As noted in Chapter 1, it is well documented that the Court often devises its own rendition of the original understanding by selecting those portions of the historical record that suit the justices' purposes, while disregarding those portions of the historical record that the justices find less palatable.[67] By manipulating constitutional fact, whether current or historical, the Court is able to obscure the personal value judgments that underlie its constitutional decisions. Those decisions thus are imbued with the appearance of being factually compelled rather than personally chosen by the justices. The manipulation of constitutional fact may occur on a conscious level or an unconscious one, but it does occur. Its roots go deep, and like those of a weed, will be difficult to extirpate.

THE MANIPULATION OF CONSTITUTIONAL FACT AND THE LEVELS OF SCRUTINY

At times the constitutional doctrine expounded by the Supreme Court can be misleading by making it appear that the various provisions of the Constitution call for different tests or rules of constitutionality. Certainly the tests and rules verbalized by the Court for various constitutional provisions differ, at least somewhat in their wording, although in recent years even the wording of tests used for various provisions has tended to become more similar. For instance, in free speech cases, rather than refer to the language of the "clear and present danger" test, the Court often will refer to the "compelling state interest" standard used under the Equal Protection Clause. Whatever difference of wording still may exist, beneath the wording and regardless of the particular constitutional provision involved, there is a paradigm constitutional issue in every case: Is there sufficient justification for what the government has done? Despite the fancy dress rules or tests ostensibly applied by the Court, that question is the essential constitutional question in all cases. It is, unavoidably, a question of both constitutional policy and constitutional fact. When the Supreme Court examines the ends of government action, it is making a policy determination; when it examines the means of government action, it is making a factual determination. The issue of constitutionality is thus made up of two components: ends and means, or values and facts.

Consider, for example, the laws enacted by several states that place limits on the size or weight of trucks that are permitted on state highways.[68] These laws usually are adopted in order to promote the state interest in traffic safety. They place a burden, however, on the free flow of interstate commerce, which is an interest of national concern. To properly evaluate the constitutionality of these laws, it is necessary to make a value judgment about their ends: Is the promotion of traffic safety a strong enough state interest to override the national interest in the free flow of interstate commerce? It also is necessary, to properly determine the constitutionality of such laws, to make factual judgments about them: Do they, in fact, enhance traffic safety? To what extent do they interfere with the free flow of interstate commerce?

Policy and facts, then, make up the core of constitutional decision making. That is, policy judgments and factual determinations are an inherent part of making constitutional decisions.

The Levels of Scrutiny

In examining the policy (ends) and factual (means) support for government action, the Supreme Court uses three distinct modes of judicial review, which are described and analyzed in Chapter 3. These modes are alternatively referred to as "levels," "tiers," or occasionally "tracks." When using minimal scrutiny, the Court is extremely deferential to the legislature. In this mode, the Court begins its review with a presumption that legislation is constitutional and the Court will not strike down legislation unless the party challenging it can prove that it bears absolutely no reasonable relationship to a legitimate state interest. Minimal scrutiny usually amounts to no scrutiny at all; even when invested with a bit of "bite," it remains true to its name, minimal.

The presumption of constitutionality that prevails under minimal scrutiny is extremely difficult to overcome. It thus provides a high degree of constitutional indulgence for legislation. It did not take the Supreme Court long to appreciate that this sort of indulgence is not appropriate for all situations. The Court was quick to see that minimal scrutiny does not provide adequate protection when legislation is based on an invidious classification, such as race or ethnic origin.[69] The Court also realized that minimal scrutiny is not appropriate when legislation impinges on a "preferred" constitutional right, such as freedom of speech,[70] or on a fundamental right, such as the right to privacy.[71] In these three situations, the Court has retained a more exacting mode of judicial review that requires strict scrutiny of the government action in question. Under strict scrutiny, governmental action is not presumed to be constitutional and will not be upheld by the Court unless shown to be necessary to achieve a compelling state interest.[72] Under strict scrutiny, a merely legitimate state interest is not enough to sustain a law, and even when a compelling state interest can be shown for a law, the law will not be upheld unless it is tailored as narrowly as possible.

As utilized by the Warren Court, there was a "sharp difference" between strict and intermediate scrutiny.[73] Scrutiny that was supposed to be strict in theory turned out to be fatal in practice, while scrutiny that was supposed to be minimal in theory turned out to be nonexistent in practice.[74] In reaction to this rigid structure, the Burger Court developed a third mode of judicial review, which operates as an intermediate form of scrutiny.[75] When using intermediate scrutiny the Court will uphold government action if it is shown to be substantially related to an important government interest.[76] Intermediate scrutiny made its initial appearance in a First Amendment case, *United States v. O'Brien*, involving symbolic expression.[77] Thereafter, it was further refined in equal protection cases as a means of evaluating government classifications that are somewhat invidious, such as those based upon gender or illegitimacy.[78] It also has been used in freedom of speech cases involving commercial speech, which the Court believes to be less fragile than other forms of expression, and in other free speech cases in which restrictions on expression are unrelated to its ideological content.[79] Intermediate scrutiny allows the Court to take a more neutral stance that favors neither the government nor the individual challenging government action. Although less exacting than the strict form of review, intermediate scrutiny is not nearly so deferential as the minimal mode of review. While minimal scrutiny operates with a heavy hand on the side of the scale favoring the government, so to speak, and strict scrutiny operates with a heavy hand on the side of the scale favoring the individual, intermediate scrutiny functions with a relatively even balance.[80]

Thus, there are three distinct modes of judicial review that are invoked in their respective spheres. The differences between each mode of review are real; they are not merely rhetorical. Under each mode, the Court takes a different posture in evaluating the policy and factual support for governmental action.

Heightened Scrutiny of Constitutional Fact

Unlike minimal scrutiny, the more heightened modes of scrutiny—intermediate and strict—do not begin with a stance of deference to the legislature. Under heightened scrutiny, there is no presumption that governmental action is constitutional. Therefore, when heightened scrutiny is operative, government action will not be upheld unless shown to be properly related to a sufficiently strong governmental interest. Under intermediate scrutiny, government action will be struck down unless shown to be substantially related to an important government interest, and under strict scrutiny, government action will be struck down unless shown to be necessarily related to a compelling government interest. Under heightened scrutiny, then, the Court, by its own standards of review, should not sustain government action unless it is shown to be sufficiently justified both as a matter of constitutional policy and as a matter of constitutional fact.

In a case calling for heightened scrutiny, especially strict scrutiny, the Court would not be expected to uphold governmental action that rests upon dubious constitutional facts. After all, whether or not government action is substantially or necessarily related to an important or compelling state interest is a matter of fact as well as a matter of policy. For example, in *Metromedia, Inc. v. San Diego*,[81] when the City of San Diego sought to justify an ordinance prohibiting billboards on the ground that the ordinance would reduce traffic accidents, two questions arose: (1) the policy question of whether the reduction of traffic accidents is a strong enough state interest to warrant this restriction upon freedom of speech, and (2) the factual question of whether the prohibition of billboards actually reduces traffic accidents. Unless the second question is examined and answered, there is no way to determine whether the ordinance in question is in fact sufficiently related to the requisite state interest. The *Metromedia* case is one of those cases that is primarily about factual matters rather than policy. That is so because it seems beyond dispute that as a policy matter the prevention of traffic accidents—that is, saving life and limb—is an extremely strong state interest sufficient to warrant a restriction upon billboards, at least a content-neutral restriction. Would anyone seriously argue that if in fact billboards do cause traffic accidents they may not be restricted by a content-neutral law? The question that remains—the real question in *Metromedia*—is whether billboards do in fact cause accidents. Or, to state it the other way around, will the San Diego ordinance prohibiting billboards in fact prevent traffic accidents and thereby save life and limb? To uphold the ordinance without determining that it will in fact reduce traffic accidents would be inconsistent with the principles of heightened scrutiny. Indeed, it would transform heightened scrutiny into minimal scrutiny by presuming governmental action to be factually sound.

The Supreme Court has frequently recognized that meaningful evaluation of constitutional fact is a critical element of heightened scrutiny.[82] The Court has stated that it will not uphold governmental regulations on the basis of speculative or hypothetical facts.[83] Important constitutional rights, the Court has ruled, may not be circumscribed by imaginary state interests.[84] Nothing less than a genuine factual basis for governmental action would seem to be acceptable under heightened scrutiny.[85] Nevertheless, this principle is one that the Court has been willing to ignore when to do so suits its purposes.

In the cases discussed in the previous section,[86] one or the other mode of heightened scrutiny supposedly was in effect, yet the Court readily accepted one questionable constitutional fact after another. According to well-established precedent,[87] the governmental action in *Branzburg, Yoder*, and *Zurcher* was subject to strict scrutiny, while the government action in *Michael M.* and *Heffron* was subject to intermediate scrutiny. Thus, in all those cases the Court should have carefully evaluated the basis of the government's claim to ensure not only that it was important or compelling, but also that it was factually genuine. Yet in these five cases the Court willingly acceded to highly doubtful assertions of constitutional fact; failing to comport with the prescribed requirements of heightened scrutiny or of proper adjudicative procedure did not in the least deter the Court.

In these cases, the manipulation of constitutional fact also functions as a manipulation of the mode of scrutiny. The Court claims to be applying strict or intermediate scrutiny, but in reality it is applying minimal scrutiny. This is accomplished by giving undue deference to some assertions of constitutional fact and giving undue disdain to others, according to the whim of the Court. This process is carried to its extreme through the alternative use of negativism and the suspension of disbelief. In *Branzburg*, for example, the Court was extremely negative toward many factual assertions made against the state's conduct whereas the Court suspended its disbelief almost entirely for factual assertions made in favor of the state's conduct.[88] This technique turns strict scrutiny, which was the appropriate mode of review in *Branzburg*, completely on its head. In effect, it reinstates the presumption of constitutionality for government action, which supposedly only obtains in a minimal scrutiny setting. In *Branzburg*, the Court presumed the state's action to be constitutional and then scrutinized it in the most minimal way. What should have been strict scrutiny was transmogrified into minimal.

In *Yoder*, unlike the other cases and although the Court's use of selective negativism might well have been discriminatory, at least the tenets of heightened scrutiny were not violated. Under heightened scrutiny, the state has the burden of showing proper justification for its action. Therefore, in a heightened scrutiny situation, if the Court must be disdainful of one set of constitutional facts, it should be the set of facts that favor the state. To do the reverse, as the Court did in *Branzburg*, is to divest heightened scrutiny of its vitality. It may be preferable for the Court to be evenhanded in its approach to all constitutional facts in any particular case. The Court could treat constitutional facts on a principled, nondiscriminatory basis that shows the same degree of skepticism or acceptance to all factual assertions. However, to suspend disbelief only in regard to constitutional facts favorable to the state's position derogates heightened scrutiny into minimal. This error is compounded when accompanied by negativism directed toward constitutional facts unfavorable to the state. It is by these devices that the Court simultaneously manipulates constitutional fact and the mode of scrutiny.

Minimal Scrutiny of Constitutional Fact

For many years, minimal scrutiny, as practiced by the Supreme Court, operated as virtually no scrutiny at all.[89] This occurred because the Court paid no more than lip service to the requirement under minimal scrutiny that governmental action must be reasonably related to a legitimate state interest.[90] In more recent years two varieties of minimal scrutiny have evolved, one with a bit of "bite" and the other "biteless."[91] The fact remains, however that in the vast majority of cases wherein no more than the minimal level of scrutiny is employed, the Court absolutely defers to the judgment of the legislature.[92] As far as the Court is concerned in the high majority of cases where minimal scrutiny obtains, there is a strong presumption—usually an irrefutable one—that whatever the government does is reasonably related to a legitimate state interest.[93] At times this is carried to the extreme of sustaining legislation based on factual assumptions that are extremely dubious or even demonstrably false.[94]

The Court may adopt this absolutely deferential posture toward either the policy consideration of the government's ends or the factual consideration of the government's means, or toward both of them. The Court's opinion in the *Dandridge v. Williams*[95] illustrates the extreme deference that the Court is capable of showing to both constitutional policy and constitutional fact. In *Dandridge*, the Court upheld a Maryland regulation, challenged as violative of the Equal Protection Clause, that limited the amount of welfare benefits for which larger families were eligible. In upholding the regulation, the Court deferentially accepted the policy determination of the state legislature that it is more important to encourage gainful employment among members of indigent large families than to relieve their more immediate financial plight.[96] *Dandridge*, however, also presented a factual question as to whether the state law at issue did in fact foster gainful employment. Evidence presented in the case, and acknowledged by the Court, revealed that in the families who were party to the litigation, as well as in many other indigent families subject to the regulation, there were no employable persons.[97] As a factual matter, then, it seemed to be highly dubious whether the regulation would go very far toward accomplishing its putative purpose of encouraging gainful employment. Surely a more reasonable alternative, from a factual standpoint, would have been to limit the application of the regulation to families in which there was an employable person. The factual deficiency of the regulation, though, was of no moment to the Court, which was quick to defer to the legislative judgment of fact that the regulation would effectuate more gainful employment. Thus, in *Dandridge* the Court deferred absolutely not only to a policy consideration, but also to an assertion of constitutional fact that may well have been incorrect.

The Court can effect absolute deference by manipulating policy or by manipulating constitutional fact. The former usually is done by inventing extremely tenuous or even imaginary state interests.[98] It is not unusual, however, for the Court to effectuate absolute deference to the legislature through the manipulation of constitutional fact. When minimal scrutiny is operative, the Court will not strike down legislation so long as "any state of facts reasonably may be conceived to justify it."[99] By itself, that standard is extremely easy to meet, satisfied as it is by the slightest factual rationalization. Yet even that minimal standard has been further weakened by the Court's pronouncement that under minimal scrutiny a party challenging legislation must "negate every conceivable basis which might support it."[100] Logically, this is an impossible burden because it demands proof of a negative.[101] Actually, it requires a good deal more than the proof of a negative; it requires a party challenging legislation to imagine every conceivable reason for the legislation and then negate each and every reason. This inordinate task, imposed upon the party challenging legislation, reduces minimal scrutiny to no scrutiny at all.

An example of how the Supreme Court manipulates constitutional fact through the application of minimal scrutiny can be observed in the case of *Vance v. Bradley*,[102] in which the Court sustained the constitutionality of a Foreign Service regulation mandating retirement for certain members of the Foreign Service at age sixty. The regulation had been challenged as a form of age discrimination violative of the Equal Protection Clause, but the Court upheld the regulation on the ground that it helped to maintain the quality of work performed by members of the Foreign Service. As the Court saw it, this mandatory retirement regulation was justified because at age sixty a decline begins in the physical and mental abilities needed for job performance.[103]

It is, of course, no small irony that the decision in *Vance* upholding a mandatory retirement regulation on the rationale that a person's abilities begin to fade at a certain age was rendered by a small group of elderly persons who enjoy the unique privilege of possessing no less than a constitutional right to life tenure in their jobs.[104] Still, there can be little argument with the proposition that maintenance of job performance in the Foreign Service is a legitimate state interest; it may even be a strong enough state interest to prevail under heightened scrutiny. However, there is a serious question of constitutional fact concerning the decline of physical and mental skills at age sixty. In *Vance*, a considerable amount of medical testimony and a variety of studies were presented to the Court showing that advancing age had no correlation to declining job performance.[105] Indeed, some studies showed that older workers may be more competent than younger ones in the type of work done by the Foreign Service.[106] The Foreign Service's mandatory retirement regulation had been enacted by Congress in 1946,[107] before most of this research had been done, and apparently was adopted with no empirical study of the effects of advancing age.[108] In later years, Congress, in conjunction with the Age Discrimination in Employment Act, produced several reports concluding that older workers perform just as well or even better than younger ones.[109] As a result of this empirical background, the government was unable to submit any evidence in *Vance* to counter the substantial data showing that advancing age is unrelated to decline in job performance.

The Court's reaction to this factual record was to proclaim that under minimal scrutiny the government had no obligation whatsoever to demonstrate the validity of its assumptions of constitutional fact.[110] Rather, the Court stated, the obligation was upon those challenging the legislation to show that Congress had "no reasonable basis for believing that . . . at age 60 or before many persons begin something of a decline in mental and physical reliability."[111] In other words, in a minimal scrutiny setting the party challenging legislation has the burden of proving that the constitutional facts upon which the legislation is based "could not reasonably be conceived to be true by the government decision maker."[112] The factual record in the case appears to show that the persons challenging this regulation had proven exactly that. If the voluminous amount of unrebutted current information presented by the plaintiffs did not amount to a demonstration that there was no reasonable factual basis for the regulation, then such a demonstration is well nigh impossible.

And therein lies the nub of the matter. The Court's treatment of constitutional fact under minimal scrutiny in *Vance* makes it virtually impossible to challenge the factual assertions of the government. What the Court requires of those challenging the government is an insurmountable burden: proof of a negative.[113] This means that nothing will ever suffice to convince the Court that the government has made an incorrect factual assumption. Under the approach taken in *Vance*, it would never be possible to demonstrate that the government had no reasonable basis for its action. Those challenging government action could never do enough to convince the Court that there was no reasonable factual foundation for legislation. Minimal scrutiny of constitutional fact, no less than minimal scrutiny of policy, turns out to be no scrutiny at all. Just as the Court manipulates fact to transform heightened scrutiny into minimal,[114] the Court also manipulates fact to transform minimal scrutiny into none.

This state of affairs should not exist. Under minimal scrutiny, the Court's total deference to legislative policy does not necessitate the same degree of deference toward legislative assumptions about constitutional fact. Cases like *Dandridge* and *Vance* illustrate that policy and fact often are two separate questions that need not be treated with the same apprehensiveness. As originally conceived, minimal scrutiny did not require the Court to give absolute deference to legislative assumptions concerning constitutional fact. According to the original version of minimal scrutiny, as described in the *Carolene Products* case,[115] the presumption that legislation had a sound factual basis could be challenged and made the subject of judicial inquiry.[116] This meant that in practice as well as in theory, judicial scrutiny of constitutional fact was truly minimal rather than nonexistent, and judicial deference to factual assumptions made by the legislature was extreme but not absolute. However, the original form of minimal scrutiny has devolved into no scrutiny at all either of policy or of fact.

In 1972, a seminal article written by Gerald Gunther advocated what would be a return to the original version of minimal scrutiny.[117] Professor Gunther advanced a model of judicial review that, in some circumstances, called for heightened scrutiny of the means of governmental action while retaining minimal scrutiny of its ends. The Gunther model was designed for cases arising under the Equal Protection Clause, and, in accordance with traditional equal protection analysis, it emphasized the distinction between scrutinizing governmental ends and governmental means.[118] It is possible, however, to give the model a wider application to all constitutional provisions and also possible to conceive of it as distinguishing between scrutiny of policy and scrutiny of fact. In other words, in minimal scrutiny cases involving any constitutional issue, it is not necessary for the Supreme Court to defer unconditionally to determinations or assumptions of constitutional fact made by the legislature. Minimal scrutiny may be applied with absolute deference to policy considerations while allowing more flexibility in regard to factual considerations.

In recent years, the Court occasionally upgrades minimal scrutiny by granting something less than absolute deference to the legislature.[119] Although absolute deference remains the rule in the vast majority of minimal scrutiny cases, the Court has been willing to put just a bit of "bite" into minimal scrutiny in a few instances. In doing so, the Court usually puts some bite into its review of legislative policy,[120] but it certainly would be possible for the Court to put some bite into its review of legislative fact as well. This would allow the Court to be slightly more critical of legislation founded on factual conclusions that are obviously misguided.

In an opinion written by Justice Oliver Wendell Holmes in 1924, the Court once stated that it was "not at liberty to shut its eyes to an obvious mistake, when the validity of [a] law depended upon the truth of what is declared."[121] Even under minimal scrutiny, it may not be appropriate for the Court to accede to blatantly erroneous assumptions of constitutional fact. Some cases almost cry out for more meaningful review of constitutional fact. Modern advances in knowledge may reveal previous factual beliefs to be clearly mistaken. For example, the mandatory retirement regulation in *Vance*, adopted in 1946 and based upon the putative beliefs of that day, are belied by more current medical knowledge.[122] By 1979 when the case was decided, it was extremely doubtful that those beliefs were still held by Congress, which in 1967 had been moved by more contemporary knowledge to enact a law prohibiting age discrimination in employment.[123] Even if Congress still held the old beliefs, judicial deference to them was inappropriate. After all, the Supreme Court should not acquiesce to the legislative mistakes of the past. Blind obedience to the errors of yesteryear hardly makes for effective decision making, even when minimal scrutiny is the appropriate mode of judicial review.

There are other instances, not necessarily due to advances in knowledge, in which the legislative or executive branch of government makes egregious factual errors. Whether due to prejudice, misinformation, a lack of information, or other causes, such errors do occur. Even the legislature, which is commonly supposed to be well equipped to gather factual information, can make blatant errors of constitutional fact. Cases such as *Dandridge* and *Vance* cast doubt on the presumed ability of the legislature to obtain and act upon factual data, and that doubt is not dispelled by closer examination of the legislative process.

In the first place, the supposition that the legislature is highly capable of gathering data takes Congress as its model, and it fails to consider that many state legislatures have considerably less resources than Congress to obtain information.[124] Even in Congress and the more well-equipped state legislatures, there are substantial problems with the gathering and use of information. Studies reveal that legislators often vote on bills about which they know little or nothing.[125] Furthermore, as described by observers of the legislative process, most legislators make their decisions in a manner that is far from open-minded.[126] Legislators have been known to be bribed to vote in a certain way, and they often are influenced by special interest groups who donate to their campaigns or inundate them with one-sided biased views.[127] Legislators also frequently make decisions about pending legislation before they have studied it or collected information about it.[128] When they supposedly are still in the process of gathering data about a bill, many legislators have already decided how they will vote on it, and may even be actively pursing its passage or defeat.[129] Theoretically, it is at legislative hearings that the legislators can obtain the information that is thought to be so vital to proper evaluation of pending legislation. Attendance at hearings, however, is poor,[130] and when legislators do attend hearings, usually their purpose is not to obtain data, but to propagandize their prepossessed views.[131] Legislators often use hearings as a propaganda device by inviting friendly witnesses and questioning them in a manner that emphasizes the merits of the legislator's position, while unfriendly witnesses, who must seek permission to testify, have their testimony obscured by interruptions and obtrusive questions. Describing several studies of the legislative process, Professor William Morrow reports that it is a rare situation indeed when legislators act as impartial judges and interpreters of the facts confronting them.[132] This is exactly why judges, when reviewing legislation, need to act as *impartial judges* rather than favoring the legislature.

If there is any force to the notion that the Supreme Court should defer entirely to the legislature due to the latter's superior ability to gather facts, that force obtains only in those instances when the legislature actually has exercised its potential ability to gather facts. In other instances when the legislature takes action based solely on factual assumptions or on outdated, incomplete, or biased information, there is no justification for total deference by the Court to the legislature. That is, insofar as constitutional fact is concerned, minimal scrutiny should be genuine though minimal rather than no scrutiny at all. If there is truly a reasonable factual basis for governmental action, it should be accepted by the Court. The Court may even begin its review with a rebuttable presumption that a reasonable factual basis does exist for legislation. But there is no need to irrebuttably presume that reasonableness is present in every case. The Court goes too far when it completely disregards reality by exchanging fact for fantasy.

If genuine though minimal scrutiny was applied to questions of constitutional fact, it would no longer be possible for the Court to rationalize decisions through the manipulation of fact. This would not obviate all of the methods of subterfuge available to the Court, but it would obviate one of the more prominent ones. The Court could still manipulate policy by hypothesizing tenuous or imaginary state interests,[133] but it would no longer be able to manipulate constitutional fact. This would make a critical difference in those cases in which the Court was unwilling or unable to hypothesize tenuous or imaginary state interests. In those situations, a different result may well obtain. It is possible, that *Vance* would have been decided differently had the Court been more true to the record of constitutional fact. Adherence by the Court to a principled and honest treatment of constitutional fact when minimal scrutiny is being used would make for definite improvement in the Court's decision-making process.

CONCLUSION

The Supreme Court's treatment of constitutional fact is problematic in several significant respects. The Court improperly manipulates constitutional fact through the use of a variety of devices, including a highly selective negativism and disregard of facts, alternated with the suspension of disbelief. By resort to these artifices, the Court manipulates its decisions and, along the way, transmutes heightened scrutiny into minimal and minimal scrutiny into none.

The manipulation of constitutional fact manifests a serious lack of discipline on the part of the Supreme Court. This lack of discipline may be traceable to the traditional notion that "legislative" (*i.e.*, constitutional) facts are beyond the legitimate purview of the judiciary.[134] The very phraseology of the term "legislative facts" more than implies that these facts are in the domain of only the legislature and not the courts. Although this notion possesses little, if any, relationship to the reality of adjudication, it nevertheless once reigned as prevailing dogma.[135] Since it was believed to be illegitimate for the Court to consider constitutional facts in the course of making a decision, perhaps we should not have expected the Court to articulate principles for dealing with constitutional facts. It would not be asking too much, though, for the Court to rise above the illusions of myth that surround the judicial process. Constitutional facts could not always be suppressed or disguised, so they would show up from time to time in the Court's opinions, but deliberation of a proper methodology for dealing with them would have to wait until their presence gained legitimacy. Although incipient recognition of that legitimacy appeared in the early 1960s,[136] it is still far from complete, and a disciplined basis for treating constitutional fact is still needed.

Through the manipulation of constitutional fact, the Supreme Court obscures its own creative function in interpreting the Constitution.[137] The Court has always been more or less reluctant to openly display its role of originating meaning for the document.[138] It prefers the appearance of discovering constitutional law rather than making it. In its earlier days, the Court utilized an assortment of natural law concepts to disguise its constitutional creativity. At one time or another, the Court invoked "the divine ordinance,"[139] "the natural order,"[140] "the fundamental laws of government,"[141] "the lessons of history,"[142] "the norms of civilization,"[143] "the concept of ordered liberty,"[144] and "the sense of justice,"[145] all in the name of proclaiming constitutional doctrine. When employing these natural law conceptions, the Court gave the impression that rather than creating law, it was discovering or revealing law that preexisted. With the breakdown of the natural law tradition in the United States,[146] the Court increasingly relied upon the manipulation of historical fact to disguise its constitutional creativity.[147] By twisting the historical record or inventing its own version of it, the Court pretended to find meaning for the Constitution in the intent of the framers of the document. Intentions were devised for the framers in order to cloak the Court's creative function.[148]

Manipulation of current constitutional fact performs the same service. It provides a facade for the Supreme Court's constitutional decisions, and gives them the illusion of being discovered by the Court rather than created by it. In order to maintain this illusion, the Court condescends to the manipulation of constitutional fact. This requires no less from the Court than its scorn for the factual record of a case, as well as disregard of the principles of sound adjudication. It also requires a disdain for reality—a refusal to perceive the world as it is. "How to inform the judicial mind," Justice Felix Frankfurter remarked, "is one of the most difficult problems."[149] And all the more difficult when that mind is closed.

NOTES

1. *See generally* Henry Wolf Bikle, *Judicial Determination of Questions of Fact Affecting the Constitutional Validity of Legislative Action*, 38 HARV. L. REV. 6 (1924); Kenneth Karst, *Legislative Facts in Constitutional Litigation*, SUP. CT. REV. 75 (1960); Dean Alfange, Jr., *The Relevance of Legislative Facts in Constitutional Law*, 114 U. PA. L. REV. 637 (1966).

2. *See generally* Bikle, *supra* note 1; Karst, *supra* note 1; Alfange, *supra* note 1.

3. Id.

4. Arthur Miller & Jerome Barron, *The Supreme Court, the Adversary System, and the Flow of Information to the Justices: A Preliminary Inquiry*, 61 VA. L. REV. 1187, 1193–99 (1975).

5. *See* Chapter 2 *supra*.

6. *See* Plessy v. Ferguson, 163 U.S. 537 (1896); Brown v. Board of Educ., 347 U.S. 483 (1954).

7. *See* Prince v. Massachusetts, 321 U.S. 158 (1973).

8. *See* Paris Adult Theatre I v. Slaton, 413 U.S. 49 (1973).

9. *See* Raymond Motor Transp., Inc. v. Rice, 434 U.S. 429 (1978); Kassel v. Consolidated Freightways Corp., 450 U.S. 662 (1981).

10. *See* Karst, *supra* note 1, at 84–86.

11. United States v. Kras, 409 U.S. 434, 460 (1973) (Marshall, J., dissenting).

12. Heffron v. International Soc'y for Krishna Consciousness, Inc., 452 U.S. 640, 662 (1981) (Brennan, J., concurring and dissenting).

13. Korematsu v. United States, 323 U.S. 214, 236 (1944) (Murphy, J., dissenting).

14. Bates v. State Bar of Arizona, 433 U.S. 350, 392 (1977) (Powell, J., concurring and dissenting); Zurcher v. Stanford Daily, 436 U.S. 547, 572 (1978) (Stewart, J., dissenting).

15. Prince v. Massachusetts, 321 U.S. 158, 175 (1944) (Murphy, J., dissenting).

16. Parker v. Levy, 417 U.S. 733, 762 (1974) (Blackmun, J., concurring).

17. *See* A. Lindesmith & A. Strauss, SOCIAL PSYCHOLOGY ch. 7 (3d ed. 1968), and the sources cited therein at 173–75.

18. *Id.*

19. Bradwell v. State, 83 U.S. (16 Wall.) 130, 141 (1873) (Bradley, J., concurring).

20. Lochner v. New York, 198 U.S. 45, 58 (1905).

21. Buck v. Bell, 274 U.S. 200, 207 (1927).

22. Lochner v. New York, 198 U.S. at 45.

23. Planned Parenthood of Southeastern Pennsylvania v. Casey, 505 U.S. 833, 861–62 (1992).

24. *Id.* at 862.

25. Plessy v. Ferguson, 163 U.S. 537 (1896).

26. Planned Parenthood of Southeastern Pennsylvania v. Casey, 505 U.S. at 863.

27. Zurcher v. Stanford Daily, 436 U.S. 547, 566 (1978).

28. *Id.* at 562, 566; Branzburg v. Hayes, 408 U.S. 665, 697 (1972).

29. Zurcher v. Stanford Daily, 436 U.S. at 561; Wisconsin v. Yoder, 406 U.S. 205, 224–25 (1972).

30. Wisconsin v. Yoder, 406 U.S. at 225.

31. Branzburg v. Hayes, 408 U.S. at 693.

32. *Id.*

33. *Id.* at 693–95; Zurcher v. Stanford Daily, 436 U.S. at 561; Wisconsin v. Yoder, 406 U.S. at 224–25.

34. Branzburg v. Hayes, 408 U.S. at 665. For a discussion of the Court's opinion in Branzburg, see Anthony Amsterdam, *Tuning Out on Civil Liberties*, TULANE LAWYER 3 (The Dreyfuss Lecture of 1979) (1980).

35. Branzburg v. Hayes, 408 U.S. at 730–33 (Stewart, J., dissenting).

36. *In re* Caldwell, 311 F. Supp. 358, 361 (1970).

37. Branzburg v. Hayes, 408 U.S. at 693–95.

38. Wisconsin v. Yoder, 406 U.S. at 205.

39. *Id.* at 224.

40. *Id.*

41. *Id.*

42. *Id.* at 245 n.2 (Douglas, J., dissenting).

43. Michael M. v. Sonoma County Superior Court, 450 U.S. 464 (1981).

44. *Id.* at 474.

45. *Id.* at 492–93 (Brennan, J., dissenting).
46. Branzburg v. Hayes, 408 U.S. at 665, 698–99.
47. *Id.*
48. Zurcher v. Stanford Daily, 436 U.S. 547 (1978).
49. *Id.* at 566.
50. *See* Amsterdam, *supra* note 34, at 7.
51. Branzburg v. Hayes, 408 U.S. at 698–99.
52. *See id.* at 733 (Stewart, J., dissenting).
53. Wisconsin v. Yoder, 406 U.S. 205, 224–25 (1972).
54. *See* text *supra*, at notes 39–42.
55. Wisconsin v. Yoder, 406 U.S. at 224–25.
56. *Id.*
57. *Id.* at 222.
58. *Id.* at 225.
59. *Id.*
60. *Id.* at 222.
61. *Id.* at 247 n.5 (Douglas, J., dissenting). Justice Douglas notes in his opinion that the Amish have problems with "drinking among youth," a high rate of suicide, preoccupation with filthy stories, and that they display "rowdyism and stress" (quoting J. Hostetler, AMISH SOCIETY 281–300 [1968]).
62. Heffron v. International Soc'y for Krishna Consciousness, Inc., 452 U.S. 640 (1981).
63. *Id.* at 653.
64. *Id.* at 661 (Brennan, J., dissenting).
65. *See* Allen Edwards, *Political Frames of References as a Factor Influencing Recognition*, 36 J. ABNORMAL & SOC. PSYCH. 34, 49 (1941); Albert. Hastorf & Hadley Cantril; *They Saw a Game: A Case Study*, 49 J. ABNORMAL & SOC. PSYCH. 129, 129 (1954); Hans Toch & Hadley Cantril, *Readiness to Perceive Violence as a Result of Police Training*, 52 BRIT. J. PSYCH. 389, 392 (1961); Hans Toch & Malcolm MacLean, *Perception and Communication: A Transactional View*, in FOUNDATIONS OF COMMUNICATIONS THEORY 125, 133 (K. Sereno & C. D. Mortensen eds. 1970).
66. *See* Chapter 1 *supra*, at notes 96–162.
67. *See* Chapter 1 *supra*, at notes 144–50 and sources cited therein.
68. *See* South Carolina State Highway Dep't v. Barnwell Bros., 303 U.S. 177 (1938); Raymond Motor Transp., Inc. v. Rice, 434 U.S. 429 (1978); Kassel v. Consolidated Freightways Corp., 450 U.S. 662 (1981).
69. *See, eg.*, Brown v. Board of Educ., 347 U.S. 483 (1954); Anderson v. Martin, 375 U.S. 399 (1964); Loving v. Virginia, 388 U.S. 1 (1967).
70. *See, e.g.*, Schneider v. Irvington, 308 U.S. 147, 161 (1939); Bridges v. California, 314 U.S. 252, 235 (1941); Board of Educ. v. Barnette, 319 U.S. 624, 639 (1943).
71. *See, e.g.*, Skinner v. Oklahoma, 316 U.S. 535, 541 (1942); Griswold v. Connecticut, 381 U.S. 479, 497 (1965); Roe v. Wade, 410 U.S. 113, 154 (1973).
72. *See* Chapter 3 *supra*, at notes 1–2.
73. The apt phrase "sharp difference" is from Gerald Gunther, *The Supreme Court, 1971 Term—Foreword: In Search of Evolving Doctrine on a Changing Court: A Model for a Newer Equal Protection*, 86 HARV. L. REV. 1, 17 (1972).
74. *See* Chapter 3 *supra*, at notes 58–81, 119–30.
75. *See* Chapter 3 *supra*, at notes 139–47.

76. *See* Chapter 3 *supra*, at note 141.

77. United States v. O'Brien, 391 U.S. 367 (1968). The O'Brien debut of intermediate scrutiny is discussed in Chapter 3 *supra*, at notes 140–42.

78. *E.g.*, Reed v. Reed, 404 U.S. 71 (1971); Weber v. Aetna Cas. & Sur. Co., 406 U.S. 164 (1972); Craig v. Boren, 429 U.S. 190 (1976).

79. *E.g.*, Central Hudson Gas & Elec. v. Public Serv. Comm'n., 447 U.S. 557 (1980); City Council v. Taxpayers for Vincent, 466 U.S. 789 (1984).

80. *See* Chapter 3 *supra*, at notes 144–45.

81. Metromedia, Inc. v. San Diego, 453 U.S. 490 (1981). An earlier case that raises a similar issue is Railway Express Agency v. New York, 336 U.S. 106 (1949), in which a New York ordinance banned certain advertising on vehicles, supposedly in order to prevent traffic accidents. Although there was no explanation as to why some vehicular advertising was singled out for prohibition while other advertising just as likely to cause traffic accidents was not, the Court upheld the ordinance by applying an extremely mild version of minimal scrutiny. The Railway Express case is discussed in Chapter 3 *supra*, at notes 66–67.

82. *See, e.g.*, Shapiro v. Thompson, 394 U.S. 618, 629 (1969); Eisenstadt v. Baird, 405 U.S. 438, 447–53 (1972); Wisconsin v. Yoder, 406 U.S. 205 (1972); Roe v. Wade, 410 U.S. 113, 148–50 (1973); Frontiero v. Richardson, 411 U.S. 677, 688–90 (1973); Craig v. Boren, 429 U.S. 190, 199–204 (1976); Metromedia, Inc. v. San Diego, 453, 490, 503 (1981); Schad v. Borough of Mount Ephraim, 452 U.S. 61, 71 (1981); United States v. Virginia, 518 U.S. 515, 555 (1996).

83. *See* United Mine Workers v. Illinois Bar Ass'n, 389 U.S. 217, 225 (1967); Williams v. Rhodes, 393 U.S. 23, 31–34 (1968); Tinker v. Des Moines Sch. Dist., 393 U.S. 503, 509 (1969); Healy v. James, 408 U.S. 169, 188–91 (1972).

84. *See* Califano v. Goldfarb, 430 U.S. 199, 212–17 (1977); Trimble v. Gordon, 430 U.S. 762, 774–76 (1977); United States v. Virginia, 518 U.S. at 516.

85. United States v. Virginia, 518 U.S. at 516.

86. *See* text *supra*, at notes 34–64.

87. *See* text *supra*, at notes 69–79.

88. *See* text *supra*, at notes 34–37, 51–52.

89. *See* Chapter 3 *supra*, at notes 59–82.

90. *Id.*

91. *Id.* at notes 82–88.

92. *Id.* at notes 106–109.

93. *Id.* at notes 54–59.

94. *Id.* at notes 76–81.

95. Dandridge v. Williams, 397 U.S. 471 (1970).

96. *Id.* at 483, 486.

97. *Id.* at 486.

98. *See, e.g.*, Kotch v. Board of River Pilot Comm'rs, 330 U.S. 552 (1947); Goesaert v. Cleary, 335 U.S. 464 (1948); Railway Express Agency v. New York, 336 U.S. 106 (1949); United States R.R. Retirement Bd. v. Fritz, 449 U.S. 166 (1980).

99. McGowan v. Maryland, 366 U.S. 420, 426 (1961).

100. *See, e.g.*, Madden v. Kentucky, 309 U.S. 83, 88 (1940); Lehnhausen v. Lake Shore Auto Parts Co., 410 U.S. 356, 364 (1973); FCC v. Beach Communications, Inc., 509 U.S. 307, 308 (1993).

101. In a different context where the Supreme Court was intent upon upholding legislation, it has recognized the difficulty of proving a negative. *See* Miller v. California, 413 U.S. 15, 22 (1973).

102. Vance v. Bradley, 440 U.S. 93 (1979).

103. *Id.* at 105–108.

104. Article III, section 1 of the Constitution provides that federal judges "both of the supreme and inferior Courts, shall hold their Offices during good Behaviour."

105. Vance v. Bradley, 440 U.S. at 119 (Marshall, J., dissenting).

106. *Id.*

107. *Id.* at 98–99.

108. *Id.* at 120 n.6 (Marshall, J., dissenting).

109. *Id.* at 119–20 (Marshall, J., dissenting).

110. *Id.* at 110–11.

111. *Id.* at 111.

112. *Id.*

113. *See* text *supra*, at notes 99–102.

114. *See* text *supra*, at notes 82–89.

115. United States v. Carolene Prods. Co., 304 U.S. 114 (1938).

116. *Id.* at 153.

117. *See generally* Gunther, *supra* note 73.

118. *Id.* at 20–25.

119. *See* Chapter 3 *supra*, at notes 82–107.

120. *See id.* at notes 82–87, 92–97.

121. Chastleton Corp. v. Sinclair, 264 U.S. 543, 547 (1924); *see also* United States v. Carolene Prods. Co., 304 U.S. 144, 153–54 (1938).

122. *See* Vance v. Bradley, 440 U.S. 93, 117–21 (1979) (Marshall, J., dissenting).

123. *See id.* at 114 (citing congressional reports); Age Discrimination in Employment Act of 1967, Pub. L. No. 90–202, 81 Stat. 602 (codified as 29 U.S.C. § 621) (1967).

124. *See* American Political Science Association, AMERICAN STATE LEGISLATURES 141–42 (1969); The Citizens Conference on State Legislatures, STATE LEGISLATURES: AN EVALUATION OF THEIR EFFECTIVENESS 39–90 (1971); The Citizens Conference on State Legislatures, THE SOMETIMES GOVERNMENTS: A CRITICAL STUDY OF THE 50 STATE LEGISLATURES 1–36 (1973); The Council of State Governments, AMERICAN STATES LEGISLATURES: THEIR STRUCTURES AND PROCEDURES 27–68 (1977); A. Rosenthal, LEGISLATIVE PERFORMANCE IN THE STATES: EXPLORATIONS OF COMMITTEE BEHAVIORS 36–65, 146–65 (1974); James A. Garner, *The Positive Revolution That Wasn't: Constitutional Universalism in the States*, 4 ROGER WILLIAMS U.L. REV. 109, 116 (1998); Roger Kersh, *et al.*, *"More A Distinction of Words than Things": The Evolution of Separated Powers in the American States*, 4 ROGER WILLIAMS U.L. REV. 5, 38 (1998).

125. *See* Charles M. Lamb, *Judicial Restraint on the Supreme Court*, in SUPREME COURT ACTIVISM AND RESTRAINT 12–13 (S. Halpern & C. Lamb eds. 1982).

126. *See* William Morrow, CONGRESSIONAL COMMITTEES 91–99 (1969); David Truman, THE GOVERNMENTAL PROCESS 369–86 (2d ed. 1971).

127. *See* Morrow, *supra* note 126, at 91–96; Truman, *supra* note 126, at 372–74.

128. *Id.*

129. *Id.*

130. *See* Truman, *supra* note 126, at 376.

131. *See* Truman, *supra* note 126.

132. *See* Morrow, *supra* note 126, at 93.

133. *See* text *supra*, at note 98.

134. *See* Paul A. Freund, *Review of Facts in Constitutional Cases*, in SUPREME COURT AND SUPREME LAW 47 (E. Cahn ed. 1954).

135. *See* Alfange, *supra* note 1, at 640; Karst, *supra* note 1, at 77.

136. This recognition is evidenced by the Alfange and Karst articles, *supra* note 1.

137. Concerning the Court's creative function, *see* Chapter 1 *supra*.

138. *See* Chapter 1 *supra*, at notes 61–83.

139. Bradwell v. State, 83 U.S. (16 Wall.) 130, 141 (1872) (Bradley, J., concurring).

140. Plessy v. Ferguson, 163 U.S. 537, 544 (1896).

141. Terret v. Taylor, 13 U.S. (9 Cranch.) 43, 52 (1815).

142. *Ex Parte* Milligan, 71 U.S. 2, 126 (1866).

143. Reynolds v. United States, 98 U.S. 145, 164 (1878).

144. Palko v. Connecticut, 301 U.S. 319, 325 (1937).

145. Rochin v. California, 342 U.S. 165, 173 (1952).

146. *See* Benjamin Fletcher Wright, AMERICAN INTERPRETATIONS OF NATURAL LAW 330 (1931); John Hart Ely, DEMOCRACY AND DISTRUST: A THEORY OF JUDICIAL REVIEW 50–52 (1980).

147. *See* Chapter 1 *supra*, at notes 70–74, 96–161.

148. *See* Chapter 1 *supra*, at 96–161.

149. Oral Argument, Brown v. Board of Educ., 347 U.S. 483 (1954), *quoted in* L. Friedman, ARGUMENT: THE ORAL ARGUMENT BEFORE THE SUPREME COURT IN *BROWN V. BOARD OF EDUCATION OF TOPEKA* 63 (1969).

Chapter 5

The Puzzle of Legislative Motive

From a very early date, the Supreme Court has taken the position that the motive of the legislature for enacting a statute is irrelevant to the statute's constitutionality.[1] In other words, in reviewing a statute to determine if it is constitutional, the Court supposedly will not inquire into the motive that animated the legislature to enact the statute. Apparently, even the most base of legislative motivations is of no concern to the Court; that the legislature was moved to act by racism[2] or even bribery[3] has no place in judicial review of legislation.

This is problematic in several respects. First, there are some laws that "fairly cry out for invalidation but cannot be declared unconstitutional without referring to motivation."[4] Consider, for example, the Supreme Court's decision in *Palmer v. Thompson*,[5] ruling that the Equal Protection Clause was not violated by a decision made by the city authorities of Jackson, Mississippi, to close all of its publicly owned swimming pools. In so ruling, the Court turned aside the plaintiffs' assertion that the motivation for the closing the pools was to avoid integrating them. This illicit motive was suggested by the fact that Jackson officials had decided to close the swimming pools shortly after a federal court struck down the city's tradition of segregation in municipal services and made clear its expectation that public facilities would be integrated.[6] In addition, the record showed a continuing resistance to desegregation by the city,[7] as well as several contemporaneous statements made by the mayor of Jackson clearly showing an aversion to desegregating the city pools.[8] After a suit was filed by black citizens of Jackson to compel desegregation of city facilities, the mayor pledged that there would be no "intermingling" at the pools.[9] A year later, he proclaimed that "neither agitators nor President Kennedy will change the determination of

Jackson to retain segregation."[10] After deciding to close the pools, city officials changed their tune. For the first time, the mayor asserted that the closing was "due to some minor water difficulty."[11] Subsequently in litigation, city officials claimed that the pools were closed because they could not be operated peacefully or economically on an integrated basis.[12] This claim was entirely speculative, as no evidence was offered to support it.[13] All of this was irrelevant as far as a majority of the Court was concerned, because illicit motive has no bearing on the constitutionality of government action.

Taken as a whole, the evidence in *Palmer* indicates overwhelmingly that the underlying motivation for closing the Jackson pools was to avoid desegregating them. If a majority of the Supreme Court had been willing to take motivation into account, surely the weight of the evidence was more than sufficient to raise the suspicion of racial animus, which would evoke strict scrutiny by the Court. *Palmer* is a case that "cries out" for the Court to consider legislative motive, because a record that so strongly suggests improper racial motivation on the part of government officials deserves much more in the way of explanation than a mere shrug of the shoulders that motive is irrelevant.

The second problem about the Court's refusal to consider legislative motive is that there are some individual Supreme Court decisions that cannot be explained if legislative motive is left out of the equation.[14] The Court's decision in *Griffin v. County School Board*[15] is a striking illustration. There the Court ruled that it was unconstitutional for Prince Edward County, Virginia, to close its public schools rather than comply with a court order to desegregate them. The heart of the Court's decision was its conclusion that the county had decided to close the schools "for one reason and one reason only," namely, to ensure that its schools would not be integrated.[16] A finding of illicit motive, then, was the linchpin of the Court's decision in *Griffin*. Other decisions arouse a strong suspicion that the Court did take legislative motivation into account, but instead of saying so, manipulated other constitutional doctrine in order to find a law unconstitutional. This had led to the criticism that the Court's purported refusal to consider legislative motivation is a "transparent and absurd fiction."[17]

Finally, as discussed in more detail below, there are several areas of constitutional law where the Court has decided that it is entirely appropriate to assess legislative motive in determining the constitutionality of a statute. Ascertaining legislative motivation plays an important role in Establishment Clause and Free Exercise Clause cases[18] and certain free speech cases,[19] as well as in reviewing laws based on nothing more than a bare desire to harm persons,[20] and in deciding what level of scrutiny to use to review legislation that is neutral on its face, but has a disparate impact on the basis of race or gender.[21] In these areas the Court simply ignores its stance against considering the motivation of the legislature. Obviously, this creates a blatant inconsistency in the law and casts doubt on the validity of the Court's frequent pronouncements that legislative motive is irrelevant to a statute's constitutionality.

Before further consideration of the puzzle of legislative motive, some terms need to be defined. Although one esteemed commentator has thought it advisable to use the term "motivation" in lieu of "motive" in order to avoid the baggage carried by the latter,[22] I have chosen to do otherwise, preferring to unpack the baggage rather than stow it away. Because the commonly understood definitions of motivation and motive are virtually the same,[23] those terms will be used interchangeably. It also should be noted that motive (or motivation) has a similar meaning to another pertinent term, "intent," although the latter usually is used in a different context than the former. While motive ordinarily is used in the context of determining the constitutionality of a law, intent normally is employed in the context of statutory or constitutional interpretation, as in the "intent of the framers." Although generally used in different contexts, motive and intent have very similar meanings. They both refer to a state of mind of legislators. That is, motive and intent both refer to thoughts held by legislators.

There is some misunderstanding about the relationship of the concept of legislative motive to yet another concept, that of legislative "purpose." To some degree, the two concepts are similar to one another, which has led the Supreme Court to use them interchangeably on a regular basis.[24] Because the Supreme Court is prone to blurring the distinction between purpose and motive, one must be especially careful in reading the Court's opinions that refer to these concepts. In referring to legislative purpose, the Court often, though not invariably, means the same thing as when it refers to legislative motive. Although some commentators have suggested that it is impossible to articulate a principled distinction between legislative motive and legislative purpose,[25] I believe that it is possible to differentiate the two concepts in a meaningful way. Given the confusion generated by the Supreme Court about legislative motive and legislative purpose, it is important to understand how the concepts may differ, despite the Court's tendency to confuse them.

Legislative motive should be understood as referring to a state of mind of *legislators*, while legislative purpose should be understood as referring to a property of *legislation*. Motive resides within legislators, while purpose resides outside them as an attribute of legislation.[26] Motive tends to be subjective; purpose is objective. In many instances, the motive of the legislature may be taken as evidence of the purpose of legislation, but the latter still exists as a thing apart from the former. The purpose of legislation may be "evident in the character of the [law] itself."[27] It may be expressly stated as part of the text of a law, or it may be implied by the text of a law or perhaps by its known effects in the real world. Usually, the best evidence of the purpose of a law will be its language, although the known effects of a law also may be helpful in determining its purpose. Legislative motive also may be an aid to ascertaining the purpose of a law as long as it is remembered that motive is evidence of legislative purpose, but not necessarily determinative of it. Some people believe that, at most, legislative motive plays a small role in the assessment of legislative purpose. Justice David Souter, for example, says that in ascertaining the purpose of a statute, the "appropriate focus is not an empirical enquiry into the actual intent of the enacting legislature, but rather the existence or not of a current governmental interest."[28] Still, there will be many times when legislative motive is strong evidence of legislative purpose. Ultimately, it is for a court to decide what purpose a statute serves, taking into account its explicit and implicit meaning, its impact upon reality, and frequently the motivation of legislators for enacting it.

Often legislative motive and purpose will be one and the same, but in some instances they will differ. For example, in *U.S. Department of Agriculture v. Moreno* a law denying food stamps to hippies has but one and the same motive and purpose: "a bare desire" to harm a politically unpopular group.[29] On the other hand, in *McGowan v. Maryland* a law requiring businesses to be closed on Sundays, while religiously motivated, was found to have a nonreligious purpose of establishing a uniform day of rest and recreation.[30]

Admittedly, the distinction between motive and purpose offered here is not perfect. Perhaps it is impossible to articulate an entirely neat and clean distinction between the two concepts. Nonetheless, I believe that the distinction has some validity and is useful in thinking about the Supreme Court's treatment of legislative motive. The Court itself may be well advised to reassess its treatment of motive and purpose, toward the end of recognizing that legislative purpose is a relevant judicial inquiry and that one of the factors that may appropriately be considered in determining legislative purpose is the motivation of the legislature. The Court, however, has not yet done this and still frequently uses the concepts of motive and purpose interchangeably.

THE TAINTED HERITAGE OF ASSESSING LEGISLATIVE MOTIVE

Similar to many other constitutional doctrines that have persisted over the years, the notion that the Supreme Court will not inquire into the motivation of the legislature was first enunciated by Chief Justice John Marshall.[31] Yet, some years later Marshall also stated that if the legislature used its authority as a "pretext" to enact a law to accomplish an objective that actually was beyond legislative authority, the Court would be obligated to declare the law unconstitutional.[32] To strike a law down because it is based on a pretext of legislative authority obviously requires an inquiry into legislative motive, an exercise that Marshall professed was anathema to the Supreme Court. Despite this contradiction, Marshall's statement about pretext has enjoyed occasional influence on later decisions.[33] There is little doubt that the predominant maxim, as far as judicial review is concerned, is that legislative motive is irrelevant and therefore should not be considered at all by the Court. Still, Marshall's dictum regarding pretext on the part of the legislature cannot be entirely dismissed because there is more than a grain of truth to it. It certainly seems to be unethical, if not unconstitutional, for the legislature to take action based on a mere pretext that conceals an improper motive. Even Justice Oliver Wendell Holmes, who believed that it was no business of the Court to assess legislative motive, admitted that if he were a legislator, he would think it "dishonest" to use legislative authority as a pretext to accomplish an improper goal.[34]

Holmes, though, was a dissenter when a majority of the Supreme Court, beginning in the early 1900s, became more willing to consider the propriety of legislative motivation. During that time, the concept of legislative motive was enlisted by a majority of the Court to play a significant part in determining whether state or federal legislatures had exceeded their constitutional authority in regulating economic matters. In fact, the issue of judicial review of legislative motive was part of the heated controversy that culminated in the New Deal Court crisis.[35] It will be remembered that the controversy arose around the turn of the century when federal and state legislatures began to enact statutes regulating business in order to improve working conditions. These efforts often were thwarted by a Supreme Court majority bent on maintaining a *laissez-faire* economic system, for the most part unrestricted by government regulation. With Holmes and Louis Brandeis usually dissenting (and joined on occasion by other justices), the majority struck down one statute after another on the ground that they impermissibly restricted the prerogatives of business or property.[36] The most infamous of these decisions, *Lochner v. New York*,[37] in which the Court struck down a law setting maximum hours of work for bakers, became the symbol of overzealous judicial review tied to an outmoded and profoundly conservative ideology devoted to protecting business from government regulation.

The Court used a variety of devices in the service of Lochnerism, and one of them was the practice of assessing legislative motive. While the Court continued to profess that it had no authority to evaluate legislative motive,[38] the Court did not always practice what it preached. During this period, both federal and state laws fell to the Court's axe when the justices suspected an illicit legislative motivation. In the "Child Labor Tax Case,"[39] for instance, the Court struck down a federal law taxing employers of child labor, because in the Court's view the "primary motive" of Congress for enacting the law was not to obtain revenue but rather the then-impermissible motive of discouraging the employment of children.[40] "A court must be blind," declared an indignant Chief Justice William Howard Taft in his opinion for the majority, "not to see that the so-called tax is imposed to stop the employment of children."[41] The attempt by Congress to enact the law under its taxing authority was nothing more than a "pretext" that the Court was obligated to condemn.[42] In *Lochner* itself, the Court turned to legislative motive as one of its reasons for striking down the New York maximum hour law. In response to the contention that the law was a health law within the police power of the state to enact, the Court retorted that the state's assertions "[gave] rise to at least a suspicion that there was some other motive dominating the legislature than the purpose to subserve the public health or welfare."[43]

Decisions like the ones in *Lochner* and the Child Labor Tax Case gave a bad name to the Court's practice of assessing the legitimacy of legislative motive.

That practice was seen as part and parcel of Lochnerism, a device of overactive and misguided judicial review. The fact that Holmes, a staunch opponent of Lochnerism, often objected to his colleague's inquiries into legislative motive was strong evidence to the next generation of jurists that assessments of legislative motive should have no place in judicial review. Making Holmes their champion, the subsequent majority of justices took many of his views as their own, including the one that legislative motive should be irrelevant in determining the constitutionality of a law. Perhaps this was precipitate, especially since denial of the relevance of legislative motive was not necessary to overrule prior decisions that had unduly restricted government authority to regulate business. That much was accomplished by rulings expanding congressional authority under the Interstate Commerce Clause and state authority under the police power to regulate health, welfare, and morals. Those rulings sufficed to redress the constitutional balance and give adequate regulatory authority to both Congress and the states. Therefore, perhaps it would have been wiser to simply increase the scope of federal and state authority without also repudiating the practice of reviewing legislative motivation.

Nevertheless, after resolution of the New Deal Court crisis, the Supreme Court became very reluctant to review legislative motive in cases involving economic legislation. In cases involving federal economic legislation, the Court deferred entirely to Congress, granting that body carte blanche to regulate business as it saw fit, regardless of motive. In cases involving state economic legislation, the Court was similarly deferential unless faced with protectionist legislation that discriminated against interstate commerce. Even in the case of protectionist legislation, however, the Court remained reluctant to review legislative motive, preferring to invalidate laws on the basis of their discriminatory effect rather than ascribing an improper discriminatory motive to the legislature.[44] Although not often, on occasion this led the Court to debatable decisions upholding laws that appeared to be enacted on the basis of improper motivation.[45]

WHY LEGISLATIVE MOTIVE SUPPOSEDLY IS IRRELEVANT

Difficulty

The Supreme Court has advanced several reasons to explain the judicial reluctance to inquire into the motives of the legislature. Foremost, there is the matter of the competence of a court to determine legislative motive. Justice Benjamin Cardozo observed in 1935 that judges are unaccustomed to psychoanalysis and therefore should avoid any attempts to assess the motivation of a legislature.[46] Psychoanalysis was then a relatively new field, and later judges may well have become more accustomed to it. More to the point, however, Justice Cardozo surely overstates the case by suggesting that an ability to practice psychoanalysis is necessary to inquiry into motive. One does not have to be a psychoanalyst or a psychic to ascertain motive. Even prior to 1935, judges were called upon to assess motive in various circumstances. More recently it is not unusual at all for judges to appraise motive. There are numerous criminal laws and civil causes of action that turn upon the presence of a particular motive on the part of private individuals or government officials.[47] In fact, the courts routinely inquire into the motive of administrators in a variety of contexts.[48] With or without psychoanalysis, taking the measure of motive is a familiar enterprise to judges.

Determining the motive or intent that underlies legislation frequently does not involve the formidable obstacles attendant upon determining the original intent that underlies the Constitution.[49] Legislative motivation is not tied to the past in the same sense as is the original understanding of the Constitution. Whereas the original understanding of the Constitution was formulated in the context of a past reality that no long exists, legislative motive usually is considerably more contemporary. The more recent a legislative enactment, the more amenable it is to current interpretation disclosing its underlying motivation. In addition, legislative provisions tend to be much more specific than the general mandates of the Constitution, and the more specific a provision, the more revealing it is of the intent that motivated it. While it may be a virtually impossible task to reconstruct the original understanding of the Constitution, ascertaining legislative motive is a significantly more attainable undertaking.

Still, assessing legislative motive can be a "hazardous matter."[50] An individual member of the legislature may have a number of reasons for voting in favor of a statue, some of which may be proper and others of which may not. This problem is vastly compounded when one considers that the legislature is a collective body composed of many individuals, each of whom may be moved by a different motive (or motives) to enact legislation. As a multi-member body, the legislature may possess a multitude of motives for enacting a particular law.[51] Indeed, the legislature rarely, if ever, will possess a single reason for enacting a law. Frequently, the legislative record only adds to the confusion. The record may include no more than the thoughts of a very small number of legislators, who are speaking only for themselves.[52] As the Supreme Court has pointed out, what motivates one legislator to make a speech about a statute is not necessarily what motivates scores of others to vote in favor of it.[53] These problems have led the Supreme Court to conclude that "[I]t is difficult or impossible for any court to determine the 'sole' or 'dominant' motivation behind the choices of a group of legislators.[54]

It would be foolhardy to deny that in some instances it is difficult or even impossible to discover a sole motivation underlying legislative action. Often there is not a single reason that motivated the legislature, and in those cases it simply makes no sense to search for one. Trying to find a dominant legislative motive also can be a tricky. Because legislative motive is a qualitative matter, not a quantitative one, the determination of a dominant motive is likely to be an extremely subjective and slippery exercise. It seems, then, that by looking for a sole or dominant legislative motive, the Court has chosen an unrealistic standard.

Antithetically, the dominant motivation of the legislature is not always impossible or difficult to ascertain. In fact, by the Supreme Court's own admission, there are times when the dominant motive of a legislature can be determined with a good degree of certainty from the legislative record.[55] For example, in *Church of Lukumi Babalu Aye v. City of Hialeah*,[56] a dominant legislative motive comes across loud and clear. Even if legislative motive may be difficult to determine in some cases, there is no reason to preclude its examination in other cases where that difficulty is not present. It would seem to be enough to allocate the burden of proving improper legislative motive to the party challenging the constitutionality of a law. Where the motive of the legislature is so difficult to ascertain that the challenging party cannot carry that burden, the law in question will survive a claim that it was the product of an illicit legislative motive. On the other hand, if the challenging party can prove the existence of an improper legislative motivation, it hardly can be objected that motive should not be considered because it is too difficult to discover. The difficulty in some instances to determine a dominant legislative motive is not a good reason to adopt a blanket refusal to examine legislative motive, especially when it can be reliably ascertained.[57]

Others have pointed out that the difficulty in determining legislative motive can be reduced if, rather than looking for the sole or dominant legislative motive, the inquiry is whether the legislature was motivated in substantial part by an illicit motive.[58] If so, under this approach, the burden would shift to the legislature to prove that it had an overriding proper reason strong enough to justify its action. This certainly seems to be a more realistic as well as a more appropriate calculus than one based on sole or dominant legislative motivation. If it can be demonstrated that the legislature was moved to act in substantial part by an illicit motive, such as racial animus or religious antagonism, the Court's suspicion should be aroused enough to evoke a heightened degree of judicial review. Where the legislature was motivated in significant part by an improper motive, it is not too much to call upon the legislature to explain its action. When the legislature can properly explain its action, no constitutional violation will be found. Under this approach, there would not be an unrealistic barrier to demonstrating the presence of illicit legislative motivation, yet there would not be an undue burden on the government to justify its action.

Despite its purported difficulty, ascertaining the dominant legislative motivation is exactly what the Court has chosen to do in several contexts. The Court routinely considers the intent of legislators as an aid to statutory interpretation. Chief Justice Earl Warren's opinion in *United States v. O'Brien* acknowledges this practice, but attempts to brush it aside by asserting that the risk of misreading the intent of the legislature is worth taking in order to benefit statutory interpretation, but not in order to decide if a statute is unconstitutional.[59] Nevertheless, that the Court regularly assesses legislative intent as a means of interpreting statutes makes one wonder if it really is all that difficult to determine legislative motive when evaluating the constitutionality of a statute.

Furthermore, it is not easy to brush aside those areas in which the Court does, indeed, turn to legislative motive when evaluating the constitutionality of statutes. As already noted, there are several areas where the Court has decided that it is quite suitable to consider legislative motive in deciding the constitutionality of a statute. Certainly, there are those who would object to this practice. They would assert that in these areas, like others, it is difficult or impossible to ascertain the dominant motive of the legislature. They would further argue that in the vast majority of cases, there is no such thing as dominant legislative motive. Rather, there are multiple legislative motives, none of which can be said to predominate over the others. While these objections might be well-founded, they have not moved a majority of the Court to abandon its pursuit of primary legislative motive. In certain areas, the Court continues on its merry way, attempting to ascertain dominant legislative motive, while in other areas it continues to insist that it is difficult or impossible to determine the dominant motivation of the legislature. Of course, this is not the first time, nor will it be the last, that the Supreme Court has spoken out of both sides of its mouth.

Futility

The Supreme Court also has suggested that there is an "element of futility" in a court striking down a law on the ground that the legislature was swayed by faulty motivation.[60] "If the law is struck down for this reason, rather than because of its facial content or effect, it would presumably be valid as soon as the legislature or relevant governing body repassed it for different reasons."[61] This argument, which is little more than a rationalization, is the weakest one the Court makes for declining to review legislative motive.

To enact a law that would stand constitutional muster the second time around, the legislature would be obligated to demonstrate that it had a sound motive for the law. In some instances the legislature would not be able to do this, and the law would not be re-enacted. In *Griffin v. County School Board*,[62] for instance, it simply is not plausible to argue that the state could find a permissible reason for re-enacting the law closing its schools. In those sort of cases, there is no futility whatsoever in striking down on a law on the basis that it was improperly motivated.

In those instances where the legislature is able to show a sound motive for re-enacting a law, to do so will require the legislature to deliberate as a body and to act rationally. The legislature, realizing upon sober second thought that its original motivation for a law was improper, may decide not to re-enact the law, even though a proper motive for it might be found. The legislature might believe that, although proper, the reasons for the law in question are not that compelling to call for its re-enactment. Although perhaps rare, there are times when the legislature finds its conscience and acts honorably. For the Court to strike down a law because it was inspired by an illicit motive may provoke the legislature to realize that it is not in favor of re-enacting that law. Even in those instances where the legislature decides to re-enact a law, it should not be said that the Court's original action in striking the law down was futile; the Court's action required the legislature to go through the process of rational deliberation. Legislative deliberation and rationality are essential aspects of democracy. Judicial review of legislative motive, then, functions to correct the legislative process.[63] It hardly seems futile for the Court to cleanse the legislative process of illicit motive in order to ensure that laws enacted can be supported by valid reasons. Indeed, on occasion the Court has elevated standards of correct legislative procedure to constitutional status, in one case striking down an administrative rule because it had not been afforded "considered evaluation."[64] For the Court to assess legislative motivation as a means of encouraging thoughtfulness and deliberation on the part of the legislature enhances the government process, and therefore is not a futile act.

Judicial willingness to review legislative motive enhances the democratic process in yet another way. The Court diminishes its own reputation when it closes its eyes to legislative motive that the public perceives to be improper. If it is correct that "[a]lmost everyone in Jackson, Mississippi, knew that the city closed its public swimming pools solely to avoid integration,"[65] it does neither the Court's repute nor the city government's any good to proclaim from on high that motive is irrelevant. In the public view, all the Court does by refusing to consider legislative motive is to make itself complicitous in the sin of the legislature.[66] On the other hand, a greater willingness on the part of the Court to review legislative motivation assures the public of the independence and integrity of the judiciary. Surely, the public must appreciate a judiciary that is strong enough to acknowledge the existence of improper legislative motivation.

Judicial Restraint

It sometimes is argued that the notion of judicial restraint calls for the Supreme Court to avoid inquiries into legislative motivation. According to this argument, the Court should not review legislative motive because it is indecorous for one branch of government to question the good faith of another branch of government. Assessing legislative motive, then, is seen as undue judicial activism that intrudes upon the legislative domain.

Apparently, this argument is one of the offshoots of the bad reputation garnered by judicial review of legislative motive from its association with Lochnerism, which was widely perceived as judicial activism run rampant. Whatever may be true about Lochnerism, however, the argument that review of motive is unduly activist makes little sense. As Professor Theodore Eisenberg points out, if it is necessary to examine legislative motive to measure laws against constitutional requirements, the Court is obligated to do so, notwithstanding niceties about respect for the good faith of the legislature.[67] The Court's role, after all, is to enforce constitutional standards against the other branches of government; hence, it should not be considered intrusive of legislative prerogatives for the Court to assess legislative motivation. When properly understood, the idea of judicial restraint does not call for the Supreme Court to refrain from enforcing constitutional standards against the legislature, even when that entails judicial review of legislative motive. Indeed, the Court's responsibility in our constitutional scheme is to correct the legislature when it acts on the basis of an illicit motive, such as racial or religious bias, that is offensive to the Constitution.

There are times when the legislature does act in bad faith, and the Court should not pretend otherwise. It bears repeating that it does neither the Court nor the legislature any good in the public eye for the Court to be an accomplice to the wrongdoing of the legislature.

Moreover, judicial review of legislative motive should not be considered unduly intrusive of the legislative domain because even when the Court finds the presence of an illicit legislative motive, the legislation in question would not automatically be struck down as unconstitutional. The presence of illicit motive does not necessarily signal a constitutional violation. Rather, it calls for the application of heightened judicial scrutiny. Under heightened scrutiny the burden would then shift to government officials to show that they did, in fact, have proper justification for their action. For example, in *Palmer v. Thompson*, this would mean that once the plaintiffs showed illicit racial animus underlying the city's closing of its swimming pools, city officials would have to provide some factual support for their predictions of violence and economic ruin. If they could provide that factual support, their action should be upheld. But mere speculation should not suffice to sustain their action in the face of such compelling evidence of illicit motivation. In any event, a judicial finding of improper motive still allows the government an opportunity to show a proper reason for its action. This is a fair accommodation of all the interests concerned, including that of the legislature, and therefore does not unduly interfere with legislative prerogatives.

Necessary Extent of Illicit Motive

There also is the supposed quandary of deciding the extent of illicit motive that would be necessary to evoke strict scrutiny of a statute.[68] Before a court may strictly review a statute on the ground of improper motive, must all of the members of the legislature who voted in favor of the statute be tainted by improper motivation? What about a majority of those who voted for the statute, or a substantial portion of them? Should a court subject a statute to heightened scrutiny if it gained passage by a margin of ten votes and of the legislators who voted in favor of it, ten did so for illicit motives? Should a court be suspicious of a statute passed by a margin of one vote and one of those legislators voting aye had an improper motive? Would the equation change if some of the tainted legislators also had a proper motivation? What exactly is the degree of illicit motive that is necessary to make a statute unconstitutional?

This quandary, however, has been artificially constructed by transforming what should be a qualitative matter into a quantitative one. As the Supreme Court itself has explained, "Discriminatory intent is simply not amenable to calibration. It either is a factor that has influenced the legislative choice or it is not."[69] This overstates the case a bit. While it certainly is correct that intent or motive cannot be quantitatively measured, it can be qualitatively appraised. The inquiry should not focus on the number of legislators who may have been moved by an illicit motive, but on the qualitative extent to which the legislature was influenced by an illicit motivation. Moreover, this qualitative inquiry can be easily guided by choosing what one believes is the most appropriate standard from several already available. The Supreme Court could decide to apply heightened scrutiny if the *dominant* legislative motive was illicit or if the legislature was moved *in substantial part* by an illicit motive, or if a statute would not have been enacted *but for* an improper motivation. None of these standards are unduly difficult to apply. Nor are others, whether a bit more strict or a bit more lenient. When all is said and done, it is not difficult to set an appropriate and workable qualitative criterion to decide the necessary extent of illicit legislative motive that will evoke heightened judicial scrutiny. The fuss about the degree of illicit motive necessary to taint a statute is nothing more than a makeweight argument. This is one quandary that does not need to exist and can be readily resolved.

WHY SHOULD MOTIVE MATTER?

The question remains, however, of why legislative motive should be taken into account in determining the constitutionality of a law. If a law is constitutionally proper except for its underlying motive, what harm does it cause? If a law is otherwise constitutional, what reason could there be to strike it down solely because it was inspired by an illicit motive?

Actually, there are several reasons why motive should matter. Foremost, even though otherwise proper, a law that is the product of an illicit motive deprives individuals of something of which they would not be deprived *but for* the legislature's improper motivation. Admittedly, it is true that an individual may possess no right to a certain thing, in the sense that the legislature could deprive an individual of it so long as the legislature acts for a proper reason. Still, a deprivation is a deprivation, and one that might not have occurred but for an improper motivation. In *Palmer v. Thompson*, for instance, individuals were deprived of the use of public swimming pools. Certainly, there is no right to the use of a public swimming pool. There is a right, however, to not be deprived of the use of a public swimming pool *on account of* race. Similarly, there may be no right to a public education, but there certainly is a right not to be denied a public education on account of race, gender, or religion. It matters *why* a person is being deprived of something. A deprivation for an improper reason is harmful and should be considered an affront to constitutional norms.

Furthermore, even though otherwise proper, a law that is the result of an illicit legislative motive causes the harm of stigmatizing its objects.[70] There can be no doubt in *Palmer v. Thompson* that the closing of the swimming pools by city officials was perceived by the public as a horrendous slap in the face of African-Americans. In fact, to call it a horrendous slap in the face does not begin to describe how harmful it was. If the city's history of segregation and the timing of the closing of the pool (shortly after a court decision ordering desegregation) were not enough to convey the message of racial bias, certainly the mayor's statement made that message crystal clear. Fueled as it was by racial animus, the city's action in *Palmer* spread a hostile message that stigmatized and hurt African-Americans, not to mention poisoning the minds of other persons. The harmful impact of this sort of message "is greater when it has the sanction of the law."[71]

In addition, the public often perceives when a law is the product of an improper legislative motive and this creates a deep public distrust of government.[72] Whatever excuses they might offer, the city officials who closed the swimming pools in *Palmer* will be perceived by members of the public—and rightly so, it might be added—as acting out of racial animus. Moreover, by acquiescing to this action, the Supreme Court will be perceived by members of the public as countenancing racism. Indeed, a decision similar to the one in *Palmer* engenders an extremely negative public reaction; to the public, city officials and the Court appear racist and dishonest. In short, by refusing to consider illicit motive, especially when it may well exist, the Supreme Court engenders public cynicism and mistrust of government.

WHEN LEGISLATIVE MOTIVE IS RELEVANT

While the Supreme Court often professes that legislative motive is not to be considered in determining a law's constitutionality, the fact is that the Court frequently does not practice what it preaches about legislative motive. To the contrary, there are at least four areas in which the Court regularly turns to legislative motive in reviewing the constitutionality of laws.

The Religion Clauses

The First Amendment contains two religion clauses: one prohibits the government from establishing religion and another prohibits the government from restricting the free exercise of religion. These clauses require governmental neutrality toward religion.[73] They disallow the government to favor one religion over another, or to favor religion in general over non-religion. In the course of enforcing these constitutional norms, the Court frequently assesses the motivation of the legislature. In fact, reviewing legislative motive has become a customary practice in cases involving the Establishment and Free Exercise Clauses of the First Amendment.

This practice began in Establishment Clause cases in 1963 in *Abington School District v. Schempp*[74] when the Court first ruled that a law does not have the requisite degree of religious neutrality if its purpose is to either advance or inhibit religion. Following *Schempp*, in 1971 the Court announced the so-called "*Lemon* test," which is a three-pronged test used to determine if a statute amounts to an unconstitutional establishment of religion.[75] According to the first prong of the *Lemon* test, a statute will be found to violate the Establishment Clause if it does not have a secular purpose, or as the Court itself has said, if it was not "motivated" by a secular purpose.[76] One of the laws that failed under this standard was an Arkansas statute that prohibited teachers in state schools from teaching about the theory of evolution.[77] The Court struck down that law because "fundamentalist sectarian conviction was and is the law's reason for existence."[78] This illustrates that legislative motivation is an important factor in determining a law's constitutionality under the *Lemon* test.

Moreover, the Supreme Court will not be swayed by statutory declarations of neutrality that are nothing more than pretext. Thus, in *Stone v. Graham*,[79] where the Court struck down a Kentucky statute requiring the Ten Commandments to be posted in public school classrooms, the Court was not dissuaded by the fact that the statute required each display of the Ten Commandments to include a notation stating that "[t]he secular application of the Ten Commandments is clearly seen in its adoption as the fundamental legal code of Western Civilization and the Common Law of the United States."[80] Unmoved by this avowal, the Court found that the pre-eminent purpose of the Kentucky law was "plainly religious in nature."[81] This case demonstrates that in religion cases the Court is not only willing to assess legislative motivation, but will do so to the extent of rejecting what the legislature claims to be its purpose. The Court should be commended for doing this, at least in cases like *Stone v. Graham*, where the avowed purpose of the legislature is so blatantly pretextual. The Court honors its role of enforcing the Constitution when it corrects legislative duplicity.

While Chief Justice William Rehnquist has criticized the *Lemon* test[82] and Justice Antonin Scalia has advocated that it be overruled,[83] a majority of the Court remains committed to it.[84] In one case, Justice Scalia argued in dissent that the number of possible motivations of legislators "is not binary, or indeed even finite."[85] He added, "To look for *the sole purpose* of even a single legislator is probably to look for something that does not exist." None of this, however, swayed the majority, which continues to assess legislative motive under the *Lemon* test.

Judicial review of legislative motive also plays a dominant part in Free Exercise Clause cases. The Court's decision in *Church of the Lukumi Babalu Aye v. City of Hialea*[86] illustrates the extent to which the Court will probe legislative motive in order to decide if a law is adequately neutral toward religion as required by the Free Exercise Clause. This case saw the Court strike down a city ordinance prohibiting ritual sacrifice of animals because the Court concluded that the ordinance was directed solely against the Santeria religious faith. *Lukumi Babalu* is a case, similar to *Stone v. Graham*, where the Court dug beneath the wording of a law to evaluate whether the legislative motivation was sufficiently neutral toward religion. In *Lukumi Babalu*, the Court said that the fact that a law is facially neutral toward religion is not determinative of its constitutionality. "([The]) Free Exercise Clause protects against governmental hostility which is masked, as well as overt."[87] A plurality of the Court turned to the legislative record, citing not only statements made by city council members and other government officials but also to reactions of members of the public at a city council meeting, all of which showed a hostile motive toward a particular religion. Thus, the plurality focused on the motivation of not only those who enacted the ordinance (the city council), but also on the motivation of other government officers and members of the public.

While the extent of this in-depth analysis of motivation may be somewhat unusual, it is not unusual at all for the Court to assess legislative motive in both Free Exercise Clause and Establishment Clause cases. The religion clauses are one area of the law where it is a well-established practice for the Court to review legislative motive.

Freedom of Speech

One of the Supreme Court's leading pronouncements that legislative motive is irrelevant to a law's constitutionality came in a free speech case, *United States v. O'Brien*. In that case, the Court flatly stated, "It is a familiar principle of constitutional law that this Court will not strike down an otherwise constitutional statute on the basis of an alleged illicit legislative motive."[88] Despite that statement, however, examination of First Amendment doctrine and decisions reveals that judicial review of legislative motivation is no stranger to the Free Speech Clause.

Board of Education v. Pico is a vivid illustration of why motivation may be extremely relevant to First Amendment principles. In *Pico*, a plurality of the Court explicitly and repeatedly referred to motivation in finding that the First Amendment was violated by a board of education's removal of certain books from public high school and junior high school libraries.[89] While recognizing that local school boards have broad discretion in the management of school affairs, including the management of school libraries, the plurality stressed the undeniable principle that a school board's discretion must be exercised in a manner that comports with the imperatives of the First Amendment.[90] Furthermore, as the plurality explained, motivation may well be relevant to First Amendment dictates:

If a Democratic school board, motivated by party affiliation, ordered the removal of all books written by or in favor of Republicans, few would doubt that the order violated the constitutional rights of the students denied access to those books. The same conclusion would surely apply if an all-white school board, motivated by racial animus, decided to remove all books authored by blacks or advocating racial equality and integration. Our Constitution does not permit the official suppression of *ideas*. Thus whether petitioners' removal of books from their school libraries denied respondents their First Amendment rights depends upon the motivation behind petitioners' actions. If petitioners *intended* by their removal decision to deny respondents access to ideas with which petitioners disagreed, and if this intent was the decisive factor in petitioner's decision, then petitioners have exercised their discretion in violation of the Constitution.[91]

While *Pico* demonstrates how motive can be relevant in an individual case involving freedom of speech, motive also may be relevant to free speech principles on a more general basis. In free speech cases, like many other areas of the Constitution, the Court has developed a multi-tier system of judicial review. In some instances, the operative level of scrutiny will hinge upon the nature of the regulation of speech in question. Regulations of speech that are content-neutral ordinarily are subject to an intermediate level of scrutiny, whereas regulations of speech that are content-based evoke strict scrutiny. Whether a law is content-based or content-neutral may depend upon the motivation of the legislature. Laws motivated by a desire to suppress a particular message are subject to strict scrutiny. Accordingly, in *Texas v. Johnson*, the Court applied strict scrutiny and struck down a Texas law making it a crime to desecrate the American flag.[92] The Court found the Texas law constitutionally deficient because it was motivated by a desire to suppress a disagreeable message. "If there is a bedrock principle underlying the First Amendment," the Court said, "it is that the Government may not prohibit the expression of an idea simply because society finds the idea itself offensive or disagreeable."[93] Similarly, in *United States v. Eichman*, the Court struck down a federal statute prohibiting defacement or mutilation of the American flag, on the ground that it was improperly motivated by a desire to suppress offensive speech.[94] In this case, the government argued that the Court should reconsider its previous decision in *Johnson* because there was a national consensus favoring the prohibition of flag destruction. In declining to reconsider *Johnson*, the Court noted that "any suggestion that the Government's interest in suppressing speech becomes more weighty as popular opposition to that speech grows is foreign to the First Amendment."[95]

These two cases illustrate that a desire to suppress speech because it is offensive to society or to the government is an improper legislative motive, and one that the Court will indeed take into account when deciding the constitutionality of laws regulating freedom of speech. Moreover, in these two cases the Court, much as it did in *Lukumi Babalu*, considered not only the motivation of the legislature, but the motivation of the public as well.

Legislative motive also may be taken into account in cases involving regulations of commercial speech. Professor Ashutosh Bhagwat points out that in a series of cases the Court has adopted the principle that a regulation of commercial speech enacted with the purpose of keeping consumers in ignorance (even supposedly for their own good) is per se invalid.[96] According to this principle, even if otherwise constitutional, a law regulating commercial speech that is tainted with an illicit purpose or motive will be struck down by the Court.

Legislative motive, then, will be taken into account by the Court in several areas concerning freedom of speech. In fact, one commentator, Elena Kagan, sees motive playing an even more pervasive, though covert, role in First Amendment jurisprudence,[97] In Professor Kagan's view, the Supreme Court has developed a body of First Amendment law over the past several decades that "has as its primary, though unstated, object the discovery of improper governmental motives."[98] She asserts that First Amendment doctrine is comprised of "a series of tools to flush out illicit motives and invalidate actions infested with them."[99] She even goes so far as to claim that "First Amendment law is best understood and most readily explained as a kind of motive-hunting."[100] In reaching this conclusion, Professor Kagan goes through a convoluted analysis, which reads a good deal more into First Amendment doctrine than the Supreme Court meant to put there. As a result, she tends to exaggerate the role of motive in free speech cases. Nonetheless, there is some degree of accuracy in what Professor Kagan says about motive and First Amendment doctrine, and her conclusions, although somewhat exaggerated, are not entirely off the mark.

It is undeniable that the Supreme Court does take legislative motive into account in First Amendment cases. In some instances, the Court does so expressly, while in other instances it does so more covertly. In either case, motive is relevant to deciding whether laws comport with the Free Speech Clause of the First Amendment.

Laws Motivated by a Bare Desire to Harm

Chapter 3 describes the development of an important constitutional principle that first emerged in *U.S. Department of Agriculture v. Moreno*.[101] In this case the Court struck down an amendment to the Food Stamp Act that barred eligibility for food stamps for unrelated persons living together. Although using minimal scrutiny in the case, the Court departed from its usual practice under minimal scrutiny of deeming legislative motive absolutely irrelevant to determining a law's constitutionality. Instead, the Court delved into the legislative record and found that the amendment in question was motivated by nothing more than a desire to penalize "hippies" for their lifestyle. This, the Court ruled, was an impermissible legislative motive. "A bare congressional desire to harm a politically unpopular ground cannot constitute a *legitimate* governmental interest," the Court proclaimed.[102] In *Moreno*, then, an illicit legislative motive was not only relevant, it was enough to provoke the Court to put some teeth into minimal judicial scrutiny and to strike down the law in question. After all, the Court did invalidate the law in question in *Moreno* for no other reason than that it was tainted by an illicit motive.

The principle enunciated by the Court in *Moreno* is an important one. It is important to recognize that the government is restricted by the Constitution from taking action if its only reason for doing so is to cause harm to an unpopular group of people. This principle should be self-evident, but unfortunately it is not. In fact, it was not until the 1973 decision in *Moreno* that the Supreme Court first enunciated the principle that a bare desire to harm a group of persons is not a legitimate government interest. Previously, the Court had recognized that religious, racial, or ideological antagonism, standing alone, was not a proper government purpose, but otherwise had not indicated that antagonism against a group of persons was an improper governmental objective.

Professor Cass Sunstein has suggested that the Constitution should be read as prohibiting the government from granting individuals "naked preferences," that is, special favors which have no general benefit to the public.[103] In Professor Sunstein's view, a predilection against the exercise of raw political power is a significant theme underlying the Constitution and is reflected in the constitutional principle of separation of powers, as well as a number of constitutional provisions, including the Privileges and Immunities Clause, the dormant Commerce Clause, the Contracts Clause, the Eminent Domain Clause, and the Equal Protection Clause.[104] This conception of the Constitution also can be seen as implying that the government should be barred from acting on nothing more than a bare desire to harm persons. After all, the other side of the coin of a naked preference is a "naked disadvantage." By granting special privileges to those whom it favors, the government at the same time denies privileges to those whom it disfavors. Therefore, it is not too difficult to expand Professor Sunstein's theory to prohibit "naked harms" as well as "naked preferences." There is much to be said for this idea. Naked preferences and harms would seem to be offensive to several constitutional principles, particularly those underlying the Equal Protection Clause and the Bill of Attainder Clause.[105] Even so, the theory remains Professor Sunstein's theory and not one that the Supreme Court has embraced. To the contrary, the Court has on a number of occasions turned a blind eye to naked preferences. Indeed, the Court's customary practice under minimal scrutiny is to be completely deferential to the legislature, allowing it to grant whatever special favors it so desires.[106]

As a result, it was not until the 1973 *Moreno* decision that the Court first announced what should have been self-evident all along, namely, that it is illegitimate for the legislature to enact a law motivated by nothing more than a desire to harm an unpopular group of people. Even then the principle received relatively little attention until twelve years later in *City of Cleburne v. Cleburne Living Center, Inc.*, which saw the Court strike down a city zoning ordinance that barred a home for persons who were mentally retarded[107] In *Cleburne*, the Court, while professing to again use minimal scrutiny, nonetheless found that the ordinance violated the Equal Protection Clause, because it was motivated by "a bare desire to harm a politically unpopular group," which is not a legitimate governmental interest[108] The *Moreno* principle gained even more prominence in the Court's 1996 decision in *Romer v. Evans*, which struck down a Colorado state constitutional amendment that prohibited the state or any state subdivision from enacting or enforcing any law under which homosexual, lesbian, or bisexual orientation is the basis of a claim of entitlement or protection.[109] Claiming once again to be using nothing stronger than minimal scrutiny, the Court found that the amendment violated the Equal Protection Clause because it was based on "a bare desire to harm a politically unpopular group."[110]

This principle lies at the heart of these three decisions. In each of these cases, the Court struck down laws because they were motivated by nothing more than a bare desire to harm an unpopular group of persons. Legislative motivation, then, will be taken into account, and, in fact, will be enough to strike down a law as unconstitutional, in those instances where the law is based on a bare desire to harm an unpopular group.

Discriminatory Impact

Although the Supreme Court often professes that legislative motive is irrelevant to deciding the constitutionality of a law, the Court has never made the same claim about the effect or impact of a law. Unlike legislative motivation, the effect that a law has in the real world may be considered as a relevant factor in determining the law's constitutionality. For example, in *Gomillion v. Lightfoot*, the Court found that the Fifteenth Amendment of the Constitution was violated by a state law redrawing the boundaries of the City of Tuskegee, Alabama, to alter its shape from a square to a "strangely irregular twenty-eight-sided figure," with the result that almost all the black voters, but none of the white voters, were excluded from the city boundaries.[111] Making no mention of race, the state law was racially neutral on its face, yet its impact was racially discriminatory to an extreme degree. Although there could be no doubt that this law was motivated by an illicit racial animus, the Court's opinion striking down the law spoke more to the discriminatory impact of the law than to the motive underlying it. True, the Court did describe the law as "a device to disenfranchise Negro citizens,"[112] which could be taken as referring to legislative motive. But the Court placed more emphasis on the "inevitable effect" of the law to establish its unconstitutionality.[113] Accordingly, today *Gomillion* is viewed as a decision about the discriminatory impact of a law rather than about the discriminatory motive of the legislature.[114]

It has been suggested that as long as the effect of a law may be considered in deciding its constitutionality, the Supreme Court's refusal to consider motive is of little consequence. The impact of law, according to this suggestion, can function as a kind of stand-in for motive, which will reveal laws that were motivated by improper reasons. Justice John Paul Stevens, for one, has asserted that the difference between motive and effect is not so bright or critical as it may seem to be.[115] In Justice Stevens' view, it can normally be assumed that the legislature intends the natural and probable consequences of its acts.[116] If that is correct, there will be little need to consider legislative motive if the discriminatory effect of legislation can be taken into account. Unfortunately, a majority of the Supreme Court has seen this matter quite differently than Justice Stevens and has expressly rejected the idea that the legislature intends the natural and probable consequences of its acts.[117] As far as a majority of the Court, is concerned, a discriminatory impact, even though prominently foreseeable, ordinarily does not render a law itself discriminatory. In *Personnel Administrator v. Feeney*, the Court ruled, " 'Discriminatory purpose' . . . implies more than intent as volition or intent as awareness of consequences."[118] Under this approach, the discriminatory impact of a law usually has no bearing on its constitutionality, and legislative motive remains irrelevant to a law's constitutionality. As a result, impact does not function as a stand-in for motive, and usually neither a discriminatory impact nor a discriminatory motive, standing alone, will be taken into account by the Court to decide a law's constitutionality.

To make matters worse, in 1976 the Supreme Court moved to limit the significance of impact in determining the constitutionality of a law that is neutral on its face when it ruled in *Washington v. Davis* that only intentional racial discrimination was subject to heightened judicial scrutiny.[119] Moreover, the Court held, a law's racially disproportionate impact, standing alone, was not sufficient to demonstrate intentional discrimination and therefore would not evoke heightened scrutiny. The Court did allow that intentional discrimination could be established by showing a disparate impact so extreme that it amounted to systematic discrimination. Otherwise, a racially disproportionate impact standing alone will be considered unintentional. Thus, while some laws, for example, the one in *Gomillion*, will still be subject to heightened scrutiny because they amount to systematic discrimination, other laws that have a disparate racial impact, but not to the same extent as the one in *Gomillion*, will be subject to mere minimal scrutiny, which virtually always leads to a finding that the laws are constitutional.

In *Personnel Administrator v. Feeney*[120] the Court extended the rule of *Washington v. Davis* to statutes that were facially neutral but had a disproportionate impact on the basis of gender. The Court held in *Feeney* that a law's disproportionate impact on the basis of gender, even when it was very foreseeable, was not, of itself, sufficient to demonstrate intentional discrimination that would evoke heightened scrutiny. Intent, the Court ruled, means something more than "awareness of consequences."[121] As far as a majority of the Court was concerned, neither disparate impact nor foreseeability was sufficient to establish discriminatory intent. And in the absence of discriminatory intent, only minimal scrutiny would be applied, thus insulating the law in question from any meaningful review.

The Court's rulings in *Davis* and *Feeney* are highly questionable. They effectively insulate laws that have a racially disparate impact from meaningful judicial review. They also make it more difficult, perhaps unduly so, to expose intentional discrimination that may in fact be present. Moreover, if a law does have a disparate impact yet is not intentionally discriminatory, subjecting it to heightened scrutiny would not result in a finding that the law is unconstitutional unless the government could not show an important or compelling state interest for it. If a law has an unequal effect upon individuals, why shouldn't the government have to demonstrate a good reason for the law? After all, the only way to determine if a law is intentionally discriminatory is to test it under heightened scrutiny, and it does not seem to be an unfair burden to ask the state to show a good reason for its law.

The decisions in *Davis, Feeney*, and other cases[122] take the stance that disproportionate impact *standing alone* is not enough to evoke heightened scrutiny. These decisions, however, allow that discriminatory legislative motive may be used in conjunction with disparate impact to show the presence of an intent to discriminate. Hence, legislative motive may be considered when deciding what level of scrutiny to use to review legislation that is neutral on its face but has a disparate impact on the basis of race or gender. The Supreme Court has offered no explanation as to why legislative motive may be considered in this context when its consideration supposedly is disdained in others. Perhaps the Court turned to taking legislative motive into account to fill the void that was left by limiting the significance of disparate impact. By restricting the use of disparate impact, the Court made it more difficult—perhaps unreasonably so—to reveal the existence of intentional discrimination. Allowing motive to be considered is a way of redressing that imbalance to some degree. Still, this does not adequately explain why the Court was willing to turn to legislative motive in some instances, when in other instances the Court has turned away from legislative motive on the rationale that is too difficult to ascertain and also an exercise in futility. Perhaps, as the Court has claimed when it comes to using legislative intent for statutory interpretation, it is worth taking the risk with legislative motive to determine if a law is intentionally discriminatory. Yet the perception remains that the Court simply is being unprincipled; legislative motive is too difficult to be bothered with except when the Supreme Court feels otherwise.

Unfortunately, there are still more complications in this area of the law. While the Court has allowed the consideration of legislative motive in conjunction with disproportionate impact, even here it has severely restricted what constitutes motive. As previously mentioned, the Court ruled in *Personnel Administrator v. Feeney* that "discriminatory purpose" implies more than intent as volition or intent as awareness of consequences.[123] The Court further explained that discriminatory purpose "implies that the decision maker . . . selected or reaffirmed a particular course of action at least in part 'because of,' not merely 'in spite of,' its adverse effects upon an identifiable group."[124] It should be noted that this is an extremely unrealistic definition of intentional conduct. Nonetheless, it is the Court's definition and therefore legally authoritative. Still, it is a strange definition of intent that makes it very difficult to demonstrate an improper legislative motive. According to the Court, if a legislative act will have a foreseeably discriminatory effect, it does not demonstrate that the legislature had a discriminatory intent (motive). In the view of the Court, discriminatory legislative intent is only present when the legislature enacts a law "because of" its discriminatory effect, rather than "in spite of" it.

The upshot is that legislative motive may be used in combination with disparate impact to establish intentional discrimination by the legislature, but only when legislation is enacted specially to cause discrimination. Even though a discriminatory effect is the natural and foreseeable consequence of legislation, it does not establish improper motive as far as the Supreme Court is concerned. While the Court will allow motive to be considered in conjunction with disparate impact, what the Court means by motive in this context is quite limited.

In addition to the four areas—discriminatory impact, a bare desire to harm, freedom of speech, and religion—where the Court regularly reviews legislative motive, there are a number of individual cases in which the Court takes legislative motive into account. For instance, in *Califano v. Goldfarb* the Court struck down a federal benefits program that provided survivors' benefits to widows but not to widowers regardless of dependency, because an "inquiry into the actual purposes" of the program revealed that there was no "deliberate congressional intention" to remedy economic disabilities suffered by women.[125] In contrast, in *Califano v. Webster* the Court upheld a federal program that provided a higher level of retirement benefits for women than for men, because its legislative history demonstrated that it was "deliberately enacted to compensate for particular economic disabilities suffered by women."[126] Thus, in selected cases as well as in the general areas described above, the Court will not hesitate to look into the mind of the legislature, notwithstanding the professed dogma that legislative motive is none of the Court's business.

ASCERTAINING PUBLIC MOTIVE—THE INITIATIVE AND REFERENDUM

It would seem especially difficult to determine the legislative motive underlying state statutes or state constitutional amendments enacted through the process of initiative or referendum. With both processes, it is the state's electorate that votes for a statute or constitutional amendment. Hence, the voters perform the ultimate legislative function of enacting laws. In fact, the voters perform even more of the legislative function through an initiative than through a referendum. With the former the voters both initiate statutory or constitutional proposals and vote on them, whereas with the latter the voters vote on proposals after they have been referred to them by the legislature. In either case, the electorate performs the act of legislating, that is, enacting laws. The relevant legislative motive behind a law enacted by initiative or referendum is the motive of the voters—a multi-member group so large as to apparently make it next to impossible to ascertain motivation.

Next to impossible, though, is not quite the same as impossible, and on occasion the Supreme Court has taken on the task of trying to determine the legislative motive that moved an electorate to enact a state statute or constitutional amendment. As previously discussed, on occasion in free speech or religion cases the Supreme Court will consider the motivation of the public as a factor in deciding the constitutionality of a law enacted through the usual legislative process. The Court may be even more inclined to consider public motive in reviewing the constitutionality of a law enacted through a referendum or initiative. After all, if motive should be taken into account at all, it is the motive of the public that should be considered in the case of a law enacted through referendum or initiative.

On occasion, the Supreme Court has considered public motive in determining the constitutionality of laws enacted through a referendum or initiative. For example, in *Reitman v. Mulkey* the Court took public motive into account in deciding that a California constitutional amendment initiated and enacted by the voters of the state amounted to state involvement with private discrimination that contravened the Equal Protection Clause of the federal Constitution.[127] To show the necessary degree of state involvement with private action, the Court repeatedly noted that the amendment was "intended" to encourage private discrimination.[128] The Court's finding of an improper discriminatory motive on the part of the public was a crucial element that led to the conclusion that the state constitutional amendment violated the Equal Protection Clause.

More recently, in *Romer v. Evans* the Court struck down a Colorado constitutional amendment, adopted in a statewide referendum, that prohibited any legislative, administrative, or judicial action designed to protect individuals from discrimination based on their sexual orientation. The Court's opinion in *Romer* did not shy away from assessing the legislative motive of the voters of Colorado. Describing the amendment as "born of animosity" and inexplicable by anything but "animus" toward the class of persons that it affected, the Court concluded that "if the constitutional conception of 'equal protection of the laws' means anything, it must at the very least mean that a bare . . . *desire* to harm a politically unpopular group cannot constitute a legitimate governmental interest."[129]

So, in *Romer*, as in *Reitman* before it, the Supreme Court turned to public motivation to evaluate the constitutionality of a law enacted by the public through a referendum or initiative. This seems to be entirely appropriate as long as it is appropriate to consider legislative motive. If the public is performing the function of a legislature, then it is the public's motive that should be considered to determine if a law was inspired by an illicit motive. While the motivation of the public may be especially difficult to ascertain, the Court should not turn away from that task in those instances, such as in *Reitman* and *Romer*, when the public motive can be ascertained reliably. Just as the difficulty in determining the motivation of the legislature does not justify a hard and fast rule against considering legislative motive, similarly the difficulty in determining the motivation of the public should not justify an automatic rule against taking public motive into account. In those situations where public motive can be ascertained with a reasonable degree of certainty, there is no reason for the Court to shy away from doing so. Decisions such as *Reitman* and *Romer* illustrate that there are times when public motivation can appropriately and successfully be assessed by the Supreme Court.

CONCLUSION

Although the Supreme Court has long professed that legislative motive is irrelevant to determining a law's constitutionality, the Court has honored that tenet more in its breach than its observance. In fact, given how frequently the Court does consider legislative motive, it is more accurate to say that in actual practice legislative motive is relevant to a law's constitutionality and may be taken into account in reviewing a law. If for no other reason than the sake of honesty, the Court should repudiate the doctrine that legislative motive is irrelevant and should openly admit that the opposite is true.

The Court also would be well advised to acknowledge that there is a conceptual difference between legislative motive and legislative purpose. Legislative purpose is an attribute of legislation, which may be indicated by the express wording of a law, the implications of its wording, its effect in the real world, and the motivation of legislators for enacting it. Legislative motive is an attribute of the legislature, which often, although not invariably, will correspond to legislative purpose. Legislative purpose is always relevant to a law's constitutionality. The Court should admit that legislative motive is indicative of legislative purpose and therefore is not irrelevant to determining a law's constitutionality.

There is no good reason why legislative motive should be ignored in deciding the constitutionality of a law. The best reason that can be advanced for disregarding legislative motive is that it may be difficult to ascertain. However, this in no way calls for a rule automatically precluding the consideration of legislative motive. At most, it calls for a rule that the party challenging government action has the burden of proving that the action in question was inspired by an illicit legislative motive. When the challenging party cannot satisfactorily prove an illicit legislative motive, the government action will remain subject only to minimal judicial scrutiny (unless other reasons for evoking heightened scrutiny are present). There is no reason to disallow the challenging party the opportunity to prove an illicit legislative motive, and when the challenging party can meet the burden of doing so, the Court should not turn a deaf ear to the presence of improper legislative motive. The showing of an illicit legislative motive should evoke heightened judicial scrutiny, which calls for the government to offer justification for its action. If that is not forthcoming, the law in question should be struck down. Laws motivated by an illicit purpose should not be winked at by the Supreme Court, because they are harmful. They deprive individuals of benefits that they would otherwise receive. They stigmatize individuals by conveying an illicit message of disapproval. They engender public mistrust of a legislature that acts for shameful reasons and of a court that acquiesces to legislative impropriety.

The simple fact is that it does no good whatsoever for the Supreme Court to continue to pretend that legislative motive is irrelevant. It is neither intellectually honest nor analytically sound to do so. Illicit legislative motive causes harm to individuals, creates public mistrust of the government, and taints the law. The Court should finally admit that legislative motive does matter in determining a law's constitutionality.

NOTES

1. Fletcher v. Peck, 10 U.S. (6 Cranch.) 87 (1810); *Ex Parte* McCardle, 74 U.S. (7 Wall.) 506, 514 (1868). *See also* United States v. O'Brien, 391 U.S. 367, 383 (1968): "It is a familiar principle of constitutional law that this Court will not strike down an otherwise constitutional statute on the basis of an alleged illicit legislative motive."

2. *See* Palmer v. Thompson, 403 U.S. 217 (1971).

3. *See* Fletcher v. Peck, 10 U.S. (6 Cranch.) 87 (1810).

4. John Hart Ely, *Legislative and Administrative Motive in Constitutional Law*, 79 YALE L.J. 1205, 1207 (1970).

5. Palmer v. Thompson, 403 U.S. 217 (1971).

6. *Id.* at 241 (White, J., dissenting).

7. *Id.* at 250.

8. *Id.* at 250–51.

9. *Id.* at 250.

10. *Id.*

11. *Id.* at 251.

12. *Id.* at 253.

13. *Id.* at 253–54.

14. "Some of [the Supreme Court's] decisions, however, can be explained only in terms of motive analysis." Theodore Eisenberg, *Disproportionate Impact and Illicit Motive: Theories of Constitutional Adjudication*, 52 N.Y.U.L. REV. 36, 106 (1977).

15. Griffin v. County Sch. Bd., 377 U.S. 218 (1964).

16. *Id.* at 231.

17. Henry Abraham, THE JUDICIAL PROCESS 322–23 (1962) (quoting Max Radin, *Statutory Interpretation*, 43 HARV. L. REV. 863, 870 [1930]).

18. *See* text *infra*, at notes 73–87.

19. *See* text *infra*, at notes 88–100.

20. *See* text *infra*, at notes 101–110.

21. *See* text *infra*, at notes 111–126.

22. Ely, *supra* note 4, at 1207 n.1.

23. *See, e.g.*, the latest edition of THE OXFORD ENGLISH DICTIONARY or MERRIAM-WEBSTER'S COLLEGIATE DICTIONARY.

24. *See, e.g.*, United States v. Darby, 312 U.S. 100, 115 (1941); United States v. O'Brien, 391 U.S. 367, 383–85 (1968).

25. *See* Note, *Legislative Purpose and Constitutional Adjudication*, 83 HARV. L. REV. 1887, 1887–88 n.1 (1970); Ely, *supra* note 4, at 1221.

26. *See* Ira Michael Heyman, *The Chief Justice, Racial Segregation, and the Friendly Critics*, 49 CAL. L. REV. 104, 115–16 (1961).

27. Radin, *supra* note 17, at 875.

28. Barnes v. Glen Theatre, Inc., 501 U.S. 560, 582 (1991) (Souter, J., concurring).

29. United States Dep't of Agric. v. Moreno, 413 U.S. 528, 534 (1973).

30. McGowan v. Maryland, 366 U.S. 420 (1961).

31. Fletcher v. Peck, 10 U.S. (6 Cranch.) 87, 130 (1810).

32. McCulloch v. Maryland, 17 U.S. (4 Wheat.) 316 (1819).

33. *See, e.g.*, Bailey v. Drexel Furniture Co., 259 U.S. 20 (1922), discussed *infra*, at note 39.

34. *See* Oliver Wendell Holmes to Learned Hand, April 3, 1919, on file in the Hand Papers, Box 103, folder 24, Harvard Law Library, Treasure Room; *quoted in* Gerald Gunther, *Learned Hand and the Origins of Modern First Amendment Doctrine*, 27 STAN. L. REV. 719 (1975).

35. *See* Chapter 3 *supra*, at notes 15–57.

36. *See, e.g.*, Lochner v. New York, 198 U.S. 45 (1905); Hammer v. Dagenhart, 247 U.S. 251 (1918); New York State Ice Co. v. Liebmann, 285 U.S. 262 (1932).

37. *Id.*

38. *See, e.g.*, Hammer v. Dagenhart, 247 U.S. at 276.

39. Bailey v. Drexel Furniture Co., 259 U.S. 20 (1922).

40. *Id.* at 38.

41. *Id.* at 37.

42. *Id.* at 37.

43. Lochner v. New York, 198 U.S. 45, 63 (1905).

44. *See, e.g.*, Hunt v. Washington Apple Adver. Comm'n, 432 U.S. 333, 352–53 (1977): "However, we need not ascribe an economic protection motive to the North Carolina Legislature to resolve this case; we conclude that the challenged statute cannot stand insofar as it prohibits the display of Washington State grades even if enacted for the declared purpose of protecting consumers from deception and fraud in the marketplace."

45. *E.g.*, Exxon Corp. v. Governor of Maryland, 437 U.S. 117 (1978); Minnesota v. Clover Leaf Creamery Co., 449 U.S. 456 (1981).

46. *See* United States v. Constantine, 296 U.S. 287, 299 (1935) (Cardozo, J., dissenting).

47. *See* Palmer v. Thompson, 403 U.S. 217, 241–42 (1971) (White, J., dissenting); Wisconsin v. Mitchell, 508 U.S. 476, 484–85 (1993).

48. Laurence H. Tribe, AMERICAN CONSTITUTIONAL LAW 814–15 (2d ed. 1988).

49. *See* Chapter 1 *supra*, at notes 95–161.

50. United States v. O'Brien, 391 U.S. 367, 383 (1968).

51. Justice Scalia claims that the number of possible legislative motivations is not even finite. Edwards v. Aguillard, 482 U.S. 578, 636–37 (1987) (Scalia, J., dissenting). This is an exaggeration, perhaps, but one that contains more than a grain of truth.

52. *See* United States v. O'Brien, 391 U.S. at 384.

53. *Id.*

54. Palmer v. Thompson, 403 U.S. 217, 225 (1971).

55. *See* Hunter v. Underwood, 471 U.S. 222, 228–29 (1985).

56. Church of Lukumi Babalu Aye v. City of Hialeah, 508 U.S. 520 (1993). See text *infra*, at notes 86–87.

57. *See* Paul Brest, *Palmer v. Thompson: An Approach to the Problem of Unconstitutional Legislative Motive*, SUP. CT. REV. 95, 119–20 (1971).

58. *See id.* at 120; Tribe, *supra* note 48, at 823.

59. *See* United States v. O'Brien, 391 U.S. at 383–84.

60. Palmer v. Thompson, 403 U.S. at 225.

61. *Id.*

62. Griffin v. County Sch. Bd., 377 U.S. 218 (1964) (described *supra*, at notes 15–16).

63. *See* Sheila Foster, *Intent and Incoherence*, 72 TUL. L. REV. 1065, 1101–1105 (1998).

64. Hampton v. Mow Sun Wong, 426 U.S. 88, 115 (1976); *see also* Regents of Univ. of California v. Bakke, 438 U.S. 265, 304–305, 307–10 (1978) (plurality opinion of Powell, J.); Fullilove v. Klutznick, 448 U.S. 448, 549–53 (1980) (Steven, J., dissenting).

65. Brest, *supra* note 57, at 95.

66. *See* Tribe, *supra* note 48, at 822–23.

67. Eisenberg, *supra* note 14, at 117.

68. *See* Fletcher v. Peck, 10 U.S. (6 Cranch.) 87, 130 (1810).

69. Personnel Adm'r v. Feeney, 442 U.S. 256, 277 (1979).

70. *See* J. Morris Clark, *Legislative Motivation and Fundamental Rights in Constitutional Law*, 15 SAN DIEGO L. REV. 953, 964–67 (1978).

71. *See* Brown v. Board of Educ., 347 U.S. 483 (1954).

72. *See* Clark, *supra* note 70, at 967.

73. Abington Sch. Dist. v. Schempp, 374 U.S. 203, 222 (1963).

74. *Id.*

75. Lemon v. Kurtzman, 403 U.S. 602, 612–13 (1971).

76. Wallace v. Jaffree, 472 U.S. 38, 56 (1985). *See also* Epperson v. Arkansas, 393 U.S. 97, 107–109 (1968) (especially at 109 where the Court expressly refers to "motivation"); Stone v. Graham, 449 U.S. 39, 41–43 (1980); Edwards v. Aguillard, 482 U.S. 578, 590–93 (1987).

77. Epperson v. Arkansas, 393 U.S. 97 (1968).

78. *Id.* at 108.

79. Stone v. Graham, 449 U.S. 39 (1980).

80. *Id.* at 40.

81. *Id.* at 41.

82. *See* Wallace v. Jaffree, 472 U.S. at 108–112 (Rehnquist, J., dissenting).

83. *See* Edwards v. Aguillard, 482 U.S. at 637 (Scalia, J., dissenting); Lee v. Weisman, 505 U.S. 577, 644 (1992) (Scalia, J., dissenting); Lamb's Chapel v. Center Moriches Union Free Sch. Dist., 508 U.S. 384, 399 (1993) (Scalia, J., concurring).

84. *See, e.g.*, Lamb's Chapel v. Center Moriches Union Free Sch. Dist., 508 U.S. at 384.

85. Edwards v. Aguillard, 482 U.S. at 637 (Scalia, J., dissenting).

86. Church of the Lukumi Babalu Aye v. City of Hialeah, *supra* note 56.

87. *Id.* at 534.

88. United States v. O'Brien, 391 U.S. 367, 383 (1968).

89. Board of Educ. v. Pico, 475 U.S. 871 (1982).

90. *Id.*

91. *Id.* at 870–71 (underlining added; italics in original).

92. Texas v. Johnson, 491 U.S. 397 (1989).

93. *Id.* at 414.

94. United States v. Eichman, 496 U.S. 310 (1990).

95. *Id.* at 318.

96. Ashutosh Bhagwat, *Purpose Scrutiny in Constitutional Analysis*, 85 CAL. L. REV. 297, 317 (1997).

97. Elena Kagan, *Private Speech, Public Purpose: The Role of Governmental Motive in First Amendment Doctrine*, 63 U. CHI. L. REV. 413 (1996).

98. *Id.* at 414.

99. *Id.*

100. *Id.*

101. United States Dep't of Agric. v. Moreno, 413 U.S. 528 (1973).

102. *Id.* at 534 (emphasis in original).

103. Cass R. Sunstein, *Naked Preferences and the Constitution*, 84 COLUM. L. REV. 1689 (1984).

104. *Id.* at 1689–92.

105. *See* Akhil Reed Amar, *Attainder and Amendment 2: Romer's Rightness*, 95 MICH. L. REV. 203 (1996).

106. *See, e.g.*, Kotch v. Board of River Pilot Comm'rs, 330 U.S. 552 (1947); Williamson v. Lee Optical, 348 U.S. 483 (1955); United States R.R. Retirement Bd. v. Fritz, 449 U.S. 166 (1980).

107. City of Cleburne v. Cleburne Living Ctr., Inc., 473 U.S. 432 (1985).

108. *Id.* at 446–47.

109. Romer v. Evans, 517 U.S. 620 (1996).

110. *Id.* at 634.

111. Gomillion v. Lightfoot, 364 U.S. 339–40 (1960).

112. *Id.* at 341.

113. *Id.*

114. Professor Eisenberg claims that *Gomillion* originally was seen as a case that turned on motive, and that the Supreme Court's attempts in *Palmer* and *O'Brien* to recast *Gomillion* as turning on effect persuaded no one. Eisenberg, *supra* note 14, at 137. While it may be correct that *Gomillion* originally was viewed as turning on motive, the fact remains that the opinion places more emphasis on effect than on motive. Moreover, with the passing of time and the wisdom of hindsight, it is clear today that *Gomillion* is best understood as being more about effect than about motive.

115. Washington v. Davis, 426 U.S. 229, 254 (1976) (Stevens, J., concurring).

116. *Id.* at 253.

117. Personnel Adm'r v. Feeney, 442 U.S. 256, 279 (1979).

118. *Id.*

119. Washington v. Davis, 426 U.S. 229 (1976).

120. Personnel Adm'r v. Feeney, 442 U.S. at 256.

121. *Id.* at 279.

122. *See, e.g.*, Village of Arlington Heights v. Metropolitan Hous. Dev. Corp., 429 U.S. 252 (1977); Mobile v. Bolden, 446 U.S. 55 (1980); McCleskey v. Kemp, 481 U.S. 279 (1987).

123. Personnel Adm'r v. Feeney, 442 U.S. at 279.

124. *Id.*

125. Califano v. Goldfarb, 430 U.S. 199, 212, 217 (1977).

126. Califano v. Webster, 430 U.S. 313, 320 (1977).

127. Reitman v. Mulkey, 387 U.S. 369 (1967).

128. *Id.* at 374–80.

129. Romer v. Evans, 517 U.S. 620, 634 (1996) (quoting United States Dep't of Agric. v. Moreno, 413 U.S. 528, 534 [1973]) (emphasis added).

Chapter 6

Case Study: The Theory of Low-Value Speech

In the course of interpreting the First Amendment, the Supreme Court has created a network of rules to maintain freedom of speech. Within this structure, regulations of speech are subject to searching judicial scrutiny, which allows speech to be restricted only when it is the cause of serious harm.[1] The harm must be real and demonstrably so.[2] The expression of an idea may not be prohibited merely because it is offensive or disagreeable.[3] Any regulation of speech must be narrowly tailored to accomplish its purpose, and an overbroad regulation of speech will be struck down on its face.[4] Content-based restrictions of speech are considered particularly suspect and are unconstitutional unless necessary to achieve a compelling governmental interest.[5] Content-neutral restrictions, although somewhat less suspicious, are unconstitutional unless closely related to accomplishing an important governmental interest.[6] These rules, along with others that amplify them, provide considerable protection for the First Amendment right of free speech.

This network of rules, however, is not operative in all cases concerning freedom of speech. In the view of the Supreme Court, "not all speech is of equal First Amendment importance."[7] The Court has taken the position in various cases that some kinds of speech have less value than others, and therefore are not entitled to the same quality of First Amendment protection as that given to more valued types of speech.[8]

The Court's use of the theory that some categories of speech have less value than others has been marked by vacillation and uncertainty. This makes it difficult to say exactly what kinds of speech the Court believes to be low in value. At one time or another, the Court has ruled that fighting words, obscenity, and child pornography are of low value.[9] Some members, although not quite a majority, of the Court would add non-obscene sexually explicit expression to that list.[10] On occasion, a few members of the Court have expressed doubt about the value of profanity, but profane speech still clings to a valued position in the minds of a majority of the Court.[11] In the area of libel, the Court has said that "there is no constitutional value in false statements of fact,"[12] and that libelous speech on purely private matters is of less First Amendment concern.[13] The Court also has stated that there are "commonsense" differences between commercial speech and other kinds of expression, and that commercial speech occupies a "subordinate position in the scale of First Amendment values."[14]

As explored in this chapter, the applicability of the low-value speech theory to various forms of expression, not to mention the basic validity of the theory itself, is subject to considerable question. Therefore, it is important not to confuse the theory of low-value speech with other doctrines used by the Supreme Court to sustain restrictions upon expression. Some kinds of speech are said to be beyond the protection of the First Amendment strictly because of the harm they cause. In these instances the Court has been able to uphold regulations of speech by focusing entirely upon the harm resulting from the speech rather than its value or lack thereof.

Occasionally commentators see the low-value speech theory in places that it really has not been. For example, it has been claimed that the Court affords low value to speech that expressly incites lawless action;[15] in fact, the Court has given this kind of speech the protection of highly valued political speech.[16] Examination of the Court's opinions in this area reveals a harm-based analysis of this sort of speech that allows its regulation only upon a demonstration that the speech in question is in fact likely to produce unlawful action.[17] This is an approach that looks to the harm occasioned by the speech without assessing the merit of the speech.

Speculation also has been raised that the Supreme Court thinks speech that is part of a labor dispute is low in value.[18] Certainly, the Court has upheld various restrictions on that sort of speech and has treated it with less solicitude than other forms of expression. The Supreme Court opinions upholding the regulation of labor dispute speech, however, contain precious few statements indicating that the speech is low in value, and for the most part those opinions are concerned with the harm caused by such speech.[19] Moreover, the Court has expressly said that the dissemination of information concerning labor relations is "indispensable" to the public.[20]

Thus, there are many times when the Court upholds restrictions upon speech or affords certain kinds of speech an inferior brand of First Amendment protection without implicating the low-value speech theory. In other instances, the theory is implicated with significant impact upon the right of freedom of speech. Indeed, the low-value speech theory has had a "curious persistence,"[21] and in recent years has a gained a renewed currency. In a case decided in 1992, one of the Court's concurring opinions referred approvingly to the notion that the

First Amendment does not apply to certain kinds of speech because its "expressive content is worthless or of *de minimis* value to society."[22] Moreover, some commentators have urged quite strenuously that even more categories of speech—pornography and "hate" speech—be added to the registry of low-value expression.

The theory of low-value speech provokes some very fundamental questions, beginning with questions about its application. What kinds of speech are, in fact, of low social value? Can it be said that any category of speech is, in fact, low in value? While particular instances of speech may be of low value, to say that all instances of speech within a general category are low in value is quite another matter.

Serious questions also exist about the basic validity of the low-value speech theory. Constitutional scholars have said that it is a theory at odds with the fundamental First Amendment principles that the government has no business evaluating the content of speech and may regulate speech only when it is the cause of serious harm. By focusing upon the merit of speech, the low-value speech theory seems to fly in the face of well-established First Amendment precepts. Other scholars disagree and have defended the low-value speech theory as a necessary element for a rational system of free expression.

The theory of low-value speech operates through the process of categorizing certain kinds of speech and giving them a low degree of constitutional protection. Because it eschews the balancing process and allows speech to be restricted with little or no showing that it causes harm, categorization is a questionable technique. It, too, has been the subject of debate among constitutional scholars, and its use in conjunction with the low-value speech theory in particular raises a number of questions.

Despite the questions that it has provoked, the low-value speech theory has never been seriously examined by the Supreme Court and constitutional scholars have not fully assessed it.[23] Some scholars have criticized the theory while other have supported it, but usually in cursory fashion.[24] A fair amount of scholarly attention has been devoted to the use of the categorization technique in First Amendment cases, through which the low-value speech theory operates, but much less attention has been given to the theory itself. Thus, the low-value speech theory and the role it plays in First Amendment adjudication deserve to be thoroughly examined.

DEVELOPMENT OF THE LOW-VALUE SPEECH THEORY

Fighting Words

The low-value speech theory traces its genesis to a Supreme Court dictum in the 1942 case of *Chaplinsky v. New Hampshire*.[25] In *Chaplinsky* the Court upheld the constitutionality of a conviction under a statute that prohibited addressing a person by "any offensive, derisive, or annoying word."[26] Mr. Chaplinsky had been convicted of violating the statute by calling a city marshall a "God damned racketeer" and a "damned Fascist."[27] There is little doubt today that any statute like the one in *Chaplinsky* would be struck down on its face as unconstitutionally vague and overbroad.[28] More significantly, by contemporary standards there is not much question that even under a more narrowly drawn statue, it would violate the First Amendment to regulate Chaplinsky's words. In the last twenty-five years, the Supreme Court has consistently given constitutional shelter to words much more offensive than those uttered by Mr. Chaplinsky.[29] The Court has made it crystal clear that if there is "a bedrock principle underlying the First Amendment," it is that speech may not be prohibited simply because it is offensive.[30]

The *Chaplinsky* dictum, which was destined to have a longer, if tortured, existence than the decision itself, is no more than a paragraph:

> There are certain well-defined and narrowly limited classes of speech, the prevention and punishment of which have never been thought to raise any Constitutional problem. These include the lewd and obscene, the profane, the libelous, and the insulting or "fighting" words—those which by their very utterance inflict injury or tend to incite an immediate breach of the peace. It has been well observed that such utterances are no essential part of any exposition of ideas, and are of such slight social value as a step to truth that any benefit that may be derived from them is clearly outweighed by the social interest in order and morality.[31]

Several points are worth noting about the Court's statement in *Chaplinsky*. First, the limited role that the Court saw for the low-value speech theory is a role that would obtain only for "certain well-defined and narrowly limited classes of speech."[32] However limited the Court may have believed that role to be, the Court surely was wrong in its assertion that the designated classes of low-value speech were "well-defined and narrowly limited." To the contrary, some of the classes of speech referred to by the Court in *Chaplinsky*—the lewd and obscene, the profane, the libelous, and fighting words—have proven remarkably resistant to precise definition. The Court has struggled for years trying to define obscenity, and it eventually gave up the struggle by more or less handing the problem over to the states. Lewdness, like obscenity, is especially difficult to define because, as the Court has noted, "one man's vulgarity is another's lyric."[33] While profanity may be defined more easily than obscenity and lewdness, it, too, raises definitional problems. Should the words "Fuck the Draft," which were the subject of a later decision, *Cohen v. California*, be treated as low-value profanity or as political speech that garners the highest protection under the First Amendment? At the time of *Chaplinsky* the concept of fighting words was not well-defined and narrowly limited; in fact, it was not until some years after *Chaplinsky* that the Supreme Court redefined and narrowed the concept of fighting words.

As recently as June 1992 the Court was still describing the *Chaplinsky* approach as operative only in "a few limited areas,"[34] but, as discussed later, the Court has not been as faithful as it professes to have been in complying with those limits.

Second, it should be noted that the Supreme Court has had serious second thoughts about the *Chaplinsky* dictum. Indeed, the Court has since given the highest First Amendment protection to lewd speech and profanity. The Court has also given substantial constitutional protection to some forms of libel, and even fighting words have been treated by the Court quite differently than they were in *Chaplinsky*. While the Court has never expressly overruled *Chaplinsky* and has not expressly recanted the fighting words doctrine, it has made a point of confining the fighting words doctrine to a more narrow scope and for many years has not used it to uphold a regulation of speech. Given a number of more recent decisions, it is highly probably that today the kind of words spoken in *Chaplinsky* would not be considered of low value by the Court and in fact would be well within the protection of the First Amendment. Thus, the low-value speech theory has its roots in a case, *Chaplinsky v. New Hampshire*, which in all probability would be decided differently today, and which is based upon a good deal of reasoning that has since been repudiated by the Supreme Court itself.

Perhaps most interesting about the *Chaplinsky* calculus is that it looks not only to the value of speech, but also to the harm caused by the speech. The *Chaplinsky* dictum states that there are some categories of speech that are not essential to the exposition of ideas and have slight social value. It also says that these same kinds of speech inflict injury or tend to incite immediate breaches of the peace. This led the Court to conclude in *Chaplinsky* that the slight social value that might be derived from the words is "outweighed" by the social interest in preventing the harm that they cause. The *Chaplinsky* calculus, then, is one that weighs or balances the benefit of speech against the social interest in proscribing it. This aspect of the *Chaplinsky* dictum, however, is often ignored.

In a 1992 decision, *R.A.V. v. St. Paul*,[35] the Supreme Court once again encountered the fighting words doctrine and came away from the encounter with a fair amount of disagreement, not to mention confusion, about the regulation of fighting words. A concurring opinion in *R.A.V.* written by Justice Byron White reiterated the *Chaplinsky* rationale and stressed the view that fighting words have little expressive value.[36] On the other hand, the majority opinion, written by Justice Antonin Scalia, readily admitted that some fighting words are extremely expressive and possess worthwhile content.[37] The majority opinion said that fighting words are unprotected by the First Amendment, not because of the ideas communicated by their content, but rather because "their content embodies a particularly intolerable (and socially unnecessary) mode of expressing whatever idea the speaker wishes to convey."[38] That is, "despite their verbal character," fighting words are "analogous to a noisy sound truck" and are excluded from the scope of the First Amendment due to their " 'nonspeech' element of communication."[39]

This is disingenuous, at best. Unlike the regulation of sound trucks, the regulation of fighting words is not directed at their mode of expression, but rather is directed exactly at their content. Regulation of fighting words typically is aimed at all modes of expression including the purest forms of speech, the spoken word and the printed page. Many fighting words are not characterized by a "nonspeech" element, and laws restricting fighting words target the verbal content of the words rather than any "nonspeech" element they may manifest.

While stating that fighting words are unprotected by the First Amendment, however, the majority went on to treat them as if they were, by ruling that the First Amendment does not permit content-based regulations of fighting words that selectively restrict particular fighting words (hate speech) because of their message. So, the present Supreme Court is severely splintered in regard to the value of fighting words, and while all the members of the Court purport to claim that fighting words are unprotected under the First Amendment, a bare majority of the Court does in fact give some measure of First Amendment protection to fighting words.

Obscenity

The balancing aspect of the *Chaplinsky* approach was abandoned by the Court in 1957 when it ruled in *Roth v. United States*[40] that to prohibit the distribution of obscene materials does not violate the First Amendment. Though it has struggled over the years to adequately define obscenity, the Court has generally characterized it as including any material that appeals to a prurient interest, is patently offensive, and lacks redeeming social value.

In reaching the conclusion in *Roth* that the First Amendment is not offended by the prohibition of obscenity, the Court stated, "All ideas having even the slightest redeeming social importance—unorthodox ideas, controversial ideas, even ideas hateful to the prevailing climate of opinion—have the full protection of the [First Amendment]."[41] The Court also stated that obscenity is not protected by the First Amendment because it is "utterly without redeeming social importance."[42] After holding that obscenity was "not within the area of constitutionally protected speech,"[43] the Court found it unnecessary to determine whether obscene materials pose any harm that might justify their regulation. Obscene materials may be regulated, the Court made clear, without showing a need for the regulation because such materials have no value as speech and therefore possess no protection under the First Amendment.

It is apparent in *Roth* that the Supreme Court was treating obscenity as a separate category of speech that had no protection under the First Amendment because, in the Court's view, it had no value. The Court's approach in *Roth* is a manifestation of the low-value speech theory in pristine form. The Court's opinion eschews any discussion of balancing, flatly rejects the need for any showing of harm caused by obscenity, and rests its decision that obscene materials have no First Amendment protection strictly on the ground that such materials have no value.

The Court's statement in *Roth* that obscenity has utterly no redeeming social value is hyperbole. Michael Perry observes that "there is no denying that obscene pornography constitutes a political-moral vision" and that it "communicates . . . certain ideas, values, and sensibilities."[44] Ideas conveyed by obscene materials may be hateful but that does not make them any less ideational; as stated in *Roth* itself, even hateful ideas have the full protection of the First Amendment.[45] To use Professor Perry's example, even reprehensible ideas such as Nazi ideology are nonetheless ideas and hence recognized as having expressive value under the First Amendment.[46]

Sexually explicit material, even if offensive, nevertheless may convey information. In fact, in 1970 the President's Commission on Obscenity and Pornography concluded that substantial numbers of persons used sexually explicit materials as a source of information, and that such materials often facilitate constructive communication about sexual matters among individuals.[47]

Sexually explicit material, despite being offensive, may have artistic value. After all, odious ideas can be expressed in an artistic manner. To create a book, movie, drawing, or photograph usually requires some degree of artistic ability, and it would seem to be a rare work that could be described accurately as being "utterly" lacking in artistic quality.

Thus, if taken seriously, the Supreme Court's description of obscenity in *Roth* as utterly lacking in redeeming social value would encompass very few, if any, works. No doubt it would include the "extreme example of 'hard core pornography' " that Frederick Schauer asks us to imagine: a ten-minute motion picture that consists entirely of "a close-up colour depiction of the sexual organs of a male and a female who are engaged in sexual intercourse," and that "contains no variety, no dialogue, no music, no attempt at artistic depiction, and not even any view of the faces of the participants."[48] As Schauer says, however, that is the extreme example; one can also imagine pornographic material that does include variety, dialogue, music, artistic endeavor, and even a view of the participants' faces, not to mention the ideas, values, and sensibilities noted by Professor Perry.

Almost all books, movies, and other creative works have at least slight value as ideas, information, or artistic expression. Perhaps that explains why, sixteen years after *Roth*, the Court decided in *Miller v. California* to readjust its definition of obscenity by ruling that obscenity is not necessarily "utterly" lacking in redeeming social value, but rather "lacks serious literary, artistic, political, or scientific value."[49] However, this is not much of a change in the definition of obscenity, and even this definition of obscenity, if taken for what it seems to mean, would leave a great deal of material that is both prurient and offensive within the protection of the First Amendment. That material is prurient and offensive does not preclude it from being ideational, informative, or artistic.

In a companion case to *Miller, Paris Adult Theatre I v. Slaton*, the Court also revisited the question of why obscenity may be regulated and took a different tack in trying to constitutionally justify the prohibition of distribution of obscene materials.[50] This time the Court said that the distribution of obscene materials could be prohibited because there is a connection between obscenity and crime and other anti-social conduct.[51] However, the Court's attempt to demonstrate a link between obscenity and harmful behavior was feeble, at best. The Court cited the minority report of the 1970 Commission on Obscenity and Pornography for the proposition that "there is at least an arguable correlation between obscene material and crime."[52] Ignoring that correlation is quite different from causation, the Court also neglected to say that a majority of the Commission had found that the empirical evidence indicated that exposure to erotic material had "little or no effect" on attitudes about sex or morality, and did not significantly affect sexual behavior.[53]

The empirical findings of the Commission's majority were downplayed by the Court. While admitting that there was "no scientific data which conclusively demonstrate that exposure to obscene materials adversely affects men and women or their society," the Court said that "it is not for us to resolve empirical uncertainties underlying state legislation, save in the exceptional case where that legislation plainly impinges upon rights protected by the Constitution itself."[54] The latter half of that statement made it clear that the Court would continue to treat obscenity as a category of speech that did not raise First Amendment concerns. Whatever one may think of the result in *Slaton*, the reasoning in the opinion is nothing if not circular. The *Slaton* tautology proceeds as follows:

(1) obscene material is not speech so far as the First Amendment is concerned because
(2) the legislature has decided that obscene material causes crime and anti-social behavior, and
(3) it is not for the Court to review this legislative determination because
(4) obscene material is not speech so far as the First Amendment is concerned.

Thirteen years later in a report from a new commission, the Court could have found stronger—though still questionable—empirical support for the assertion that some obscene material causes harmful behavior. The 1986 report of the Attorney General's Commission on Pornography distinguished among three different kinds of sexually explicit material: (1) material that contains graphic displays of violence, (2) material that contains no violence but that depicts women in a degrading way, and (3) material that is sexually explicit but is neither violent nor degrading to women.[55] The report concluded that research showed that there is a causal relationship between sexually violent material and aggressive behavior toward women.[56] The commission also reported that there was some, although less, evidence suggesting that nonviolent sexually explicit materials depicting women in a degrading manner caused aggressive behavior.[57] Finally, the report concluded that there was no evidence showing a causal relationship between nonviolent, nondegrading sexually explicit material and aggressive behavior.[58]

However, the commission's conclusions have been subject to a great deal of criticism, and the debate still rages as to whether obscenity causes anti-social behavior. The commission's report, not to mention the *Slaton* case, focuses upon the harmful effects obscenity may have, rather than its value as expression. Although the logic of *Slaton* is seriously flawed and the empirical findings of the 1986 commission report are debatable, they both represent a departure from the reasoning in *Roth* that originally excluded obscenity from the aegis of the First Amendment on the ground that obscenity had no expressive value.

Shortly after the decision in *Roth*, the eminent First Amendment scholar Harry Kalven noted that the Court had created a "two-level" approach to the First Amendment.[59] At one level were communications, even though "odious to the majority opinion of the day," that could not be regulated unless shown to cause significant harm; at another level were communications "apparently so worthless as not to require any extensive judicial effort to determine whether they can be prohibited."[60]

Professor Kalven had strong doubts about the soundness of the two-level theory. Like Justice William Douglas, who had dissented in *Roth*, Professor Kalven thought that the basic flaw of the two-level approach was that "[t]he First Amendment . . . was designed to preclude courts as well as legislatures from weighing the values of speech against silence."[61] In Professor Kalven's view the two-level theory of speech afforded the Court a diplomatic way to deal with the dilemma of obscenity, but was "difficult to accept as doctrine," and was "a strained way to trap a problem."[62] He warned that the two-level approach "may have unhappy repercussions on the protection of free speech generally," and hoped that the Court would not find any other categories of speech to be lacking in redeeming social value.[63]

In more recent times it is still said that "the Court has adhered generally to a 'two-level' theory of free expression in its interpretation of the first amendment."[64] This, however, is an oversimplification. In the years since its decision in *Roth*, the Court's use of the low-value speech theory has become increasingly intricate. The Court had developed a hierarchy of speech, within which there are a number of different categories of speech that in the Court's view have diminishing levels of social value and receive respectively diminishing degrees of constitutional protection. Obscene speech, however, remains at the bottom of the totem pole, having, as the Court sees it, no value and therefore being entitled to no protection under the First Amendment.

Child Pornography

In *New York v. Ferber* the Supreme Court upheld a statute prohibiting the distribution of material depicting children engaged in sexual conduct. Although the statute applied to some material beyond the Court's definition of obscenity, Justice White's majority opinion noted that the standard of obscenity did not circumscribe the authority of a state to regulate child pornography and that the states were "entitled to greater leeway in the regulation of pornographic depictions of children."[65] The Court was willing to give that leeway to the states primarily because it believed there was a compelling interest in safeguarding the physical and psychological well-being of minors.[66] The use of children, the Court said, to produce pornographic materials is harmful to the physiological, emotional, and mental health of the children.

The majority opinion, however, also "echoed the *Chaplinsky* approach by 'classifying child pornography as a category of material outside the protection of the First Amendment,' "[67] not only because of the harm it caused, but also because the Court thought that "[T]he value of permitting live performances and photographic reproductions of children engaged in lewd sexual conduct is exceedingly modest, if not *de minimis*."[68] Although the majority opinion placed decidedly greater emphasis on the harm caused by child pornography to justify the regulation of such material, the opinion did not stop short of adding that child pornography has very little value. It was, however, unnecessary for the majority to take that additional step of evaluating the merit of the speech in question, because the same result could have been reached in the case based solely on the harm caused by child pornography.

Sexually Explicit Expression

The Supreme Court's treatment of speech that is sexually explicit but not within the definition of obscenity has been marked by vacillation and splintered opinions. Some members of the Court, although not a majority of them, have taken the position that certain sexually explicit expression, even though not within the Court's definition of obscenity, is nonetheless of low value under the First Amendment. To a few justices, non-obscene but sexually explicit "adult entertainment," although not as low in value as obscenity, still ranks rather poorly in the First Amendment hierarchy.

A majority of the Court, however, has thought otherwise, and in certain instances has been willing to accord high constitutional value to some forms of non-obscene, sexually explicit expression. In two cases decided in 1975, *Erznoznik v. City of Jacksonville*[69] and *Southeastern Promotions, Ltd. v. Conrad*,[70] the Court applied a searching degree of judicial scrutiny in invalidating restrictions on sexually explicit expression. In *Erzonznik*, the Court struck down on its face an ordinance prohibiting drive-in movies from showing motion pictures containing scenes of human nudity if the movie screens are visible from the street. In reaching its decision, the Court emphasized that the government may not selectively censor some kinds of speech on the ground that they are more offensive to the public than other kinds of speech.[71] In the *Southeastern Promotions* case, the Court found that it was unconstitutional for city officials to bar the musical *Hair* from a municipal auditorium because it contained scenes of nudity. In this case, the Court treated the expression in question as a highly valued form of speech as far as the First Amendment was concerned.

Other cases involving non-obscene sexually explicit expression have seen the Court splintered along several lines. In *Young v. American Mini Theatres, Inc.*,[72] the Court upheld a city ordinance that compelled the dispersal of adult theaters and bookstores by limiting the sites where they could be located. Justice John Paul Stevens' plurality opinion in the case utilized a form of minimal judicial scrutiny quite unlike the searching scrutiny the Court uses to review regulations of highly valued speech. Applying minimal scrutiny, the plurality readily accepted the city's assertion that the concentration of adult theaters and bookstores causes an area to deteriorate and become a focus of crime. Although that assertion was rather questionable, the plurality deferred to the city by stating, "It is not our function to appraise the wisdom of its decision."[73]

In adopting this deferential stance, the plurality noted that the ordinance did not ban adult theaters or bookstores, or even limit their number; it merely restricted the places where they may be located.[74] But the plurality opinion also stated that even though the First Amendment would not allow a total ban of "erotic materials that have some arguably artistic value, it is manifest that society's interest in protecting this type of expression is of a wholly different, and lesser, magnitude than the interest in untrammeled political debate."[75] Adult entertainment, the plurality continued, was the sort of speech that "few of us would march our sons and daughters off to war" to protect.[76]

There were four dissenters in the *Young* case, and they viewed the Court's decision as an "aberration."[77] As far as the dissenters were concerned, the plurality's statement—"few of us would march our sons and daughters off to war" to protect this sort of speech—was a drastic departure from well-established First Amendment principles and was "wholly alien to the First Amendment."[78]

The Court's decision in *Young* was by a vote of 4–1–4. The Justice in the middle providing the crucial fifth vote to support the judgment was Justice Lewis Powell, who wrote a concurring opinion pointedly critical of the plurality approach because it treated non-obscene erotic expression differently under the First Amendment than other forms of speech.[79] In fact, a few years later in a case involving profanity,[80] Justice Powell would again concur in a judgment while refusing to join the plurality opinion written by Justice Stevens, and would take strong objection to the low-value speech theory. "I do not subscribe to the theory," stated Justice Powell, "that the Justices of this Court are free generally to decide on the basis of its content which speech protected by the First Amendment is most 'valuable' and hence deserving of the most protection, and which is less 'valuable' and hence deserving of less protection."[81]

Another ordinance regulating the location of adult theaters was upheld by the Court in *City of Renton v. Playtime Theatres, Inc.*,[82] but in this case a majority of the justices found it unnecessary to say anything about the value of the speech subject to the ordinance. Avoiding any comment about the value of adult entertainment, the Court found that the ordinance was not directed at the suppression of adult entertainment and was justified as a means of preventing crime, protecting retail trade, maintaining property values, and preserving the quality of urban life.[83]

In *Schad v. Mt. Ephraim*,[84] though, a majority of the Court did have something to say about the value of adult entertainment that was quite different from the position taken in Justice Stevens' plurality opinion in *Young*. In *Schad*, a majority of the Court accorded high value to nude dancing at an adult entertainment establishment and used heightened judicial scrutiny in striking down a zoning ordinance that banned live entertainment. Noting that entertainment, as well as political and ideological expression, is protected by the First Amendment, the Court declared that an entertainment program may not be prohibited solely because it displays the nude human figure.[85] Even Justice Stevens, the author of the plurality opinion in *Young*, concurred in the result in *Schad*, although not without adding the metaphorical statement that "even though the foliage of the First Amendment may cast protective shadows over some forms of nude dancing, its roots were germinated by more serious concerns."[86]

Justice Stevens' metaphor foreshadowed the plurality opinion in *Barnes v. Glen Theatre, Inc.*,[87] a case in which the Court upheld the constitutionality of applying a public indecency statute to ban nude dancing at lounges and adult entertainment stores. Grudgingly admitting that "[s]everal of our cases contain language suggesting that nude dancing of the kind involved here is expressive conduct protected by the First Amendment,"[88] the plurality nonetheless went on to say that "we view it as only marginally so."[89]

Ironically, in *Barnes* a majority of the Court did not think that nude dancing was merely at the margin of First Amendment concerns. Justice White's dissenting opinion, joined by Justices Thurgood Marshall, Harry Blackmun, and Stevens, began by stating that, according to precedent, there was no question but that nude dancing was within the protection of the First Amendment. The opinion also pointed out that dancing was an ancient art form that inherently communicates ideas and emotions.[90]

Similarly, Justice David Souter allowed that performance dancing was inherently expressive and that nudity can enhance the expressive function of dancing.[91] Nevertheless, Justice Souter concurred in the judgment upholding the ban on nude dancing, because in his view the ban was directed not at the message conveyed by nude dancing, but rather at the "secondary effects" of the dancing, such as prostitution, sexual assault, and associated crimes.[92] Although Justice Souter showed little concern that scant evidence actually showed that nude dancing in fact leads to these secondary effects, he did suggest in a footnote that it would be difficult to sustain a prohibition of nude dancing in a theatrical production such as *Hair* or *Equus* on the ground of preventing harmful secondary effects.[93]

Justice Souter, then, seemed willing to assume, with little or no proof, that nude dancing at the Kitty Kat Lounge is the cause of prostitution, sexual assault, and other crimes, but he was not willing to make the same assumption about nude dancing in a theatrical production of *Hair* or *Equus*. Although one may suspect that Justice Souter does not think that nude dancing at the Kitty Kat Lounge is quite as expressive as it is in *Hair* or *Equus*, the fact remains that Justice Souter did not say that in his opinion. What he did say was that nude dancing, wherever it may occur, has expressive value and therefore is entitled to protection under the First Amendment.[94] On that particular point, he and the dissenting judges formed a majority who agreed that nude dancing is a valuable form of expression.

The Court has been more willing to protect sexually explicit speech that is conveyed through some forms of the electronic media, but here, too, the Court has wavered on occasion. There was no wavering, though, in *Sable Communications, Inc. v. FCC*, in which the Court achieved a rare unanimity in striking down part of a federal law that attempted to restrict "dial-a-porn" services by prohibiting indecent telephone messages.[95] While upholding another provision in the same law that banned obscene telephone messages, the Court stated, "Sexual expression which is indecent but not obscene is protected by the First Amendment."[96] In fact, the Court in *Sable* granted the fullest degree of constitutional protection to non-obscene indecent speech.[97] However, in *Denver Area Educational Telecommunications Consortium, Inc. v. FCC*,[98] a badly splintered Court was unable to attain a majority opinion in upholding one provision while striking down two others; all allowed various restrictions of patently offensive sexually oriented material on cable television. Yet, just one year later in *Reno v. American Civil Liberties Union*.[99] Justice Stevens wrote for a 7–2 majority of the Court in striking down a federal statutory provision that prohibited communicating indecent speech on the Internet. The opinion in *Reno* made it clear that the level of First Amendment protection that the Court is willing to extend to sexually explicit speech will depend significantly on the nature of the medium through which it is conveyed. The Court has often observed that each medium of expression presents its own First Amendment problems[100] and this seems to be especially so when the Court is dealing with sexually explicit speech.

Profanity

According to the *Chaplinsky* dictum, profanity is one of those "certain well-defined and narrowly limited classes of speech . . . [that] are no essential part of any exposition of ideas, and are of such slight social value as a step to truth that any benefit that may be derived from them is clearly outweighed by the social interest in order and morality."[101]

Twenty-nine years later, in *Cohen v. California*,[102] the Supreme Court would decisively repudiate that aspect of *Chaplinsky*. In *Cohen* the Court held that it was a violation of the First Amendment for a state to make it a crime for a person to wear a jacket in public emblazoned with the words "Fuck the Draft." Offensiveness of speech, the Court proclaimed, furnishes no reason to regulate it, because otherwise the government's power to ban speech would be "inherently boundless."[103] Transcending its own limits, the Court was able to comprehend that "one man's vulgarity is another's lyric."[104]

Thus, *Cohen v. California* squarely brought profanity back into the ambit of First Amendment protection, and treated it as speech of the highest constitutional order. Several subsequent Supreme Court decisions took a similarly tolerant approach of profanity,[105] which by then seemed to be securely situated in the First Amendment hierarchy. And then . . . along came the comedian George Carlin with his seven dirty words that you can never say on radio or television to find a splintered audience in the halls of the Supreme Court.

The Supreme Court met up with George Carlin and his seven dirty words monologue, which is replete with profanity, in a case entitled *FCC v. Pacifica Foundation*,[106] in which a severely divided court upheld a penalty imposed by the Federal Communications Commission on a radio station for broadcasting the Carlin monologue in the early afternoon hours when, according to the Court, children might be listening. Although there was no majority opinion in the case, five justices of the Court did agree that the FCC action was constitutionally justified on the grounds of protecting the right of privacy in the home and protecting the right of parents to shield their children from what the FCC referred to as "indecent" language.

Justice Stevens, who wrote the Court's plurality opinion, certainly emphasized reasons other than the nature of the speech for upholding the FCC action. Nonetheless, he could not resist commenting that the place of profanity in the hierarchy of First Amendment values was "aptly sketched" in *Chaplinsky*.[107] While he admitted that the Carlin monologue would be constitutionally protected in other contexts, he still maintained that the words in question "ordinarily lack literary, political, or scientific value."[108]

It was over that very point that Justice Stevens lost majority approval for his opinion, as Justice Powell wrote his concurring opinion, joined by Justice Blackmun, objecting to the "theory" that Supreme Court justices may make determinations about the value of speech in deciding how much protection it has under the First Amendment.[109]

Notwithstanding the decision in *Pacifica* and the splintered views of the justices, in later cases such as the aforementioned *Sable Communications, Inc. v. FCC*[110] and *Reno v. American Civil Liberties Union*,[111] the Court has given constitutional shelter to profanity in some electronic venues by striking down statutes that prohibit indecent speech over the telephone or the Internet. Profanity, then, so far as the Supreme Court is concerned, has its place. It may not be banned from public places, telephone communications, or the Internet, but it may be stricken from commercial radio and television broadcasting during daylight hours.

Libel

In 1952 the Supreme Court decided *Beauharnais v. Illinois*,[112] sustaining, by the slimmest of majorities, a so-called "group libel" statute that made it a crime to exhibit in public any publication that "portray[ed] depravity, criminality, unchastity, or lack of virtue of a class of citizens of any race, color, creed or religion, [or which] expos[ed] the citizens of any race, color, creed or religion to contempt, derision, or obloquy."[113] Most of the Court's opinion, authored by Justice Felix Frankfurter, was devoted to deferring to the legislative judgment that the statute in question prevented racial strife and violence.[114] However, quoting from *Chaplinsky*, the Court also noted that libel is one of those "narrow classes of speech" which is "no essential part of any exposition of ideas" and which has "slight social value."[115]

Although *Beauharnais* has never been expressly overruled, it is of extremely dubious validity by contemporary standards. It was decided by a 5–4 vote, with dissenting opinions by Justices Hugo Black, William Douglas, Robert Jackson, and Stanley Reed, which "were a precursor to the future position of the Court concerning libel."[116] Since *Beauharnais* was decided in 1952, the Supreme Court has significantly revised and rewritten the doctrine regarding freedom of speech in general and libel in particular. The majority opinion in *Beauharnais* was characterized by a brand of minimal scrutiny that gave great deference to the legislature; since then the Court has continuously expanded its application of stricter scrutiny to statutes that regulate speech. As the Court stated more recently, "Deference to a legislative finding cannot limit judicial inquiry when First Amendment rights are at stake."[117] Thus, the basic approach to First Amendment issues used in *Beauharnais* no longer comports with the prevailing law.

Even more pertinent, however, is the fact that *Beauharnais* was decided prior to *New York Times Co. v. Sullivan* and its progeny, in which the Supreme Court completely revamped the constitutional law of libel. *Beauharnais* rests upon the rationale that libel lies outside the protection of the First Amendment—a rationale that possesses little validity since the decision in *New York Times*. Accordingly, it has been noted that "while the Court has never explicitly overruled *Beauharnais*, it should be impossible to reach its results under the modern cases."[118]

The genesis of the modern approach to libel was *New York Times Co. v. Sullivan*,[119] a case that has been extolled as one of the most important First Amendment decisions ever made by the Supreme Court.[120] In the *New York Times* case, the Court repudiated the dictum in *Chaplinsky* that libelous utterances "are no essential part of any exposition of ideas," and brought libel back within the ambit of First Amendment protection, at least to some degree. Noting that "debate on public issues should be uninhibited, robust, and wide-open," and that "erroneous statement is inevitable in free debate," the Court insisted that free speech needed "breathing space if it is to survive."[121] To provide that breathing space for freedom of speech, the Court ruled in *New York Times* that a public officer may not recover damages for a defamatory falsehood relating to his or her official conduct unless the officer can prove the statement was made with actual malice, that is, the knowledge that it was false or with reckless disregard that it may have been false.

In the view of Harry Kalven, in *New York Times Co. v. Sullivan* the Supreme Court captured the "central meaning of the First Amendment," namely, the notion that seditious libel is not subject to sanction by the government.[122] This has been confirmed in subsequent cases, which have seen the Supreme Court adhere to and even reaffirm[123] the *New York Times* ruling in regard to libel of public officials and public figures, but to draw back First Amendment protection in cases involving libelous statements in the private arena beyond the public interest.

In *Gertz v. Robert Welch, Inc.* the Court adopted a different calculus for cases involving defamation of private individuals, rather than public officials or public figures. In *Gertz*, the Court readily acknowledged that under the First Amendment there is no such thing as a false idea. However pernicious an idea may seem, the Court said, it should be dealt with in the marketplace of ideas and not by government regulation. On the other hand, the Court continued "there is no constitutional value in false statements of fact." Although the Court continued to acknowledge the importance of robust and uninhibited debate on matters of public concern, it also noted that false statements of fact are harmful; they wrongfully harm an individual's reputation and integrity. While the Court reaffirmed the actual malice standard of *New York Times Co. v. Sullivan* for dealing with defamation of public officials or public figures, it thought that a different criterion should apply to defamation of private individuals, who have not thrust themselves voluntarily into the public spotlight and who are more vulnerable to injury from defamation because they lack the same sort of access to the media that public personalities have to correct defamatory statements made about them. Therefore, the Court was unwilling to extend the full scope of the actual malice standard to defendants accused of making defamatory comments about purely private persons about whom there was no genuine public concern.

Accordingly, the Court ruled in *Gertz* that when a private individual seeks to establish a cause of action of defamation, actual malice need not be shown as an element of the cause of action. If, however, the private plaintiff seeks to recover either presumed damages or punitive damages, actual malice must be proved as a condition of recovering such damages. The cause of action itself and actual damages, though, do not depend on any showing of actual malice, so far as the First Amendment is concerned.

If in *Gertz* the Court had followed its own reasoning to its logical extreme, it should have come to the conclusion that punitive and presumed damages are constitutionally impermissible even if actual malice could be shown. The Court stated in *Gertz* that the only justification for regulating libel is that it wrongfully harms an individual's reputation and integrity. Neither punitive nor presumed damages, however, are directed to that harm. The purpose of punitive damages, obviously, is to punish the wrongdoer and not to compensate for harm; in fact, they are a windfall for the plaintiff. Presumed damages are intended to compensate for harm that is difficult to prove or quantify and that may not in fact have occurred. Thus, if the Court had been true to its own reasoning in *Gertz v. Welch*, it would have ruled that the First Amendment precludes punitive and presumed damages in defamation actions (even if actual malice is shown), because they are not based upon a showing of harm that is the very justification for allowing defamation to be regulated.

Still, speech on matters of public concern is of high constitutional order, and even false statements about public matters enjoy a substantial degree of constitutional protection. Defamatory statements regarding a matter of public concern are only subject to liability when they can be shown to be accompanied by actual malice—that is, knowledge that they were false or reckless disregard that they may have been false. On the other hand, false statements of fact about purely private matters have no constitutional value and therefore enjoy only slight protection under the First Amendment. They may be subject to liability without a showing of actual malice, and may even be subject to punitive and presumed damages if actual malice is proven.

Commercial Speech

On various occasions the Supreme Court has described commercial speech as speech that does "no more than propose a commercial transaction"[124]—a meager definition if not a circular one. Subsequently, the Court has pointed to three factors, which, when they exist in combination, are strongly indicative of the commercial nature of expression: (1) the speech is an advertisement, (2) it mentions a specific product by name, and (3) it is economically motivated.[125] Justice Stevens has challenged the latter definition of commercial speech, arguing that some forms of "promotional advertising" that fall within the definition should not be considered in the same category as other commercial speech.[126] He believes that some expression related solely to the economic interests of a speaker and audience may nonetheless relate to issues of public significance and therefore should be entitled to the maximum protection provided by the First Amendment.[127] Furthermore, he says, the economic motivation of a speaker should not diminish his or her constitutional protection; "even Shakespeare may have been motivated by the prospect of pecuniary reward."[128]

In 1942 in *Valentine v. Christensen*, the Supreme Court ruled that the First Amendment placed no limitation whatsoever on the authority of the legislature to restrict the dissemination of commercial advertising.[129] The Court offered little explanation for its conclusion that commercial advertising was not protected by the First Amendment, except to imply that commercial advertising was a business activity rather than a form of expression.[130] In subsequent years that ruling was criticized, and the Court saw fit to chip away at it in several cases. Eventually, in *Virginia State Board of Pharmacy v. Virginia Citizens Consumer Council, Inc.*,[131] a 1976 decision, the Court reversed its previous position and welcomed commercial speech back into the arms of the First Amendment, although some portion of that welcome was retracted in following cases.[132]

In *Virginia State Board of Pharmacy*, the Court stated that consumers and society at large have a strong interest in the free flow of commercial information. "Advertising," the Court said, "however tasteless and excessive it sometimes may seem," nonetheless disseminates information that is indispensable to intelligent decision making about purchasing products and services.[133] In subsequent opinions the Court expanded on this theme, noting that while the "speaker's" interest in commercial speech is primarily economic, the "listener's" interest is substantial and in fact may be more important to him or her than political dialogue.[134] Advertising, even though thoroughly commercial, may also carry information about issues important to the public.[135] Thus, the Court came to view commercial advertising as a valuable form of expression, because it provides information about consumer goods and services to the public and conveys other information as well.

The Court, however, has not remained quite so sanguine about the value of commercial speech. In later cases the Court said that there are "commonsense" differences between commercial speech and other varieties of expression.[136] The Court also has suggested that, because commercial speech is linked to the economic well-being of a business, it is less vulnerable than other forms of expression to overboard regulations that have a chilling effect on speech. And the Court has even echoed *Valentine* by alluding, albeit briefly, to the economic character of commercial speech.[137]

All of this has led the Supreme Court to place commercial speech at a middle level of the constitutional hierarchy,[138] and then on occasion to further retract the scope of constitutional protection afforded to commercial speech.[139] While more valuable forms of speech are entitled to the protection of strict judicial scrutiny, commercial speech receives the protection of intermediate scrutiny, a step up from minimal scrutiny but a significant step down from strict scrutiny. For a while the Court withdrew some portion of even that constitutional protection by applying a combination of intermediate and almost minimal scrutiny in commercial speech cases,[140] but later the Court restored the full force of intermediate protection to commercial speech.[141] In addition, the Court further has ruled that commercial speech is not entitled to the protection of the overbreadth doctrine (see p. 201) as are more valued categories of speech,[142] and that because the First Amendment's solicitude for commercial speech is based on the informational aspects of advertising, false or misleading advertising and advertising about unlawful activities are entitled to no constitutional protection.[143]

As far as the Supreme Court is currently concerned, then, commercial speech possesses an intermediate degree of value, but precariously so.

PROPOSALS TO ADD NEW VARIETIES OF LOW-VALUE SPEECH

In recent years several commentators have suggested that several new categories of expression should be added to the list of low-value speech, which garners little or no protection under the First Amendment. Some commentators point to non-obscene pornography as low-value speech, while others point to racist "hate speech" as being low in value. The commentators also argue that these kinds of speech cause harm, but they are not content to rest their proposals on a harm-based analysis. They also claim that the value of the speech in question should be examined, and they find pornography and hate speech lacking in the kind of value that entitles speech to First Amendment protection.

Pornography

Some of these commentators have suggested that certain sexually explicit pornographic expression, even though not within the Supreme Court's definition of obscenity, nonetheless ought to be subject to regulation or even prohibition without violating the First Amendment. These commentators argue that non-obscene pornography should be amenable to prohibition or regulation without offending the First Amendment, because it causes harmful behavior and has little value as speech.

One of the more prominent proponents of the anti-pornography movement is Catharine MacKinnon, who has frequently written and spoken against pornography. Professor MacKinnon and Andrea Dworkin are the co-authors of a model ordinance to regulate pornography. The ordinance was approved twice by the City Council of Minneapolis, but vetoed each time by that city's mayor on the ground that it violated the First Amendment. The ordinance also was enacted by the City of Indianapolis, only to be found unconstitutional by the federal Seventh Circuit Court of Appeals,[144] and was adopted by referendum in Bellingham, Washington, only to be found unconstitutional by a federal district court.[145] Other versions of the MacKinnon-Dworkin ordinance, in statutory form, have been proposed in several other localities.

The MacKinnon-Dworkin position has found more acceptance in Canada, where the Supreme Court of Canada interpreted a criminal statute prohibiting the sale of obscene material as applicable to the kind of pornographic material targeted in the ordinance.[146] Moreover, that Court also ruled that to ban the sale of pornography was not a violation of the free speech clause in the Canadian Charter of Rights and Freedoms.[147]

The issue of pornography has divided the feminist community, and the MacKinnon-Dworkin ordinance has been the focus of that division.[148] While many feminists support the regulation of pornography, others do not and have responded to the anti-pornography movement by forming the Feminist Anti-

Censorship Taskforce, which has participated in challenging the MacKinnon-Dworkin ordinance and other efforts to ban pornography.[149]

To Professor MacKinnon, pornography and obscenity are two very different things. The MacKinnon-Dworkin ordinance defines pornography as:

> the graphic sexually explicit subordination of women through pictures and/or words that also includes one or more of the following: (i) women are presented dehumanized as sexual objects, things or commodities; or (ii) women are presented as sexual objects who enjoy pain or humiliation; or (iii) women are presented as sexual objects who experience sexual pleasure in being raped; or (iv) women are presented as sexual objects tied up or cut up or mutilated or bruised or physically hurt; or (v) women are presented in postures or positions of sexual submission, servility, or display; or (vi) women's body parts—including but not limited to vaginas, breasts, or buttocks—are exhibited such that women are reduced to those parts; or (vii) women are presented as whores by nature; or (viii) women are presented as being penetrated by objects or animals; or (ix) women are presented in scenarios of degradation, injury, torture, shown as filthy or inferior, bleeding, bruised, or hurt in a context that makes these conditions sexual.[150]

Professor MacKinnon believes that pornography causes harmful behavior and therefore should be be regulated. However, she also seems to reject First Amendment analysis altogether and has made a laborious effort to remove pornography from the realm of speech entirely. It is a mistake, she claims, to "miscast" the regulation of pornography "into obscenity's old drama of ideas."[151] In her view, the concepts of pornography and obscenity are so different from one another that they have "literally nothing in common."[152] Obscenity, she claims, is a moral idea that deals with the abstract, while pornography is a political practice that deals with the concrete.[153] "Obscenity as such probably does little harm; pornography causes attitudes and behaviors of violence and discrimination which define the treatment and status of half of the population."[154] To Professor MacKinnon, pornography, unlike obscenity, "is not imagery. . . . It is sexual reality."[155]

In attempting to recast the concept of pornography, Professor MacKinnon simply denies the essential attributes of pornographic material. Notwithstanding her view, words and pictures, including pornographic ones, are abstractions that represent ideas, and they are not concrete practices. They may well have a political content, but that does not exclude the possibility that they also have a moral content. Despite Professor MacKinnon's protestations to the contrary, the concept of pornography is not as different from the concept of obscenity as she would like to think; pornographic books, movies, and other materials, like obscene ones, are in fact imagery and not reality.

Profession MacKinnon further believes that pornography "constructs the social reality of gender,"[156] and that the reality it constructs is one of male dominance, sex discrimination, and gender inequality.[157] Pornography itself, she concludes, "is a systematic act against women on every level of its social existence."[158]

Steven Gey has pointed out that this is a view that "ascribe[s] extraordinary powers to expression."[159] It makes pornography the first source and the principal cause of discrimination against women.[160]

The assertion that pornography constructs reality recalls the debate about whether art reflects reality or creates it. When all is said and done, it probably does both, and the same is true of many kinds of speech. Each individual has his or her own vision of reality, and expression of those visions may have an effect—in some cases greater, in other cases lesser—in constructing reality for those around us. The shamefully negative portrayal of African-Americans, Native Americans, Hispanics, and other groups in newspapers, magazines, movies, books, television, and other forms of popular culture, not to mention textbooks and more serious works of fiction, throughout much of history "constructed reality" and affected "attitudes and behaviors" no less than pornography does. While eventually these materials were harshly criticized (and justifiably so), it was never suggested that they were not speech, and only the most constrained interpretation of the First Amendment would have allowed them to be banned.

If pornographic materials construct reality, so do communist, socialist, and anarchist leaflets, speeches, and meetings. So does flag burning and the editorial advertisement in *New York Times Co. v. Sullivan*. So do sit-ins and civil rights marches, anti-war armbands and Paul Cohen's jacket. The political cartoons of Thomas Nast or Herb Block, as well as the vicious satire in *Hustler v. Falwell*, all may play a part in constructing reality. That does not make them any less speech. Indeed, it confirms their expressive nature. They all are forms of expression, just as pornography is a form of expression. By its nature, speech reflects and constructs reality.

The irony of Professor McKinnon's position is that the more artistic the content of what she defines as pornography, the greater the impact it is likely to have in "constructing" a reality that she opposes. Accordingly, the more meaningful the expression, the more reason she would see to regulate it—a position it goes without saying, exactly at odds with the First Amendment.[161]

There are others, however, who admit that pornography is speech but deny that it has much value as speech. Cass Sunstein argues that pornography causes harmful behavior and has such slight social value that it should not be protected by the First Amendment.[162] Professor Sunstein defines pornography that he believes should be subject to regulation as including any material that (1) is sexually explicit, (2) depicts women as enjoying or deserving some form of physical abuse, and (3) has the purpose and effect of producing sexual arousal.[163]

Professor Sunstein sets forth a "four-factor analysis," which he admits is controversial, according to which he finds pornography to have little value.[164] The analysis focuses on these factors: (1) political speech that relates to matters of public concern has more First Amendment value than speech that concerns other matters; (2) cognitive speech is more valuable than noncognitive speech; (3) the purpose of the speaker is relevant—if his or her intent is to communicate a message, more constitutional value is present; and (4) speech is less apt to be valuable if the government regulation directed at it reflects a judgment that in certain areas government is likely to be acting for constitutionally permissible reasons.[165] The general validity of these four factors, some of which have been suggested by other commentators, as applied to other kinds of speech will be examined more fully in a subsequent section; at this point, however, some comment is appropriate regarding the application of the factors to the category of pornography defined by Professor Sunstein.

Sunstein sees the paradox that arises from Professor McKinnon's view that pornography manifests an ideology with significant social consequences. For the very reason that pornography expresses a significant ideology, it could well be considered political speech lying at the core of the First Amendment.[166] However, Sunstein claims that this is not a paradox, but a mistake about what entitles speech to the highest degree of constitutional protection.[167] "The question instead turns more generally on the speaker's purpose and on how the speaker communicates the message."[168] As Professor Sunstein views it, the pornographer's purpose is sexual arousal, a purpose of low value as far as the First Amendment is concerned.[169] Nevertheless, it might be pointed out that sexual arousal is also the purpose of a good deal of mainstream books, magazines, motion pictures, television programs, advertisements, and other forms of expression in the mass media.

Professor Sunstein additionally suggests that the ideological content of pornography has little value because it is directed to noncognitive functions rather than cognitive ones.[170] This distinction is one that has been questioned by modern psychological knowledge,[171] and it has been pointed out that "[m]uch pornography does indeed possess cognitive elements, especially as those elements are understood by the depth psychologies such as psychoanalysis."[172] If pornography is as noncognitive as Sunstein seems to think, so is much of the world's great art, not to mention a good deal of the world's popular culture.

Perhaps the most questionable of Professor Sunstein's assertions is his suggestion that when the government regulates pornography, it should be assumed that the government is acting for the constitutionally permissible purpose of preventing the harm pornography causes rather than acting for the impermissible purpose of disapproval of the content of pornographic expression.[173] This assumption flies in the face of a long and dishonorable history of government censorship, especially directed at materials with a sexual content, that has been motivated by nothing more than disapprobation of the content of the materials. When it comes to censorship of pornography, history suggests that the government is particularly undeserving of deference, and suspicion of government motive should be the standard.[174]

After examining the Sunstein four factors of low-value speech, Donald Downs, a political scientist and author of a comprehensive study of pornography, came to the conclusion that "[u]sing [the Sunstein] criteria, much pornography would be entitled to constitutional protection despite evidence that certain forms are related to harm."[175]

Hate Speech

In recent times, several commentators also have suggested that "hate" speech should be accorded little protection under the First Amendment.[176] Hate speech is usually considered to be highly offensive speech that vilifies, insults, or stigmatizes an individual on the basis of race, ethnicity, national origin, religion, gender, age, handicap, or sexual orientation.[177] Many people who attempt to justify restrictions on hate speech would add that before hate speech may be restricted, it must be shown that the speaker intended his or her words to vilify, insult, or stigmatize or reasonably should have known that the words would have that effect.[178]

It should be emphasized that most of the commentators who assert that hate speech should not be protected by the First Amendment base their theories on the harm they believe to be caused by hate speech; some, however, supplement a harm-based approach with the notion that hate speech has little value. Mari Matsuda, for instance, offers an extensive harm-based discussion of racist speech, while further asserting that "collective historical knowledge" has led to "universal acceptance of the wrongness of the doctrine of racial supremacy."[179] "Racial supremacy," she says, "is one of the ideas we have collectively and internationally considered and rejected."[180]

Another and more recent proponent, Alon Harel, not only echoes Professor Matsuda, but is perhaps unique is basing his approach almost entirely on the premise that racist speech has virtually no value. Moreover, Professor Harel makes the same claim about pornographic speech. He asserts that neither racist nor pornographic speech should be protected under the First Amendment because each possesses extremely little value.[181] Professor Harel approaches his theory of unprotected speech with a recognition that the current state of the law affords high First Amendment protection to racist and pornographic speech because they are perceived to be part of the political dialogue.[182] He argues, however, that racist and pornographic speech are so abhorrent and morally unacceptable that they should not be regarded as part of the political dialogue.[183] In his view, racist and pornographic speech are not a "legitimate" part of the political discourse because they have no "morally binding force."[184]

As Professor Harel admits, his theory is based on "a value-laden characterization of political discourse."[185] It is also a theory at odds with long-standing basic First Amendment principles. Under the First Amendment, there has been a thorough rejection of the notion that the government can decide what speech is suitable for public discourse. To endow the government with power to decide whether speech is acceptable for discourse is a decidedly more dangerous risk than to allow an "uninhibited, robust, and wide-open" marketplace of ideas.[186]

Moreover, defining low-value hate speech, similar to defining obscenity or pornography, presents a tremendously difficult line-drawing task that poses a threat to the kinds of speech that should not be excluded from the protection of the First Amendment. Consider, for example, the novel *Huckleberry Finn*—a work that a number of people have suggested should be banned. Certainly, there is no denying that the word "nigger" appears repeatedly throughout the book and that Mark Twain's novel otherwise reflects, in some respects, the racial bigotry of its time. However, there also is no denying that in other respects *Huckleberry Finn* transcends that bigotry and stands as a great celebration of the essential worth and dignity of all individuals. And there is no denying that *Huckleberry Finn* is a great work of art, a classic American novel.

Yet there are those who see it as an instance of hate speech that should be censored or banned. There are those who have labeled Bernard Malamud's award-winning *The Fixer* as anti-Semitic,[187] while a more discerning eye might perceive it as an homage to Jewish people. Therein, of course, lies the problem. Offensiveness, like beauty, often lies in the eye of the beholder, and the censor can almost always be counted on to see offensiveness and to ban expression again and again.

Contemporary attempts to define hate speech, or even pornography, that should be excluded from First Amendment protection often are plagued by the fundamental flaw of over-including a good deal of very important speech. When that flaw is addressed by refining the definitions, the result is such narrow definitions of regulable speech that little, if any, impact is made toward achieving their goals.[188]

Perhaps Rodney Smolla has offered the most sensible approach to hate speech.[189] In a measured examination of the topic, he recognizes that hate speech is an abomination that should be opposed vigorously by all means permitted under the Constitution.[190] Nevertheless, he continues, the appropriate balance for an open society is the one presently set by First Amendment rules, which allow the regulation of hate speech only in very narrow circumstances such as when the speech presents a clear and present danger of physical violence or is intertwined with actual discriminatory conduct.[191] Professor Smolla concludes that beyond those narrow circumstances, the fight against hate speech is more effectively waged through persuasion and education than by punishment and coercion.[192]

The proposals to regulate hate speech suffered a severe, although not entirely fatal, set-back in 1992 when the Supreme Court decided *R.A.V. v. City of St. Paul*,[193] ruling that the St. Paul Bias-Motivated Crime Ordinance violated the First Amendment. The ordinance made it a crime to display a symbol that one knows or has reason to know will arouse anger, alarm, or resentment in others on the basis of race, color, creed, religion, or gender.[194] In the view of a bare majority of the Supreme Court, the ordinance was unconstitutional on its face because it discriminated against speech on the basis of its message. The Court suggested though, that some hate speech could be constitutionally proscribed under a more content-neutral law that generally prohibited fighting words.[195]

Tolerating Loathsome Speech

At their core, the contemporary proposals seeking to suppress either hate speech or pornography are founded on the notion that the ideas expressed by such speech are intolerable.[196] This is not the first time there has been a debate about whether "words matter." Alexander Bickel argued that we should not think that "words don't matter, that they make nothing happen and are too trivial to bother with."[197] He believed that offensive speech, such as the phrase "Fuck the Draft" printed on Paul Cohen's jacket, was a kind of verbal "assault" that "create[s] a climate, an environment in which conduct and actions that were not possible before become possible."[198] This argument is echoed by Professor MacKinnon's notion that pornography "causes attitudes and behaviors of violence and discrimination."[199] Professor Bickel's argument also is echoed by the contention that racist speech creates stereotypes that inflict emotional distress on the people they are directed at and that create stereotypes affecting attitudes and behavior.

It is undeniable that a good deal of speech—and not just pornography or hate speech—does matter; it may construct reality, create stereotypes, or affect attitudes and behavior. According to First Amendment doctrine, however, that has never been reason enough to regulate speech. The fact that some speech may convey offensive, even pernicious, messages that contribute to generating an ugly reality has never been enough under the First Amendment to justify the regulation of speech. As Justice Oliver Wendell Holmes said, "[w]e should be eternally vigilant against attempts to check the expression of opinions that we *loathe and believe to be fraught with death*."[200] And should there be any doubt that Holmes meant what he said, let the doubtful know that he said much the same thing again ten years later, proclaiming that the most imperative constitutional principle was "the principle of free thought—not free thought for those who agree with us but freedom for the thought that we *hate*."[201] In a similar vein, Justice Louis Brandeis stated that "discussion affords ordinarily adequate protection against the dissemination of noxious doctrine."[202] And even Justice Jackson, who was no great First Amendment advocate, noted that "the freedom to differ is not limited to things that do not matter much."[203] In more recent times, the Supreme Court has pointedly stated that "[i]f there is a bedrock principle underlying the First Amendment, it is that the Government may not prohibit the expression of an idea simply because society finds the idea itself offensive or disagreeable."[204]

One of the reasons for this "bedrock principle" is that there is no stopping place for the notion of offensiveness; if speech could be suppressed because it is offensive, little would remain of the First Amendment. There is no denying that hate speech is extremely offensive or that pornography can be pernicious. There is no denying that some of the contemporary proposals to regulate these kinds of expression go to elaborate lengths to demonstrate just how offensive they are. But if pornography or hate speech can be restricted because they are so offensive, then so can flag burning,[205] the *Hustler* satire of Jerry Falwell,[206] the words of George Carlin[207] and Paul Cohen,[208] and the black armbands worn by Mary Beth and John Tinker to protest the war in Viet Nam.[209] All of these are extremely offensive forms of expression to many people. Indeed, if offensiveness is the standard, the civil rights marches of the 1950s and 1960s[210] could have been restrained because they were an affront to the "fine and upstanding" citizens who opposed desegregation.

In response to Professor Bickel, Daniel Farber has eloquently reminded us why it is better to tolerate offensive speech than to suppress it.[211] Offensive speech, Professor Farber points out, reveals something that we should know: Some people have offensive thoughts.[212] Suppressing this kind of speech "violates a cardinal principle of a free society, that truths are better confronted than repressed."[213] Banning speech is a repressive act that drives attitudes underground, rather than addressing or redressing them. Allowing the expression of offensive speech has the positive function of provoking responses to it, which can lead to change. The suppression of offensive speech does little to alter the odious attitudes that spawn it, while a free marketplace of ideas is more likely to point the way to reform.

HOW HIGH-VALUE AND LOW-VALUE SPEECH ARE TREATED

The two-level approach to freedom of expression that the Supreme Court originally developed in *Chaplinsky* and *Roth* has evolved into a more intricate structure composed of a number of tiers and a variety of rules. At each tier, the speech in question is viewed by the Court to have diminishing value and therefore is accorded diminishing measures of constitutional protection. Within the hierarchy of speech, the Court employs several different modes of constitutional review for various categories of speech, several different overall approaches to speech, and a number of special rules for different categories of speech.

Levels of Scrutiny

The essential difference between the Supreme Court's treatment of high- and low-value speech concerns what the Court will accept as justification for regulating speech. As previously noted, a majority of the Court has never taken an absolutist approach to the First Amendment, even when dealing with the most valued kinds of speech. High-value speech is not beyond restriction if a sufficiently serious state interest can be shown for its regulation. However, the Court requires much less to sustain the regulation of low-value speech.

In First Amendment cases, as in cases involving other constitutional provisions, the Supreme Court has developed a multi-level system of judicial review.[214] At the highest tier, the Court applies strict judicial scrutiny, which requires government action to be justified by a compelling state interest achieved through the least restrictive means possible.[215] The Court employs this strict level of scrutiny when dealing with regulations that affect high-value speech; obviously, this provides a substantial degree of constitutional protection.

Somewhat less, though still a fair degree, of protection is afforded by intermediate scrutiny, which requires government action to be justified by an important state interest achieved through carefully selected, although not necessarily perfect, means.[216] The Court uses this intermediate tier of scrutiny when dealing with speech that it finds to be of middling value. Shortly after bringing commercial speech back into the ambit of the First Amendment, the Court decided to use intermediate scrutiny in dealing with regulations of commercial speech.[217] Then, for a while the Court became more grudging about the protection afforded commercial speech and decided to use intermediate scrutiny only in reviewing the ends, and not the means, of regulations of commercial speech.[218] Later, however, the Court restored the full force of intermediate protection to commercial speech.[219]

Minimal scrutiny is the lowest level of judicial review. It grants a great deal of deference to actions of the other branches of government and requires only that they justify their actions by a valid or legitimate state interest achieved through reasonable means.[220] In practice, minimal scrutiny usually operates as no scrutiny at all and grants total deference to the other branches of government.[221] However, on occasion (although it is nearly impossible to predict when), the Court will put some "bite" into minimal scrutiny, and upgrade it from no scrutiny at all.[222] Minimal scrutiny without bite is the kind of scrutiny that the Court employs in obscenity cases.

In the eyes of the Supreme Court, regulations of high-value speech that focus on the content of speech are especially suspect and presumptively unconstitutional unless they are shown to be necessary to achieve a compelling governmental interest.[223] Even content-neutral regulations of high-value speech are considered with a fair degree of suspicion and are unconstitutional unless closely related to accomplishing an important governmental interest.[224] On the other hand, content-based regulations of low-value speech are regarded by the Court so deferentially that they ordinarily will be sustained as constitutional on the most meager showing of governmental interest.[225]

Approaches

In addition to the different levels of scrutiny, the Court has different approaches for dealing with different kinds of speech. When dealing with high-value speech, the Court uses what has been called "ad hoc balancing,"[226] which is an approach that "focuses upon each particular case individually, weighing the interest served by the speech in each particular instance against the asserted state interest in regulating the speech."[227] Ad hoc balancing, although not absolutely protective of speech, tends to be highly protective of it, allowing speech to be regulated only upon a showing that the particular speech in question will cause a serious harm that cannot be avoided by an alternative regulation less restrictive of speech.

Still, a regulation of highly valued speech may be constitutional if it is demonstrated that the particular speech causes a serious harm that the government has a compelling state interest in preventing. Thus, even political speech, which the Supreme Court has always recognized as the most highly valued kind of speech, nevertheless may be regulated if it is shown to cause a clear and present danger, or if a compelling state interest is demonstrated to support its regulation.

Ad hoc balancing should be distinguished from "definitional balancing,"[228] a technique the Court uses for some forms of speech that are lower, although not at the very bottom, on the Court's totem pole. Definitional balancing might just as well as called "categorical balancing," because it focuses upon a category or class of speech, such as libel, and inquires whether the category of speech causes a sufficiently serious harm to justify restricting the speech. When using definitional balancing, the Court will uphold a regulation of speech if the Court is convinced that the class of speech in question is sufficiently harmful. No showing is required that the individual instance of speech in that particular case is harmful, as long as the Court believes that the kind of speech involved tends to cause harm.[229]

It has been pointed out that whether ad hoc or definitional balancing provides more protection for speech depends upon the specific content that the Court chooses to provide for each of those balancing approaches.[230] Certainly the Court could devise a definitional balancing test that is highly protective of speech and could devise an ad hoc balancing test that is less so. In practice, however, it is clear that, as used by the Court, ad hoc balancing provides decidedly more protection for speech than definitional balancing does. Definitional balancing is the primary method the Court uses for giving less constitutional protection to speech, such as libel, that the Court feels has some but not full constitutional value. Speech that is lower, but not the lowest, in value receives diminished protection by denying it the safeguard of ad hoc balancing.

Still, definitional balancing does provide some constitutional protection, and even that much is denied to speech that the Court views as lowest in value. When dealing with the least valued speech, such as obscenity, the Court does not balance at all; that is, because the Court sees the speech as having little or no value, the Court designates it as a category of speech that receives no First Amendment protection. In effect, the Court "categorizes out" certain kinds of speech to deny them First Amendment protection. This use of the categorization technique requires no showing of any harm, whether of the particular speech or of the class of speech. All the Court looks to is the value of the speech; if the Court is convinced that the speech has no value, the Court gives no constitutional protection to the speech.

In comparing these three approaches, it is clear that when either of the balancing approaches is used, the constitutionality of a regulation of speech turns on an assessment of the harm caused by the speech. On the other hand, when the technique of categorization is used, the constitutionality of a regulation of low-value speech turns on an assessment of the value of the speech.

Rules

Speech that is deemed high in value by the Supreme Court also enjoys the protection of the rule against overbreadth.[231] According to this rule, an overbroad regulation of speech is considered unconstitutional on its face and therefore cannot be applied even to regulate speech that could be proscribed under a more precisely drawn statute.[232] The purpose of the rule against overbreadth is to prevent a "chilling effect" upon constitutionally protected, valuable speech.[233] However, the Court has withdrawn the protection of the rule against overbreadth from a less valuable form of speech, namely, commercial speech, and has expressly said that "the overbreadth doctrine does not apply to commercial speech."[234] Similarly, the Court uses an extremely truncated version of the overbreadth doctrine in cases involving child pornography, another category of speech low in value.

For some categories of low-value speech, special rules are devised to give them a modicum of First Amendment protection. For example, while child pornography is low in value and certainly may be restricted, regulations prohibiting it must be adequately defined and may be applied only to material that actually involves the participation of children.[235] In defamation cases involving matters of public concern, a showing of actual malice is required to establish a cause of action; in defamation cases involving private affairs, actual malice only needs to be shown to recover presumed or punitive damages.

Thus, a complex hierarchy of speech has been created by the Supreme Court over the years. It is a hierarchy that encompasses three very different levels of constitutional review, three very different overall approaches to expression, and a number of special rules for various kinds of speech.

DETERMINING THE VALUE OF SPEECH

First Amendment theory has been greatly influenced by the scholarly works of Alexander Meiklejohn. His view was that the central purpose of freedom of speech and the press is to enable individuals to participate in our democratic system of self-government.[236] Meiklejohn believed that freedom of expression was an aspect of self-government that derived from the basic democratic premise that the people shall make decisions about their own governance for themselves.[237] As Meiklejohn explained, the free flow of information and opinion about matters of public concern is essential to effective self-government.[238] Therefore, the central function of freedom of expression is to ensure the discussion of public issues.

Meiklejohn posited that speech about public matters was entitled to absolute protection under the First Amendment.[239] Although at first he applied his theory of absolute protection to a somewhat limited range of public issues,[240] he later expanded its application to a broad range of expression that included all "human communications from which the voter derives the knowledge, intelligence, sensitivity to human values . . . [and] the capacity for sane and objective judgment which, so far as possible, a ballot should express."[241] Meiklejohn specified that this expression encompassed all phases of education, philosophic and scientific understanding, literature and the arts, and public discussion of public issues.[242]

Meiklejohn's principal intent was to expand and protect freedom of speech by providing absolute First Amendment protection for all expression about matters of public concern. However, there are those who see an implication in Meiklejohn's theory that limits freedom of speech. The range of public speech that Meiklejohn thought was within the core of the First Amendment, although wide, was not without limits. Beyond those limits, non-public speech impliedly is not of central concern under the First Amendment and should enjoy considerably less constitutional protection.

Some commentators see this implication as unduly restricting freedom of speech. They assert that the First Amendment serves purposes other than enhancing democratic self-regulation. Thomas Emerson, for example, suggests that a primary purpose of the First Amendment is to foster individual self-fulfillment, and therefore expression about matters, public *or* private, is within the ambit of the First Amendment.[243] Martin Redish makes a strong argument that the ultimate purpose of the First Amendment is to enhance "individual self-realization," a concept that includes individual self-fulfillment as well as autonomy in making decisions about one's own destiny.[244] When the First Amendment is viewed in this light, Professor Redish points out, participation in public affairs is one, but not the only, means to the broader goals served by freedom of speech.[245]

Although a majority of the Supreme Court, despite the exhortations of former Justices Black and Douglas, has never adopted an absolutist view of the First Amendment, it has accepted the Meiklejohn view that the central purpose of the First Amendment is to ensure discussion of public matters. On a number of occasions, the Court has said that discussion of public issues lies "at the heart of the First Amendment's protection,"[246] and therefore freedom of expression embraces discussion of "all matters of public concern."[247] Conversely, discussion of matters of no concern to the public has less importance under the First Amendment and therefore is given less constitutional protection.

By this criterion a good deal of the expression said to be low in value should, in fact, be recognized as highly valuable. Some commercial speech, such as the prices of prescription drugs,[248] the availability of legal services,[249] and information about condoms, family planning, and the prevention of venereal disease,[250] are of considerable concern to the public. And as pernicious as it is, hate speech often relates to political issues or matters of public concern.

Even the sort of "fighting words" the Court originally found to be of low value in *Chaplinsky* may be a matter of public concern. Indeed, in a Ninth

Circuit decision in which an individual directed profane gestures and speech at a police officer, the court observed, "Inarticulate and crude as [the individual's] conduct may have been, it represented an expression of disapproval toward a police officer with whom he had just had a run-in. As such, it fell squarely within the protective umbrella of the First Amendment."[251]

Aside from the general stance that issues of public concern lie at the core of the First Amendment, the Supreme Court has never precisely explained what characteristics it considers in determining the value of speech under the First Amendment.[252] Commentators have noted the Court's failure to articulate a principle that unifies the various categories of speech it considers low in value. This "absence of a unifying principle is a source of continuing frustration to scholars of free speech law."[253]

Several commentators have attempted to designate other factors that make speech more or less valuable. Some have asserted that the value of speech depends upon its ability to communicate a mental stimulus that is directed to reason or to the intellect.[254] In a similar vein, it has been argued that cognitive material has more value as speech than non-cognitive material.[255] Steven Gey, who is less than persuaded by these arguments, notes that they harken back to the ancient distinction between "reason" and "passion," a distinction that has been shaken, if not completely toppled, by modern psychological analysis.[256] Similarly, Professor Redish notes that individuals often respond to expression with varying degrees of physical, emotional, and intellectual reaction, which are often inseparable.[257] He therefore concludes that the purported distinction between the "physical" and non-physical impact of speech has no basis in reality and is unjustifiable.[258]

Even if one adheres to the distinction, there is little support for the claim that intellectual expression is more valuable that emotive expression. A good portion of the world's great art, especially music and painting, could be described as appealing to "passion" rather than "reason." To exclude that sort of expression from the protection of the First Amendment on the ground that it has little value is absurd and certainly would have disastrous results for freedom of speech.[259]

The notion that there is little First Amendment value to non-cognitive expression is one that has been decisively rejected by the Supreme Court:

> [W]e cannot overlook the fact . . . that much linguistic expression serves a dual communicative function: it conveys not only ideas capable of relatively precise, detached explication, but otherwise inexpressible emotions as well. In fact, words are often chosen as much for their emotive as their cognitive force. We cannot sanction the view that the Constitution, while solicitous of the cognitive content of individual speech, has little or no regard for that emotive function which, practically speaking, may often be the more important element of the overall message sought to be communicated.[260]

Professor Sunstein points to additional factors that he claims are characteristic of low-value speech. He says that a speaker who intends to communicate a message should be treated more favorably than one who does not.[261] This factor seems to prove either too little or too much, because virtually all speakers intend to communicate a message. They may have other intentions as well, such as wanting to influence a vote, foment rebellion, reform government, stop the draft, increase sales of a product, save the environment, produce sexual arousal, or provoke laughter, but they intend to accomplish those goals by communicating a message.

Later in his analysis, Professor Sunstein seems to equate the intent to communicate a message with cognitive speech.[262] If, however, he means to suggest that we should only value a speaker's intention to communicate cognitive messages, he is merely repeating the questionable notion, discussed above, that noncognitive speech is low in value.

Finally, Professor Sunstein suggests that in some areas, such as those involving commercial speech, private libel, fighting words, and pornography, it should be assumed that the government is acting for permissible reasons and therefore should be granted more latitude to regulate speech.[263] Others, however, are not so willing to make that assumption about government, especially in light of the historical tendency on the part of government to over-censor speech.[264] Perhaps it is correct that the government's tendency to over-censor has not been operative in regard to particular kinds of speech. No doubt many would agree with Professor Sunstein that the government usually is acting for permissible reasons in regulating commercial speech and private libel. It is difficult to say the same about government regulation of fighting words—witness *Chaplinsky* itself—and even more difficult to say the same about government regulation of sexually explicit material, which historically has been characterized by constitutionally impermissible intent on the part of the government.[265] Moreover, the question remains why, in any area involving freedom of expression, the government should be presumed to be acting for proper reasons. If government has good reason to regulate speech, why shouldn't it be expected to explain what that reason is? Indeed, if the government has good reason to regulate speech, it should be quite willing to say what that reason is.

THE BASIC VALIDITY OF THE LOW-VALUE SPEECH THEORY

Several Supreme Court justices and a number of prominent constitutional scholars have expressed serious doubts about the basic validity of the low-value speech theory. In his dissenting opinion in the *Roth* case, Justice Douglas expressed his belief that the First Amendment was designed to preclude courts as well as legislatures from weighing the value of speech.[266] Some years later, Justice Powell would declare that he did not subscribe to the theory that Supreme Court justices could evaluate the content of speech and decide which expression was more or less deserving of First Amendment protection.[267]

One of the foremost First Amendment scholars, Thomas Emerson, believed that the *Chaplinsky* theory of low-value speech was fundamentally incompatible with First Amendment principles.[268] Professor Emerson pointed out that the *Chaplinsky* approach requires the Supreme Court to make value judgments about the content of expression, a role that Emerson believed is "foreclosed . . . by the basic theory of the First Amendment."[269] The same point was made by Justice Douglas in his dissenting opinion in the *Roth* case,[270] and by Professor Kalven, who thought that Justice Douglas had "put his finger firmly on the fundamental difficulty of the two-level theory."[271]

Steven Shiffrin is a contemporary First Amendment scholar who believes that the low-value speech theory is basically inconsonant with First Amendment principles. According to Professor Shiffrin:

> [T]he very concept of low-value speech is an embarrassment to first amendment orthodoxy. To say that government cannot suppress speech unless the speech is of low value sounds like a parody of free speech theory. The censor will always be inclined to say that the speech suppressed is of low value. Thus, the low-value exception mocks the rule. It seems almost like saying that [under apartheid] South Africa ha[d] a humane racial policy except for its treatment of the blacks.[272]

The most devastating critique of the low-value speech theory comes from the work of Kenneth Karst.[273] In Professor Karst's perceptive vision of the First Amendment, the central principle of the Amendment is equality of expression—that is, "equal liberty of expression, not merely in the political arena, but throughout all the interdependent 'decisionmaking' processes of a complex society."[274] Although Professor Karst believes that the principle of equality of expression is inherent in the First Amendment, he acknowledges that it was not crystallized until 1972 in the case of *Police Department of Chicago v. Mosley*.[275] While it took the Court until then to fully articulate the principle, it finally did so in no uncertain terms:

> [A]bove all else, the First Amendment means that government has no power to restrict expression because of its message, its ideas, its subject matter, or its content . . . To permit the continued building of our politics and culture, and to assure self-fulfillment for each individual, our people are guaranteed the right to express any thought, free from government censorship. The essence of the forbidden censorship is content control.[276]

Professor Karst believes that the *Chaplinsky* two-level approach to the First Amendment is "radically inconsistent with the principle of equal liberty of expression."[277] He explains that even though the equality principle does not preclude all content-based regulation, it does begin with a presumption against content-based regulations that can be overcome, but only by a showing of a strong probability of serious harm.[278] Accordingly, Professor Karst joins the ranks of those who think that the theory of low-value speech is fundamentally at odds with the meaning of the First Amendment.[279]

Others, however, disagree. In fact, some constitutional scholars believe that the low-value speech theory is an essential element of First Amendment doctrine. Geoffrey Stone, for example, asserts:

> The low value theory, or some variant thereof, is an essential concomitant of an effective system of free expression, for unless we are prepared to apply the same standards to private blackmail, for example, that we apply to public political debate, some distinctions in terms of constitutional value are inevitable.[280]

This assertion is echoed by Cass Sunstein, who says that "It would be difficult to imagine a sensible system of free expression that did not distinguish among categories of speech in accordance with their importance to the underlying purposes of the free speech guarantee.[281] The alternative, he asserts, would be to apply the standards for political speech to all speech, thereby requiring the government to meet a test "so stringent as to preclude most forms of regulation that are currently accepted."[282] More recently, Professor Sunstein has acknowledged that the Supreme Court has provided no clear principle to unify the various categories of speech that it designates as low-value, but he still maintains that any well-functioning system of free expression must distinguish between low- and high-value expression.[283]

Frederick Schauer makes a similar argument. He points out that there are a number of activities accomplished through speech that the government should be able to regulate.[284] "Not only do we fix prices with speech, but we also make contracts with speech, commit perjury with speech, discriminate with speech, extort with speech, threaten with speech, and place bets with speech."[285] These classes of speech, or at least some of them, Professor Schauer claims, do not present the kind of harm that amounts to a clear and present danger, and there is no particularly compelling governmental interest in prohibiting them.[286] Thus, the only way of explaining why they may be regulated by the government without violating the First Amendment is the low-value speech theory—that is, these forms of speech "are to be tested under drastically different standards of protection" than other kinds of speech that are more valued under the First Amendment.[287]

The justification proffered for the low-value speech theory by Stone, Sunstein, and Schauer is what used to be derogatorily referred to as "result-oriented." The justification begins with a desired result, namely, that there should be a system of freedom of speech that provides a good deal of constitutional protection to most forms of expression, and also allows for the regulation and even prohibition of some kinds of expression, such as price-fixing, blackmail, perjury, libel, commercial speech, and obscenity. The only method of reaching the result Stone, Sunstein, and Schauer envision is to distinguish among various kinds of speech according to their value. This sort of result-oriented approach to legal analysis, although at one time considered illegitimate by some, should not be so quickly scorned as it once was; in fact, it does find more acceptance in contemporary legal circles than it did in the past.

Other questions, however, remain about the arguments made in support of the low-value speech theory. The arguments are somewhat convincing, but not entirely. Certainly an effective system of free expression should proscribe some regulations of speech and uphold others. However, it is not at all clear that such a system necessitates measuring the value of different categories of speech. After all, it may be possible to have an effective system of free expression that focuses upon the consequences of speech rather than the value of its content. Notwithstanding claims to the contrary, it is possible to imagine a sensible system of free expression that avoids any assessment of the value of expression, but also upholds regulations of speech upon the showing of a substantial or even a compelling state interest. Such a system might well allow the regulation of private blackmail and other speech that causes harm while prohibiting the regulation of speech that does not cause harm. In other words, an effective system of freedom of expression might focus on the effects of speech rather than the putative value of its content. It may be a mistake to assume that an effective system of speech regulation must focus on the content of speech; it is altogether possible that an effective theory of free expression could ignore the content of speech and focus solely on its impact.

The examples given by various commentators to demonstrate the need for the low-value speech theory are rather weak. Blackmail, price fixing, perjury, and extortion are properly subject to regulation either because they pose a clear and present danger of a harm that the government has authority to prohibit or because there is a compelling state interest to regulate them. And to the extent that contracts may be regulated, discrimination and threats prohibited, and betting restricted, there also is a compelling state interest for regulation. The regulation of libel already is based, at least partially, on the harm—wrongful damage to individual reputation and integrity—it causes. By adopting a definitional balancing approach, the Supreme Court has shown that it is possible to regulate libel on the basis of its consequences rather than its value.

It also would seem that a harm-based analysis could well be used to assess regulations of commercial speech without addressing the value of such speech. False or misleading advertising could be regulated because it is harmful; it deceives people into taking action they would not otherwise take. Advertising for dangerous products, such as cigarettes or alcohol, could be constitutionally restricted on the basis of the harm the products cause. Similarly, advertising for products that are harmful to the environment could be prohibited.

Indeed, if highly valued speech can be regulated on the basis of harm, it seems possible to envision the same sort of system for low-value speech. After all, the most highly valued political speech may be restricted if it is shown to incite violence, damage the environment,[288] cause visual blight,[289] threaten pedestrian safety,[290] violate privacy, or cause other sorts of harm, and there is no apparent reason why low-value speech could not be regulated on the same basis.

The low-value speech theory rests on the questionable premise that it is somehow necessary to evaluate the merit of speech in order to be able to regulate some kinds of speech. A sensible system of free expression does seem possible by focusing on the harm of speech, rather than evaluating its content. Indeed, the only justification for restricting speech is to prevent harm, and it is harm, therefore, that should be the key to the system.

THE LOW-VALUE SPEECH THEORY AND THE TECHNIQUE OF CATEGORIZATION

The Practice of Categorization

The low-value speech theory operates through the technique of categorization. That is, the Supreme Court designates different kinds or categories of speech and assigns them high or low value. It can be said that the Court "categorizes" some kinds of speech as beyond First Amendment protection or at the fringes of the First Amendment and therefore entitled to little of its protection.

In *R.A.V. v. City of St. Paul*, decided in 1992,[291] the Supreme Court found itself in serious disagreement regarding the categorization approach in First Amendment cases. The majority opinion, written by Justice Scalia, abruptly dismissed the categorization approach as nothing more than a metaphor.[292] According to Justice Scalia's opinion, the metaphor of categorization literally means that the First Amendment is not violated by the regulation or prohibition of certain categories of speech.[293]

Justice White, believing that the majority was abandoning the categorization technique, wrote a defense of it in a concurring opinion.[294] The Court has long held, said Justice White, that certain categories of speech may be proscribed on the basis of their content.[295] Moreover, he continued, the "categorical approach has provided a principled and narrowly focused means for distinguishing between expression that the government may regulate freely and that which it may regulate . . . only upon a showing of compelling need."[296]

Justice Stevens, who joined the other parts of the White concurrence, pointedly declined to join the part concerning categorization. In his own concurring opinion, Justice Stevens described the categorization approach as "unworkable" and "ultimately futile."[297] In Justice Stevens' view, categories correspond poorly to the complex reality of expression.[298] Categories, he said, are too fuzzy and do not account for the context in which speech occurs.[299]

While Justice Scalia may be correct to say that the term "categorization" is a metaphor, it is nevertheless a metaphor, like many others, that has a certain accuracy that more literal statements lack. The Court does on occasion classify speech into categories and place some of those categories of speech beyond the protection of the First Amendment.

Frederick Schauer has written what is probably the most thorough attempt to justify First Amendment categorization.[300] He correctly notes that categorization often is presented as an alternative to balancing.[301] But categorization is necessary in First Amendment cases, Professor Schauer argues, because balancing does not provide a complete picture of First Amendment methodology and obscures the full importance of categorization in the structure of First Amendment doctrine.[302]

Professor Schauer also points out that the First Amendment itself sets up the category of speech, and that when defining the word "speech" to determine if a certain activity is within the scope of the First Amendment, we are categorizing.[303] This is undeniably true. The Constitution, like other laws, is replete with categories. Categorization can never be entirely eliminated from the process of constitutional interpretation. Indeed, it can never be entirely eliminated from any form of human thought. Words themselves are categories. Human beings inescapably think and communicate in categories, and when we define something, we are engaged, as Professor Schauer tells us, in the act of categorizing. Thus, a certain amount of categorizing is unavoidable in constitutional decision making as well as in any other form of human decision making.

Nonetheless, there are various ways to formulate categories, and not all of them are equally useful. *A priori* categories are particularly dangerous because they tend to be thoughtlessly devised. They have a beguiling appeal because they seem to be natural or even supernatural, handed down by some transcendental authority.[304] At base, however, *a priori* categories provide nothing more than a false security. They can be neither proven nor disproven, as they are founded upon neither empirical observation nor policy considerations.[305] Having no basis in reality or policy, *a priori* categories tend to be non-teleological—lacking in purpose—and therefore the results to which they lead are random and desultory.

Other categories that are devised according to reason or to accomplish certain purposes tend to be much more thoughtful and useful, depending upon the validity of the reasons or purposes that support them. Definitional or categorical balancing makes use of categories, although not *a priori* ones; even ad hoc balancing makes use of categories, although they tend to be relatively concrete and narrow. Categories can be useful, but only to the extent that they are devised in terms of the purposes they are meant to serve. It has been said that categorical definitions of speech are plausible only if there is a single normative value served by freedom of speech or if several normative free speech values can coincide in a single category of speech.[306] Unfortunately, the Supreme Court has not yet been able to achieve that sort of unified vision of the First Amendment; it seems that no group of human beings is capable of agreement concerning what values underlie the First Amendment and exactly how those values should be delineated in the categorization of expression.

Categorization can be emphasized or de-emphasized in a human thought process, and it can be maximized or minimized in constitutional interpretation.

There is an essential difference between categorization and balancing; the former looks to definitions, the latter to reasons, and that difference makes balancing the preferred method of constitutional interpretation.

Legal historian Morton Horwitz has pointed out that "Nothing captures the essential difference between the typical legal minds of nineteenth- and twentieth-century America quite as well as their attitude toward categories."[307] Nineteenth-century legal thought, he continues, was overwhelmingly under the sway of categorical thinking, whereas twentieth-century thought emphasizes balancing of values and policies.[308] Twentieth-century thought recognizes that the differences of kind presumed to be at the foundation of categories are actually differences in degree.[309] Thus, we have come to see reality "not as a series of mutually exclusive black-white bright-line boundaries . . . but rather as a series of continua involving shades of gray requiring line-drawing."[310] Categories, then, have a certain inherent fallibility.

Moreover, the efficacy of any category depends on how it is defined, and categories have a tendency to be over- or under-inclusive, or both. The Court's definition of commercial speech, for example, is so broad that it includes wildly different kinds of expression. Professor Sunstein's definition of pornography seems to be so narrow that it would exclude the regulation of a good deal of material that he no doubt believes to cause violent behavior.[311] Professor MacKinnon's definition of pornography is so extensive that it would allow the regulation of a good deal of material that has substantial artistic merit.[312]

Although it may be unavoidable to some degree, categorization has a number of deficiencies that should not be overlooked. One of the obvious deficiencies of categorization, because categories are abstract and general, is that they cannot adequately account for all of the specific instances within their scope. Low-value speech categories certainly are plagued by that deficiency. Probably all the low-value categories of speech—commercial speech, libel, obscenity, etc.—are broad enough to encompass a fairly wide array of speech that may vary considerably in nature and communicative value. The category of commercial speech, for example, encompasses a wide variety of material that ranges from being barely to highly informative. A sign painted on barns throughout the country reading "Chew Mailpouch" conveys very little in the way of information, but brochures about family planning or venereal disease distributed by a company that produces condoms contain a useful information about important social issues.[313] The same point can be made about pornography. Some expresses very little in the way of ideas or information, but some does express ideas and information. In fact, the same point can be made about virtually any category of speech, including highly valued categories. Traditionally, political expression about public issues has enjoyed the highest constitutional value; it is considered to lie at the very core of the protection afforded by the First Amendment. Certainly, political speeches, articles, and debates express the kinds of ideas and data that are essential to an informed electorate. But a sign that reads "Roland Vincent—City Council"[314] conveys about the same measure of information as one that says "Chew Mailpouch." Indeed, as our political campaigns become more and more like the packaging and advertising of products, the difference between political and commercial speech begins to pale.

A related drawback of the low-value speech theory is that it depends on categories of speech that often overlap to a great extent and thus make it difficult, if not impossible, to determine the value of speech. For example, the category of political speech is highly valued; the category of profanity at one time was less valued. What about the speech in *Cohen v. California*?[315] Is it political speech or profanity? Obviously it is both. Throughout history, political ideas often have been expressed in sexual, scatological, profane, or offensive imagery. The political satires of Jonathan Swift are replete with scatological images. The great works of William Shakespeare and Mark Twain include racist and anti-Semitic language. The parody in *Hustler Magazine v. Falwell*[316] is undeniably gross and offensive, but it also skewers political and religious hypocrisy. To many individuals, burning the American flag is "profoundly offensive" and to some it may be nothing more than "an inarticulate grunt or roar,"[317] but it is also a profound political protest that could be said to lie at the very heart of protection afforded by the First Amendment. All these examples illustrate that the categories of speech designated by the Supreme Court, like most other categories, cannot be neatly separated. They tend to overlap one another, making it problematic to assess the value of speech.

A further problem in assessing the value of speech is that whatever value speech may or may not possess varies according to its context.[318] Value, like beauty, resides in the eye of the beholder, and the meaning of any particular book, article, film, etc., changes from situation to situation. Expression has no constant value; rather, its value changes and shifts from one context to another. In one setting speech may be taken as profane, racist, or obscene, whereas in another setting the very same speech may be taken in a very different way.

Categorization, then, has its pitfalls.

The Basis of Categorization

To acknowledge that some degree of categorization inevitably will occur is not to say that every act of categorization is done correctly or justifiably. To define First Amendment "freedom of speech" as encompassing only printed materials such as books and newspapers would surely be an act of categorization, albeit one that would be most difficult, if not impossible, to justify.

And therein lies the greater problem about the category of low-value speech. It is problematic not only because it engages in categorization, but more so because of the specific content of the categories, which is based upon evaluating the social worth of speech. Unlike the approach of definitional or categorical balancing, which looks to the harm caused by speech, low-value categorization looks to the value of speech, which is a highly questionable, uncertain, and subjective enterprise.

Moreover, these matters become more complicated. As Professor Schauer readily acknowledges, although the First Amendment itself designates the category of speech, it does not designate any subcategories of speech.[319] The First Amendment speaks of "speech," but says nothing of "high-value" or "low-value" speech. The First Amendment speaks of "speech," but makes no mention of "political," "public," or "private" speech. Nor does it refer to "fighting words," "obscenity," "libel," "commercial speech," or any other kind of speech. These refinements, which are not found within the text of the First Amendment, have been devised by the Supreme Court. Therefore, while some categorization may be inevitable in determining what is and is not speech, the further subcategorization the Court has formulated is neither inevitable nor unavoidable.

Professor Schauer admits this, but asserts that the subcategorization that has occurred at the hands of the Court is justifiable.[320] Although he wishes the subcategories employed by the Court were more well-defined,[321] he advances several arguments "in favor of categorization within the First Amendment."[322] First, he says, in the absence of subcategories of speech, "there may be pressure to keep troublesome categories completely outside. When the choice is all or nothing, the difficulties of 'all' may lead courts to choose 'nothing.' "[323]

This argument appears a bit sophistic. It overlooks that the courts may choose "all," which is, indeed, the proper choice unless some justification for the subcategory can be shown. Furthermore, the argument pretends to be protective of freedom of speech by claiming to allow the suppression of some speech in order to protect other speech. Yet the argument has a hollow ring because the list of low-value speech is growing longer, contrary to early warnings that it should be kept strictly confined to a few well-defined and narrowly limited categories of speech.

Next, Professor Schauer argues that not all forms of speech are amenable to the same analytic approach.[324] For example, the "clear and present danger" test used in cases dealing with advocacy of rebellion is not appropriate for dealing with libel or false advertising.[325] Schauer believes most First Amendment doctrine has been formulated in response to cases dealing with advocacy of rebellion, and other lines of analysis are needed for other categories of speech.[326]

The assertion that most First Amendment doctrine has been formulated in regard to advocacy of rebellion ignores the scope and complexity of that doctrine. While the genesis of First Amendment doctrine occurred in advocacy cases, since then the Supreme Court has developed an extensive body of law dealing with many other kinds of speech. Professor Schauer may be on firmer ground when he suggests that not all forms of speech are amenable to the same analysis, but considerable question remains as to whether it is necessary to categorize speech, and, if so, whether it should be categorized according to its presumed value or according to the harm that it demonstrably causes.

Finally, Professor Schauer argues that the refusal to categorize is "frightfully counter-intuitive."[327] "Political argument," he says, "is simply more important than 'Specified Sexual Activities,' and *Hamlet* is simply better literature than

'Dance With the Dominant Whip.' . . . Anyone who holds otherwise is just plain wrong."[328] Although Professor Schauer's assessment, at least of those particular examples, is in all probability correct, nonetheless there is a certain risk in making such an unqualified pronouncement, especially when it comes to a matter of taste. Taste, it should be remembered, is something for which there is no accounting. It is worth noting, too, that a good deal of political argument hardly reaches the level of *Hamlet*. Even Professor Schauer admits:

> [T]hings are not this simple. Our commonsense categories have fuzzy edges, and there is much more agreement that *Hamlet* is good literature and 'Dance With the Dominant Whip' is bad literature than there is about in which category to put *Memoirs of a Woman of Pleasure* or George Carlin's 'Seven Dirty Words' monologue.[329]

What makes the fuzzy edges of the categories even more problematic is that it will be government officials who enforce the categories and who decide which speech falls into which category. Given the historical tendency of government to over-censor, fuzzy-edged categories pose a significant threat to freedom of speech.

Whatever the relative merits and demerits of the categorization technique, it should be emphasized that if categorization of speech does occur, it need not be based on the value of speech. Martin Redish points out,

> [A]lthough it may well be appropriate to distinguish among different forms of expression on the ground that some of them present greater danger of harming society, it is considerably more doubtful that an arm of the state should have the authority to decide for the individual that certain means of mental development are better than others.[330]

Speech can be categorized by standards other than its value. In fact, it could be categorized according to whether it causes harmful effects beyond its communicative impact. This is the approach taken, for example, in Justice William Brennan's concurring opinion in *Ferber*.[331] If this approach were taken toward obscenity or pornography, there would be a stronger case for regulating violent sexually explicit materials than for regulating sexually explicit materials that contain little or no violence. Moreover, if the category were based on the harmful effects of speech, the specific content of the category might be changed by stressing the component of the material—violence—that causes the harm, rather than the sexual component, which appears to have no harmful effects.

Although categorization may not be completely avoidable, it is a mode of thought that has serious flaws. Moreover, categories of speech can be formulated based on the effects of expression without reference to its value.

CONCLUSION

The difficulties of categorizing speech on the basis of its value should not be underestimated. Lawrence Alexander points out that attempts to "distinguish speech of different value leads to intractable difficulties of classification."[332] Moreover, categorizing speech on the basis of its supposed value is a dubious practice that seems to contradict basic First Amendment principles. To the extent that fighting words, commercial speech, pornography, or other kinds of speech may be subject to regulation, it should be because they cause harm and not because they are presumed to be low in communicative value.

Perhaps the greatest danger of the low-value speech theory is the temptation it poses for expanding its application to new kinds of speech. From the very beginning of the theory[333] to the Supreme Court's most recent pronouncement about it[334] the Court has always described it as applicable only in "limited" areas. But whenever another kind of expression—be it flag burning or hate speech—gains a renewed disfavor, there is a strong temptation to devalue it and restrict it on that basis. It is quicker and easier to deal with disfavored speech by denigrating its value than by making real assessments about the harm it supposedly causes. And certainly some kinds of speech seem, as Professor Schauer puts it, "intuitively" to be low in value.

However, it is one matter to designate one or two categories of speech as low in value and attempt to keep those categories narrowly defined, and quite another matter to expand the list of low-value categories first to one new area and then to another. After all, there are serious questions about the basic compatibility of the low-value speech theory with First Amendment principles, and its expansion may amount to a serious threat to freedom of expression. If not properly cabined, it is a theory that could swallow large chunks of the First Amendment and lead to extensive suppression of free speech. Over thirty years ago Harry Kalven cautioned that the two-level approach to the First Amendment "may have unhappy repercussions on the protection of free speech generally."[335] That caution still pertains.

NOTES

1. *See, e.g.*, Brandenburg v. Ohio, 395 U.S. 444 (1969) (holding statute punishing mere advocacy of use of force violates First Amendment); Tinker v. Des Moines Sch. Dist., 393 U.S. 503 (1969) (holding school policy prohibiting wearing armbands to school in protest of Viet Nam war violates First Amendment); Cohen v. California, 403 U.S. 15 (1971) (wearing jacket with words "Fuck the Draft" in public is speech protected by the First Amendment and may not be prosecuted as breach of the peace); New York Times Co. v. United States, 403 U.S. 713 (1971) (holding government carries heavy burden to justify prior restraint enforcement); Landmark Communications, Inc. v. Virginia, 435 U.S. 829 (1978) (holding judicial inquiry beyond legislative determination required in determining existence of First Amendment violation); Texas v. Johnson, 491 U.S. 397 (1989) (burning American flag in public as means of political protest protected by First Amendment).

2. *See* cases cited, *supra* note 1.

3. "If there is a bedrock principle underlying the First Amendment, it is that the

government may not prohibit the expression of an idea simply because society finds the idea itself offensive or disagreeable." Texas v. Johnson, 491 U.S. at 414.

4. *See* Jeffrey M. Shaman, *The First Amendment Rule Against Overbreadth*, 52 TEMP. L.Q. 259 (1979).

5. *See* Geoffrey R. Stone, *Content Regulation and the First Amendment*, 25 WM. & MARY L. Rev. 189 (1983).

6. *Id.*

7. Dun & Bradstreet, Inc. v. Greenmoss Builders, Inc., 472 U.S. 749, 758 (1985) (holding credit report matter of purely private concern and therefore of lesser constitutional value than matter of public concern).

8. *See* text *infra*, at notes 25–143.

9. *See* text *infra*, at notes 25–68.

10. *See* text *infra*, at notes 69–100.

11. *See* text *infra*, at notes 101–111.

12. Gertz v. Robert Welch, Inc., 418 U.S. 323, 340 (1974) (holding lesser standard of liability exists for private libel actions than for public figures).

13. Dun & Bradstreet, Inc. v. Greenmoss Builders, Inc., 472 U.S. at 749, 758.

14. Ohralik v. Ohio State Bar Ass'n, 436 U.S. 447, 456 (1978) (holding state may proscribe in-person attorney solicitation of contingent fee employment without a showing of actual harm).

15. *See* Stone, *supra* note 5, at 194.

16. Brandenburg v. Ohio, 395 U.S. 444 (1969).

17. *Id.*

18. *See* Geoffrey R. Stone *et al.*, CONSTITUTIONAL LAW 1200–03 (2d ed. 1991).

19. *See* NLRB v. Gissell Packing Co., 395 U.S. 575, 616–19 (1969) (holding First Amendment does not prohibit NLRB from regulating employer's retaliatory speech as unfair labor practice).

20. Thornhill v. Alabama, 310 U.S. 88, 102 (1940) (holding peaceful picketing protected by First Amendment).

21. *See* Kenneth L. Karst, *Equality as a Central Principle in the First Amendment*, 43 U. CHI. L. REV. 20, 31 (1975).

22. R.A.V. v. City of St. Paul, 505 U.S. 377, 400 (1992) (White, J., concurring and dissenting, joined by Blackmun, J., & O'Connor, J.).

23. Some scholarship, such as Daniel A. Farber, *Commercial Speech and First Amendment Theory*, 74 NW. U.L. REV. 372 (1979), has focused on the value of particular kinds of speech, but there have been few, if any, comprehensive studies of the low-value speech theory. The beginnings of a scholarly examination of the theory can be seen in the short exchange between Lawrence Alexander, *Low Value Speech*, 83 NW. U.L. REV. 547 (1989), and Cass R. Sunstein, *Low Value Speech Revisited*, 83 NW. U.L. REV. 555 (1989).

24. *See* text *infra*, at notes 266–85.

25. Chaplinsky v. New Hampshire, 315 U.S. 568 (1942).

26. *Id.* at 569.

27. *Id.*

28. *See, e.g.*, Coates v. Cincinnati, 402 U.S. 611 (1971) (holding ordinance prohibiting assembly on sidewalk and annoying conduct unconstitutionally vague and overbroad); Rosenfeld v. New Jersey, 408 U.S. 901 (1972) (holding statute prohibiting public

use of offensive and indecent language overbroad); Lewis v. New Orleans II, 415 U.S. 130 (1974) (holding statute prohibiting public use of lascivious language overbroad).

29. *See, e.g.*, Brandenburg v. Ohio, 395 U.S. 444 (1969); Cohen v. California, 403 U.S. 15 (1971); Texas v. Johnson, 491 U.S. 397 (1989); Cantwell v. Connecticut, 310 U.S. 296 (1940) (holding First Amendment protects religiously offensive speech); Kunz v. New York, 340 U.S. 290 (1951) (holding ordinance vesting administrative officer with discretionary power to restrict public speaking about religion violated First Amendment); Rosenfeld v. New Jersey, 408 U.S. 901 (1972); Lewis v. New Orleans II, 415 U.S. 130 (1974); Hustler Magazine v. Falwell, 485 U.S. 46 (1988) (holding public figure's recovery for tort dependent on showing of actual malice); *see also* Note, *The Demise of the Chaplinsky Fighting Words Doctrine: An Argument for Its Interment*, 106 HARV. L. REV. 1129 (1993).

30. *See* cases cited *supra* note 1; Coates v. Cincinnati, 402 U.S. 611 (1971).

31. Chaplinsky v. New Hampshire, 315 U.S. 571–72 (1942); *see also* Beauharnais v. Illinois, 343 U.S. 250, 255–57 (1952) (sustaining criminal group libel statute).

32. Chaplinsky v. New Hampshire, 315 U.S. at 571.

33. Cohen v. California, 403 U.S. at 25.

34. R.A.V. v. City of St. Paul, 505 U.S. 377, 382–83 (1992).

35. *Id.*

36. *Id.* at 398–403 (White, J., concurring and dissenting).

37. *Id.* at 384–85.

38. *Id.* at 393.

39. *Id.* at 386.

40. Roth v. United States, 354 U.S. 476 (1957).

41. *Id.* at 484.

42. *Id.*

43. *Id.* at 485.

44. Michael J. Perry, *Freedom of Expression: An Essay on Theory and Doctrine*, 78 NW. U.L. REV. 1137, 1182 (1983).

45. "All ideas having even the slightest redeeming social importance—unorthodox ideas, controversial ideas, even ideas hateful to the prevailing climate of opinion—have the full protection of the [First Amendment], unless excludable because they encroach upon the limited area of more important interests." Roth v. United States, 354 U.S. at 484. *See also* Gertz v. Robert Welch, Inc., 418 U.S. 323, 339 (1974): "Under the First Amendment there is no such thing as a false idea. However pernicious an opinion may seem, we depend for its correction not on the conscience of judges and juries but on the competition of other ideas."

46. Perry, *supra* note 44, at 1182–83.

47. THE REPORT OF THE PRESIDENT'S COMMISSION ON OBSCENITY AND PORNOGRAPHY 53 (1970).

48. Frederick Schauer, FREE SPEECH: A PHILOSOPHIC ENQUIRY 181 (1982).

49. Miller v. California, 413 U.S. 15, 24–25 (1973).

50. Paris Adult Theatre I v. Slaton, 413 U.S. 49 (1973).

51. *Id.* at 58.

52. *Id.*

53. THE REPORT OF THE PRESIDENT'S COMMISSION ON OBSCENITY AND PORNOGRAPHY 27 (1970).

54. Paris Adult Theatre I v. Slaton, 413 U.S. at 60.

55. Attorney Gen.'s Comm'n on Pornography, U.S. Dept. of Justice, Final Report 320–49 (1986).

56. *Id.*

57. *Id.*

58. *Id.*

59. Harry Kalven, *The Metaphysics of the Law of Obscenity*, 1960 Sup. Ct. Rev. 1, 11.

60. *Id.*

61. *Id.* at 19 (quoting Justice Douglas dissenting in Roth v. United States, 354 U.S. 514 [1957]).

62. *Id.* at 10–11.

63. *Id.* at 17–19.

64. Stone *et al., supra* note 18, at 1144; *see also* Cass R. Sunstein, *Free Speech Now*, 59 U. Chi. L. Rev. 255, 301–302 (1992).

65. New York v. Ferber, 458 U.S. 747, 753–56 (1981).

66. *Id.* at 756–57.

67. Gerald Gunther & Kathleen M. Sullivan, Constitutional Law 1146 (13th ed. 1997) (quoting *Id.* at 763).

68. New York v. Ferber, 458 U.S. at 762.

69. Erznoznik v. Jacksonville, 422 U.S. 205 (1975).

70. Southeastern Promotions v. Conrad, 420 U.S. 546 (1975).

71. Ernoznik v. Jacksonville, 422 U.S. at 209–10.

72. Young v. American Mini Theatres, 427 U.S. 50 (1976).

73. *Id.* at 71.

74. *Id.* at 62–63.

75. *Id.* at 70.

76. *Id.*

77. *Id.* at 87 (Stewart, J., dissenting, joined by Brennan, J., Marshall, J., & Blackmun, J.).

78. *Id.* at 84–87 (Stewart, J., dissenting, joined by Brennan, J., Marshall, J., & Blackmun, J.).

79. *Id.* at 73 (Powell, J., concurring).

80. FCC v. Pacifica Found., 438 U.S. 726 (1978).

81. *Id.* at 761 (Powell, J., concurring).

82. City of Renton v. Playtime Theatres, Inc., 475 U.S. 41 (1986).

83. *Id.* at 47–51.

84. Schad v. Mt. Ephraim, 452 U.S. 61 (1981).

85. *Id.* at 65–66.

86. *Id.* at 80 (Stevens, J., concurring).

87. Barnes v. Glen Theatre, Inc., 501 U.S. 560 (1991).

88. *Id.* at 565.

89. *Id.* at 566.

90. *Id.* at 587 (White, J., dissenting).

91. *Id.* at 581 (Souter, J., concurring).

92. *Id.* at 582–86 (Souter, J., concurring).

93. *Id.* at 585 n.2 (Souter, J., concurring).

94. *Id.* at 581 (Souter, J., concurring).

95. Sable Communications, Inc. v. FCC, 492 U.S. 115 (1989).

96. *Id.* at 126.

97. *Id.*

98. Denver Area Educational Communications Consortium Inc. v. FCC, 518 U.S. 727 (1996).

99. Reno v. ACLU, 521 U.S. 844 (1997).

100. *See, e.g.*, Joseph Burstyn, Inc. v. Wilson, 343 U.S. 495, 502–503 (1952); Erznoznik v. Jacksonville, 422 U.S. 205 (1975).

101. Chaplinsky v. New Hampshire, 315 U.S. 568, 571–72 (1942).

102. Cohen v. California, 403 U.S. 15 (1971).

103. *Id.* at 25.

104. *Id.*

105. Rosenfeld v. New Jersey, 408 U.S. 901 (1972); Lewis v. New Orleans II, 415 U.S. 130 (1974); Brown v. Oklahoma, 408 U.S. 914 (1972) (holding statute prohibiting obscene or lascivious language overbroad).

106. FCC v. Pacifica Found., 438 U.S. 726 (1978).

107. *Id.* at 746.

108. *Id.*

109. *Id.* at 761 (Powell, J., concurring).

110. Sable Communications, Inc. v. FCC, 492 U.S. 115 (1989).

111. Reno v. ACLU, 521 U.S. 844 (1997).

112. Beauharnais v. Illinois, 343 U.S. 250 (1952).

113. *Id.* at 251.

114. *Id.* at 258–63.

115. *Id.* at 256–57.

116. John E. Nowak & Ronald D. Rotunda, CONSTITUTIONAL LAW 1036 (4th ed. 1991).

117. Landmark Communications, Inc. v. Virginia, 435 U.S. 829, 843 (1978).

118. Nowak and Rotunda, *supra* note 116, at 1036.

119. New York Times Co. v. Sullivan, 376 U.S. 254 (1964) (holding public official must prove actual malice to recover damages for defamatory falsehood regarding his official conduct).

120. See Anthony Lewis, MAKE NO LAW: THE SULLIVAN CASE AND THE FIRST AMENDMENT (1991); Harry Kalven, Jr., *The New York Times Case: A Note on "The Central Meaning of the First Amendment*," SUP. CT. REV. 191 (1964).

121. New York Times v. Sullivan, 376 U.S. at 270–72.

122. Kalven, *supra* note 120, at 221.

123. *See, e.g.*, Gertz v. Robert Welch, Inc., 418 U.S. 323, 339 (1974); Bose Corp. v. Consumers Union of United States, Inc., 466 U.S. 485, 503–504 (1984) (holding appellate court must independently review lower court's actual malice finding in defamation case); Hustler Magazine v. Falwell, 485 U.S. 46, 50–51 (1988).

124. Pittsburgh Press v. Human Rel. Comm'n, 413 U.S. 376, 385 (1973) (holding employment ad is proposal of possible employment not protected by First Amendment); Virginia State Bd. of Pharmacy v. Virginia Citizens Consumer Council, Inc., 425 U.S. 748, 762 (1976) (striking down statute making it illegal to advertise prescription drug prices).

125. Bolger v. Youngs Drug Prods. Corp., 463 U.S. 60, 66–67 (1983) (holding contraceptive ad mailings constitute commercial speech).

126. Central Hudson Gas & Elec. v. Public Serv. Comm'n, 447 U.S. 557, 579–81

(1980) (Steven, J., concurring) (holding statute banning electrical utility promotional advertising violates First Amendment).

127. *Id.*

128. *Id.*

129. Valentine v. Chrestensen, 316 U.S. 52 (1942) (upholding provision of sanitary code prohibiting distribution of advertisements in the streets).

130. *See id.* at 54.

131. Virginia State Bd. of Pharmacy v. Virginia Citizens Consumer Council, Inc., 425 U.S. 748 (1976).

132. *See* text *infra*, at notes 134–41.

133. Virginia State Bd. of Pharmacy v. Virginia Citizens Consumer Council, Inc., 425 U.S. at 765.

134. Bates v. State Bar of Arizona, 433 U.S. 350, 364 (1977) (prohibiting attorney price advertising for routine legal services violates First Amendment).

135. *Id.*

136. *Id.* at 380–81 (1977); Central Hudson Gas & Elec. v. Public Serv. Comm'n, 447 U.S. at 557, 562.

137. Central Hudson Gas & Elec. v. Public Serv. Comm'n, 447 U.S. at 561–62.

138. *Id.*; Metromedia, Inc. v. San Diego, 453 U.S. 490 (1981).

139. *See* Bates v. State Bar of Arizona, 433 U.S. at 364; Posadas de Puerto Rico Assocs. v. Tourism Co., 478 U.S. 328 (1986); Board of Trustees of the State Univ. of New York v. Fox, 492 U.S. 469 (1989).

140. *See* Posadas de Puerto Rico Assocs. v. Tourism Co., 478 U.S. at 328; Board of Trustees of the State Univ. of New York v. Fox, 492 U.S. 469 (1989).

141. *See* City of Cincinnati v. Discovery Network, Inc., 507 U.S. 410 (1993); Edenfield v. Fane, 507 U.S. 761 (1993); Rubin v. Coors Brewing Co., 514 U.S. 476 (1995); 44 Liquormart, Inc. v. Rhode Island, 517 U.S. 484 (1996).

142. Bates v. State Bar of Arizona, 433 U.S. at 380–82.

143. Central Hudson Gas & Elec. v. Public Serv. Comm'n, 447 U.S. at 557, 563–64.

144. American Booksellers Ass'n v. Hudnut, 771 F.2d 323 (7th Cir. 1985); *aff'd*, 47 U.S. 1001 (1986).

145. Village Books v. City of Bellingham, Docket No. 88–1470 (W.D. Wash. Feb. 9, 1989).

146. Regina v. Butler, SCC at 62 (Feb. 27, 1992) (unreported).

147. *Id.* The objective of the ban, to prevent the harm fostered by pornography, was considered to be of sufficient importance to warrant overriding the free speech guaranteed by the Charter. *Id.* at 480.

148. *See* Ronald J. Berger, FEMINISM AND PORNOGRAPHY (1991).

149. *Id.* at 120–22. *See also* WOMEN AGAINST CENSORSHIP (V. Burstyn ed. 1985).

150. Andrea Dworkin, *Against the Male Flood: Censorship, Pornography and Equality*, 8 HARV. WOMEN'S L.J. 1, 25 (1985).

151. Andrea Dworkin & Catharine A. MacKinnon, PORNOGRAPHY AND CIVIL RIGHTS 58 (1988).

152. Catharine A. MacKinnon, *Not A Moral Issue*, 2 YALE L. & POL'Y REV. 321, 329 (1984).

153. *Id.* at 322–23.

154. *Id.* at 323–24.

155. *Id.* at 326–27.

156. Catharine A. MacKinnon, *Pornography, Civil Rights, and Speech*, 20 HARV. C.R.-C.L.L. REV. 1, 7 (1985).

157. MacKinnon, *supra* note 150, at 321–29.

158. Dworkin & MacKinnon, *supra* note 149, at 62.

159. Steven G. Gey, *The Apologetics of Suppression: The Regulation of Pornography as Act and Idea*, 86 MICH. L. REV. 1564, 1606 (1988).

160. *Id.* at 1607.

161. *Id.* at 1605–06.

162. Cass R. Sunstein, *Pornography and the First Amendment*, 1986 DUKE L.J. 589 (1986).

163. *Id.* at 592.

164. *Id.* at 603–608.

165. *Id.* at 603–604.

166. *Id.* at 607.

167. *Id.*

168. *Id.*

169. *Id.* at 606–607.

170. *Id.*

171. *See* Gey, *supra* note 157, at notes 100–148 and sources cited therein.

172. Donald A. Downs, THE NEW POLITICS OF PORNOGRAPHY 164 (1989).

173. *Id.* at 604, 611–16.

174. *Id.* at 164.

175. *Id.*

176. Richard Delgado, *Words That Wound: A Tort Action for Racial Insults, Epithets, and Name Calling*, HARV. C.R.-C.L.L. REV. 133 (1982); Mari J. Matsuda, *Public Response to Racist Speech: Considering the Victim's Story*, 87 MICH. L. REV. 2320 (1989); Charles R. Lawrence, *If He Hollers Let Him Go: Regulating Racist Speech on Campus*, DUKE L.J. 431 (1990); Alon Harel, *Bigotry, Pornography, and the First Amendment: A Theory of Unprotected Speech*, 65 S: CAL. L. REV. 1887 (1992).

177. *See* Doe v. University of Michigan, 721 F. Supp. 852, 855 (E.D. MICH. 1989) (holding campus speech code overbroad and overly vague under First Amendment).

178. *See, e.g.*, Delgado, *supra* note 174, at 145–46, 179.

179. Matsuda, *supra* note 176, at 2359.

180. *Id.* at 2360.

181. Harel, *supra* note 176, at 1889.

182. *Id.* at 1888–89.

183. *Id.* at 1889.

184. *Id.*

185. *Id.*

186. The phrase is from New York Times Co. v. Sullivan, 376 U.S. 254, 270 (1964).

187. *See* Board of Educ. v. Pico, 457 U.S. 853 (1982) (disapproving removal of books from school library by board of education).

188. *See* Nadine Strossen, *Regulating Racist Speech on Campus: A Modest Proposal?*, 1990 DUKE L.J. 484, 491–93 (1990).

189. See Rodney Smolla, FREE SPEECH IN AN OPEN SOCIETY ch. 6 (1992).

190. *Id.* at 167–69.

191. *Id.*

192. *Id.*

193. R.A.V. v. City of St. Paul, 505 U.S. 377, 400 (1992).

194. St. Paul Bias-Motivated Crime Ordinance, St. Paul, Minn. Legis. Code § 292.02 (1990).

195. R.A.V. v. City of St. Paul, 505 U.S. at 395–96.

196. *See* Franklin S. Haiman, *The Remedy Is More Speech*, THE AMERICAN PROSPECT, Summer 1991, at 30.

197. Alexander M. Bickel, THE MORALITY OF CONSENT 71 (1975).

198. *Id.* at 72.

199. MacKinnon, *supra* note 150, at 324.

200. Abrams v. United States, 250 U.S. 616, 630 (1919) (Holmes, J., dissenting) (emphasis added).

201. United States v. Schwimmer, 279 U.S. 644, 654–55 (1929) (Holmes, J., dissenting) (emphasis added).

202. Whitney v. California, 274 U.S. 357, 375 (1927) (Brandeis, J., concurring).

203. Board of Educ. v. Barnette, 319 U.S. 624, 642 (1943) (punishing failure to salute U.S. flag violates First Amendment).

204. Texas v. Johnson, 491 U.S. 397, 414 (1989).

205. *See* Texas v. Johnson, 491 U.S. at 397.

206. *See* Hustler Magazine v. Falwell, 485 U.S. 46 (1988).

207. *See* FCC v. Pacifica Found., 438 U.S. 726 (1978).

208. *See* Cohen v. California, 403 U.S. 15 (1971).

209. *See* Tinker v. Des Moines Sch. Dist., 393 U.S. 503 (1969).

210. *See, e.g.*, Cox v. Louisiana, 379 U.S. 536 (1965) (holding peaceful march to protest jailing of picketers protected by First Amendment); Gregory v. Chicago, 394 U.S. 111 (1969) (holding peaceful protest advocating school desegregation protected by First Amendment).

211. Daniel A. Farber, *Civilizing Public Discourse: An Essay on Professor Bickel, Justice Harlan, and the Enduring Significance of Cohen v. California*, 1980 DUKE L.J. 283 (1980).

212. *Id.* at 302.

213. *Id.*

214. *See* Chapter 3 *supra*, at notes 1–195.

215. *Id.* at notes 119–150.

216. *Id.* at notes 151–195.

217. Central Hudson Gas & Elec. v. Public Serv. Comm'n, 447 U.S. 557 (1980).

218. Posadas De Puerto Rico Assocs. v. Tourism Co., 478 U.S. 328 (1986); Board of Trustees of the state Univ. of New York v. Fox, 492 U.S. 469 (1989).

219. *See* City of Cincinnati v. Discovery Network, Inc., 507 U.S. 410 (1993); Edenfield v. Fane, 507 U.S. 761 (1993); Rubin v. Coors Brewing Co., 514 U.S. 476 (1995); 44 Liquormart, Inc. v. Rhode Island, 517 U.S. 484 (1996).

220. *See* Chapter 3 *supra*, at notes 16–118.

221. *Id.*

222. *Id.* at notes 82–118.

223. Geoffrey R. Stone, *Content Neutral Restrictions*, 54 U. CHI. L. REV. 46, 47–54 (1987).

224. *Id.*

225. *Id.*

226. Melville B. Nimmer, NIMMER ON FREEDOM OF SPEECH 2–9 to 2–14 (1984).

227. Pierre J. Schlag, *An Attack on Categorical Approaches to Freedom of Speech*, 30 UCLA L. REV. 671, 673 (1984).

228. Nimmer, *supra* note 224, at 2–15 to 2–24.

229. Compare Ohralik v. Ohio State Bar Ass'n, 426 U.S. 447 (1978), in which the Supreme Court upheld a regulation of lawyer solicitation in a commercial setting, with *In re* Primus, 436 U.S. 412 (1978), in which the Court struck down a regulation of lawyer solicitation in a political setting.

230. Steven H. Shiffrin, THE FIRST AMENDMENT, DEMOCRACY, AND ROMANCE 15–17 (1990).

231. *See* Shaman, *supra* note 4.

232. *Id.* at 260–61.

233. *Id.* at 260.

234. Village of Hoffman Estates v. Flipside, Hoffman Estates, Inc., 455 U.S. 489, 497 (1982) (upholding ordinance requiring business license to allow sale of items designated for use with illegal drugs).

235. New York v. Ferber, 458 U.S. 747, 764–65 (1981).

236. Alexander Meiklejohn, FREE SPEECH AND ITS RELATION TO SELF-GOVERNMENT ch. IV (1948).

237. Alexander Meiklejohn, POLITICAL FREEDOM 20–27 (1960).

238. *Id.* at 116–18.

239. Alexander Meiklejohn, *The First Amendment Is An Absolute*, SUP. CT. REV. 245, 256 (1961).

240. Meiklejohn, *supra* note 234, at 18–27.

241. Meiklejohn, *supra* note 237, at 256.

242. *Id.* at 256–57.

243. Thomas I. Emerson, TOWARD A GENERAL THEORY OF THE FIRST AMENDMENT 4–7 (1966).

244. Martin H. Redish, FREEDOM OF EXPRESSION: A CRITICAL ANALYSIS 11–14 (1984).

245. *Id.* at 19–26.

246. First Nat'l Bank of Boston v. Bellotti, 435 U.S. 765, 776 (1978).

247. *Id.*; Thornhill v. Alabama, 310 U.S. 88, 101 (1940); Dun & Bradstreet, Inc. v. Greenmoss Builders, Inc., 472 U.S. 749, 758–59 (1985).

248. *See* Virginia State Bd. of Pharmacy v. Virginia Citizens Consumer Council, Inc., 425 U.S. 748 (1976).

249. *See* Bates v. State Bar of Arizona, 433 U.S. 350 (1977).

250. *See* Bolger v. Young Drugs Prods. Corp., 463 U.S. 60 (1983).

251. Duran v. City of Douglas, 904 F.2d 1372, 1378 (9th Cir. 1990) (holding profanity and obscene gesture directed toward police officer protected by First Amendment).

252. "The precise factors that the Court considers in determining whether a particular class of speech occupies a 'subordinate position in the scale of First Amendment values' remain somewhat obscure. The Court apparently focuses, however, on the extent to which the speech furthers the historical, political, and philosophical purposes that underlie the first amendment." Stone, *supra* note 5, at 194 (footnote omitted); *see also* Sunstein, *supra* note 162, at 602–03.

253. Sunstein, *supra* note 64, at 302.

254. *See* John M. Finnis, *"Reason and Passion": The Constitutional Dialectic of Free*

Speech and Obscenity, 116 U. PA. L. REV. 222 (1967); Schauer, *supra* note 48, at 178–88.

255. Sunstein, *supra* note 162, at 603.

256. Gey, *supra* note 159, at 1587.

257. Redish, *supra* note 244, at 76.

258. *Id.*

259. *See* Miller v. Civil City of South Bend, 904 F.2d 1081, 1092–96 (7th Cir. 1990) (Posner, J., concurring).

260. Cohen v. California, 403 U.S. 15, 25–26 (1971).

261. Sunstein, *supra* note 162, at 603–04.

262. "Speech that is not intended to communicate a substantive message or that is directed solely to noncognitive capacities may be wholly or largely without the properties that give speech its special status." *Id.* at 606.

263. *Id.* at 604, 611–16.

264. *See* Vincent Blasi, *The Checking Value in First Amendment Theory*, AM. B. FOUND. RES. J. 521 (1977).

265. "[C]ensorship of sexual expression is indeed often laden with 'constitutionally impermissible' motives. Although there are reasons to be concerned about the effects of pornography, it is too simplistic to stress these concerns without also acknowledging the more ideological motives of censorship." Downs, *supra* note 172, at 164.

266. Roth v. United States, 354 U.S. 476, 514 (1957) (Douglas, J., dissenting).

267. FCC v. Pacifica Found., 438 U.S. 726, 761 (1978) (Powell, J., concurring).

268. Thomas I. Emerson, THE SYSTEM OF FREEDOM OF EXPRESSION 326 (1970).

269. *Id.*

270. *See supra* note 266 and accompanying text.

271. Kalven, *supra* note 59, at 19.

272. Shiffrin, *supra* note 230, at 244. Professor Shiffrin's statement was made when apartheid still prevailed in South Africa; hence the parenthetical phrase was editorially added to the text to more accurately express the author's meaning.

273. Karst, *supra* note 21, at 20.

274. *Id.*

275. Police Dep't of Chicago v. Mosley, 408 U.S. 92 (1972) (holding ordinance barring all picketing near school but labor dispute picketing violates First Amendment).

276. *Id.* at 95.

277. Karst, *supra* note 21, at 31.

278. *Id.*

279. *See also* Alexander, *supra* note 23, at 552: "The 'high value,' 'low value,' 'no value' taxonomy is completely wrongheaded, if not incoherent."

280. Stone, *supra* note 5, at 252 n.24.

281. Sunstein, *supra* note 162, at 605.

282. *Id.*

283. Sunstein, *supra* note 64, at 301–04.

284. Frederick Schauer, *Categories and the First Amendment: A Play in Three Acts*, 34 VAND. L. REV. 265, 270–72 (1981).

285. *Id.* at 270.

286. *Id.* at 271.

287. *Id.* at 271–72.

288. *See* Clark v. Community for Creative Non-Violence, 468 U.S. 288, 298 (1984) (upholding application of public park use regulation to prohibit demonstration).

289. *See* City Council v. Taxpayers for Vincent, 466 U.S. 789, 803–17 (1984) (upholding ordinance prohibiting sign posting on public property).

290. *See* Cox v. New Hampshire, 312 U.S. 569 (1941) (upholding law proscribing permitless public street procession); Heffron v. International Soc'y for Krishna Consciousness, Inc., 425 U.S. 640 (1981) (upholding rule confining merchandise sale or distribution to rented state fair booths).

291. R.A.V. v. City of St. Paul, 505 U.S. 377 (1992).

292. *Id.* at 384–85.

293. *Id.*

294. *Id.* at 398–403 (White, J., concurring).

295. *Id.* at 398–401 (White, J., concurring).

296. *Id.* at 399–401 (White, J., concurring).

297. *Id.* at 428 (Stevens, J., concurring).

298. *Id.* at 426–27 (Stevens, J., concurring).

299. *Id.*

300. Schauer, *supra* note 284.

301. *Id.* at 265.

302. *Id.* at 265–66.

303. *Id.* at 267–73.

304. Felix S. Cohen, *Transcendental Nonsense and the Functional Approach*, 35 COLUM. L. REV. 809, 814–21 (1935).

305. *Id.*

306. Schlag, *supra* note 227, at 695.

307. Morton J. Horwitz, THE TRANSFORMATION OF AMERICAN LAW 1870–1960 17 (1992).

308. *Id.*

309. *Id.*

310. *Id.* at 199.

311. In a letter-to-the-editor responding to a review of his book, Professor Sunstein wrote: "In fact, my approach would probably allow less regulation of sexually explicit speech than does current law." Cass R. Sunstein, *Exchange*, THE NATION, December 27, 1993, at 786.

312. *See* text *supra*, at notes 150–61.

313. *See* Bolger v. Young Drugs Prods. Corp., 463 U.S. 60 (1983).

314. *See* City Council v. Taxpayers for Vincent, 466 U.S. 789 (1984).

315. *See* text *supra* at notes 102–4.

316. Hustler Magazine v. Falwell, 485 U.S. 46 (1988).

317. Texas v. Johnson, 491 U.S. 397, 432 (1989) (Rehnquist, C. J., dissenting).

318. *See* Alexander, *supra* note 23, at 551.

319. Schauer, *supra* note 284, at 282–83.

320. *Id.*

321. *Id.* at 288.

322. *Id.* at 286.

323. *Id.*

324. *Id.*

325. *Id.* at 287.

326. *Id.*
327. *Id.*
328. *Id.* at 288.
329. *Id.*
330. Redish, *supra* note 244, at 57.
331. *See* New York v. Ferber, 458 U.S. 747, 775 (1981) (Brennan, J., concurring).
332. Alexander, *supra* note 23, at 551.
333. *See* text *supra*, at notes 25–34.
334. R.A.V. v. City of St. Paul, 505 U.S. 377, 384–85 (1992).
335. Kalven, *supra* note 59, at 17–19.

Chapter 7

The Vicissitudes of the Fourteenth Amendment

> All persons born or naturalized in the United States and subject to the jurisdiction thereof, are citizens of the United States and of the State wherein they reside. No State shall make or enforce any law which shall abridge the privileges or immunities of citizens of the United States; nor shall any State deprive any person of life, liberty, or property, without due process of law; nor deny to any person within its jurisdiction the equal protection of the laws.
>
> —Amendment XIV, United States Constitution

Enacted in 1868, following the Civil War, the Fourteenth Amendment ordains national citizenship for all persons born or naturalized in the United States. The amendment contains three great clauses: the Privileges or Immunities Clause, the Due Process Clause, and the Equal Protection Clause. Each of these clauses stands as a potential guardian against oppression and inequity, a constitutional promise of justice throughout the land. Yet the vicissitudes of each clause have been nothing short of astounding. The three clauses have been sapped of vitality by the Supreme Court, only to be revitalized years later, before being enervated yet again, and then revived again.

THE DISCARDED CLAUSE: PRIVILEGES OR IMMUNITIES

It did not take the Supreme Court long to begin its handiwork on the Fourteenth Amendment. In fact, in the very first case involving the Amendment to reach the Court, known as the *Slaughter-House Cases*,[1] the Court gave restrictive readings to all three clauses of the Fourteenth Amendment, severely limiting their effectiveness. The Court was especially hostile to the Privileges or Immunities Clause, diluting its promise beyond recognition. The *Slaughter-House Cases* involved a Louisiana statute chartering a corporation and granting it a monopoly to maintain slaughter-houses. The law was challenged by a group of butchers not included in the monopoly who claimed that the law deprived them of the right "to exercise their trade" in violation of the Fourteenth Amendment. It is unfortunate that the first case involving the Fourteenth Amendment was not aimed at ensuring racial equality. After all, the primary purpose of the Fourteenth Amendment, for which the nation had gone through a Civil War, was to eliminate the racial injustice flowing from slavery. As the Court pointed out in the *Slaughter-Houses Cases*, the "one pervading purpose . . . lying at the foundation" of all three of the Civil War amendments was to remedy the oppression suffered by the recently freed slaves.[2] Yet, while that noble cause was the *primary* purpose of the Fourteenth Amendment, it was not the *sole* purpose. In the words of the Court, "We do not say no one else but the negro can share in this protection."[3] Thus, in later cases the Supreme Court, while consistently adhering to the historical foundation of the Fourteenth Amendment to eliminate racial discrimination,[4] has nonetheless applied the amendment to rectify other forms of injustice.

While the butchers in the *Slaughter-House Cases* were not complaining of racial discrimination, they did seem to have a valid gripe; in granting a monopoly to a corporation composed of seventeen persons,[5] the Louisiana law deprived a thousand butchers of the ability to pursue their occupation.[6] Although Louisiana claimed that the law was a health measure, aimed at removing "noxious slaughter-houses" from densely populated areas,[7] there seemed to be no reason why this needed to be accomplished through the granting of a monopoly that denied so many people the ability to work in their chosen profession. In chartering the monopoly, the Louisiana legislature certainly appeared to be parceling out special favors to its friends, if not trading in out-and-out corruption. The butchers' chief argument was that the Louisiana law violated the Privileges or Immunities Clause by abridging their privilege to engage in a lawful profession.[8] Their claim was that the Privileges or Immunities Clause protected fundamental rights, among which was the right to work, that is, the right to exercise their trade. They pointed to an 1823 decision, *Corfield v. Coryell*,[9] concerning the Privileges and Immunities Clause of Article IV, which prohibits a state from discriminating against out-of-staters by providing that "[t]he Citizens of each State shall be entitled to all Privileges and Immunities of Citizens in the several States." The Fourteenth Amendment protects federal privileges or immunities; Article IV protects state privileges and immunities. In *Corfield* the Court ruled that the phrase "privileges and immunities" referred to those fundamental rights that belonged to the citizens of all free governments, including the right to acquire and possess property and to pursue and obtain happiness and safety.[10] Surely this must include, the butchers asserted, the right to pursue a lawful occupation. Indeed, in enacting the Civil Rights Act of 1866, Congress repeatedly referred to *Corfield*,[11] thus suggesting that Congress believed the right to engage in a trade was a privilege within the meaning of the Fourteenth Amendment. In addition, eminent authorities, such as Adam Smith, the author of *Wealth of Nations*, and Sir William Blackstone, the esteemed English jurist, were quoted for the notion that the right to work was fundamental to a free society.[12]

None of this, however, was convincing to the slim 5–4 majority of the Supreme Court in the *Slaughter-House Cases*. In the majority's view, the Privileges or Immunities Clause could not be read as protecting fundamental rights, because to do so would produce consequences "so serious, so far-reaching and pervading, so great a departure from the structure and spirit of our institutions."[13] To do so would make the Court itself "a perpetual censor upon all legislation of the States," and further would "fetter and degrade" the states by subjecting them to the control of Congress.[14] This would "radically change the whole theory of the relations of the State and Federal governments to each other and of both these governments to the people."[15] This the Court was not willing to do.[16]

When one gets past the Court's hyperbolic language, it can be seen that the problem with the Court's stance is that it is exactly contrary to the import of the Fourteenth Amendment. In its three clauses, the Fourteenth Amendment mandates federal constitutional restrictions upon state authority. It is the responsibility of the Supreme Court to enforce the constitutional mandate of the Fourteenth Amendment against the states. This makes the Court a "censor," although not a perpetual one, of some, although not all, state legislation. To use less pejorative wording, the Fourteenth Amendment makes the Court a judicial reviewer of state action. That is exactly what the amendment is supposed to do. In addition, the Fourteenth Amendment does in fact subject the states to the control of Congress. That is explicitly what section 5 is supposed to do. Yes, this "fetters and degrades" the states, or, again to use less pejorative language, this places restrictions upon the states, which is expressly what the Fourteenth Amendment mandates. Yes (and in this instance the language is correct), this "radically changes" federal-state relations. That is why the Civil War was fought!

In perverting the meaning of the Fourteenth Amendment, the Court seriously injured the effectiveness of the Privileges or Immunities Clause to protect the rights of individuals. Indeed, by refusing to use the clause to protect fundamental rights, the Court rendered it useless. The Court, however, attempted to deny the harm it was doing to the Privileges or Immunities Clause. In a display of bluster, the Court proclaimed that the clause protected a number of rights, which the Court listed as follows:

> [T]he right of the citizen . . . to come to the seat of government to assert any claim he may have upon that government, to transact any business he may have with it, to seek its protection, to share its offices, to engage in administering its functions. He has the right of free access to its seaports, through which all operations of foreign commerce are

conducted, to the subtreasuries, land offices, and courts of justice in the several States. . . . Another privilege of a citizen of the United States is to demand the care and protection of the Federal government over his life, liberty, and property when on the high seas or within the jurisdiction of a foreign government. . . . The right to peaceably assemble and petition for redress of grievances, the privilege of the writ of habeas corpus, are rights of the citizen guaranteed by the Federal Constitution. The right to use the navigable waters of the United States . . . all rights secured to our citizens by treaties with foreign nations, are dependent upon citizenship of the United States. . . . [A] citizen of the United States can, of his own volition, become a citizen of any State of the Union.[17]

This is an impressive list of rights, perhaps, but only to the uninitiated; to the more knowledgeable, the list is highly problematic. The problem is that all of the rights enumerated by the Court existed prior to the enactment of the Fourteenth Amendment, and thus hardly needed the Privileges or Immunities Clause to secure them. So, the Court's decision in the *Slaughter-House Cases* reduced the Privileges or Immunities Clause to a mere redundancy. The decision nullified the Privileges or Immunities Clause, making it superfluous.[18] As Justice Stephen Field put it in his dissenting opinion, the majority's decision made the clause "a vain and idle enactment, which accomplished nothing, and most unnecessarily excited Congress and the people on its passage."[19]

THE SUBSTITUTE CLAUSE: DUE PROCESS OF LAW

The Privileges or Immunities Clause laid vain and idle for 126 years, ignored by the Supreme Court as a source of constitutional rights.[20] What the Supreme Court did do, however, beginning not too long after its decision in the *Slaughter-House Cases*, was to use the Due Process Clause of the Fourteenth Amendment as a kind of occasional substitute for the Privileges or Immunities Clause. By its wording, the Due Process Clause seems to be directed to ensuring fair procedures in the law, rather than to protecting substantive rights. At first the Supreme Court viewed the Due Process Clause as a procedural directive, not a substantive one. After the decision in the *Slaughter-House Cases*, the Court gradually converted the Due Process Clause into a means of protecting substantive rights.[21] Most particularly, the Court used the Due Process Clause to protect the right of liberty of contract, which the court was now willing to deem a fundamental right, despite the fact that it was nowhere mentioned in the Constitution. In 1897, in the case of *Allgeyer v. Louisiana*,[22] the slow drift to substantive due process review was completed when the Court struck down a state law on substantive due process grounds for the first time.[23] In *Allgeyer*, the Court declared,

The liberty mentioned in [the Fourteenth Amendment] means not only the right of the citizen to be free from the mere physical restraint of his person, as by incarceration, but the term is deemed to embrace the right of the citizen to be free in the enjoyment of all his faculties; to be free to use them in all lawful ways; to live and work where he will;

to earn his livelihood by any lawful calling; to pursue any livelihood or avocation, and for that purpose to enter into all contracts which may be proper, necessary and essential to his carrying out to a successful conclusion the purposes above mentioned.[24]

Interestingly, the *Allgeyer* Court's formulation of the rights protected by the Due Process Clause repeatedly included the right to pursue a livelihood, the very right rejected by the Court in interpreting the Privileges or Immunities Clause in the *Slaughter-House Cases*. In *Allgeyer*, though, the right to pursue a livelihood was definitively ensconced within the scope of the Fourteenth Amendment's Due Process Clause. The right to work, still barred from the Privileges or Immunities Clause, nonetheless found a happy home in the Due Process Clause.

By the time the Court decided *Lochner v. New York*,[25] a mere eight years after *Allgeyer*, substantive due process review was in full bloom and used repeatedly by the Court to strike down laws regulating property rights or business practices.[26] Liberty of contract had become the Court's favorite conceit, an *idee fixe* that the Court elevated to the divine constitutional status of a fundamental right. Although the Court liked to pretend that liberty of contract was a means to protect the rights of the common person, such as the right to work, in truth the Court used liberty of contract to guard the prerogatives of property and business owners, which most often were used to the disadvantage of the common people. *Lochner* is a prime example of this. In *Lochner*, while professing to uphold the right of workers to contract on their own terms,[27] the Court ignored that in the real world where equality of bargaining power could be found in few quarters, workers had precious little capability to contract on their own terms. So, the Court struck down a maximum hours law designed to protect the health of workers on the pretense that the rights of workers were being upheld.

From the 1897 *Allgeyer* decision to 1937, the Supreme Court invalidated approximately 200 state laws on the ground that they violated the Due Process Clause.[28] Laws regulating prices, wages, and working conditions were the most susceptible to the Court's axe.[29] Although the Court just as often rebuffed due process attacks on economic regulations,[30] the fact remains that the Court made active and frequent use of the Due Process Clause to strike down laws that the Court perceived as interfering with its favorite fundamental right—liberty of contract.

This would come to a screeching halt, however, as old notions about law and economic policy began to crumble.[31] It was becoming increasingly apparent that the Supreme Court's conception of "liberty of contract" was little more than a shibboleth used to shield the prerogatives of business owners. In the Court's hands, it seemed, liberty of contract had little to do with the right of an individual to pursue a livelihood. Moreover, with the onset of the Great Depression, it became increasingly apparent that economic regulation was in the best interests of workers and the common people. Thus, economic regulation became more widely accepted as essential to the well-being of society.[32]

At first, the Supreme Court resisted the new order. Progressive economic legislation designed to ameliorate the urgent conditions of the Depression was initially struck down by a slim majority of the Court still devoted to safeguarding liberty of contract.[33] After President Roosevelt attacked the Court for its retrogressive ways and proposed his Court-packing plan to bring the Court into the twentieth century, one of the justices had a constitutional change of heart, thus shifting the majority view.[34] Not long after that, other justices left the Court to be replaced by Roosevelt appointees who were decidedly more hospitable to economic regulation.[35]

The strategy adopted by the newly constituted Court was to withdraw from judicial oversight of economic regulations by reviewing them with the most deferential variety of judicial scrutiny—so deferential, in fact, as to be virtually nonexistent.[36] "So far as the requirement of due process is concerned," the Court declared, a "state is free to adopt whatever economic policy may reasonably be deemed to promote public welfare."[37] And so far as freedom of contract was concerned, the Court proclaimed:

> What is this freedom? The Constitution does not speak of freedom of contract. It speaks of liberty and prohibits the deprivation of liberty without due process of law. In prohibiting that deprivation, the Constitution does not recognize an absolute and uncontrollable liberty. . . . [R]egulation which is . . . adopted in the interests of the community is due process.[38]

Rather than completely rejecting the constitutional status of liberty of contract, the Court moved to severely restrict it. As the Court now saw it, liberty of contract, unmentioned in the Constitution, was far from absolute, and, in fact, could be restricted by any regulation adopted in the interest of the community. Furthermore, as the Court made clear in later cases, what was or was not in the interest of the community was a matter for the legislature to decide, not the Court.[39] Henceforth, the Court would grant extreme deference to any legislative determination that the public interest called for restricting liberty of contract. The result was to severely undermine the constitutional status of liberty of contract. If not quite explicitly denying the fundamental status of liberty of contrast, the Court certainly no longer treated liberty of contract as a fundamental right. Indeed, the Court treated liberty of contract as if it possessed no special station at all.

Thus, whereas sixty-some years before in the *Slaughter-House Cases* the Court had expressly ruled that the right to work had no special status under the Privileges or Immunities Clause of the Fourteenth Amendment, the Court now was more indirect in implicitly ruling that liberty of contract had no special status under the Due Process Clause of the Fourteenth Amendment. In both situations, however, the effect was to rein in the scope of the Fourteenth Amendment, and thereby restrict its potential for protecting various rights.

Before that occurred in the due process arena, liberty of contract temporarily enjoyed a privileged rank in the eyes of the Supreme Court. During the *Lochner* era, liberty of contract was by far the Supreme Court's preferred fundamental right. Still, in this period of time there was another fundamental right that the Court recognized, albeit on rare occasion; the first of which occurred in *Meyer v. Nebraska*, decided in 1923.[40] In *Meyer* the Court struck down, as violative of the Due Process Clause, a state law that prohibited the teaching of foreign languages to students below the eighth grade in any school. Although admitting that it had not previously attempted to exactly define the scope of liberty protected by the Due Process Clause,[41] the Court noted,

> Without doubt, it denotes not merely freedom from bodily restraint but also the right of the individual to contract, to engage in any of the common occupations of life, to acquire useful knowledge, to marry, establish a home and bring up children, to worship God according to the dictates of his own conscience, and generally to enjoy those privileges long recognized at common law as essential to the orderly pursuit of happiness by free men.[42]

The Court then concluded that the Nebraska laws interfered "with the calling of modern language teachers, with the opportunities of pupils to acquire knowledge, and with the power of parents to control the education of their own."[43] A few years later, in *Pierce v. Society of Sisters*, in striking down an Oregon law requiring students to attend public schools, the Court again recognized the fundamental right of parents to control the upbringing of their children.[44]

In recognizing, if only in dicta, the right to marry, establish a home, and bring up children, the Court in *Meyer* and *Pierce* initiated a fundamental right that would some years later come to be known as the right of privacy or the right of individual autonomy. It eventually would encompass the right to use contraceptives[45] and the right of a woman to decide for herself to have an abortion.[46] While far along the path of repudiating Lochnerism and the deification of liberty of contract,[47] the Court in 1942 decided a case once again safeguarding, and, in fact, expanding, the right of privacy, although this time under the Equal Protection Clause, rather than the Due Process Clause.[48] In *Skinner v. Oklahoma*, the Court struck down a state law providing for compulsory sterilization after a third-time conviction of a felony involving moral turpitude.[49] While the Court in *Skinner* was still chary enough of Lochnerism to avoid due process substantive review in favor of an equal protection analysis, the Court was not reluctant to continue an enhanced constitutional protection for the right of privacy. "We are dealing here," the Court stated, "with legislation which involves one of the basic civil rights of man. Marriage and procreation are *fundamental* to the very existence and survival of the race."[50]

Lingering wariness of Lochnerism probably explains why in 1965, in *Griswold v. Connecticut*, the Court chose to fashion the "penumbra theory" in lieu of due process to strike down a law prohibiting the distribution or use of contraceptives.[51] According to the penumbra theory, the right of privacy was implicit in a variety of constitutional provisions "suggest[ing] that specific guarantees in the Bill of Rights have penumbras . . . that help give them life and substance."[52] The soundness of the penumbra theory has been the subject of considerable debate, but whatever its cogency may be, the fact remains that in *Griswold*, the Court once again expanded the fundamental right of privacy, this time to include the right of an individual to obtain and use contraceptives.

Seven years after *Griswold*, in *Eisenstadt v. Baird*,[53] the Court specifically upheld the right of an unmarried individual to use contraceptives. In *Baird*, like *Skinner* before it, the Court relied upon the Equal Protection Clause to protect the right of privacy. The stage was now set for *Roe v. Wade*.[54] The right of privacy was an established fundamental right, with a pedigree dating back to 1923. For some years after the downfall of Lochnerism, the Court eschewed the Due Process Clause as a means of protecting the right of privacy, but nevertheless showed an abiding conviction that privacy was a fundamental right. By 1973, when the Court decided *Roe*, it was ready to return to the Due Process Clause as the source of constitutional protection for the right of privacy. In *Roe*, the Court squarely ruled that the right of privacy is a "fundamental"[55] right "implicit in the concept of ordered liberty"[56] that is grounded in the Due Process Clause of the Fourteenth Amendment.[57] Moreover, the Court stated, the due process fundamental right of privacy was "broad enough to encompass a woman's decision whether or not to terminate her pregnancy."[58] Despite attempts to overrule *Roe v. Wade* by various justices on the Court, a majority of the justices have reaffirmed this ruling in *Roe* on numerous occasions, most notably in *Planned Parenthood of Southeastern Pennsylvania v. Casey*, where the Court repeatedly stated that it was reaffirming the "essential holding" of *Roe v. Wade* that prior to viability a woman has a right to choose to have an abortion.[59] The right of privacy, then, including the right of a woman to decide to have an abortion, remains a fundamental right protected by the Due Process Clause of the Fourteenth Amendment. As the Court eloquently explained in *Casey*:

> It is a promise of the Constitution that there is a realm of personal liberty which the government may not enter. . . . Our law affords constitutional protection to personal relations relating to marriage, procreation, contraception, family relationships, child rearing, and education. These matters, involving the most intimate and personal choices a person may make in a lifetime, choices central to personal dignity and autonomy, are central to the liberty protected by the Fourteenth Amendment. At the heart of liberty is the right to define one's own concept of existence, of meaning, of the universe, and of the mystery of human life.[60]

In addition to upholding the reproductive rights of individuals, the Court has decided a number of cases upholding other family rights of individuals, such as the right to marry[61] and the right to live together as an extended family.[62] Clearly, the Court considers procreational and family matters to be fundamental rights protected by the Fourteenth Amendment. The right of privacy, then, includes the right to marry, the right to divorce, the right to have children, the right to use contraceptives, the right to have an abortion, the right to live together as a family, and the right to control the upbringing of one's children.

Due to the fundamental importance of family rights, the Supreme Court has allowed that there is a concomitant right of access to the justice system, when family rights are at stake. In *Boddie v. Connecticut*, the Court ruled that it was a violation of the Due Process Clause to deny indigent persons access to the courts to obtain a divorce solely because they could not pay the filing fee.[63] The Court noted that the marriage relationship occupies a basic position in our society and the state monopolizes the means for legally dissolving marriage. Given these circumstances, the precept of due process of law prohibits a state from denying access to its courts, solely based on inability to pay, to individuals who seek judicial dissolution of their marriages.[64] In subsequent cases, though, it became apparent that if *Boddie* established any right of access to the courts, it was only in situations involving family matters. Thus, the Court ruled that due process does not require the waiver of filing fees so that indigent persons might have access to the courts in order to file bankruptcy petitions[65] or seek review of administrative reduction of their welfare payments.[66] In *Little v. Streater*, however, the Court ruled that under the Due Process Clause an indigent defendant in a paternity action was entitled to blood tests paid for by the state.[67] More recently, in *M.L.B. v. S.L.J.*, the Court ruled that in an appeal from an order terminating parental rights, an indigent person was entitled to waiver of fees charged to prepare the record for appeal.[68] In this instance, the Court relied upon the Equal Protection Clause to protect an individual's right of access to the justice system when family rights are at stake.

As noted in Chapter 3, by lionizing privacy as a fundamental right, the Court left itself open to the charge that it was reading its own values into the Constitution, just as it had done in the days of *Lochner*.[69] Now, however, the Court's values had changed; in the hierarchy developed by the justices, liberty of contract had given way to the right of privacy. Perhaps mindful of that criticism, the Court turned to the past as a source of fundamental rights. Thus, in *Moore v. City of East Cleveland*, a 1977 decision, Justice Lewis Powell's plurality opinion concluded that the right to live together in an extended family was fundamental because it was a liberty "deeply rooted in this Nation's history and tradition."[70] A reluctant majority of the Court in 1990 would again turn to history to "assume" that under the Due Process Clause an individual possessed a right to bodily integrity, which encompassed the right to refuse unwanted medical treatment.[71] In time, however, the Court's historical approach would prove to be a double-edged sword, even in the sphere of family rights,[72] because the Court would learn to use history as a means of derogating the constitutional status of various rights on the ground that they were not firmly established in our history and tradition—at least not in the Court's reading of our history and tradition.

History was wielded to cut short the promise of due process in *Bowers v. Hardwick*, which saw the Court rule, by a vote of 5–4, that the right of privacy does not encompass the right of a consenting adult to engage in homosexual conduct, even in the privacy of his or her home.[73] Justice Byron White's opinion for the majority drew a strict distinction "between family, marriage, or procreation on the one hand and homosexual activity on the other."[74] Taking an historical approach to constitutional interpretation, the Court refused to give constitutional countenance to a right to engage in homosexual conduct because such a right was neither "deeply rooted in this Nation's history and tradition" nor "implicit in the concept of ordered liberty."[75]

The Court's decision in *Bowers* has been described as "the second death of substantive due process"; the first death was the abandonment of liberty of contract.[76] This is an exaggeration, however. Whereas liberty of contract has been completely forsaken, the right of privacy has not. Limits certainly have been set, but unlike liberty of contract, the right of privacy has persevered. Still, the point is well taken that the Supreme Court's decision in *Bowers* reins in the promise of the right of privacy in a startling fashion. *Bowers* put a freeze on the expansion of the right of privacy, but it did not retract previously recognized aspects of the right of privacy, which the Court has continued to uphold in cases subsequent to *Bowers*.[77]

In cases after *Bowers*, at the prompting of Chief Justice William Rehnquist and more particularly Justice Antonin Scalia, the Court increasingly turned to history as a means of delineating the scope of fundamental rights protected by the Due Process Clause. History and tradition have proven to be, for the Court, a convenient means of restricting the recognition of fundamental rights. In the Court's view of history, there appear to be precious few fundamental rights. In *Michael H. v. Gerald D.*, for instance, the Court ruled that a biological father did not have a right to visit his child because no such right could be found in the traditions of our society.[78] In *Washington v. Glucksberg*, the Court ruled an individual did not have a right to physician-assisted suicide, once again because none could be found in the traditions of our society.[79]

The Court's historical approach in these cases is profoundly conservative in the true sense of that term. That is, it preserves the old ways of doing things. Only those rights that are "deeply rooted in this Nation's history and tradition" will be allowed by the Court; new rights will never be able to gain constitutional approval. This is a static, rather than evolutionary, view of the Constitution that greatly reduces its ability to deal with changing conditions or attitudes. It was exactly this sort of historical approach that the Court followed ninety years earlier in *Plessy v. Ferguson* in ruling that "separate but equal" facilities for whites and blacks did not violate the Constitution.[80] In *Plessy*, the Court took the position that the reasonableness, and hence constitutionality, of legislation should be determined "with reference to the established usages, customs, and traditions of the people,"[81] according to which there was nothing objectionable about racial segregation. *Plessy*, however, was eventually overruled by *Brown v. Board of Education*, in which the Court observed, "In approaching this problem, we cannot turn the clock back to 1868 when the [Fourteenth] Amendment was adopted, or even to 1896 when *Plessy v. Ferguson* was written."[82] Notwithstanding that observation, at the dawning of the twenty-first century, the Court was more inclined to turn the clock ever further back than to face the new millennium.

THE LAST REFUGE: EQUAL PROTECTION OF THE LAWS

With the scope of the Due Process Clause frozen and the effectiveness of the Privileges or Immunities Clause completely nullified, the only remaining provision in the Fourteenth Amendment available for the potential protection of rights was the Equal Protection Clause, the very clause that Justice Oliver Wendell Holmes once prophetically described as "the usual last resort of constitutional arguments."[83]

Classifications

The Equal Protection Clause is directed toward the interdiction of unjust discrimination. As such, the primary focus of the Equal Protection Clause is on the ways in which laws classify individuals.

Racial classifications are especially questionable under the Equal Protection Clause. As envisioned by its framers, the central purpose of the Equal Protection Clause was to eliminate racial discrimination against the newly freed slaves.[84] In 1944 the Supreme Court declared that racial classifications are suspect and therefore subject to the most exacting judicial scrutiny.[85] Accordingly, racial classifications will be struck down unless shown to be necessary to achieve a compelling governmental interest.[86] The Court also considers classifications based upon national origin[87] or alienage[88] to be suspect and subject to strict scrutiny.

Race is the prototypical suspect classification, and as such it exemplifies the essential characteristics of a suspect classification. A classification may be considered suspect when it is directed at a "discrete and insular minority"[89] that has been subject to a "history of purposeful unequal treatment."[90] Suspect classifications often operate to stigmatize people with a "badge of inferiority."[91] Frequently, they are the result of prejudice and are based upon group stereotypes that are not truly indicative of an individual's abilities.[92] Suspect classifications may focus on an immutable trait that is an accident of birth for which an individual should bear no responsibility.[93] They tend to be irrational and irrelevant to any proper governmental purpose.[94] Given their history of abuse, their irrelevance to any bona fide purpose, and their prejudicial and discriminatory nature, certain classifications are suspicious and therefore should be examined carefully by the Supreme Court in determining their constitutionality.

In the 1970s, the Supreme Court began to see that classifications based on gender bear many of the invidious characteristics of a suspect classification. In 1973, a plurality opinion authored by Justice William Brennan pointed out that in the United States there has been "a long and unfortunate history of sex discrimination" that has been "rationalized by an attitude of 'romantic paternalism' which, in practical effect, put women not on a pedestal but in a cage."[95] The opinion also noted that many laws across the nation were based on "gross, stereotyped distinctions between the sexes,"[96] and that women still faced pervasive discrimination in education, the job market, and the political arena.[97] Nonetheless, a majority of the Court was unwilling to declare that gender was a suspect classification, in all probability because at that time some of the newer members of the Court were wary of expanding the scope of strict scrutiny. As the Warren Court was being transformed into the Burger Court, the new majority moved toward curtailing some of its predecessor's egalitarian urges. The justices thus found themselves on the horns of a dilemma. While it was difficult to deny the long history of irrational and prejudicial discrimination against women, the new majority was loathe to embrace the judicial activism of the Warren era. The dilemma was finally resolved by a compromise; gender classifications were placed in the intermediate tier of scrutiny, which had been created just a few years earlier to deal with symbolic speech.[98] In effect, the Court decided to treat gender as a "semi-suspect" classification to be reviewed under a heightened, although not strict, standard of scrutiny.

A few years later, the Court decided to take the same tack with classifications of non-marital children by ruling that although such classifications were not suspect enough to warrant the most exacting scrutiny, they certainly were irrational enough to call for more than minimal review.[99] Thus, classifications of non-marital children also were considered semi-suspect and hence subject to intermediate scrutiny.

That, however, marked the end of the heightened review, whether strict or intermediate, of classifications. Henceforth, the Court would adamantly refuse to recognize any new suspect or semi-suspect classifications. Classifications based on race, national origin, or alienage were suspect; classifications based on gender or against non-marital children were semi-suspect; and there the list ended. This brought to an end the possible expansion of protection provided by the Equal Protection Clause that previous decisions had suggested.

In several cases decided while Earl Warren was Chief Justice, the Court came close to declaring, if not actually declaring, that classifications based on wealth that burden the poor were suspect. This trend was suggested by decisions striking down poll taxes that burdened the poor[100] and striking down laws that abridged the rights of indigent persons to equality of treatment in the criminal justice system.[101] The use of strict scrutiny in these cases might be explicable by the presence of what the Court considered at that time to be fundamental interests rather than, or in addition to, the presence of a suspect classification. Still, in these cases the Court often likened classifications on the basis of wealth to invidious racial classifications.[102] In fact, in one case the Court stated, "Lines drawn on the basis of wealth and property, like those of race, are traditionally disfavored."[103] In another case the Court stated, albeit in dicta, that "a careful examination on our part is especially warranted where lines are drawn on the basis of wealth or race, two factors which would independently render a classification highly suspect and thereby demand a more exacting judicial scrutiny."[104]

Despite these statements, when Warren Burger became Chief Justice, the Supreme Court had a change of heart about classifications based on wealth and refused to admit that they were suspect. In *James v. Valtierra*, decided in 1971, the Court saw no equal protection violation in a California law that barred low-rent housing projects unless approved in a local referendum.[105] Over the dissent's assertion that the law explicitly classified on the basis of wealth,[106] a majority of the Court refused to apply strict scrutiny, noting that the law did not involve "distinctions based on race."[107] A few years later, in *San Antonio Independent School District v. Rodriguez*, the Court was more direct in rejecting the notion that classifications based on wealth were suspect.[108] There, the Court stated that "this Court has never heretofore held that wealth discrimination alone provides an adequate basis for invoking strict scrutiny."[109]

In cases following *Rodriguez*, the Court continued to take the position that wealth was not a suspect classification.[110] Moreover, decisions like *Rodriguez* signaled that the Supreme Court was unwilling to recognize any new suspect or semi-suspect classifications. After *Rodriguez*, the Court ruled, for example, that classifications based on age were not suspect enough to evoke heightened scrutiny. In concluding that mandatory retirement laws did not violate the Equal Protection Clause, the Court stated that while the elderly in the nation have suffered some unfair discrimination, they have not experienced "a history of purposeful unequal treatment," nor have they "been subjected to unique disabilities on the basis of stereotyped characteristics not truly indicative of their abilities."[111] In making this assessment, the Court was not entirely realistic about the degree of discrimination inflicted upon elderly persons or its nature. As noted by Justice Thurgood Marshall in a dissenting opinion, when it comes to employment, the elderly certainly have been subject to repeated arbitrary discrimination based on overly general stereotypes that stigmatize the elderly as physically and mentally deficient.[112] Still, a majority of the Court ruled that age is not a suspect classification and therefore classifications based on age were to be reviewed with the most minimal scrutiny.

More recently in *Cleburne v. Cleburne Living Center, Inc.*, the Court ruled that classifications based upon mental retardation are neither suspect nor quasi-suspect.[113] In fact, the Court expressly overturned a Court of Appeals decision holding that mental retardation was a quasi-suspect classification.[114] Brushing aside the long history of purposeful invidious discrimination against persons who are mentally retarded, the Court made clear that it was antipathetic to the recognition of any new suspect or semi-suspect classifications.[115]

Yet in *Cleburne* the Court did strike down a zoning ordinance that discriminated against persons who were mentally retarded. Unlike the case involving age classifications in which the Court used the most minimal form of judicial scrutiny, in *Cleburne* the Court was willing to put some bite into its application of minimal scrutiny. This at least provides some degree of constitutional protection for persons who are mentally retarded, whereas the elderly have virtually no constitutional protection at all.

As noted in Chapter 3, in *Cleburne* the Court was able to provide some protection for persons who are mentally retarded by following the principle that a bare legislative desire to harm a politically unpopular group does not amount to even a legitimate government interest.[116] The Court also relied upon this principle in *Romer v. Evans* to conclude that the Equal Protection Clause was violated by a Colorado state constitutional amendment that prohibited the enactment of any laws providing protection or entitlement on the basis of a person's sexual orientation.[117] The principle followed in *Romer* has been described as the "Pariah Principle," according to which the government may not target people for who they are rather than what they do.[118] In other words, the government should not treat persons differently on the basis of a disfavored status. In *Romer*, the Court accepted this principle and thereby was able to provide protection under the Equal Protection Clause without finding a suspect or quasi-suspect classification.[119] While avoiding the issue of whether classifications on the basis of sexual orientation are suspect or semi-suspect, the Court still was able to provide constitutional protection for persons who are discriminated against on the basis of their sexual orientation.

Sexual orientation, then, while never deemed a suspect or quasi-suspect classification, nonetheless garners protection under the Equal Protection Clause. Mental retardation, explicitly rejected as a suspect or semi-suspect classification, gets some protection; age and poverty, both rejected as suspect classifications, get virtually no protection. The Supreme Court has put a halt to its recognition of suspect or quasi-suspect classifications and is extremely grudging when it comes to widening the scope of protection afforded by the Equal Protection Clause.

Fundamental Rights

As discussed above, the primary focus of the Equal Protection Clause is on the basis by which laws classify individuals. That focus need not be exclusive, and the Equal Protection Clause also may be used with an eye to protecting fundamental rights. Even in the absence of an invidious classification, the Supreme Court may apply strict judicial scrutiny under the Equal Protection Clause if a law impinges upon a fundamental right. At first, the Court was reluctant to use the Equal Protection Clause as a means of safeguarding fundamental rights. Just as the Court was initially inclined to use the Due Process Clause to ensure proper procedure rather than to protect substantive rights, the Court also was initially inclined to use the Equal Protection Clause to ensure proper classification rather than to protect substantive rights. That began to change, however, in the 1940s, after the first rise and fall of substantive due process review. At this period of time the Privileges or Immunities Clause of the Fourteenth Amendment was long gone and unavailable as a source of protection for fundamental rights. The recent demise of Lochnerism had left the Due Process Clause similarly unavailable to protect fundamental rights,[120] and a Supreme Court peopled with at least eight New Deal sympathizers[121] was going to stay far away from any hint of reviving substantive due process review.

It was in this setting that the Court decided *Skinner v. Oklahoma*.[122] As previously mentioned, in *Skinner* the Court was faced with an Oklahoma statute that provided for compulsory sterilization after a third conviction of certain felonies involving moral turpitude. The statute was challenged on the grounds that it amounted to cruel and unusual punishment as well as violating due process of law. Both of those challenges were curtly swept aside with the remark that "[W]e pass those points without intimating an opinion on them, for there is a feature of the [statute] which clearly condemns it."[123] That condemnatory feature was its "failure to meet the requirements of the equal protection clause of the Fourteenth Amendment."[124] Because procreation was "one of the basic civil rights of man" and "fundamental to the very existence and survival of the race," the Court thought that "strict scrutiny" was the appropriate mode of review,[125] and concluded that, by imposing the penalty of sterilization upon some third time felons but not others, the statute unjustly discriminated against an individual's right to procreate. *Skinner*, then, is a case in which the Supreme Court used strict scrutiny under the Equal Protection Case to protect the fundamental right of privacy. In later cases, the Court would occasionally return to the Equal Protection Clause to protect the fundamental right of privacy,[126] but eventually would come to prefer the Due Process Clause as a means of providing protection for that right.[127]

Skinner v. Oklahoma is the first case in which the Supreme Court used the Equal Protection Clause to protect a fundamental right. It would not, however, be the last. The Court also has used the Equal Protection Clause to protect other fundamental rights: the right to vote,[128] the right of equal access to the courts,[129] and the right of interstate migration.[130]

Various aspects of the right to vote in a federal election are expressly protected by the Constitution. Article I provides that the members of the House of Representatives shall be chosen "by the people of the several States," and the Seventeenth Amendment provides that the members of the Senate shall be "elected by the people" of each state. In addition, the Twenty-Fourth Amendment prohibits poll taxes in federal elections. Other constitutional provisions protect different aspects of the right to vote in both federal and state elections. The Fifteenth Amendment mandates that the right to vote "shall not be denied or abridged by the United States or by any State on account of race, color, or previous condition of servitude." The Nineteenth Amendment declares that the right to vote "shall not be denied or abridged by the United States or by any

State on account of sex." And the Twenty-Sixth Amendment provides that the right to vote of citizens who are eighteen years of age or older "shall not be denied or abridged by the United States or by any State on account of age." Otherwise, however, there is no general right to vote expressly guaranteed by the Constitution.

Nonetheless, the Supreme Court has ruled that the right to vote is a fundamental right within the scope of protection afforded by the Equal Protection Clause. As explained by the Court, the right to vote is fundamental because it is the "essence of a democratic society."[131] The right to vote lies at the "heart of representative government"[132] and is "preservative of other basic civil and political rights."[133] The fundamental importance of the right to vote was recognized in *Reynolds v. Sims*, the 1964 decision that established the constitutional principle of "one [person], one vote."[134] *Reynolds* concerned a constitutional challenge to the gross malapportionment that then existed of the Alabama legislature. Proclaiming that "[U]ndoubtedly, the right of suffrage is a fundamental matter in a free and democratic society,"[135] the Court found that the Alabama apportionment scheme violated the Equal Protection Clause. An individual's fundamental right to vote is unconstitutionally impaired, the Court ruled, when its weight is substantially diluted in comparison to the votes of persons living in other parts of the same state.[136]

The Supreme Court has recognized that, in addition to the one-person–one-vote principle, the Equal Protection Clause provides further protection for the fundamental right to vote. For example, the Court has ruled that the Equal Protection Clause is violated by laws that condition the right to vote on the paying of a tax[137] or the ownership of property.[138] The Court also has found that an offshoot of the right to vote is the right to be a candidate, and has struck down laws that place unduly burdensome obstacles on access to the ballot.[139]

In a group of cases involving another sort of right, the Court has found that in some circumstances there is a fundamental right to equality of treatment in the justice system. When a state engages in action that causes inequitable treatment of individuals in the justice system, the state action in question may be subject to strict scrutiny under the Equal Protection Clause. This principle was established in 1956 in *Griffin v. Illinois*, in which the Court ruled that under the Equal Protection Clause indigent defendants are entitled to free transcripts of their criminal trials so that they may appeal their convictions.[140] Seven years later, the *Griffin* ruling was extended in *Douglas v. California*, in which the Court held that on a direct appeal of right an indigent criminal defendant is entitled to free counsel.[141] As discussed above, these decisions might be explicable by the presence of discrimination against the poor rather than, or in addition to, the presence of a fundamental right of access to the justice system. Alternatively, however, *Griffin* and *Douglas* may be read as establishing a fundamental right of equality of access to the justice system in criminal cases. That reading would become particularly apt when the Court would rule in later cases that discrimination against the poor is not a suspect classification.[142] *Griffin* and

Douglas, then, can be understood as establishing a fundamental right in the criminal process to an appeal, at least to a first appeal. Eleven years after *Douglas*, however, in *Ross v. Moffitt*, the Court refused to extend that right to a second appeal.[143] In *Ross* the Court concluded that even when persons who can afford to hire their own attorneys have the opportunity of appealing their criminal convictions a second time, the Equal Protection Clause does not require that indigent defendants be afforded free counsel for a second appeal. In later decisions, the Court has made it clear that there is a right to appointed counsel only for a first appeal and not for subsequent appeals or for collateral attacks on a conviction, and this is so even in the case of a conviction that carries a sentence of death.[144] According to the Supreme Court, the dictates of equal protection of law are adequately served so long as an indigent defendant has been provided free counsel for one appeal. In the view of the Court, there is a fundamental right to some degree of equality of treatment in the criminal justice system, but far from complete equality.

The right to equal treatment in the criminal justice system also applies to the right of equality of sentencing. The Equal Protection Clause prohibits the practice of imposing harsher penalties on criminal defendants because they are indigent.[145] Therefore, it is unconstitutional to imprison criminal defendants merely because they are unable to pay a fine, which otherwise would be their only penalty.[146] It also is unconstitutional to increase a defendant's jail term beyond the maximum statutory period because the defendant cannot afford to pay a fine.[147] It is not a violation of the Equal Protection Clause, though, for a state to require an indigent defendant to later repay the state for the services of appointed counsel.[148]

Insofar as the Supreme Court has recognized a right of equal access to the justice system, it has been primarily in criminal cases. In civil cases, the Court has recognized a right of access to the courts only in extremely limited settings. As discussed above, the Court has ruled that in situations where family rights are at stake, the Due Process Clause or the Equal Protection Clause provide a right of access to the justice system, which requires a waiver of court fees for indigent persons.[149] The Court, however, has steadfastly refused to extend the right of access to the courts in civil cases to any other settings.

Although the Constitution makes no mention of a right to travel from state to state, the right to interstate travel may be inferred from various provisions. The Constitution creates a federated nation and grants citizenship to individuals on a national basis. The Fourteenth Amendment begins with a ringing declaration: "All persons born or naturalized in the United States . . . are citizens of the United States and of the State wherein they reside."[150] This certainly could be taken as implying a right to travel or migrate anywhere within the United States. After all, is not one of the rights of citizenship the right to move freely anywhere within the nation of which one is a citizen? Moreover, Article IV of the Constitution proclaims, "The Citizens of each State shall be entitled to all Privileges and Immunities of Citizens in the several States."[151] Not to be confused with the Fourteenth Amendment Privileges or Immunities Clause, which prohibits the abridgement of federal rights, the Article IV Privileges and Immunities Clause prohibits a state from discriminating against citizens of other states. As such, it was interpreted at an early date as protecting "the right of a citizen of one state to pass through or reside in any state."[152] Similarly, the Interstate Commerce Clause[153] has been interpreted as prohibiting a state from unduly interfering with the free flow of interstate movement.[154] Surely, then, Chief Justice Roger Taney was correct when he observed that "[W]e are all citizens of the United States . . . [and as such] . . . must have the right to pass and repass through every part of it without interruption, as freely as in our own states."[155]

In a series of cases that began with *Shapiro v. Thompson* in 1969, the Supreme Court has ruled that the right to interstate travel is a fundamental right protected by the Equal Protection Clause.[156] As such, state residency requirements that impinge upon the right to migrate are subject to strict judicial scrutiny and will be struck down unless proven to be necessary to achieve a compelling governmental interest. Following that approach, the Court has invalidated residency requirements that condition eligibility for welfare benefits,[157] voting,[158] and free medical care.[159] In other cases, though, the Court has sustained residency requirements that condition entitlement for lower tuition rates at a state university[160] and that condition the prerogative to file for a divorce.[161] In addition, the Court has stated that it will be more tolerant of residency requirements as long as they do not penalize the right to interstate travel by conditioning another fundamental right or a necessity of life.[162]

The Court also has protected the right to interstate migration by striking down laws that distribute government benefits according to a person's length of residence in a state. For example, in *Zobel v. Williams* the Court invalidated an Alaska statute that distributed dividends derived from oil revenue to state citizens based on their length of residence within the state.[163] And in *Hooper v. Bernalillo County Assessor*, the Court struck down a New Mexico law granting a tax exemption to Viet Nam veterans only if they were state residents before a certain date.[164]

The Court's decisions dealing with the right to interstate migration are not entirely consistent, although it is possible to derive some general principles from them. Justice Brennan explained in a plurality opinion that a "state law implicates the right to travel when it actually deters such travel, when impeding travel is its primary objective, or when it uses 'any classifications which serve to penalize the exercise of that right.' "[165]

The right to interstate migration has strong roots in the text of the Constitution and is well-established as a fundamental right under the Equal Protection Clause. Nevertheless, Justice Sandra Day O'Connor has questioned the notion that there is some "free floating 'right to migrate.' "[166] In her view, laws that treat newer residents of a state differently than other residents are most appropriately analyzed under the Privileges and Immunities Clause of Article IV.[167] As discussed later, however, in the Court's latest pronouncement concerning these matters, it has found a surprising new home for the fundamental right of interstate migration.[168]

Well before this development, however, the Court moved to seriously restrict meaningful judicial review under the Equal Protection Clause by circumscribing the concept of fundamental rights. The first step was in the 1970s with the case of *Dandridge v. Williams*.[169] This case involved an equal protection challenge to a Maryland regulation that placed a cap on the amount of welfare benefits available to a family qualifying for the Aid to Families with Dependent Children program. Under the program, the amount of aid for which a family was eligible was calculated on the basis of the family's need. Maryland had decided to put a cap on the total amount of aid that any one family could receive. As a result of the cap, the benefits received by larger families covered a smaller proportion of their needs than the benefits received by smaller families. Noting that the benefits were supposed to be based on need, the plaintiffs in the case challenged the cap, arguing that it discriminated against persons in larger families. In all probability, the cap could not survive meaningful constitutional scrutiny. Maryland claimed that it had adopted the cap in order to encourage persons receiving welfare to seek employment. For a number of reasons, however, the cap had precious little effect toward that end.[170] More telling was that Maryland could offer no explanation of why it adopted a regulation to encourage welfare recipients in larger families, but not smaller ones, to seek employment. Thus, even with a small degree of reflection, the regulation did not appear to be rationally related to a legitimate state purpose. Nonetheless, the Court upheld the regulation, spouting the old minimalist rhetoric that the Constitution "does not require that a State must choose between attacking every aspect of a problem or not attacking the problem at all."[171] The Court declined to review the Maryland legislation in any meaningful way because it dealt with a "social and economic field, not affecting freedoms guaranteed by the Bill of Rights."[172]

A few years later, in *San Antonio Independent School District v. Rodriguez*,[173] it became crystal clear what the Court was doing. In *Rodriguez*, the plaintiffs challenged, as violative of the Equal Protection Clause, the Texas system for financing public schools. Because it was based primarily on local property taxes, it resulted in disparity of funding from one school district to another. Under the Texas system, poor school districts, even though they taxed themselves at a higher rate than wealthier districts, had little to spend on education, while rich districts, taxing themselves at a lower rate, had considerably more to spend on education.[174] Despite this disparity, in the Court's view there was no violation of the Equal Protection Clause. The Court was able to reach this decision by ruling that the case involved neither a suspect classification nor a fundamental right, and therefore called for only the most minimal judicial scrutiny.

Obviously, the Court's decision in *Rodriguez* is extremely significant in regard to the quality of education in this nation. By ruling that even gross disparities in school funding do not violate the Constitution, the Court allowed the continuation of public school systems that are riddled with inequality. On the poor side of those systems, untold numbers of students throughout the nation are denied an education that by any genuine standard could be called adequate. In addition, the Court's ruling in *Rodriguez* gave the states and state officials wide latitude to run the public schools free from constitutional oversight. As long as school officials do not engage in invidious forms of discrimination or impinge upon rights specifically protected by the Constitution,[175] they are pretty much free to do as they see fit. *Rodriguez* allows the states an extremely broad scope of discretion to administer public education. Under the deferential approach taken in *Rodriguez*, even policies or practices for which a state can offer no good explanation will be rubber-stamped by the Court.[176]

But as significant as it was in regard to education, *Rodriguez* was all the more significant in regard to constitutional doctrine and constitutional rights. Indeed, in several respects the Court's opinion in *Rodriguez*, written by Justice Powell, took a profoundly meager view of constitutional doctrine that severely restricted constitutional rights. The Court ruled that education was not a fundamental right, and therefore the Texas system of financing education was subject to only the most minimal constitutional scrutiny.[177] In deciding that education was not a fundamental right within the protection of the Constitution, the Court adopted the stance that whether a right is fundamental has nothing to do with its social importance. The "key" to discovering whether a right is fundamental, the Court said, is not to be found in comparisons of the relative societal significance of rights or in weighing their importance.[178] Rather, the answer lies in assessing whether a right is "explicitly or implicitly guaranteed by the Constitution."[179] In other words, a right will be deemed fundamental by the Court only if it can be connected to the text of the Constitution implicitly or, preferably, explicitly. No matter how important a right is, it will not be recognized by the Court as fundamental unless it can be tied to the language of the Constitution. Consider, indeed, education itself. The importance of education to the individual as well as to society cannot be denied. Education is essential to a productive life, financial success, professional accomplishment, and self-fulfillment. In turn, an educated citizenry is crucial to the political, cultural, and economical viability of the nation. As the Court admitted in *Rodriguez*, a unanimous Court in *Brown v. Board of Education* stated that "education is perhaps the most important function of state and local governments."[180] That admission, however, was unavailing to the Court in *Rodriguez*. It simply did not matter to the Court in *Rodriguez* how important a right may be. Or, to put it another way, it simply did not matter to the Court how fundamental to an individual or society a right may be. As far as the Court was concerned, if it is not in the Constitution, it is not fundamental.

The Court's methodology in *Rodriguez* for determining if a right is fundamental departed from precedent and signaled a momentous shift in constitutional law. In a number of previous decisions, the Court was quite willing to recognize fundamental rights that could not be tied to the text of the Constitution. As Justice Marshall pointed out in his dissenting opinion in *Rodriguez*, nothing in the Constitution guarantees the right to procreate,[181] the right to vote in a state election,[182] or the right to appeal from a criminal conviction,[183] yet in previous decisions the Court recognized all of them as fundamental. It could be added that nothing in the Constitution guarantees the right of parents to control the upbringing of their children, yet the Court previously recognized that it was, indeed, a fundamental right.[184] In *Rodriguez*, though, the Court shut the door to the further recognition of fundamental rights.

The Court's approach in *Rodriguez* requires a particular right to be specifically connected to the Constitution—either explicitly or implicitly, but nonetheless specifically. This severely limits the use of expansive constitutional provisions, such as the Equal Protection Clause, the Due Process Clause, or the Privileges or Immunities Clause, to protect individual rights and liberties. Because those clauses are worded so broadly, it is virtually impossible to connect specific rights to them in the manner required by *Rodriguez*. In that respect, the decision in *Rodriguez* resembles the Court's decision in the *Slaughter-House Cases*, where the Court, by a bare majority, rejected the notion that the Privileges or Immunities Clause protected fundamental rights. In so ruling, the Court gave such a crabbed reading to the Privileges or Immunities Clause as to render it superfluous, thereby making it a constitutional provision that protected no rights except those already protected by other constitutional provisions. Similarly, in *Rodriguez*, the Court gave a crabbed reading to the Equal Protection Clause, restricting its reach to those rights that otherwise could be connected to something in the Constitution.

In cases following *Rodriguez*, the Court adhered to this constricted view of fundamental rights, ruling that neither housing, nor welfare, nor employment were fundamental rights, and hence had virtually no constitutional protection from being restricted by a state. Accordingly, the Court allowed the states the widest possible latitude to regulate housing, welfare, and employment. While professing that state or federal regulations in these areas would be struck down unless shown to a bear a rational relationship to some legitimate governmental interest, in truth the Court upheld one irrational regulation after another.

The Supreme Court's decision in *Rodriguez* put a freeze on the recognition of fundamental rights under the Equal Protection Clause. Rights previously recognized as fundamental would continue to enjoy that status, but henceforth only those rights that could be found residing in the text of the Constitution would be deemed fundamental. The Court simply became unwilling to further expand the concept of fundamental rights. Those fundamental rights already recognized under either the Equal Protection Clause or the Due Process Clause would retain their constitutional protection, but no longer would they be extended beyond their present reach; new fundamental rights certainly would not be ordained by the Supreme Court.

CONCLUSION: A SURPRISING REVIVAL

In the last year of the twentieth century, the Supreme Court made a surprising decision, reviving a constitutional provision, the Privileges or Immunities Clause of the Fourteenth Amendment, that had lain dormant for 126 years since being enervated by the Court itself in the *Slaughter-House Cases*.[185] The revival occurred in *Saenz v. Roe*, which presented a constitutional challenge to a California law that afforded lower welfare benefits to individuals who had not resided in the state for at least a year.[186] Thirty years before, in *Shapiro v. Thompson*, the Court had struck down state laws denying welfare benefits to persons who had not resided in the state in question for at least a year.[187] In *Saenz*, however, California asserted that its law was distinguishable from those in *Shapiro*, because it did not deny eligibility for welfare to newly arrived persons, it merely reduced the amount of the benefits.[188] The Court found that this difference was not enough to distinguish the cases, and went on to conclude that the California residency requirement impermissibly infringed the right to travel in violation of the Fourteenth Amendment.[189] While admitting that the specific source of the right to travel has not always been identified,[190] the Court insisted that the right to travel from state to state nonetheless was "firmly embedded in our jurisprudence."[191] As the Court explained, it has been long recognized that the nature of the "Federal Union" and our concepts of personal liberty combine "to require that all citizens be free to travel throughout the length and breadth of our land uninhibited by statutes, rules, or regulations which unreasonably burden or restrict this movement."[192]

Having placed the right to travel from state to state solidly somewhere within our constitutional jurisprudence, the Court next decided to locate a more exact home for the right to travel. And that home turned out to be—of all places—the Privileges or Immunities Clause of the Fourteenth Amendment. The Court pointed out that, despite fundamentally differing views of the Privileges or Immunities Clause, "most notably those expressed in the majority and dissenting opinions of the *Slaughter-House Cases*," there has always been common agreement that the clause protects the right to migrate to a new state and become a citizen of it.[193] Indeed, in the *Slaughter-House Cases*, both Justice Samuel Miller's opinion for the majority and Justice Joseph Bradley's dissenting opinion proclaimed that one of the privileges conferred by the clause is that a citizen of the United States may migrate to any state he or she chooses and become a citizen of the new state entitled to the same rights as any other citizen.[194]

It goes without saying that what is most significant about the Court's decision in *Saenz* is that the Court chose to rely upon the Privileges or Immunities Clause of the Fourteenth Amendment, rather than the Equal Protection Clause, to protect the fundamental right of interstate travel. The Court could have continued to rely upon the Equal Protection Clause, as it did in *Shapiro* and subsequent cases, to protect the right of travel, but chose instead to use the Privileges or Immunities Clause as a source of protection for that right. In so doing, the Court once again breathed life into the Privileges or Immunities Clause that had been smothered in the *Slaughter-House Cases* 126 years before. Although surprising, the Court's decision in *Saenz* was theoretically sound for several reasons. First, it resuscitated a constitutional provision that had been improperly nullified years before. The Supreme Court's decision in the *Slaughter-House Cases* extinguishing the Privileges or Immunities Clause was wrong and cried out to be corrected. Second, it makes more sense, both textually and historically, to locate the right to migrate within the Privileges or Immunities Clause than within the Equal Protection Clause. As the Court described, at the time of the *Slaughter-House Cases* there was common agreement that the right to travel was a "privilege" of citizenship. The Supreme Court, then, should be commended for relocating the right to migrate to a revitalized Privileges or Immunities Clause.

It remains to be seen, of course, what further use, if any, the Court will make of the Privileges or Immunities Clause.[195] The clause could be used to protect a variety of rights along the ideological spectrum. It could be evoked to protect property rights, the right to work, the right to intimate association, the right to an education, or other rights of the individual. More likely, however, the Supreme Court may be content to have relocated the right to travel in its more appropriate home, the Privileges or Immunities Clause, and to leave other matters as they presently stand. The current majority of the Supreme Court is not inclined to expand the scope of the Fourteenth Amendment to encompass any fundamental rights other than those few now extant. It may well be unrealistic, then, to expect much in the way of further development of the Privileges or Immunities Clause as the Court is presently disposed.

Still, constitutional law is nothing if not evolutionary. The vicissitudes of constitutional doctrine will continue on their evolutionary journey, if not with the current justices then with those who will come anew to the Supreme Court. After all, constitutional law is a vibrant, ongoing process; it is rooted in the past, existing in the present, and reaching for the future.

NOTES

1. Slaughter-House Cases, 83 U.S. (16 Wall.) 36 (1873).
2. *Id.* at 71.
3. *Id.* at 72.
4. "[W]e deal here with a classification based upon the race of the participants, which must be viewed in light of the historical fact that the central purpose of the Fourteenth Amendment was to eliminate racial discrimination emanating from official sources in the States." McLaughlin v. Florida, 379 U.S. 184, 191–92 (1964).
5. Slaughter-House Cases, 83 U.S. (16 Wall.) at 83 (Field, J., dissenting).
6. *Id.* at 89 (Field, J., dissenting).
7. *Id.* at 64.
8. *Id.* at 74.
9. Corfield v. Coryell, 6 Fed. Cas. 546 (C.C.E.D. Pa. 1823) (Washington, J., on circuit).

10. *Id.*
11. Slaughter-House Cases, 83 U.S. (16 Wall.) at 97–98 (Field, J., dissenting).
12. *Id.* at 111 nn.39–40 (Field, J., dissenting).
13. *Id.* at 78.
14. *Id.*
15. *Id.*
16. The Court further stated:

> Unquestionably [the events leading to the Civil War] added largely to the number of those who believe in the necessity of a strong National government. But, however pervading this sentiment, and however it may have contributed to the adoption of the amendments we have been considering, we do not see in those amendments any purpose to destroy the main features of the general system. Under the pressure of all the excited feeling growing out of the war, our statesmen have still believed that the existence of the States with powers for domestic and local government, including the regulation of civil rights—the rights of person and of property—was essential to the perfect working of our complex form of government, though they have thought proper to impose additional limitation on the States, and to confer additional power on that of the Nation.

Id. at 82.

17. *Id.* at 79–80 (quoting in part Crandall v. Nevada, 73 U.S. [6 Wall.] 35 [1867]).

18. Unique among constitutional provisions, the Privileges or Immunities Clause of the Fourteenth Amendment enjoys the distinction of having been rendered a "practical nullity" by a single decision of the Supreme Court within five years after its ratification. Edward Corwin, The Constitution of the United States of America 965 (1953).

19. *Id.* at 96 (Field, J., dissenting). In 1935, Justice Harlan Fiske Stone referred to the Privileges or Immunities Clause as "almost forgotten." Colgate v. Harvey, 296 U.S. 404, 443 (1935) (Stone, J., dissenting).

20. The Supreme Court relied upon the Privileges or Immunities Clause to declare a state law unconstitutional in only one case, Colgate v. Harvey, 296 U.S. at 404, which was overruled ruled five years later in Madden v. Kentucky, 309 U.S. 83 (1940).

21. *See* Gerald Gunther & Kathleen M. Sullivan, Constitutional Law 457 (13th ed. 1997).

22. Allgeyer v. Louisiana, 165 U.S. 578 (1897).
23. Gunther & Sullivan, *supra* note 21, at 460.
24. Allgeyer v. Louisiana, 165 U.S. at 589.
25. Lochner v. New York, 198 U.S. 45 (1905).
26. *See* Benjamin Wright, The Growth of American Constitutional Law 154, 176 (1942).
27. Lochner v. New York, 198 U.S. at 57.
28. Wright, *supra* note 26.
29. *See* Gunther & Sullivan, *supra* note 21, at 470–74.
30. Wright, *supra* note 26.
31. *See* Chapter 2 *supra*, at notes 41–73.
32. *See* Laurence H. Tribe, American Constitutional Law 578 (2d ed. 1988).
33. *See* Chapter 3 *supra*, at notes 38–42.
34. *Id.* at notes 48–50.
35. *Id.* at notes 51–52.
36. *Id.* at notes 53–70.
37. Nebbia v. New York, 291 U.S. 502, 537 (1934).

38. West Coast Hotel Co. v. Parrish, 300 U.S. 379, 391 (1937).

39. "We do not sit as a super legislature." Day-Brite, Inc. v. Missouri, 342 U.S. 421, 423 (1952). "The day is gone when this Court uses the Due Process Clause of the Fourteenth Amendment to strike down state laws, regulatory of business and industrial conditions, because they may be unwise, improvident, or out of harmony with a particular school of [thought]." Williamson v. Lee Optical Co., 348 U.S. 483, 488 (1955).

40. Meyer v. Nebraska, 262 U.S. 390 (1923).

41. *Id.* at 399.

42. *Id.* The Court also stated that "the individual has certain fundamental rights which must be respected." *Id.*

43. *Id.* at 401.

44. Pierce v. Society of Sisters, 268 U.S. 510 (1925).

45. Griswold v. Connecticut, 381 U.S. 479 (1965).

46. Roe v. Wade, 410 U.S. 113 (1973); Planned Parenthood of Southeastern Pa. v. Casey, 505 U.S. 833 (1992).

47. *See, e.g.*, West Coast Hotel Co. v. Parrish, 300 U.S. 379 (1937); Olsen v. Nebraska, 313 U.S. 236 (1941).

48. Skinner v. Oklahoma, 316 U.S. 535 (1942).

49. *Id.*

50. *Id.* at 541 (emphasis added).

51. Griswold v. Connecticut, 381 U.S. at 483–84. It is noteworthy that the majority opinion in Griswold, with its penumbra theory, was written by Justice Douglas. A faithful New Dealer, Douglas was a staunch opponent of Lochnerism, as can be seen in the quotes from his opinions written for the Court in Day-Brite, Inc. v. Missouri and Williamson v. Lee Optical Co., *supra* note 39.

52. Griswold v. Connecticut, 381 U.S. at 484.

53. Eisenstadt v. Baird, 405 U.S. 438 (1972).

54. Roe v. Wade, 410 U.S. 113 (1973).

55. *Id.* at 152–54.

56. *Id.*

57. "This right of privacy, whether it be founded in the Fourteenth Amendment's concept of personal liberty and restrictions upon state action, as we feel it is. . . ." *Id.* at 153.

58. *Id.*

59. Planned Parenthood of Southeastern Pa. v. Casey, 505 U.S. 833, 846, 870 (1992).

60. *Id.* at 847, 851.

61. *See* Loving v. Virginia, 388 U.S. 1 (1967); Boddie v. Connecticut, 401 U.S. 371 (1971); Zablocki v. Redhail, 434 U.S. 374 (1978).

62. *See* Moore v. City of East Cleveland, 431 U.S. 494 (1977).

63. Boddie v. Connecticut, 401 U.S. 371 (1971).

64. *Id.* at 374.

65. United States v. Kras, 409 U.S. 434 (1973).

66. Ortwein v. Schwab, 410 U.S. 656 (1973).

67. Little v. Streater, 452 U.S. 1 (1981).

68. M.L.B. v. S.L.J., 519 U.S. 102 (1996).

69. *See* Chapter 3 *supra*, at notes 219–20.

70. Moore v. City of East Cleveland, 431 U.S. at 503.

71. Cruzan v. Director, Missouri Department of Health, 497 U.S. 261, 279 (1990).

72. *See* Michael H. v. Gerald D., 491 U.S. 110 (1989) (ruling that a biological father did not have a right to visit his child).

73. Bowers v. Hardwick, 478 U.S. 186 (1986).

74. *Id.* at 190–91.

75. *Id.* at 191–94.

76. Daniel O. Conkle, *The Second Death of Substantive Due Process*, 62 IND. L. J. 215 (1987).

77. *See* Planned Parenthood of Southeastern Pa. v. Casey, 505 U.S. at 833, 846, 870.

78. Michael H. v. Gerald D., 491 U.S. at 110.

79. Washington v. Glucksberg, 521 U.S. 702, 710–19, 723–26 (1997).

80. Plessy v. Ferguson, 163 U.S. 537 (1896).

81. *Id.* at 550.

82. Brown v. Board of Educ., 347 U.S. 483, 492 (1954).

83. Buck v. Bell, 274 U.S. 200, 208 (1927).

84. "[It is an] historical fact that the central purpose of the Fourteenth Amendment was to eliminate racial discrimination emanating from official sources in the States." McLaughlin v. Florida, 379 U.S. 184, 192 (1964).

85. Korematsu v. United States, 323 U.S. 214 (1944).

86. McLaughlin v. Florida, 379 U.S. at 184; Loving v. Virginia, 388 U.S. 1 (1967).

87. Hernandez v. Texas, 347 U.S. 475 (1954).

88. Graham v. Richardson, 403 U.S. 365 (1971).

89. United States v. Carolene Prods. Co., 304 U.S. 144, 152–53, n.4 (1938).

90. San Antonio Indep. Sch. Dist. v. Rodriguez, 411 U.S. 1, 28 (1973).

91. *See* Brown v. Board of Educ., 347 U.S. at 494.

92. *See* Palmore v. Sidoti, 466 U.S. 429, 432 (1984).

93. *See* Fullilove v. Klutznick, 448 U.S. 448, 496 (1980).

94. *See* Bolling v. Sharpe, 347 U.S. 497, 500 (1954); Harper v. Virginia State Bd. of Elections, 383 U.S. 663, 668 (1966).

95. Frontiero v. Richardson, 411 U.S. 677, 684 (1973).

96. *Id.* at 685.

97. *Id.* at 685–86.

98. *See* Chapter 3 *supra*, at notes 140–47.

99. *See* Mathews. V. Lucas, 427 U.S. 495 (1976); Trimble v. Gordon, 430 U.S. 762 (1977); Lalli v. Lalli, 439 U.S. 259 (1978).

100. Harper v. Virginia State Bd. of Elections, 383 U.S. 663 (1966).

101. Griffin v. Illinois, 351 U.S. 12 (1956); Douglas v. California, 372 U.S. 353 (1963).

102. *See* Griffin v. Illinois, 351 U.S. at 17; Harper v. Virginia State Bd. of Elections, 383 U.S. at 668.

103. Harper v. Virginia State Bd. of Elections, 383 U.S. at 668.

104. McDonald v. Board of Election, 394 U.S. 802, 807 (1969).

105. James v. Valtierra, 402 U.S. 137 (1971).

106. *Id.* at 144 (Marshall, J., dissenting).

107. *Id.* at 141.

108. San Antonio Indep. Sch. Dis. v. Rodriguez, 411 U.S. 1 (1973).

109. *Id.* at 29.

110. *See, e.g.*, Maher v. Roe, 432 U.S. 464 (1977); Kadrmas v. Dickinson Public Schs. 487 U.S. 450 (1988).

111. Massachusetts Bd. of Retirement v. Murgia, 427 U.S. 307 (1976); *see also* Vance v. Bradley, 440 U.S. 93 (1979); Gregory v. Ashcroft, 501 U.S. 452 (1991).

112. *See* Massachusetts Bd. of Retirement v. Murgia, 427 U.S. at 324 (Marshall, J., dissenting).

113. City of Cleburne v. Cleburne Living Ctr., Inc., 473 U.S. 432 (1985).

114. *Id.* at 442.

115. *Id.* at 445–46.

116. *See* Chapter 3 *supra*, at notes 92–95.

117. Romer v. Evans, 517 U.S. 620 (1996).

118. Daniel Farber & Suzanna Sherry, *The Pariah Principle*, 13 CONST. COMMENTARY 257 (1996); *see also* Akhil Reed Amar, *Attainder and Amendment 2: Romer's Rightness*, 95 MICH. L. REV. 203, 208–210 (1996).

119. Romer v. Evans, 517 U.S. at 623.

120. *See* text *supra*, at notes 36–39.

121. I count among this group Chief Justice Stone, who originally was appointed to the Court by President Coolidge, but was elevated in 1941 to the Chief Justiceship by Roosevelt, after being a staunch supporter of New Deal programs. The other Roosevelt appointees were: Hugo Black (1937); Stanley Reed (1938); Felix Frankfurter (1939); William Douglas (1939); Frank Murphy (1940); James Byrnes (1941); Robert Jackson (1941); and Wiley Rutledge (1943). Rutledge replaced Byrnes, who resigned from the Court after serving one year. Owen Roberts, who had been appointed by President Hoover, remained on the Court until 1945. If not exactly a Roosevelt sympathizer, he did not actively oppose reform after 1937 when his change of mind in NLRB v. Jones & Laughlin Steel Corporation, 301 U.S. 1 (1937), shifted the Court's majority in favor of the New Deal.

122. Skinner v. Oklahoma, 316 U.S. 535 (1942).

123. *Id.* at 538.

124. *Id.*

125. *Id.* at 541.

126. Eisenstadt v. Baird, 405 U.S. 438 (1972); Zablocki v. Redhail, 434 U.S. 374 (1978).

127. *See* text *supra*, at notes 54–64.

128. *See* text *infra*, at notes 131–39.

129. *See* text *infra*, at notes 140–49.

130. *See* text *infra*, at notes 150–168.

131. Reynolds v. Sims, 377 U.S. 533, 555 (1964).

132. *Id.*

133. *Id.* at 562.

134. *Id.* at 558, quoting Gray v. Sanders, 372 U.S. 368, 381 (1963).

135. *Id.* at 561–62.

136. *Id.* at 562.

137. Harper v. Virginia State Bd. of Elections, 383 U.S. 663 (1966).

138. Kramer v. Union Free Sch. Dis., 395 U.S. 621 (1969).

139. *E.g.*, Williams v. Rhodes, 393 U.S. 23 (1968); Bullock v. Carter, 405 U.S. 134 (1972); Illinois Elections Bd. v. Socialist Workers Party, 440 U.S. 173 (1979).

140. Griffin v. Illinois, 351 U.S. 12 (1956).

141. Douglas v. California, 372 U.S. 353 (1963).

142. *See* text *supra*, at notes 104–110.

143. Ross v. Moffitt, 417 U.S. 600 (1974).

144. Pennsylvania v. Finley, 481 U.S. 551 (1987); Murray v. Giarratano, 492 U.S. 1 (1989).

145. Williams v. Illinois, 399 U.S. 235 (1970); Tate v. Short, 401 U.S. 395 (1971); Bearden v. Georgia, 461 U.S. 660 (1983).

146. Tate v. Short, 401 U.S. at 395.

147. Williams v. Illinois, 399 U.S. at 235.

148. Fuller v. Oregon, 417 U.S. 40 (1974).

149. *See* text *supra*, at notes 63–68.

150. U.S. Const. amend. XIV, § 1.

151. U.S. Const. art. IV, § 2.

152. Corfield v. Coryell, 6 Fed. Cas. 546, 551–52 (C.C.E.D. Pa. 1823) (Washington, J., on circuit).

153. U.S. Const. art. I, § 8.

154. *See, e.g.*, Baldwin v. G.A.F. Seelig, Inc., 294 U.S. 511 (1935); Kassel v. Consolidated Freightways Corp., 450 U.S. 101 (1981).

155. The Passenger Cases, 48 U.S. (7 How.) 283, 492 (1849) (Taney, J., dissenting).

156. Shapiro v. Thompson, 394 U.S. 618 (1969); Dunn v. Blumstein, 405 U.S. 330 (1972); Memorial Hosp. v. Maricopa County, 415 U.S. 250 (1974).

157. Shapiro v. Thompson, 394 U.S. at 618.

158. Dunn v. Blumstein, 405 U.S. at 330.

159. Memorial Hosp. v. Maricopa County, 415 U.S. at 250.

160. Starns v. Malkerson, 326 F.Supp. 234, *aff'd*, 401 U.S. 985 (1971).

161. Sosna v. Iowa, 419 U.S. 393 (1975). *See also* Jones v. Helms, 452 U.S. 412 (1982) (upholding a state statute that increased the penalty for child abandonment if the parent in question left the state) (discussed in Chapter 3 *supra*, at notes 135–36).

162. Memorial Hosp. v. Maricopa County, 415 U.S. 250 (1974). The Court's decision in Sosna v. Iowa, 419 U.S. 393 (1975), upholding a one-year residency requirement as a condition of filing a divorce, ignores the dictate in Maricopa that strict scrutiny should be applied to residency requirements that impinge upon other fundamental rights. The right to marry or divorce are fundamental, yet in Sosna the Court applied minimal scrutiny. *See* discussion in Chapter 3 *supra*, at notes 135–36.

163. Zobel v. Williams, 457 U.S. 55 (1982).

164. Hooper v. Bernalillo County Assessor, 472 U.S. 612 (1985); *see also* Attorney General of New York v. Soto-Lopez, 476 U.S. 898 (1986).

165. Attorney General of New York v. Soto-Lopez, 476 U.S. at 903 (citations omitted) (plurality opinion).

166. *Id.* at 918 (O'Connor, J., dissenting).

167. *Id.* at 920 (O'Connor, J., dissenting); Zobel v. Williams, 457 U.S. at 74–75 (O'Connor, J. concurring).

168. *See* text *infra*, at notes 185–94.

169. Dandridge v. Williams, 397 U.S. 471 (1970).

170. *Id.* at 526–27 (Marshall, J., dissenting).

171. *Id.* at 486–87.

172. *Id.* at 484.

173. San Antonio Indep. Sch. Dist. v. Rodriguez, 411 U.S. 1 (1973).

174. *Id.* at 79–80 (Marshall, J., dissenting).

175. Even when rights are specifically protected by the Constitution, on some occa-

sions involving public education the Supreme Court may defer to school authorities. *See, e.g.*, Hazelwood Sch. Dist. v. Kuhlmeier, 484 U.S. 260 (1988).

176. *See* Chapter 3 *supra*, at notes 58–67.

177. San Antonio Indep. Sch. Dist. v. Rodriguez, 411 U.S. at 37. The Court also ruled that there was no suspect classification present in the case to evoke a more heightened form of scrutiny. *Id.* at 25.

178. *Id.* at 33.

179. *Id.*

180. *Id.* at 29 (quoting Brown v. Board of Educ., 347 U.S. 483, 493 [1954]).

181. *Id.* at 99 (Marshall, J., dissenting, referring to Skinner v. Oklahoma, 316 U.S. 535 [1942]).

182. *Id.* (Marshall, J., dissenting, referring to Reynolds v. Sims, 377 U.S. 533 [1964]).

183. *Id.* (Marshall, J., dissenting, referring to Griffin v. Illinois, 351 U.S. 12 [1956]).

184. Meyer v. Nebraska, 262 U.S. 390 (1923); Pierce v. Society of Sisters, 268 U.S. 510 (1925).

185. *See* text *supra*, at notes 1–19.

186. Saenz v. Roe, 526 U.S. 489, 119 S.Ct. 1518 (1999).

187. Shapiro v. Thompson, 394 U.S. 618 (1969).

188. Saenz v. Roe, 526 U.S. 489, 119 S.Ct. at 1524–25.

189. *Id.* at 1527–30.

190. *Id.* at 1524.

191. *Id.* The Court noted that the right to travel discussed in previous cases embraces three different components: (1) the right to pass through (enter and leave) a state, (2) the right to be treated as a welcome visitor rather than an unfriendly alien while temporarily present in a state, and (3) the right to migrate to a state and become a resident of it, entitled to be treated like any other citizen of the state. *Id.* at 1525. Saenz, of course, involved the third component.

192. *Id.* at 1524 (quoting Shapiro v. Thompson, 394 U.S. 618, 629 [1969]).

193. *Id.* at 1526–27.

194. *Id.* (quoting Miller, J., 83 U.S. [16 Wall.] at 80 and Bradley, J. [dissenting] 83 U.S. [16 Wall.] at 112–13 in the Slaughter-House Cases, 83 U.S. [16 Wall.] 36 [1873]).

195. *See* Laurence H. Tribe, *Saenz Sans Prophecy: Does the Privileges or Immunities Revival Portend the Future—Or Reveal the Structure of the Present?*, 113 HARV. L. REV. 110 (1999).

Table of Cases

Index

About the Author

JEFFREY M. SHAMAN is Professor of Law at DePaul University. He has concentrated much of his scholarship in the area of constitutional law, and his work analyzing the constitutional process has been published in law reviews across the country. He is also a national authority on judicial ethics and has written and lectured extensively on that subject. As a scholar and an attorney, Professor Shaman has participated in a variety of activities to promote human rights both in the United States and other nations.

www.ingramcontent.com/pod-product-compliance
Ingram Content Group UK Ltd.
Pitfield, Milton Keynes, MK11 3LW, UK
UKHW020247290926
15470UKWH00002B/795

9 780313 314735